D1457627

THE WILSON W. CLARK
WITHDRAWN
MEMORIAL LIBRARY
UNIVERSITY OF PORTLAND

The Idea of Democracy
in the Modern Era

Ralph Ketcham

The Idea of Democracy
in the Modern Era

 University Press of Kansas

JC
423
.K4128
2004

#54776121
i128823788

© 2004 by the University Press of Kansas

All rights reserved

Published by the University Press of Kansas (Lawrence, Kansas 66049), which was organized by the Kansas Board of Regents and is operated and funded by Emporia State University, Fort Hays State University, Kansas State University, Pittsburgh State University, the University of Kansas, and Wichita State University

Library of Congress Cataloging-in-Publication Data

Ketcham, Ralph Louis, 1927–
   The idea of democracy in the modern era / Ralph Ketcham.
      p.   cm.
   Includes bibliographical references and index.
   ISBN 0-7006-1334-X (cloth : alk. paper)
   1. Democracy.   2. Democracy—United States.   3. Democracy—East Asia.
4. Political science.   I. Title.
   JC423. K4128   2004
   321.8—dc22   2004005383

British Library Cataloguing in Publication Data is available.

Printed in the United States of America

10 9 8 7 6 5 4 3 2 1

The paper used in this publication meets the minimum requirements of the American National Standard for Permanence of Paper for Printed Library Materials z39.48-1984.

CONTENTS

In dealing with East Asian names and materials in English translation and in romanized form, there are complex, not always consistent, but finally necessary and useful conventions to observe. With Chinese, Japanese, and Korean names, the family name comes first, though some Western sources put it last. In transliterating Chinese names and words, I use the system most familiar in Western usage. For example, I use the older Wade-Giles system for *Chiang Kai-shek* and *Chungking* but the pinyin for *Liang Qichao* instead of the Wade-Giles *Liang Chi Chao*, even though the latter is often found in older accounts and in library reference systems (I have even found him in indexes under *Chi Chao, Liang*). Generally, however, I use the pinyin system of romanization adopted officially in the People's Republic of China. I have also asked Chinese or Japanese scholars to provide the Chinese characters for some key words in their languages.

In the East Asian chapters, I have relied on materials in English, many gathered or written by scholars expert in Chinese or Japanese studies and the Japanese and Chinese languages. Most particularly, I have relied on Benjamin Schwartz's study of Yan Fu, Philip Huang's of Liang Qichao, Thomas Havens's of Nishi Amane, and Stephen Hay's of Tagore's visits to Japan and China. For general historical context, I have relied on Maruyama Masao, Edwin O. Reischauer, Nakane Chie, and Robert Scalapino for Japanese thought and government and on Tu Wei-ming, Jerome Greider, and, especially, Jonathan Spence for Chinese thought. Professor Liu Zuochang of Shandong Teacher's University and Professor Kumei Teruko of Shirayuri College in Tokyo have helped me over some of my ignorance on language questions and, to my immense advantage, read and critiqued parts of the manuscript. Closer to home, the Japanese scholars Iino Masako, Takamura Hiroko, Shimada Noriko, Ito Hisako, Kushida Hisayo, and Ohta Kazuko and the Korean scholars John Kim, Grace Yu, and Han Jongwoo, all of whom have studied at Syracuse University, have been thoughtful colleagues throughout. Ma Lan, Paul Yuan, Chen Lei, and Wang Qingjia, also all Syracuse students, have helped me with the Chinese dimensions of the study. Lily H. M. Ling, Wang Hongying, and Norman Kutcher, Maxwell School colleagues, have been wonderfully helpful in my efforts to understand something of Chinese thought and culture.

I am grateful to the staffs of the libraries at Evergreen College in Olympia, Washington, the University of Sheffield in Sheffield, England, Massey University in Palmerston North, New Zealand, Loyola University in New Orleans, and Syracuse University for support and assistance. Linda Kirk and Richard Carwardine at Sheffield, Lisa Wilkin and William Maloney at Massey, David Moore and Mark Fernandez at Loyola, John Wilson at the University of Hawaii, and especially David Marr at Evergreen, who introduced me to the seminar "Democracy in the Twentieth Century," were helpful and stimulating colleagues. Press readers Fred Dallmayr and Peter Onuf made helpful and incisive comments on a late version of the manuscript, for which I am most grateful. David Bennett, Roger Sharp, Steve Webb, Ken Pennington, Joe Levine, Betsy Lasch-Quinn, Sudipta Sen, Jeff Stonecash, Fred Frohock, Steve Macedo, Manfred Stanley, Gerald Grant, Vernon Greene, Rogan Kersh, Bob McClure, Joe Julian, Keith Bybee, and others of the Maxwell School faculty have listened patiently and responded helpfully to my musings about the idea of democracy. Students past and present of my seminar "Foundations of American Political Thought," including Paul Finkelman, Barbara Fairchild, Ben Fischer, Susan Gooden, Robert Udick, Barbara Franz, McGee Young, John Mero, Ermin Sinonovic, Amanda DiPaoli, Kim Kyung Hwa, and, especially, Doug Challenger and Murni Abdul Hamid, have been constant sources of stimulating and challenging discussion.

In preparing the manuscript, my faithful collaborator has been Fran Bockus, always efficient, industrious, creative, and cheerful. In fact, without her skillful assistance in word processing, organizing, and proofreading, there would be no manuscript—I am deeply grateful to her and to her family. As usual, my wife, Julia, not only has had to endure much more talk about ideas of democracy than any human being should be subjected to, but has also been a thoughtful critic and highly skilled editor of the entire work. Like my book about James Madison thirty years ago, this one is warmly dedicated to her.

I have tried in this study to offer an account of the thinking during the last four centuries about the idea of human self-government, paying particular attention to the rationales on its behalf, the axioms and arguments that have been offered to undergird and justify democratic government. Important ideas about democracy and republics have been circulating at least since classical Greece and Rome, of course, and human thinking about them has existed and developed in myriad ways in various parts of the world. There are other important patterns of thought about democracy, such as the French republican tradition and recent African conceptions of "consensual" democracy, but these on the whole have not had the wide and lasting significance of the largely Anglo-American tradition. This especially influential, "mainline" thinking about democracy has matured mainly in the West, especially in Anglo-America, since early in the seventeenth century. It arose from the work of Francis Bacon, René Descartes, and others whose inductive, scientific modes of thought "recoloured our mentality . . . [and] altered the metaphysical presuppositions of the imaginative contents of our minds," as Alfred North Whitehead put it.[1] Insofar as this pattern of thought relates to democratic government, in development since about 1600, it is the subject of this book—nothing more, and, I hope, nothing less. The theme is that the very idea of democracy itself, implicit in the nature of "modern" thought, has received various and distinctive rationales in four manifestations of modernity in the last four centuries or so.

In telling this story, after some reflections on the problem of government as the twenty-first century dawns, I identify and try to explain four episodes or configurations of "modernity" that, in turn, each spawned an understanding of and rationale for democracy. The "first modernity," following Bacon and John Locke, did not emphasize grand theories or metanarratives under which particular experiences are subordinated deductively. It starts, rather, with the study and collection of particular facts and observations, from which tentative inductive generalizations might be made. This way of thinking implies, for politics, starting with the "parts"—individual people—and then considering what would be appropriate government for them. The parts, the people, should, reasonably, somehow set their own agenda and somehow rule themselves. What other arrangement, if there was nothing to begin with (e.g., no theory of divine right or no holy book[s]) except diverse, differentiated people, could possibly be justified? Such thinking became the first rationale for democracy and found expression in the U.S. Constitution of 1787–1791 and in the thought of James Madison, Thomas Jefferson, and others.

If, however, one follows the advocacy and critique of this rationale for democracy in minds still impressed with a modern, Baconian empiricism, one finds grave objection. The Locke-Jefferson rationale itself had become, not a tentative hypothesis, but rather a natural law ideology. It then imposed a universalism about government as closed and dogmatic as those of Augustine and Aquinas themselves. Jeremy Bentham, J. S. Mill, Herbert Spencer, John Dewey, and a host of others in the nineteenth century and the early twentieth, responding especially to the reformulation of scientific thought following Charles Darwin, thus challenged the natural law foundation of democracy as "non-sense," unfaithful to modern, inductive thought. Following this logic, "second modernity" thinkers regrounded the rationale for democracy on a calculus of the greatest good of the greatest number, on social science, and on the empirically determined "felt needs" of the majority of *all* the people—nothing more, nothing less. This revision led to the "liberal corporate state" that, in the twentieth century, became a second modernity orthodoxy, an essential, universal meta-narrative of democracy.

When second modernity thought rather suddenly came to Japan and China in the late nineteenth century, however, it slowly but powerfully led toward an altered rationale for democracy. Though largely second modernity based, that rationale was, in fact, still sufficiently grounded in the Confucian thought of East Asia to be significantly different: a "third modernity" understanding of democracy. Theories and forms of government deriving from the ideas of Mill, Spencer, Dewey, and others became widespread, but they took on a different flavor in response to essentially Confucian concepts of the importance of the state in human society, of the requirement that government rest on time-honored principles and rituals ("the mandate of heaven"), and of the need for wise and firm leadership. East Asian scholars and leaders thus produced what can be considered a third modernity rationale for democracy. Though sometimes hesitant and incomplete and often contested, its impact in East Asia has been potent since the Meiji Restoration in Japan in 1868.

In the last third of the twentieth century, yet another cycle or version of modernity, a "fourth modernity," generally termed *postmodernism,* has produced yet another rationale for democracy. Following Michel Foucault, Jean-François Lyotard, and Jacques Derrida, postmodern thinkers have again called for a more faithful adherence to critical, reductionist, "deconstructive" modes of modern thought, often harking back to Baconian guidelines, just as Thorstein Veblen and Harold Laski had done a century earlier. Postmodernists scorn second modernity understandings and the institutions that they validate as further "wills to system" and metanarratives, just as coercive and illegitimately universal tending as the natural law dogma of the first modernity. They believe that twentieth-century democratic government has been, in fact, oppressive and undemocratic in every one of its hallmarks: its liberalism was a dogmatic denial of multicultural "otherness"; its corporateness was a system of coercions aimed at the marginalized and excluded; and its idea of the state, its "nationalism," was inherently and irredeemably oppressive.

This fourth modernity, like its predecessors, spawned its own rationale for a democracy substantially different from earlier modern rationales. Noticing the strong tendency for the liberal (universal) ideals of the liberal corporate state (or welfare state) to become corporatized dogma imposed by a coercive state, postmodern thinkers moved toward their total repudiation. The liberal state represented the power of a dominant majority to oppress and marginalize the very diversities and "othernesses" that it claimed to acknowledge and take into account. Since there were no universal guidelines of the sort that first and second modernity thinkers had posited or assumed, a government's claims to follow such guidelines were always a fraudulent rationalization of its own will to domination. They were aided and abetted, moreover, by the legions of experts and social scientists who produced the plans, set up the certifications, and justified the institutions that controlled the lives of the people, especially the marginalized and oppressed not part of the dominant group. Thus, insofar as it could be any government at all under noncoercive, nonuniversal guidelines, real democracy would be a group or identity politics that, first and foremost, would nourish, "presence," and empower the various marginalized groups in any society. The idea would be, not to form any new, purposeful regime such as a "dictatorship of a proletariat" (a regime that would simply create another oppressive orthodoxy), but rather, perhaps in some devolved or minimalized way, to let all groups and "others" simply be "present" to each other, released from the authority of the dominant group and its universalizing ideology. Indeed, the very idea of a state, a national government, whether democratic or not, became problematic because of an always-present tendency to become a dominant power marginalizing and excluding "others." This was the rationale for democracy attending the fourth modernity, in fact more a supermodernity than a postmodernity.

Democracy's bumpy ride up to this point, together with two concluding chapters of evaluation and synthesis, is, then, the theme and subject matter of this study. The work is, thus, both an exercise in the history of ideas and, more implicitly, a criticism and explication of democratic theory, I hope in a way that contributes to both the history and the theory without abusing either. Throughout, I have dealt partially with towering intellects about whom much more could be said for many other purposes. I have also dealt only in passing with major patterns of thought—for example, Marxism and ideas of global democracy—that relate to my theme generally in alternative or critical ways. I hope only that I have been fair in my usages and omissions for my purposes, which I want to keep sharply on the idea of democracy. Beyond that, I apologize for what some will see as abuse or neglect. This may be especially true of the long chapters on the impact of Western, post-Darwinian thought in East Asia. These are long because of the relative unfamiliarity in the West of the ideas discussed (Yan Fu is less known than J. S. Mill, Liu Shaoqi than Thomas Jefferson, the Japanese "pragmatist" Nishi Amane than John Dewey, and so on) and the more complex way in which they relate to the mainstream development of Western, mainly Anglo-American thought (see esp. chapter 12). I hope, however, that the attention to East Asian rationales for democracy not only explicates those ideas in a largely Confucian context, but also reverberates to clarify what is going on in ideas of citizenship, of representation, of leadership, and of other aspects of Western democratic thought (again, see esp. chapter 12).

In covering so much ground, I have also had to indulge in generalizations that will seem to some readers distorted and oversimplified. Even the use of the terms *modern* and *postmodern* is dubious because there are, of course, many modernities and many postmodernities. I use both terms in the broadest, most conventional way to designate large movements that contain many variations, even contradictions. Some thinkers whom I have included in some categories would not accept my designations, and others have been placed in other categories by other scholars. I have also attended only slightly to the thought of Montesquieu, Rousseau, Marx, Freud, Rawls, Habermas, and others, not because they do not stand as major thinkers, but because they contribute less as constructors of new rationales for democracy emerging from new modernities than as propounders and critics within existing modernities. I hope, however, that my usages are at least plausible and make sense in the development of my theme. Inductive, differentiating, critical, reductionist tendencies exist in each of the four modernities that I explain, and postmodernism is really a further supermodernism, properly heir to the earlier modernities. What in the late nineteenth and early twentieth centuries in the West is commonly referred to as the *modern* era of art, literature, and other elements of culture is generally what I designate as the *second modernity*. Postmodernism is, in that sense, "post" modernism, but it is in a larger sense simply a further modernism.

I have also accepted the very broad generalizations of Max Weber, Liang Qichao, Huston Smith, and others of three large cultural spheres in the world that have, in recent centuries, interacted vigorously and reciprocally with each other: the West, including the influence of Greece and Rome as well as the branches and expansions of the three Abrahamic religions, Judaism, Christianity, and Islam;

South Asia, including Hinduism and Buddhism; and the East Asian sphere of Confucian-based culture common to China, Japan, and Korea. Much more might be said about the comparison and interaction of these cultural spheres, and the generalizations are themselves frayed and problematic, especially at the edges, but keeping them largely in mind helps clarify major developments in ideas of government (see esp. chapter 3 on tensions of citizenship and chapter 9 on Rabindranath Tagore's visits to Japan and China). Also, in dealing with ideas in East Asia, I have concentrated on the shared Confucian values and concepts as most important to the political realm, even though this neglects such highly significant cultural aspects as Taoism in China, the strong recent influence of Christianity in Korea, and the immense importance of Buddhism throughout the region. My argument is simply that, so far as ideas and practices of government are concerned, the millennia-long influence of the Confucian tradition, explicitly nourished and promulgated in each country for centuries at a time, is of prime significance. The encounter of Western ideas of democracy with Confucianism, above all, has evoked the most profound and important response, perhaps because of the greater depth, longer persistence, and wider influence of Confucian thought (superior to Western thought in ethics and politics, Leibniz and Voltaire would declare [see chapter 8]).

This is a study in the history of ideas—really one idea, the idea of democracy. It takes ideas seriously, in their own right, as an interesting and significant dimension of human experience. Humans vary greatly, of course, in their attention to and capacity to handle the realm of ideas, but that realm is surely one that is, for some people, an important part—and, for a few, a very important part—of how they understand themselves and the world they live in. In this view, ideas have a sort of life of their own, responding to, elaborating on, and criticizing each other, sometimes in thesis-antithesis-synthesis form, but, in any case, presenting a substance that is of fascination and significance. Ideas are, thus, not opposite to or different from facts, but rather part of the facts, part of the reality of human experience, in varying degrees for different people. Further questions of the economic or social origins or causes of ideas, or of their impact on events, are interesting and important and, of course, require attention, but it is also useful to understand what these ideas mean in their own right and how they relate to and evolve from each other, as ideas. This opens, and perhaps invites, a critique of the central idea—that of democracy—that I make implicit throughout, indicating, in conclusion, what might be a good way to understand the idea in the twenty-first century. In this study, no claim of ideas as essential or causal in human affairs is made, merely that understanding them is both of intrinsic interest and often helpful in understanding events.

The Idea of Democracy
in the Modern Era

I

Prospects for Government in 1989

In the blood-soaked travail for humankind that the twentieth century was, three years—1914, 1945, and 1989—stand out as turning points. In 1914, when Sir Edward Grey noted "lights going out all over Europe" and the Great War began thirty-one of the worst years in human history, a season of war, terror, brutality, and depression visited the world. The 1945 scenes of surrender in ruined Berlin and on the deck of a warship in Tokyo Bay surely marked a moment when one era, of fascist militarism seeking to dominate the globe, first triumphed and then ended and another, of "superpower" rivalry, began. The opportunity was there, and expectations were there, at least, for new directions. The prodemocracy demonstrations in Beijing's Tiananmen Square, the Gorbachev reforms in Moscow, and the sudden, seemingly spontaneous fall of the Berlin Wall, all in 1989, just as surely marked another propitious turning point. A new era had arrived perhaps as momentous for the future as that begun two centuries earlier with the fall of the Bastille. But what *was* the significance of 1989, and how can we understand its place in the larger patterns of Western and world history? What speculations might be in order about possible needs and directions in government, especially democratic government, for the third millennium?

"The End of History?"

By century's end, a number of scenarios had been proposed. Perhaps most likely, and unimaginatively, the so-called world capitalist economy might simply go on. The (highly? over?) developed nations of "the North," led by the United States and protected by its military power, but perhaps to be overshadowed by the shift of transnational economic power toward East Asia, might sustain their domination indefinitely. In a more vivid evocation, the "Lexus" of globalization might lift traditional (backward) "olive tree" societies toward a more prosperous modernity complete with effective "integrative" and "social safety net" policies. Though these projections might benefit the current hegemony, the looming threats of uprisings among "the wretched of the earth," violent strife among imperialist nations, international terrorism, and ecological catastrophe, all viewed by some as implicit and inevitable given the "contradictions" within the existing system, complicate and cloud the future.[1] In any event, emphasis on the hegemony of the world capitalist economy, whether one sees it as constructive or exploitative, leaves vast regions and realms of human potential and aspiration unfulfilled. Cultural critics inside and outside the "hegemon" make this point repeatedly and poignantly.

A broader view of the prospects for the "winners" of the cold war sees the steady worldwide spread of liberal, democratic ideas and practices as "the end of history." History has "ended," in this argument, because the market economies and liberal democratic governments of the Western world have triumphed, not only through their firm implantation in the trilateral (North America, Western Europe, and Japan) heartland, but also through their steady spread to the less developed world. And, after the collapse of communism both in theory and in practice, even the former Second World is shifting. In this view, the dialectic is over because the uniquely successful liberal corporate state synthesis of capitalism and socialism, at least for the foreseeable future, breeds no antithesis capable of making history go on. Instead, as the Communist bloc, after the disappearance of the Soviet Union, continues its metamorphosis into market-oriented, more or less democratic states (including, eventually, China and other Second World leftovers), and as the rest of the world continues its sometimes stagnated, sometimes backsliding, but nonetheless relentless movement in the same direction, the globe will experience a spreading convergence, not necessarily of equitable plenty, but at least of rising prosperity, diminished political oppression, and relative international peace.[2]

Another scenario supposes that the epochal change marked by the events of 1989 will find the cold war between the superpowers replaced by a "clash of civilizations." The divisive, dangerous, violence-prone conflicts in the world will no longer be either propelled or restrained by cold war imperatives but instead be driven by revived and heightened ethnic, religious, nationalistic, and regional animosities. Ancient and deep-seated fault lines between Roman Catholics, Orthodox Christians, and Muslims in the Balkans, between Nordic and Slavic energies around the Baltic Sea, between Confucian and Buddhist orientations in Southeast Asia, between Catholics and Protestants in Ireland, between Hindus and Muslims on the Indian subcontinent, between Muslim, Christian, and animistic cultures, between Hutu and Tutsi in sub-Saharan Africa, between Turkic and Iranian peoples in Central Asia, between whites and people of color in North and South America, between Jews and Arabs in the Middle East, and so on around the world will furnish abundant sources of conflict. Perhaps most ominous of all might be the explosive energies of Islam in confronting both the modernizing (often imperialistic) forces from without and the counterpoise of Sunni and Shia rivalries within. Any glance around the world reveals further sources of potential conflict.[3]

A final series of outlooks finds only gloom and decline in the future. Driven by unbearable demographic pressure, ecological decline, nuclear accidents or assaults, tendencies toward malgovernment and the "failed state" syndrome, and militaristic authoritarian regimes claiming unique capacities to cope with the poverty and disarray, the "human prospect [is] a deterioration of things, even an impending catastrophe of fearful dimensions."[4] Though the "catastrophe of fearful dimensions" is differently envisioned by demographers, ecologists, social critics, moralists, and political leaders, a sense of problems relentlessly outrunning solutions is a common thread. In this analysis, after some glimpses upward for the human species and some experiences of a better existence, Hobbes's famous dictum reclaims the future, leaving "the life of man solitary, poor, nasty, brutish, and short" or, no less dreadfully in the modern counterpart, "solitary, rich, nasty, brutish, and long."

Crisscrossing demographic, ecological, economic, and cultural analyses and projections are multiple examples of political malfunction and failure. The problems at nearly every stage are either caused by, exacerbated by, or at least unresolved by the incapacities of government. Though one can find drought, ecological disaster, overpopulation, imperialist leftovers, and ethnic strife beneath some of the world's recent catastrophes, the collapse or failure of the state has often been the more immediate cause. Put oppositely, in the most notable cases of the 1990s—Somalia, Rwanda, Bosnia, Haiti, Liberia, Chechnya, Albania, Zaire, and Kosovo, for example—had governments retained support and effectiveness, the worst events and the most dismal prospects seem unlikely to have ensued. Even in East Central Europe and the former Soviet Union, where government and the state have generally not collapsed, it is abundantly clear that preservation of some form of state effectiveness is crucial to the prevention of strife and chaos. Beyond that, as Václav Havel and others have said poignantly and eloquently, the creation of a civil society that in turn can sustain good self-government seems to be the most fundamental need in the former empire of Nicholas II, Lenin, Stalin, and Brezhnev.

But, if the obvious failure and need of the former Soviet Empire did not sufficiently make the point, the difficulties with various forms of self-government in the rest of the world ("First," "Third," and "Fourth") underscore the awesome *political* dimension of the problem. According to one calculation (made in 1991),[5] in two "waves" since World War II—1942–1962 and 1974–1990—there have been fifty-two generally democratic regimes installed around the world, with perhaps twenty or so more since that estimate. (Recall that, in the late 1930s, under assaults from left and right, there had been left not more than a dozen effectively democratic nations.) It does seem that some form of democratic government, accompanied generally by at least a partial market economy, is the purposeful objective of almost all the peoples on earth. The throngs in Tiananmen Square in 1989, in Djakarta in 1998, in Lima in 2000, and in Tehran in 1999 and 2003 and ongoing popular surges in Africa, in Latin America, and in the Muslim world underscore the point even where authoritarian regimes have remained in power. Yet difficulties, false starts, and regressions often loom larger than stable achievement. Remarkable shifts in the 1990s toward more popular governments in, to take major examples, South Africa, Mexico, Russia, Indonesia, and the Republic of Korea all seem endangered by debilitating weaknesses in the institutions, processes, ideologies, skills, and habits of democracy among leaders as well as citizens. The same question looms in all cases: Can democratic aspirations be translated into effective forms of good government?

Self-Government and Good Government

Even in the First World, the developed or trilateral world (North America, Western Europe, and Japan), though the institutions and processes of democratic government seem firmly and ubiquitously in place, a sense that these nations are governing themselves well, governing in ways that fulfill potential, that "establish justice," is by no means pervasive. In the past half century, phrases such as *power elite, malaise, stagflation, gridlock, moral decay, Japan, Inc., racism, neoimperialist, capitalist hegemony, superpower,* and so on, all with pejorative, unfulfilling, oppressive connotations, cloud the account of public life in the so-called leading powers. Indeed, the record seems so problematic that many observers see it as evidence, not of a positive model, but rather of an antimodel. Instead of having learned and practiced how to govern themselves democratically and justly and well, for their own sakes as well as for that of the rest of the world, these nations seem often to have performed miserably. They have, that is, failed to be examples of how the state, in Aristotle's classic aspiration, might exist "for the sake of a good life, and not for the sake of life only"—for all its people.

The problem of government, then, generally speaking, seems to be at once simple and exceedingly difficult and complicated. Two norms seem to hold for much of the world: that some form of democracy or self government is, in Winston Churchill's formulation, preferable to anything else that humankind has tried; and that the qualities of good government can generally be agreed on. As the U.S. Constitution puts it, to "establish justice, ensure the domestic tranquility, provide for the common defense, promote the general welfare, and secure the blessings of liberty." Yet, as has been true at least since 1776, when the Declaration of Independence declared as basic principles both that certain rights were "unalienable" and that government derived its "*just* powers from the consent of the governed" (emphasis added), there seems to be a profound tension between the norms. Can democracy, self-government, really be the road to achieving in society "the good life" as outlined, for example, in the Preamble of the Constitution or in other generally similar aspirations around the world?

The point is that, beyond all the economic, ecological, cultural, and other tensions, catastrophes, and injustices that plague the world, the problem of good government, the effective resolution of the political dimension of human existence, remains a crucial and perhaps overarching concern. Deficiencies in government can cause or exacerbate economic, ecological, or social problems, and the absence of good government can foreclose opportunities for effective improvements. Good government, of course, can by no means be equated with big or strong government, which is often very *bad* government, but, on the other hand, weak government is almost always also bad, or at least ineffective or unfulfilled, government. While some societies can be said to have suffered from too much bad government (e.g., the former Soviet Union and its satellite states), others perhaps can be said to suffer from too little good government (e.g., the United States?). In any case, it seems clear that direct attention to the business of governing well—from developing an underlying political culture and civil society, to establishing ideas, forms, and institutions of government, to improving actual political behavior and performance—may be the most important and urgent task facing the world as the third millennium begins. At least it may be true that simply saying that least government is best government is a dangerous delusion. Profound attention, furthermore, is needed to the nature of and rationale for democracy if it is to fulfill the aspirations of 1776, 1789, 1848, 1918, 1945, and 1989.

2

Aristotelian and Confucian Insights

Relationships and the Political as Sacred

Two ancient perspectives on government, Aristotle's *Politics* (ca. 350 B.C.E.) and certain sections of the *Analects,* the *Great Learning,* and other Confucian classics (ca. 500 B.C.E.), can help us discern the nature of the modern need for good government. The Greek philosopher and the Chinese sage provide particular insight on the role of the political in human life and on the place, purpose, and design of government in society. The richness of their concern for the *social* nature of the human species and for the vast potential of the state in nourishing, not "life only," but "a good life"[1] makes them especially useful guides. When the deficiencies, crimes, and defaults of government make politicians in democracies campaign "against government," when residents in tyrannies incline to idolize anarchy, and when citizens suffer the trauma of "failed states," the Confucian and Aristotelian insights perhaps seem most relevant. One finds in each, for example, an indelible sense of human life in relationship rather than in isolation, of the vast increment derivable from public accord and from shared effort and purposes, and of the critically important and beneficial contribution that a well-ordered, properly empowered, and public-spirited government can make. One learns from each, then, of the inevitability of the social, the potential for the political, and the standards needed to judge the quality of government.

In the Confucian understanding, for example, one does not begin, as is common in the West (including Islam), with a conception of an autonomous individual or a sacred soul, valuable in his or her own right, and thought of as the essential part or building block in the assembling of human institutions from the family to the state. Rather, one starts with an entity (not a "self") whose being and essence are a matter of relationships. One can say that there really is no autonomous center in this understanding—the essence is a rich and complex web of connections that *are* human existence. The Confucian "self," David Hall and Roger Ames explain, is "a complex of roles and functions associated with one's obligations to the various groupings to which one belongs. . . . In the absence of the performance of these roles, nothing constituting a coherent personality remains; no soul, no mind, no ego."[2] The bond, for example, between parent and child (Confucius, of course, said literally father and son, but his point is fully present in the more inclusive terms), requiring respect from the child and responsible concern from the parent, must also be infused with affection to achieve its human-fulfilling potential. The living out of this relationship in its full moral dimension as one is, first, a respectful child and, then, a responsible parent becomes an essential element of one's being. The same fulfillment is part of the other four basic relationships: sovereign-subject (and such subsets as teacher-pupil and boss-worker), where duty is the key sentiment; husband-wife, where distinction or differentiation is crucial; older sibling–younger sibling, where precedence or order is central; and friend-friend, where faithfulness or loyalty is essential. That is, not only do the relationships define the customs and rituals appropriate to the particular connections, but each also embodies a sentiment or morality that gives the bond its rich human meaning.

Implicit are patterns and progressions of life that are obligatory if one is to experience the full meaning and potential of human existence. The respect (in extreme form even veneration) that children have for loving and caring parents, the unique sense of affection inspired on both sides of the relationship, the literally marvelous pleasure of moving from one side to the other, this is not just something that human individuals might or might not experience or choose or might find "elsewhere." Rather, it is profound, unreplaceable, indelible— something without which, when it is physically possible, life simply is not fully human. Therefore, the possessing and reveling in its incredible satisfactions, obligations, and joys is what life *is*—apart from it a person is bereft, impoverished. This Confucian understanding has its oppressive aspects and denigrates some styles of life (not forbidden necessarily, but at least devalued in some degree), but, more fundamentally, it provides a pervasive, relational morality appropriate for the biological center of life—how it ought to be experienced to be fully human.

The same rich, moral sensibility pervades the other four relationships, all attended, not only with more or less formal obligations, but also with attitudes and feelings that provide satisfaction and fulfillment. Except in some ways for the friend-friend bond, each of the five relationships is hierarchical; there is an "upper" and a "lower" part, each having associated privileges and responsibilities. The distinction essential to the husband-wife relationship, for example, of course requires the "listening" attentiveness of the wife, but it also expects the husband to be "good" and caring—without these feelings, the formal requirements of obedience and differentiation of function would be, at best, empty shells and, at worst, tyrannical impositions. Hence, though the basic relational morality is fraught with potential abuses of stagnation, mere ritual, and social domination, at its best it insists that human life be both enjoyably social and deeply moral. In fact, it collapses the two terms—to be social is to be moral, and to be moral is to be social.

An endlessly repeated and elaborated aphorism from the *Great Learning,* one of the Confucian "Four Books,"[3] declares:

> If there is righteousness in the heart, there will be beauty in the character.
> If there is beauty in the character, there will be harmony in the home.
> If there is harmony in the home, there will be order in the nation.
> If there is order in the nation, there will be peace in the world.[4]

Notice the admired qualities—righteousness, beauty, harmony, order, and peace. Notice, too, how the qualities (their Chinese written characters, of course, are infused with great depth, richness, and sublimity through millennia of use in literature, philosophy, and history) build and depend on one another. The starting point, righteousness (*li,* 理, meaning both "principle" and "ritual," both "right" and "rite"), becomes a key component of beauty. Beauty (美), that is, must also be morally grounded or meaningful—or it is not beauty. Then the endlessly invoked idea of harmony (諧) has as an essential component an element of beauty; if something is not beautiful, then it is not fully harmonious. Next, order (序; the English word connotes more mere static in-placeness than does the Chinese character) would not have its full and proper meaning unless infused with the richer idea of harmony—perhaps like that of a "philharmonic" symphony, the ordered whole being much more than the virtuoso performance of the various parts. Finally, peace (和) in the world would have little value, in fact, might be merely an oppressive tyranny, did it not also embody the rich and humane ideas of order, harmony, beauty, and righteousness.

The relentlessly social nature of the Confucian outlook is summed up in perhaps the most significant concept in all Chinese thought, *jen* (仁), composed of the characters for "two" and "human being," and variously translated as *fellow feeling, goodness, human heartedness, goodwill, empathy, love* (or *charity*), and, perhaps best, *benevolence*. In a way, *jen* includes the connotations of all the Greek words for *love—eros, philos,* and *agape.* This quality is required in all five of the relationships, implanting an affection and humaneness in what otherwise might be rather formal and oppressive obligations. It also courses through all the linkages from goodness in the heart to peace in the world. Thus, the very essence of Confucian (and, hence, Chinese, Korean, and Japanese) culture is the requirement that all life—most fundamentally the five relationships and their subsets, but also including every association, process, enterprise, and institution —be lived with an attitude and posture of *jen,* or benevolence and empathy and goodwill.

Applied to government, this places an attitude, a moral sensibility, at the center of everything. All in the society, whether emperors, imperial counselors, provincial administrators, village headmen, or ordinary people, were expected at all times to exhibit *jen,* benevolence. In the explicitly political relationship, for example, that of sovereign-subject, both the upper and the lower parts had duties. The upper must discern and respond to the needs of the people and be guided by the common good and the mandate of heaven as explained by sage counselors and had fundamentally to act always exuding benevolence. All other levels and positions were, as duty required, to obey the laws and conform to the social good, but for them, too, the benevolent, public-spirited attitude and understanding were essential. As the *Great Learning* summarizes: "All alike from Emperor to the common people should take self-cultivation (*xiushen,* 修身) as their root."⁵ That is, the very idea of self (and, in projection, of citizenship) contained a universally applicable social and moral dimension.

Now, within this configuration, the political is regarded as supremely important, and the essence of the political is a sense of justice and of the public good—the public manifestation, in a way, of *jen.* The quality and effectiveness of the political, especially the nation or the empire, are of transcendent importance to the life of the people, so much so that one cannot imagine fulfillment, or even existence, apart from them. The state or nation in East Asia is, E. O. Reischauer notes, "the highest embodiment of civilization." Thus, it is not surprising that "among the nations of the contemporary world those which first took shape as recognizably the same political units they are today are China in the third century BC and Korea and Japan in the seventh century AD."⁶

The nation, in Confucian culture, then, is really not much like any of the Western models. It is certainly more than the individually contracted for "leviathans" or "conveniences" of the Hobbesian or Lockean conceptions or even the protector of bourgeois property of Marxist-Leninist theory. On the other hand, it is different, perhaps less somehow, than in the grander Hegelian, divine right, or Islamic models of Western culture. The nation (or state or empire) is simply *there,* implicit and assumed, not very doctrinally explicit or assertive, yet pervasive and indelible in its range, significance, and moral foundation. Hence the omnipresence of Qing, Guomindang, Maoist, or Dengist authority in China; of the Koryo dynasty, Japanese-imposed colonialism, or post-1950 North or South authoritarianism in Korea; and of Tokugawa, Meiji, militarist, or postwar "Japan, Inc." state hegemonies in Japan—throughout and despite important differences among the regimes, the state looms large and endures in its paramount, paternal significance. Thus, for example, the overwhelming concern of the Chinese people, whether right, left, or center of the Dengist regime, is for the *endurance* of a state, whatever form (historically *dynasty*) it might take. The many revolutions in more than two millennia of Chinese history generally sought, not to overthrow the ancient regime, but merely to change the dynasty to one conforming to the mandate of heaven. Even Mao's establishment in 1949 of the People's Republic of China, though in a way truly revolutionary, did not by any means discard the ancient Chinese emphasis on the paternal, authoritarian state. These traditions, of course, have been highly dictatorial and have virtually nothing democratic about them, but they have everything to do with a conception of an indispensable, morally grounded, and active essence (government) in a "good society."

In this way, the Confucian understanding of the role of government reveals its closeness to the Aristotelian dictum: "A state exists for the sake of a good life, and not for the sake of life only." As Benjamin Schwartz has put it: "In the Chinese and Greek concepts of the polity, there is a shared assumption that the polity bears a maximum responsibility as the moralizing agent of the society."[7] The state, that is, has an indispensable role to play if the polity, understood as an enduring social matrix (*not* simply a summation of discrete, self-willed individuals), is to seek effectively the good of the whole. Aristotle makes the point simply in declaring that "man is by nature a political animal."[8] That is, to fulfill their natures, to become all that it means to be fully human, to reach their potential, human creatures must be *political,* must take part in the shared, public life of society. That the Greek root πολιτκ has sometimes been translated as "social," rather than "political," makes the point that Aristotle's meaning was broad, inclusive, participatory; he referred to a wide, active, and responsible engagement with all that aspect of life that has to do with deliberating, contesting, acting collectively with others: the inclusive connotations of the word *social,* yet with the governing or explicitly collective connotations of the word *political.* In any event, like the Confucian tradition, Aristotle and the classical outlook generally accept the irreducible socialness of human nature, the centrality of government in that socialness, and the vast and indispensable potential for social guidance and goodness that the state affords.

The Confucian and Aristotelian traditions, then, both regard the political itself as sacred. Government and the state are understood as more than a sort of auxiliary contrivance where mundane affairs are managed as best can be while religion, nourishing moral and spiritual capacities toward transcendent ends, receives primary attention, as Saint Paul, Augustine, Aquinas, and Calvin—and perhaps Jeremiah and Muhammad as well—might be understood to teach. Nor is the state a mere contract of convenience allowing discrete individuals to otherwise pursue with least interference their individual goals, as Hobbes, Locke, J. S. Mill, and other contract theorists and utilitarians might be understood to teach. The state exists within a matrix of moral order—what the Chinese call *the mandate of heaven*—that defines the just or good society. People (saying *individuals*, as Western habits of thought might tend to do here, would convey alien connotations) are themselves part of this order and find meaning and fulfillment within it. The state—all the constitutions and arrangements and powers and processes and offices of government—at its best is natural, indigenous, essential, active, benign, and paramount. (Both the Aristotelian and the Confucian traditions, of course, warn against the perversions and corruptions that governments often exhibit: Aristotle's "bad" forms of government and the Confucian idea of deposing "bad" rulers. The mandate is withdrawn, or, in the literal Japanese version, "heaven changes its mind.") The point is that human life is essentially relational or social, that a moral order pervades these patterns of relationship (Aristotle's *Ethics* in a way undergirds the *Politics*), and that the state has a responsibility to guide toward, not "life only," but "a good life." The guiding hand best suited for encouraging the good life might be a "mild" and carefully limited one, but it would be the responsibility of the collected polity to so decide, deliberately.

The Qualifications of Rulers

Both the Greek and the Chinese traditions, of course, would place crucial emphasis on the education of those who did and would rule. How could there be, that is, wise and good government (according, e.g., to the mandate of heaven) unless the rulers had been nurtured and educated to understand and revere the indispensable guidelines? Plato and Aristotle, and Confucius himself, were most serious, and most insistent, as teachers, especially of those who would rule. Long and elaborate parts of Plato's *Republic* explain the education appropriate for the to-be philosopher-king, and Plato often himself undertook to advise Greek rulers. Aristotle taught the future Alexander the Great before he conducted his own academy for leaders and citizens, while Confucius and his followers set patterns of study and qualification for officials that were the formal undergirding of Chinese government for two millennia. The intent was always to assure that the system of government ("the constitution") and the understanding and intention of those who would rule were in accord with standards ("mandates," 主) of wisdom and justice.

Even in traditions less focused on mundane public life, the proper training of the rulers has often received careful attention. In Judaism, Christianity, and Islam, though personal, spiritual, and moral fulfillment is always placed above temporal affairs (see chapter 3), rulers are nonetheless to be carefully nurtured and guided to be in support of the supreme religious goals of society. The role of the iman (the ayatollah in the Islamic Republic of Iran), South Asian traditions of holy men teaching and counseling in affairs of state, and nearly universal patterns all over the world of wise elders training and advising chiefs, matriarchs, or headmen make the same point: good government requires wisdom in the councils and in the seats of power. The educational process for rulers, though perhaps less elaborately and less centrally set forth than in the Greek and Confucian ways, is always an important part of ensuring the good ordering of society.

Perhaps most significant from the standpoint of modern democratic societies, attention to the need for educating "the rulers" remains, whatever the *number* who take part in governing. In the classic Aristotelian formulation, the need is to achieve *good* government whether it is by one, by a few, or by many. Since good government is essentially government attentive to the common good, this might happen under a monarchy, an aristocracy, or a constitutional polity where citizens at large govern. Likewise, bad government, government in the interests of partial or selfish entities, a tyrant, an oligarchy, or a democracy (demagogue-driven mob rule), is also possible regardless of the number of rulers.[9] The standard is always qualitative, not quantitative. In the traditional Chinese system, the number of people educated for officialdom (verified by nationwide examination) depended on the number needed to properly counsel (and, in a way, educate) the emperor and to administer government in the empire. Aristotle's understanding of liberal education had to do with the instruction appropriate for the "freeman," or citizen, qualified to take part in the government of the city. Though, in the Greek system, emphasis on education was, thus, limited to citizens qualified to participate in public affairs (for the time an unusually large number of people) and, in the Chinese system, there was no thought of widespread education (since generally there was no government role for "the people"), each system was inclusive in the sense that *all* involved in governing had to be educated, in principle and in practice, for their uniquely important role. Hence, when, following John Locke, Thomas Jefferson, John Dewey, and others, wider and wider groups of people (eventually in the twentieth century *all* adults) were regarded as *citizens* (operatives of the city, we might say), the emphasis on education became more widespread—and, eventually, universal. If one takes government seriously, in an

Aristotelian way, and also moves in a demo-cratic direction of government by the people, it is nearly inevitable that public education (i.e., education of all for public purposes) becomes a vital concern.

Just Government and the Good Society

A rich, inclusive attention given to education has always propelled an intense interest in the social web and means of livelihood that surrounded people's lives. The family system, the intricate relationships among parents and children, teachers and pupils, and so on, the architecture of public spaces and imperial conference rooms, and the nature of the occupations most valued and encouraged in society were all taken most seriously by the Chinese and the Greeks. All were calculated and arranged to promote circumstances conducive to the nourishing of good rulers, subjects, officials, or citizens, as the case might be. Both Confucius and Aristotle paid great attention to the concept of friendship, emphasizing its dependence on loyalty and goodwill and the good effect that such values had on the political. Both traditions also looked carefully at the effect of occupations on the character and socialization of the people. Though each saw the virtue of middle-class commercial life, each also valued farming or pastoral life because of its moral advantage and constructive contribution to the political realm—in the same spirit that Marx condemned the harmful, alienating aspects of industrial labor and Jefferson saw yeoman farming as the best basis for good citizenship. All emphasized the impact of social arrangements and occupation on the overall socializing, nurturing, educating function of society, which, in turn, had a fundamental impact on the quality of government.

One of the things, of course, that rulers (one, few, or many) must learn in their carefully arranged educations is an understanding of and a faithfulness to the just *processes* of government. If government is to be conducted in accord with ideals of justice or a mandate of heaven, and if these guidelines are themselves discernible and made manifest through deliberative and administrative processes, then careful attention to and training in those processes will be important. Whether one has in mind the model of sage counselors gathered around the monarch to discuss public policy and provide authoritative advice (idealized at least in the Chinese, Korean, and Japanese traditions), or the classical model of liberally educated, public-spirited citizens gathered in the public forum, or the modern democratic model of government responsive to an inclusively participatory people through channels of consent both precise and elaborate, a sense of faithfulness to a deliberative process is paramount (Al Gore's point in his gracious concession speech of December 2000 and Richard Nixon's in his orderly departure from the presidency in 1974). The larger the polity, of course, the more complex, and perhaps even problematic and tenuous, the process becomes, but a sense of the need to somehow preserve both the responsiveness and the deliberativeness has remained a constant concern as the size and inclusiveness of polities has grown.

In democratic societies, the concern for process has had to attend most fundamentally to the ways in which the basic component, the people, participates, plays its role in government. How can people, perhaps millions, tens, even hundreds of millions of them, be made both genuinely and significantly part of the governing process and, thus brought in, be so constituted as to facilitate *good* government? In the first instance, democratic polities must attend endlessly to providing meaningful access through inclusive franchise and easy registration, to encouraging civil and political organizations, to opening real choices at elections, to devising formal or informal mechanisms of referendum, initiative, and recall, to ensuring fullness and accuracy of ballot counting, to ensuring openness and fair use of means of communication, and to simplifying access to administrative and judicial apparatus. In modern democracies, immense importance has been attached to these matters, and evaluation of the genuineness or reality of self-government has generally depended on them.

Perhaps even more basic than the openness of the processes to all citizens, however, is the *quality* of the participation. Do the citizens possess the moral qualities, the knowledge and experience, and the public-spirited outlook to make their participation conducive to *good* government? The existence of the opposite, of a people found or alleged to be prejudiced, ignorant, selfish, or apathetic, has always been the grounds for either explaining the inadequacies of democratic government or opposing its institution in the first place. Well-devised and effective means of access and even a ready responsiveness from government offices is not enough if "the people" do not understand justice or have mean and narrow ideas (if any) of the public good. Thus, the most profound democratic philosophers of citizenship have followed, while taking into account far larger numbers of people, the Aristotelian and Confucian emphases on the deep, rich, essentially moral nurturing necessary for participants in government (in Confucian thought, of course, confined to a small elite). Knowledge of public affairs and administrative skill are, of course, important, but even more basic is public-spiritedness, "the virtue and public spirit of our common people," which, Benjamin Franklin said, was essential to the good operation of the republican constitution under discussion in 1787.[10] Again, good government is not essentially mechanical or quantitative but qualitative, dependent on the whole web of culture and nurture that furnishes the moral and deliberative context in which public matters are decided.

Even beyond this generally moral foundation required for good government, democracy requires an overall, substantial, down-to-earth idea of what the public dimensions of a good society for human beings living together should and might be like. What principles of justice, civil institutions, means of government, systems of social welfare, ecology, beautification, levels of prosperity, methods of education, guidelines for public health, care of the young and old, and so on would enhance the quality of life in the polity? It is not that there should or could be long-term, fixed agreement about such matters in any given society but, rather, that there might be agreement that those concerns, perhaps understood as those *questions,* were important ones, ones requiring some sort of public attention and response. The agreement, that is, is on the agenda and on a conviction that public-spirited asking of the questions will be conducive to the common good. And this circles around again to the Aristotelian and Confucian faith in the constructiveness of the properly arranged deliberative process, whether of liberally educated citizens or sage counselors. A similar faith in a benign deliberative process involving at some level and some fashion *all* members of a democratic society is just as important there in moving toward its good society. A failure to encourage and somehow make real this fulfillment of the human political nature is probably as problematic now as Pericles said it was in Athens in 428 B.C.E.: "Our ordinary citizens, though occupied with the pursuits of industry, are still fair judges of public matters; for, unlike any other nation, regarding him who takes no part in these duties not as unambitious but as useless, we Athenians are able to judge at all events if we cannot originate, and instead of looking on discussion as a stumbling block in the way of action, we think it an indispensable preliminary to any wise action at all."[11]

The Aristotelian and Confucian insights, then, instructive today in understanding good government and the role of those who govern, begin with a pervasively social, relationship-oriented understanding of human nature. In its political dimension, this requires elaborate, explicit attention to the ways and means of government and an acknowledgment of its crucial importance, for better or for worse, in human affairs. The governance of society, that is, is a prime—we might even say sacred—function that cannot safely or wisely be neglected or denigrated. Hence, those who govern (of whatever number) have a heavy responsibility to attend seriously to whatever their part in that function might be, and they must be brought, earnestly and deliberately, to that task. This concern, more or less attended to, has followed the idea of democracy as it has evolved through four stages of "modern" thought since the Baconian age four centuries ago. Formal education, institutions of civil society, opportunities to participate, and modes of economic livelihood all need to be taken into account, organized or modified, as required by the basic political imperative.

With formal processes of government attuned to these principles, and with the whole society, so to speak, thus attentive in some degree to the public interest, perhaps the twenty-first century might be more civilized than the twentieth. That problematic democracies, transitional regimes, authoritarian nations, and failed states alike somehow seek this progress may be the most urgent task facing nations around the world.

3

Tensions of Citizenship:
Judaism, Christianity, and Islam

Higher Law, Holy Books, and Prophets

In a broadly conceived, worldwide perspective, Western culture has spread with the political, moral, and social energy of Jerusalem, Rome, and Mecca, extending from Arkhangel'sk to New Zealand and from Alaska to Zanzibar. Strong tensions exist, however, in Western ideas of allegiance and citizenship that have problematic implications for a richly social Aristotelian or Confucian concept of government. Judaism, Christianity, and Islam, in all their sects and forms, begin with Yahweh, God, Allah, and a higher law found in holy books and expounded by prophets, which must be the guide on earth and a path to eternal bliss. All aspects of mundaneness, of the here and now, of existing temporal society, to be justified, must be ordered and guided by this higher law. The prototype is Mosaic: the law comes from God through the prophet to be elaborated in Scripture that then becomes the law for life on earth. Though complex societies and nations might form in pursuit of the higher law (the Israel of King David, the Holy Roman Empire, modern Iran), the pattern is always one of the "outsider," filled with the spirit and word of God (telling Jeremiah: "Behold I put My words in thy mouth" [Jer. 1:9]), setting forth precepts for the earthly city that conform to those for the heavenly city. The pattern rests, moreover, on an individual model of "superhuman" moral and spiritual faith and insight that not only comes from outside and in judgment of conventional temporal society, but also emphasizes individual regeneration that has its ultimate reward beyond the here and now. The higher law, the holy books, the prophets themselves, and the idea of the "good life" for individuals are all, in a sense, otherworldly.

Thus, though the faithful Jew, Christian, or Muslim lives (the Christian expression *sojourns* perhaps best catches the connotations) in the mundane, temporal world, has comprehensive ideas of what that should be like, and has personal obligations to make it that way, the essence of life is still one's personal relation to God and to his way, that is, one's faith in the transworldly.

This pattern sets up what Mark Roelofs has called a "tension of citizenship"[1] wherein an individual is torn between, in the Augustinian paradigm, the heavenly city and the earthly city, between that which God desires and that which human life exhibits and inhabits, between submission to Allah and submission to the ungodly, between that which one renders unto God and that which one renders unto Caesar. Though the stories that reveal this paradigm are filled with worldly and political import, they generally begin with a sinful, helpless locale needing outside inspiration and guidance for its regeneration. Thus, there is little emphasis on the (unregenerate) people or on their deliberative potential, wisdom, and public spirit as human beings in the community, apart from the divinely sent and inspired prophet and his faithful followers and designees. (A more dramatic but basically parallel model is that of the righteous Lone Ranger, the masked outsider, rescuing the frontier town lacking the resources and community effectiveness that it needs to save itself from whatever thieves or murderers or sinfulness it faces—Gary Cooper acts this part in *High Noon*.)

The pattern is set in place when God's "judge," Samuel, anoints the temporal rulers, Saul and then David, first to rescue and then to lead the "children" of Israel in God's way—and their authority lasts only as long as their commitment to that way does. The same priority is emphasized in King David's chastisement before the prophet Nathan for his disobedience of God's law and is repeated endlessly in the stories of the later prophets and rulers of God's chosen people. From his immaculate conception, through baptism by the wild and uncouth John, and then murder at the hands of sacerdotal and secular authorities, Jesus the Christ proclaimed that his kingdom was not of this world, drove the money changers from the temple, and made clear that that rendered unto Caesar was to be governed by the higher obligation to render unto God. Muhammad, though deeply immersed in worldly affairs and even in government, was preeminently a prophet of Allah, delivering his word, proclaiming faith in him as the first duty, and heralding the (otherworldly) paradise waiting for those who lived and died in his name. In the Muslim tradition, whether under caliphs, sultans, or ayatollahs, the temporal was always (at least in theory) to be under the sway and control of the faith as set forth in the holy book and as taught by the seers (see-ers).

This Judeo-Christian-Islamic paradigm, then, has for three millennia and for half the human race set a higher and essentially "from-the-outside" faith and law at the apex. The secular community, or nation, is subordinate and, perhaps more pointedly, bereft, corrupt, tyrannical, ineffective, sinful, "lost" in the absence of the voice from without. Though the infusion of faith into the people and their empowerment through commitment to God's will open the way for mass action in earthly affairs and can move toward deeply purposeful and highly organized societies, nothing much is to be expected of or is possible from "the people" until they are regenerated by a personally accepted faith. The overall effect is to denigrate the indelibly social and the deliberatively effective political dimensions of human nature—something that the Greek and Confucian traditions generally do not do. The South Asian Hindu and Buddhist traditions are, of course, often even more otherworldly, mystical, and pantheisiic than the Abrahamic offshoots. Contemporary "planet earth" consciousness, moreover, notes that forms of otherworldliness tend to make that of the earth of lesser value, thus devaluing ecological concern and policy.

Religion, Conscience, and the Purpose of Government

It is precisely at this point that the tension in any idea of leadership or citizenship arises. With the basic, higher law and inspiration coming from above, or outside, one is always, at least at first, drawn away from the mundane, creating a sense of distance, even alienation, from the earthly community. In accord with one's (new) faith, one, again initially, steps outside, viewing and judging temporal affairs in terms of one's allegiance to that faith. The empowered servant, or disciple, or apostle, so to speak, then turns with the new faith to the "city of man" to conform it to God's way. Rule on earth is then to be conducted as far as possible in accord with God's will as found in his book and understood by his faithful rabbis, priests, or mullahs.

In order to make this work in the real world, those who actually conducted the affairs of government needed to be thoroughly imbued with the higher (religious) principles that were to be their mundane guides. For centuries in the Christian monarchical tradition, for example, this required giving careful attention to "the education of the Christian prince"—Saint Thomas Aquinas and Erasmus both wrote notable and influential treatises on that subject.[2] The idea was that, if a country was to be governed properly (i.e., in accord with the higher law), then those who ruled would have to be in tune with that law. This would be achieved first, and most fundamentally, by assuring that the prince absorbed the higher law (including, of course, personal commitment to the faith) and would be sustained, as needed, by advice and even interference from religious authorities— hence the clerical offices of confessor and preceptor to the young prince, the crowning of the Holy Roman Emperor by the pope, and the scene at Canossa in 1077 A.D. when Emperor Henry IV appeared contrite, in sackcloth and ashes, before Pope Gregory VII. John Calvin's rule in Geneva, Oliver Cromwell's domination of Parliament, and John Winthrop's governorship of the Massachusetts Bay Colony were Protestant examples of the same idea of primacy even when the ancient institutions and offices had been repudiated: God's word as found in the Bible and expounded by his ministers was to be the foundation of the polity and the guide for rulers.

Even radical "protesters" who more and more repudiated the direct linkage of church and state, however, continued to insist on adherence to God's law—in fact, that insistence was the grounds for their quarrel with government as they saw it conducted. Saint Francis of Assisi left temporal society that he might attend, and show humankind how to attend, to God's way. Roger Williams resisted the intrusion of any officers of state in matters of faith because "the straining of men's *consciences* by *civil power*, is so far from making men faithful to *God* or man, that it is the ready way to render a man false to both."[3] Quakers repudiated religious offices and all temporal conventions that kept them from seeing or responding to "the inner light," and then they insisted on living strictly in accord with that conviction of conscience. Slavery, taxes to support wars, and military conscription, for example, even though lawfully ordered by civil (even democratic) power, were condemned because they violated the higher law. In faith and conscience, Quakers at times simply withdrew from the state and refused to obey its laws. In all these radical "protestations," the effect was not only to uphold a higher law of God, or of conscience, but also to denigrate government and to shift individual attention and allegiance from the mundane to the transcendent.

Three more modern figures—Henry David Thoreau, Mohandas Gandhi, and Martin Luther King—keenly aware of themselves as kindred spirits (though not all explicitly Christians), continued the same pattern of insistence on a moral and spiritual righteousness that condemns, or at least subordinates, temporal authority to uphold a prophetically articulated higher law. King in 1963 wrote from a Birmingham jail that "an unjust law is no law at all" (quoting Saint Augustine), while Thoreau in 1848 insisted that "it is not desirable to cultivate a respect for the law, so much as for the right."[4] Gandhi intended, through nonviolent disobedience, to collapse the whole unjust apparatus of British imperial government. Though there is nothing finally anarchic about any of these leaders, each gave powerful voice to the three-millennia-old Judeo-Christian tradition of temporal subordination to a higher law. Gandhi, as was King, was a modern Moses; both were leaders of their people from oppression to freedom under principles of justice. (Gandhi's complex blending of Western and Hindu thought and practice reveals an affinity that itself enlarges the sway in the world of inattention to the polis.)

Gandhi and King, of course, in a populist era far distant from the world of Thomas Aquinas and John Calvin, provided important roles for the people and, indeed, required a great deal of them. Through their own faith, sense of justice, and place in society, ordinary people were the crucial instruments of the higher law. Their courage, solidarity, discipline, and conscientious conviction were necessary to carry the day against conventional society and government powers. Yet the energy for Gandhi, King, and Thoreau came distinctly from without, from conviction of conscience attuned, not to ongoing political processes, but to a higher, prophetic voice. There is little or no cultivation of the deliberative, lawful processes of self-government that were at issue in classical times and remain fundamental to democracy in the modern era (since about 1600). The things of the public (*res publica*, "republic") arose, not from the socially considered concerns of the people (whether seeking self-interests through controversy or the common good through reason), but rather from the growing, finally overwhelming conviction of the people in the rightness and uprightness of their faith. The tendency, then, is to emphasize the charismatic power of the leader to convey the faith to the conscience of the people and, thus, not so much to derive just government from the consent of the governed as to confer it on them. In any case, the civil processes of democracy are not so much refuted as bypassed. In Thoreau's version: "That government is best which governs not at all. . . . Must a citizen ever for a moment, or in the least degree, resign his conscience to the legislator? Why has every man a conscience then? I think that we should be men first, and subjects [citizens?] afterward. . . . The only obligation I have a right to assume is to do at any time what I think right."[5]

One does not think readily, that is, of the throngs that followed Gandhi or King as *citizens,* as part of the body politic. Like Elijah or Amos, they were prophets or judges from without or above, voices of conscience to an erring land. They were, in fact, in strong tension with any idea of citizenship seen as embedded in the structure and political processes of society. Consider the difference between the circumstances of an individual in a Gandhi or a King movement and the place (theoretically at least) of a citizen in the Athens of Pericles. The Athenian citizen is immersed in, part of, active within the existing polity— even if opposed to a particular policy or even to the nature of the government itself. Change, even radical change, would come in deliberative and organizational activity with other citizens. The Socratic example, of accepting an unjust penalty rather than undermining the political community, dramatizes the difference. Socrates drank the hemlock to show his deep reverence for the idea of responsible citizenship, while Martin Luther King, and Gandhi too, went to jail to show contempt for and transcendence of temporal power. In a way, Socrates was as much the dissident and thorn in the side of the authorities as King was, but his concept of citizenship, strong, indelible, and mundane, simply could not countenance "outsideness" (exile specifically in his case). There was tension aplenty in Socrates' consideration of what he should think and do as a member of the polity—but no thought that his grounds for action might come from outside or above. Rather, they came from within his sense of what the polity was and of the responsibilities that he shared with others in it—even when and as he expressed profound dissent from existing policies and practices.

The fact that Gandhi and King (and their followers) were compelled to be outsiders, in that they were excluded from any meaningful, legitimized role in the political societies in which they lived (while Socrates was much more an insider), of course explains some of their critique and assault from without. Still, however, like Thoreau's, their subordinated idea of government and their exalted sense of individual conscience (Martin Luther facing the authorities echoes: "Here I stand, I can do no other") almost inevitably place them as prophets whose primary allegiance is to a higher law that they derive from outside and above. The tension will be intense and omnipresent throughout any sojourn in the earthly city. The essential "living" is never comfortably and unreservedly within that city. Though a Thoreau or a Gandhi or a King has a conscientious concern for justice in the earthly city and a deep commitment to its achievement, each nonetheless remains in a way "apolitical" in his preoccupation with his own moral and spiritual purposes—in a way that a Socrates (or a Confucius) would not so much repudiate as simply not even conceive. Their understanding of themselves as "political animals" is too strong and their sense of a personal, conscientious connection to an outside, higher law (or God) too weak.

In the Middle Eastern, Abrahamic tradition, the sense of outside, apoliticalness is, of course, more dramatically evident in its most thoroughly spiritual manifestations. The Hasidic rabbis, the monks and saints of Christendom, and the Islamic Sufis are so entirely imbued with the spiritual realm and so intensely aware of their personal experience of God that they seem literally otherworldly —and, in a way, pride themselves on that. They are, moreover, often viewed as the ultimate representatives of their religious traditions: experiencing and living God's way so completely that they suffer no taint from the this-worldly and are, thus, the fullest embodiment of Jew, Christian, or Muslim. At the same time, they are at the furthest remove from the political community. Though the outcome of their way is not unrelated to politics (indeed, the impact can be enormous), the effect often is to so subordinate, even denigrate the political that the public realm and the perspective and attitudes that the Aristotelian and Confucian traditions value and exalt atrophy from neglect and scorn. The conception and practice of citizenship are, thus, substantially displaced, or at least enough moved aside by moral and spiritual otherworldliness as to create in any faithful person a tension between what is rendered unto God and what is rendered unto Caesar, between the heavenly city and the earthly city. The religious life is exalted, and, insofar as government is attended to, it is required to conform to and sustain the religious higher law. Citizenship observes the same priorities.

4

The First Era of Modern Thought,
ca. 1600—1750

During the European Renaissance of the fifteenth and sixteenth centuries, the revival of classical learning, with its emphasis on political community, combined with Christian thought, with its emphasis on individual conscience (even before the Reformation), to assist the creation of a worldview and ideology that ushered in the first cycle of modernity. The essence of this first version of modernity, in the various evolutions that it has undergone in five hundred years, comes to be a kind of secular individualism, taking classical secularism, or mundaneness, from the ancient world and, thus, weakening medieval spirituality while, at the same time, sustaining the individual faith and orientation of Judeo-Christianity (and Islam) in a way that diluted classical assumptions about polity. This interacting of ideas, together with the rise of capitalism and European access to the East and the New World, marks the beginning of the modern era, which would, in turn, generate new conceptions and practices of self-government and the ideas of leadership and citizenship that might go with them.

In its first version (for second, third, and fourth versions, see below), modernity embraced a worldview that was fundamentally at odds with both ancient and medieval thought and, thus, became its own full-fledged ideology, a new paradigm. Drawing strength from Renaissance humanism, capitalistic competitiveness, and Reformation anticlericalism, an outlook emerged that placed the individual on earth at the center of the conceptual universe. In the famous Renaissance manifesto *Oration on the Dignity of Man* (1486), the Florentine Pico della Mirandola wrote: "The Supreme Maker . . . took man, made in his own individual image, . . . and placed him in the center of the world [where,] . . . restrained by no narrow bonds, according to [his] own free will . . . [he] shall define [his] nature for [himself]."[1] Yet, as Reinhold Niebuhr has observed, the classical thought that Pico celebrated "has no such passion for the individual as the Renaissance betrays." The model of individual fulfillment and responsibility "could only have grown on the soil of Christianity."[2] The essence of modernity took shape, then, when an invigorated sense of personality derived from Middle Eastern spirituality and moral athleticism combined with a classical mundaneness ("man . . . placed . . . in the center of the world") to fashion an unprecedented individuality. Oppositely, and politically, however, the new individuality contradicted much of both classical social or civic emphasis and medieval spiritual or otherworldly preoccupation.

This worldly individuality, of course, dovetailed nicely with the expansive commercial spirit that accompanied the dawning era of exploration and capitalism and reflected (or caused?) the individualism of the Protestant Reformation. (Which came first, or caused the other, is less to the point than their obvious tendency to converge or overlap.) The convergence defined, in fact, a worldview that crystallized in Western Europe and especially in England in the seventeenth century, recounted classically by Alfred North Whitehead in *Science in the Modern World*. Science, Whitehead noted, "recoloured our mentality . . . [and] altered the metaphysical presuppositions of the imaginative contents of our minds":[3] the "first modernity."

Bacon, Descartes, and "Science in the Modern World"

The key philosophers of the new habits of thought, the "modern" mentality, were Francis Bacon (1561–1626) and René Descartes (1596–1650). Bacon hailed the inductive method of inquiry beginning with the parts, the collection of evidence, that could then generate hypotheses to be tested against more evidence—the scientific method. The method was a frame of mind that departed fundamentally from the abstract dogmatizing, "full of superstition and imposture," that, Bacon wrote, had for centuries damaged classical and Christian thought alike. Instead, "for the study of truth" Bacon proposed "having a mind nimble and versatile enough to catch the resemblances of things, . . . at the same time steady enough to fix and distinguish their subtler differences; as being gifted by nature with desire to seek, patience to doubt, fondness to meditate, slowness to assert, readiness to reconsider, carefulness to dispose and set in order; and [that] . . . neither affects what is new nor admires what is old, and that hates every kind of imposture." "The human understanding," Bacon asserted, is prone to abstractions and finds its "greatest hindrance and aberration . . . [in] the dulness, incompetency, and deceptions of the senses." Yet "to resolve nature into abstractions is less to our purpose than to dissect her into parts. . . . Matter rather than forms should be the object of our attention, its configurations and changes of configuration, and simple action, and law of action or motion; for forms are figments of the human mind." (Nietzsche would call forms a "will to a system" [see chapter 10].) "Axioms established by argumentation," like the great logical, deductive treatises of Aristotle and Aquinas, could not "avail for the discovery of new works; since the subtlety of nature is greater many times over than the subtlety of argumentation. But axioms duly and orderly formed from particulars easily discover the way to new particulars, and thus render sciences active." "In ancient times there were philosophical doctrines in plenty," Bacon noted, listing a dozen thinkers from Pythagoras to Zeno: "All these invented systems of the universe, each according to his own fancy, . . . where of some were more elegant and probable, others harsh and unlikely. . . . Everyone philosophizes out of the cells of his own imagination, as out of Plato's cave. . . . By the regulation of some learned and excellent men, the sciences are confined to certain and prescribed authors, and thus restrained are imposed upon the old and instilled into the young. . . . Authority is taken for truth, not truth for authority." If humankind had "any love of truth in nature, any hatred of darkness, any desire for the purification of the understanding," Bacon pleaded, "we must entreat men again and again to discard . . . these volatile and preposterous philosophies, which have preferred theses to hypotheses, [and] led experience captive, . . . [and instead] to approach with humility and veneration to unroll the volume of Creation, to linger and meditate therein, and with minds washed clean from opinions to study it in purity and integrity." Since "the human understanding is of its own nature prone to suppose the existence of more order and regularity in the world than it finds," Bacon noted, "man, being the servant and interpreter of nature, can do and understand so much and so much only as he has observed in fact or in thought of the course of nature; beyond this he neither knows anything nor can do anything."[4] The way to understand, and then control and manage, human society as well as natural science was to set aside abstractions, theses, imposed doctrines, and other "volatile and preposterous philosophies." Then, Bacon explained, new modes of thought to improve the senses, to catch resemblances and subtle differences, modes open to all experiences and alert to "new particulars" and "dissect[ion] . . . into parts" that would "render sciences active," could come into play.

Descartes instructed simply that the starting point was "I think, therefore I am," placing the individual perceiver at the center of understanding and, therefore, reality. Scorning "the syllogisms . . . of the Schools . . . as capable only of explaining to others those things that are known," Descartes praised the Baconian method as a way of "learning what is new," thus enabling men to "render [themselves] the masters and possessors of nature." Among his rules of inquiry were "to divide up each of the difficulties which I examined into as many parts as possible" and "to make enumerations so complete and reviews so general that I should be certain of having omitted nothing."[5] Endorsed, candidly and self-confidently, was the idea that one started, not with abstract and holistic essences, traditions, or polities, but with numberless discrete parts (facts) and with autonomous, thinking, choosing individuals. Bacon and Descartes were, thus, explaining a "recolour[ing] . . . [of] mentality," what can be called a *first modernity,* that contained the seeds of a recast democracy of immense significance for the future. Politics should not rest on large abstractions and dogmas that formed religious and national imperialisms from above and, thus, imposed purposive regimes on subjects who were understood to have meaning only within those imperiums. Rather, the political aspect of humankind, detached from "preposterous philosophies," would be able to derive from the dissected parts, the people, "omit[ting] nothing," *all* the people, then move to "new particulars," in an "active," forward-looking polity, a government resting on the felt needs of the people—the defining idea of a secular, inductive modernity and a notion foreign equally to Confucius, Plato, and Aristotle, Muhammad, Aquinas, and Calvin.

Hobbes, Locke, and Modern Politics

The political implications of this "Copernican Revolution," this reordering of what is at the center, were worked out by Thomas Hobbes and John Locke. "The rights and duties of subjects," Hobbes said, could, like a watch or an engine, be known only when "considered as if they were dissolved," separated, taken apart. Government, he argued, was a contract "because we make the commonwealth ourselves," thus emphasizing the individual agreements of obedience to the sovereign who could control "the war of all against all." As one of his early critics noted, Hobbes "discourses of Men as if they were terrigene, born out of the earth, come up like seeds, without any relation one to the other."[6] No less autonomously, according to Locke's theorizing, individuals, with minds blank at birth and made infinitely varied through a Baconian process of receiving sense impressions, agreed to form government for their mutual protection and convenience. Hobbes supposed a single, rational act of agreeing to obey a sovereign to achieve social order, while Locke posited an ongoing formulation of and agreement to laws through representatives in order to achieve order and social convenience. In any case, the state was demystified and made to rest on the need of individuals for their own survival and self-protection. There was no whole, that is, other than the sum of the parts, the aggregated will of individuals. The political dimension of modernity, we might say, had been fashioned; government rested on a mundane individualism, nothing more.

Neither the Hobbesian nor the Lockean version of the foundation of government (contract), of course, precluded *strong* government. Indeed, Hobbes's version seemed to entail a great leviathan able to impose law and order on quarrelsome and selfish parts (though the presumptions remained that the writ of the sovereign extended only to the need to preserve order and that self-willed individuals would continue to seek their own ends). Locke's version placed no theoretical limit on what the contracted-for government might be authorized to do. In the British Declaratory Act of 1766, for example, Parliament asserted its power to "legislate in all matters whatsoever," and, in the New Deal formulation (1933), government (federal, state, or local) might entail large-scale management of the economy, social welfare, and other public concerns. The Lockean principle required only that those in the political community consent through some representative process. In both versions, however, the ends and means of government were mundane and limited to dealing with the quarrelsome inclinations and/or varied interests of the persons governed—there was no Holy Roman Empire, or mystical Third Rome or Third Reich, or Islamic Republic to set a higher purpose of the state.

Hobbes's use of machine analogies and the influence of Newtonian models of physical forces in dynamic equipoise highlight the tendency in this first modern political thinking to view the good society as one where interacting forces (e.g., self-willed individuals) balanced each other to create benign results. The need, then, is a political constitution, bereft of from-on-high purposes, that takes into account existing (individual, factional) interests and provides a mechanism to allow their orderly combination. The economic analogue of this process, of course, is Adam Smith's idea of the "invisible hand" creating laws of supply and demand leading to the "wealth of nations" as individual, self-interested, competitive energies interact in the marketplace. Again, the whole arrangement is mundane, individual based, and independent of any explicit ideas of grand design or national purposes (except aggregate wealth)—indeed, it is vigorously hostile to them as counterproductive, as, for example, in its hostility to the theories of mercantilism in international trade and divine right or dynastic destiny in monarchies.

Altogether, then, the elements of the first version of modernity, the version sometimes retroactively called *liberalism,* were put in place during the seventeenth and eighteenth centuries. Dovetailing with the humanism of the Renaissance, the commercial ethic of capitalism, and the moral and spiritual individuality of the Reformation, and using the empiricism and inductive thinking of Baconian science, a "new science of politics" took shape. The powerful technology and immense material wealth thus generated, mobilized by burgeoning commercial and capitalist enterprise, and undergirded by liberal, first modernity ideology, moreover, served to distance the modern (Western) world even further from millennia-old spiritual and moral traditions. Protestant ethical individualism, for example, attuned to ancient moral precepts that condemned greed and wealth often found itself overwhelmed by the more material, self-centered dimensions of modern society. The personal responsibility and con-scientiousness of Protestantism, when coupled with the economic self-assertiveness of capitalism and private property, more often than not left the mundane domi-nant. This meant that the first configuration of modernity, in its political dimen-sion, had a strong tendency toward what C. B. MacPherson has called *possessive individualism.*[7] The polity, that is, had built into it, not only an emphasis on the individual parts, but also a devotion to the commercial ethic. Though the rheto-ric of moral purpose remained, the actual practice in both economic and political life left the ethic of trade, the acquisitive emphasis, and the structure of capitalism dominant. It seemed that the attention to the parts (individualism) of Bacon, Locke, and Calvin, instead of fostering a social and political liberation, in fact simply ushered in the domination of, first, the lords of trade and, then, the cap-tains of industry—or even the leviathan to control "the war of all against all." The demystification of the state, of the political realm, seemed to open the door, not for the intended enlargement of human potential, but for a pervasive capitalism. In any case, the mundane individualism at the heart of modernity had a way of heightening emphasis on the material and economic aspects of life—or had those aspects generated the new individualism? Again, however, settling the question of cause and effect is less important than is the convergence that gave the modern era its most distinctive mark. The political dimension, developed largely in the British polity in the seventeenth and eighteenth centuries, was a form and rationale for self-government that attended to the rights and interests of the "terrigene" (earth-born) parts as they competed with each other. The fun-damentals of both democracy and liberalism, that is, were in place.

The "Ancients" and a Republican Counterpoint

When government is viewed in this broad perspective, with a modernity chal-lenging basic ways of thinking and every aspect of culture, it is not surprising that profound and eloquent voices spoke out in defense of more traditional pat-terns and ideas of government. In England, in the late seventeenth century and the early eighteenth, this challenge resulted intellectually in "the Battle of the Books" between the "Ancients" and the "Moderns."[8] When Descartes pro-claimed priority for methods of thought that "learned what is new" above "syllogisms ... [that] explained those things that are [already] known," the terms of the discourse were set. The point of detailed observation, careful collection of evidence, attention to the facts, tentative formulation of hypotheses, and further testing against more evidence was to discover, formulate, and verify the previously unknown. As scientists discovered the circulation of the blood, the nature of light, the laws of motion in the physical universe, and other basic matters, often upsetting ancient understandings, it seemed that humankind had more to learn by looking ahead than by cherishing the past, by looking down at the earth than by dreaming of transcendence. In the Royal Society's *Transactions* and other scientific publications, the new discoveries were announced and extended, one investigation building on another until it seemed that probing for the new was the way in which to understand the world.

In a way responding to tendencies in capitalism, science, and Baconian modernity to focus on the (competitive) parts and to move as well toward coherence and grand design, first modernity thinking about ethics and politics sought to derive universally valid, "natural" laws from the accumulated "facts" and differentiations in modern social life, just as Newton had done in the physical world. Locke and others argued that there were in politics and ethics universal, natural laws compatible with, indeed drawn from, an empirical understanding of human nature. Among Locke's foundational works, *An Essay concerning Human Understanding* validated the *Second Treatise on Civil Government*, which set forth the natural laws of politics. David Hume's logically powerful critique of this bypassing of the contradictions between modern and ancient thought was largely ignored as first modernity political thinking found differentiation and newly discovered facts compatible with universal laws.

Though the method of collecting evidence and formulating hypotheses seemed triumphant over Aristotelian physics, Ptolemaic astronomy, and Galenic medicine, that is, was it equally the case that ancient moral philosophy, politics, literature, aesthetics, and rhetoric were outmoded and best submitted as well to the new inductive methods? In an overtly neoclassical age, a host of English writers, led by Sir William Temple, Jonathan Swift, Alexander Pope, and Henry St. John Lord Bolingbroke, brilliantly upheld ancient wisdom and scorned the presumption that Francis Bacon, Bernard Mandeville, and Daniel Defoe had more to teach the world about philosophy, literature, and politics than did Homer, Aristotle, Cicero, and Virgil. In so arguing, of course, the ancients in the Battle of the Books were calling into question many of the assumptions and guidelines of the modern worldview in development since the Renaissance. Indeed, they insisted that a true renaissance would best attend to the *revival* of ancient wisdom rather than to an arrogant assertion of novelty everywhere. Readers of Temple's *Essay upon Ancient and Modern Learning* (1690), Swift's *Gulliver's Travels* (1726), Pope's *Dunciad* (1728), and Bolingbroke's *Idea of a Patriot King* (1738) found telling scorn for modern presumptions and profound voice for ancient learning.

This pervasive encounter provided the backdrop for a searching debate over the political implications of modernity. The great English "philosophers of the parts," Bacon, Hobbes, and Locke, began with notions of human nature and human society far different from those of the ancient authors and philosophers the study of whose learning remained pervasive in seventeenth- and eighteenth-century England. To those steeped in the wisdom of the Greeks and the Romans, much of modern thought seemed so unsocial, amoral, and autonomous (self-preoccupied) as to be wrongheaded and superficial, even absurd and calamitous. When, in *Gulliver's Travels,* Swift ridiculed and scorned the Lilliputians, the Laputans, and the Yahoos, his target was the selfish, arrogantly "scientific," commercial, nascently democratic, factious, corrupt, small-minded nation that he thought England (and Britain) was becoming in the days of Robert Walpole (1721–1742) and the Commercial Revolution. In words and examples and metaphors deliberately and vividly evoking classical values and models, Swift held up for his readers Brobdingnagians and Houghuhnmians more like Pericles and Cicero than like the rulers of contemporary England. To Swift, the Greek and Latin writers offered a wisdom about morality and politics vastly superior to the practice and the thought of the England of Bacon, Locke, Walpole, and the Whig merchants. He extolled the ancients and scorned the modern, as did Alexander Pope in the *Dunciad,* John Gay in the *Beggar's Opera,* and many other brilliant writers of the Augustan Age. In his *Cato,* a stirring drama widely popular on both sides of the Atlantic, Joseph Addison upheld the courageous, principled, public-spirited republican hero who resisted corruption, intrigue, greed, and tyranny.

What so appalled Swift and these other writers was the radical declension of the standards of the good and just society. In Walpole's England, Pope declaimed, "in Soldier, Churchman, Patriot, Man in Power, / 'Tis Avarice all, Ambition is no more!" Indeed, the denigration of the very idea of the political led to thinking, as Swift put it, that "the whole art of government consisted in the importation of nutmegs and the curing of herrings."[9] It was not that Swift and his fellow critics were especially surprised by the greed, favoritism, and corruption in public life; human fallibility and self-orientation made such conduct a more or less perennial part of politics. Much more alarming—and novel—was the *praise* and *celebration* of selfish, factional motivations as necessary and useful in economics, politics, and morality. When Bernard Mandeville insisted that the greed of merchants to become rich ("private vice") was in fact useful to a nation's prosperity ("public benefit") and that "Desires enlarg'd," "Appetites refin'd," and "Vices increas'd" were valuable qualities in public life; when Pierre Bayle asserted that, to become great and rich, a nation must "maintain avarice and ambition in all their ardor"; and when Daniel Defoe declared that the tradesman who has "thriven and grown rich, is a really valuable man" and better qualified to conduct public business than "men of ten times learning and education," a stunningly, frighteningly new public morality was in view.[10] If, instead of disinterestedness, public spirit, and patriotism being the aspirations of politics, one claims that self-interest, enhancement of trade and wealth, and advocacy of (various) special interests are the desired foundations and will lead to the only proper understanding of the common good (the aggregated "goods" of all the parts), profound revolutions in the purpose of government, the ideals of leadership, and the nature of citizenship follow. And, in the long run, the most problematic aspects were not the pursuit of private interest and the overriding of policies tending toward the common good—such pursuits and neglects were ancient facts of political life—but the *validating* of them as the *right* way to conduct the public life of the nation, thus marking them as something to be encouraged rather than resisted. If this view came to prevail, then the whole conception of citizenship and leadership, and the very idea of government itself, would be transformed. And, indeed, this unashamed ideology of autonomy, self-interest, aggregation of the parts, free trade, individual rights, and an openness that endorsed popular access to government—later generally termed *liberalism*—formed much of the political dimension of the first modernity.

As the powerful and influential voices of Pope and Swift and Bolingbroke made clear, however, the triumph of the moderns was by no means uncontested. "What expectation," Bolingbroke asked, "can be entertained of raising a disinterested public spirit among men who have no other principle than that of private interest, *who are individuals rather than fellow citizens,* who prey on one another, and are, in a state of civil society, much like Hobbes's men in the supposed state of nature?" (emphasis added).[11] Bolingbroke inveighed against the control of Walpole's government by corrupt commercial interests, upheld the benefits of a "patriot king," and looked forward (vaguely) to a republicanized government where leaders and citizens alike were guided by the paramount public virtue of concern for the common good. This harked back, of course, to ancient (Aristotelian, Ciceronian) ideals of government and citizenship, as the neoclassical English writers were well aware. Modernity, on the other hand, pointed toward a world where government would rest, not on divine right or higher law or deliberations in the public interest, but on special interests, majority rule, and convenience. The role of the more or less equalized human parts (really not conceptualized as citizens) would be to seek their own preservation and aggrandizement, whether by submitting to a leviathan state or by organizing to protect individualities. This was the political dimension of the modern worldview that caused Pope's lament:

> Lo! thy dread Empire, CHAOS! is restored;
> Light dies before thy uncreating word:

Thy hand, great Anarch! lets the curtain fall;
And universal Darkness buries All.

Thus, the first modern political ideology took shape in the presence of a brilliantly articulated ancient counterpoint that remained itself a potent part of early-modern political thought and practice. Pope encapsulated the tension in calling Bacon "the wisest, brightest, meanest of mankind."[12]

Benjamin Constant (1767–1830), a Frenchman deeply learned in Enlightenment thought yet tinged with the new Romantic mood, a century later caught the political disaccord and the fundamental ancient reservations about the ideas of citizenship and the public sphere in the first modernity in a speech entitled "The Liberty of the Ancients Compared with That of the Moderns," given at the Athénée Royal in 1819:

> The danger of ancient liberty was that men, exclusively concerned with securing their share of social power, might attach too little value to individual rights and enjoyments.
>
> The danger of modern liberty is that, absorbed in the enjoyment of our private independence, and in the pursuit of our particular interests, we should surrender our right to share in political power too easily. . . . Is it so evident that happiness, of whatever kind, is the only aim of mankind? If it were so, our course would be narrow indeed, and our destination far from elevated. There is not one single one of us who, if he wishes to abase himself, restrain his moral faculties, lower his desires, abjure activity, glory, deep and generous emotions, could not demean himself and be happy. No, Sirs, I bear witness to the better part of our nature. It is not to happiness alone, it is to self-development that our destiny calls us; and political liberty is the most powerful, the most effective means of self-development that heaven has given us.
>
> Political liberty, by submitting to all the citizens, without exception, the care and assessment of their most sacred interests, enlarges their spirit, ennobles their thoughts, and establishes among them a kind of intellectual equality which forms the glory and power of a people. . . . Far from renouncing either of the two sorts of freedom, it is necessary to learn to combine the two together. . . .
>
> The work of the legislator is not complete when he has simply brought peace to the people. Even when the people are satisfied, there is much left to do. Institutions must achieve the moral education of the citizens. By respecting their individual rights, securing their independence, refraining from troubling their work, they must nevertheless consecrate their influence over public affairs, call them to contribute by their votes to the exercise of power, grant them a right of control and supervision by expressing their opinions; and, by forming them through practice for these elevated functions, give them both the desire and the right to discharge these.[13]

5

The United States and First Modernity Democracy

The founding of the American polity in the last quarter of the eighteenth century bears the mark of the tension that accompanied the transition from ancient to modern ideas of the political—and perhaps benefited from the ambiguity of that complex origin. The new, modern ideology of Bacon, Locke, English "radical Whigs" (and, by 1776, Adam Smith and other Scots) was the clear, articulated philosophy of the American Revolution. These were the ideas that such revolutionaries as Samuel Adams, Thomas Paine, and Thomas Jefferson took seriously and set forth in *Common Sense,* the Declaration of Independence, and other manifestos. The American revolutionary leaders, like Locke himself and most eighteenth-century thinkers, did not, however, completely accept the finally fragmenting, antiuniversal implications of post-Baconian modernity. Drawing an analogy from Isaac Newton's laws of physical nature, they supposed that all the diverse details of human society and politics could also be seen as converging toward certain fundamentals that they understood as further natural law. In Carl Becker's phrase, they accepted "the heavenly city of the eighteenth-century philosophers," as much in their minds a universal cosmology as that fashioned by Saint Augustine himself. In a way sustaining this philosophically dubious idea (Becker's argument was an ironic one), an age of republican revolution was under way in the Western world that would sweep France in 1789 and soon touch most of the other nations of Europe. The American Revolution was a foreshadowing part of this republican, radicalizing, enlightened, ideologically problematic movement that forever altered the political and social landscape. No "rethinking of the American Revolution," no emphasis on the difference between the American and the

French phenomena, and no acknowledgment of the flaws, limitations, and even Thermidorian aspects of the American Revolution can offset the radical burst of 1776 and all that it entailed.[1]

The Rationale of the American Revolution

Thus, the thrust and energy of American revolutionary ideology were forward, toward modernity. That ideology emphasized securing the rights of individuals, balancing and limiting the powers of government, and establishing a polity resting on the consent of the governed. The new thinking about government that excited creative minds, the particular needs of growing colonies to throw off the restraints of the mother country, and the Enlightenment emphasis on reason and openness rather than bigotry and tradition all favored the developing ideology of individual autonomy, enlightened self-interest, and limitation on government. The American Revolution, as an intellectual movement, took place at a time when much of British thought (and its Continental parallels), in the writings of Adam Smith, Richard Price, James Burgh, Joseph Priestley, and others, emphasized individual rights and self-rule. All the major American founders responded to these works and accepted their implicit political philosophy—so much so that John Adams could declare that it had been "hackneyed" in the Continental Congresses of 1774–1776 and Jefferson could say that in the Declaration of Independence he had merely set down the "common sense" of contemporary political thinking.[2] As Abraham Lincoln would later emphasize, the Declaration thus proclaimed a new, ideologically based nation "conceived in liberty and dedicated to the proposition that all men are created equal." This endorsed the idea of "certain inalienable rights" of individual liberty that were regarded as the "property" of all members of the polity being created and gave a Lockean moral foundation—the equal rights of all, for the sake of the individuality of each member—to the polity.

The next phrase of the Declaration, however, asserted that the just powers of government derived from the consent of the governed, another Lockean notion, but one that also echoed ancient ideas about the nature and purpose of government. It was to be conducted according to "just" (principled, moral) standards, and it was also to accord with the will and needs of the people, meaning especially their *common* good (and not simply aggregated individual needs). The first charge against George III in the Declaration of Independence was that he had thwarted laws passed by colonial legislatures "wholesome and necessary for the public good." The colonies and their united polity, that is, aspired to governments that would be active and effective in pursuing, not Britain's selfish or dynastic goals, but rather common, now American, purposes. This was consistent in a way with the early stages of protests against British authorities, when colonial leaders had appealed to a higher law and to the king to sustain the common good (of the empire) against particularistic and factional interests in Parliament and the ministries in London. James Otis asserted in 1764 that, though "Parliaments are in all cases to declare what is good for the whole," any act of Parliament "contrary to eternal truth, equity, and justice [natural law] would be . . . consequently void," while in 1774 Jefferson advised George III that he was "no more than the chief officer of the people, appointed . . . to assist in working the great machine of government, erected for their use." Jefferson added that, though surrounded by "counsellors [who] are parties," the king must nonetheless adhere to "great principles of right and wrong . . . [and] no longer persevere in sacrificing the rights of one part of the empire to the inordinate desires of another." Only this could "establish fraternal love and harmony through the whole empire."[3] The American revolutionaries, then, though excited by modern ideas of liberty and independence, were at the same time still deeply imbued with ancient concepts of political purpose and harmony. They were, thus, heirs as much to Aristotle as to Locke, intent on sustaining good government as well as repudiating tyranny. They sought to understand justice and probed the purpose of the state as Plato had done (even though they did not come to his answers)—and as their earliest and most basic instruction and reading about government had taught.

This nation-building emphasis, of course, came more urgently to the fore as British authority and military power were driven out and the newly independent states sought to establish governments for themselves and for their union. After the excesses of the last royal governors, and after Thomas Paine's scorn in *Common Sense* (1776) of George III as the "royal Brute of Britain,"[4] monarchy was no longer a viable option in the new nation, but conservative ideas of government by a privileged elite remained potent. Also present were both the classical republican tradition of ordered self-government according to principles of virtue and the common good and a more radical liberal ideology looking ahead to a democratic politics of rights and interests. (These terms, however, were not part of revolutionary political dialogue, nor would participants in that dialogue have seen themselves as divided in that way; most of them held views combining elements, not inconsistently, of each.) Thus, as first the states and then the union created in 1776 sought to frame governments, they possessed a fertile legacy of traditions with which to work.

Phrases from some of the most notable state constitutions reveal the important crosscurrents of political ideas. The Continental Congress had simply proposed on May 15, 1776, that the states "adopt such government as shall, in the opinion of the representatives of the people, best conduce to the happiness and safety of their constituents in particular and America in general." (Thus, the union, the needs of "America in general," was present and central from the beginning—as Lincoln would also emphasize in 1861.) The day after the adoption of the Declaration of Independence, John Adams wrote his wife that "the new governments we are assuming . . . will require a Purification from our Vices, and an augmentation of our Virtue or they will be no Blessings." A Pennsylvania pamphleteer insisted that "a government made for the common good should be framed by men who can have no interest besides the common interest of mankind," warning especially against the influence of "great and over-grown rich men." The government, then, ought to seek "the common benefit, . . . [not] the particular emolument or advantage of any single man, family, or sett of men." And elections and offices were open to "all free men having a sufficient evident common interest with, and attachment to the community." (Thus, the defining idea was a moral and inclusive one that would, as black slaves and women and eighteen-year-olds later came to be regarded as members of the political community, of course validate their participation and responsibility.) Lest government officials miss their basic purpose, they were instructed in the Pennsylvania Constitution of 1776 that "laws for the encouragement of virtue, and prevention of vice and immorality [were to] be made and constantly kept in force"—in order to nourish good citizenship.[5]

In Massachusetts, similar underlying political ideas were evident. With the royal charter abrogated by Parliament also repudiated by the people, Massachusetts moved deliberately to establish government de novo by in 1779 calling a convention to draft a new constitution to be ratified by the people to assure its standing as higher law: "an original, explicit, and solemn compact." The convention, then, in undertaking its work sought to answer "the great inquiry . . . wherein the common interest consists." Led by John Adams, the convention devised a government of carefully arranged separation of powers and explicit declarations of the rights of the people. The Constitution provided as well for effective and energetic government that would "cherish the interests of literature and science, [establish] public schools and grammar schools in the towns, . . . [and] inculcate the principles of humanity and general benevolence, public and private . . . among the people." To this end, it created an unusually strong unitary executive who was "emphatically the representative of the whole people," capable of thwarting factional, "unsystematical," and foolish legislation. Underlying all the powers of government was the need that public and private institutions nourish "a wise, understanding, and free people" who could fulfill the high demands of republican citizenship. When Samuel Adams ventured the hope that the new United States might become a "Christian Sparta," he thus embraced the tensions in political purposes that infused the first American efforts to establish governments.[6]

These ambiguities, sustaining intentions to take government seriously, to depend on a capacity for public spirit in both leaders and citizens, *and* to protect individual rights, also found expression in the new federal Constitution of 1787–1791. The frame of government provided for in the new constitution, and most of the argument by "Publius" in the *Federalist* on its behalf, is, on the face of it, "liberal," that is, in the mode of Locke and the other modern thinkers so influential in the new United States.[7] Thus, protection of rights (now often termed *human,* or *individual,* or even *universal* rights, but in the eighteenth century generally called *natural* rights), limited powers of government, majority rule, and legislative provision to serve the needs and convenience of citizens were the foundations of the Constitution, all in accord with the Lockean dicta of equality before the law, of provision for "certain unalienable Rights," and of the "just Powers" of government deriving from "the consent of the Governed." Further, in accord with the oracular writings of Montesquieu and what David Hume had recently termed *a new science of politics,* the Constitution provided for careful separation of powers among the three branches of the federal government and between that level and the state governments. The idea was to prevent government itself from abusing the rights of individuals or from engaging in grandiose schemes (foreign conquest, holy wars, dynastic intrigue, etc.) beyond the needs and interests of private individuals and groups. The careful listing of the specific powers of Congress (and the implicit, and after the Tenth Amendment explicit, reservation of other powers to the states and to the people), the requirement that the president uphold the Constitution, and the provision for an independent judiciary further implanted "liberal" axioms of government.

Publius's explication of the Constitution emphasized this "liberalism." His defenses of the limited power to tax, of the civilian control of the armed forces, of the "numerous and indefinite" powers left to the states, of the Constitution's bicameral nature, and of the power of the federal judiciary to defend "the rights of individuals" against the "ill humor . . . of designing men" and "serious oppressions" potential in majority rule[8] all accord with the principles of Locke, "Cato," Adam Smith, Burgh, Paine, and other British theorists of limited government. Expressing the basic dynamic of the Constitution, Publius argued in *Federalist* no. 10 that the very variety of opinions and interests inevitable in the free and open society, provided for under the Constitution, would itself proscribe the tyranny of any individual or faction: the inclusion of many interests, each intent on protecting and aggrandizing itself, would prevent the undue dominance of any one group or interest. An important part of the operation of government, that is, would depend on the self-interested dynamism of its various parts. And, since the dynamic worked well in proportion to the number of interests in the polity, the Constitution implicitly welcomed the inclusion of more groups. (It would work better, e.g., if nonpropertyholders, women, and slaves were included, an important aspect of the argument for those inclusions as time went by.) Lockean autonomy and diversity of interests, the essence of "the new science of politics," thus undergirded and, in a way, found fulfillment in the new constitution.

Also present, though less explicitly, in revolutionary documents, in the Constitution itself, in its defense by the federalists, and in the arguments of the antifederalists were powerful overtones of what historians generally term *civic republican* ideology. The first six charges against George III in the Declaration of Independence complained about interference, not with the personal rights of individuals, but with the lawful processes of *government*. The king had refused "his assent to Laws, the most wholesome and necessary for the public Good" and had instructed his colonial governors to suspend or neglect enforcement of important laws. Then, the purposes of the new government of 1787, articulated in the Preamble, were broadly republican—establish justice, ensure domestic tranquility, provide the common defense, promote the general welfare, and secure the blessings of liberty, all through the formation of "a more perfect union," that is, through better government. Though these aspirations and phrases are not inconsistent with Lockean, "liberal" ideas, they echo more richly civic republican thought found in the writings of Aristotle, Cicero, other ancients, and their seventeenth- and eighteenth-century followers.

Publius began his defense of the Constitution of 1787 by asking his readers to "deliberate" on a proposed government resting, not on "accident and force," as was usual in human experience, but rather on "reflection and choice"[9]— not un-Lockean, but again echoing rich, positive ideas of government. (Liberal theory, not yet articulated in 1787–1788, would rest on self-interest, advocacy, and majority decisions.) The explanations by Publius of the need for a stronger union for purposes of defense, of the uses of the taxing power, of the merits of "loose construction," and of the contributions of an active, unitary executive all connote positive purposes going beyond a minimal, limited, rights-protecting paradigm.

The construction and defense of Congress reveal a similar dual yet expansive intent. The understanding of the House of Representatives is fundamentally "liberal": its membership to rest on a broad suffrage representing the regions of the country and to assemble bringing their varied interests to the legislative arena. The coequal Senate, however, was smaller and elected less directly and for a much longer term, in order that "wisdom and stability" might prevail over "the impulse of sudden and violent passions, and . . . intemperate and pernicious resolutions" that often characterized large, diverse, and frequently elected assemblies. The "display of enlightened policy, and attachment to the public good" likely to issue from the carefully constructed Senate, Publius argued, would act powerfully to earn the support and even the affection of the people thus well governed.[10] In Aristotelian terms, Publius clearly thought that a carefully designed bicameral legislature would not only deter invasions of rights but, perhaps more important, look toward sustaining a state that "exists for the sake of a good life, and not for the sake of life only."[11]

Even the *Federalist* paper most often cited as revealing the "liberal," conflict-of-interest nature of the Constitution, James Madison's famous no. 10, in fact rests more fundamentally on an intention to sustain the public good. *Faction* itself is defined within such an assumption: "a number of citizens, whether amounting to a majority or minority of the whole, actuated by some common impulse of passion, or of interest, adverse to the rights of other citizens, or to the permanent and aggregate interests of the community." That is, *faction* (current usage would more readily say *special interest*) is defined qualitatively, revealing partial or self-interested intent, as opposed to the long-range interest of the "community" as a whole—the public interest. Madison's goal is to control the variety of passions and interests and groups spawned inevitably by free society, much of which is corrupt, self-interested, and shortsighted. The need is to *neutralize,* render to no effect as much as possible, the public impact of these factions. The solution, especially efficacious in an "extended republic," is that the larger number of factions thereby encompassed will the more effectively check and confound each other, in that way preventing the triumph of particular "local prejudices and . . . schemes of injustice." With factions and special interests thus rendered less potent, the wiser, more just, more genuinely deliberative elements of the polity will have an opportunity to gain sway and guide toward what Madison in *Federalist* no. 10 nine times terms *the public good.* There was, indeed, in this explanation candid recognition of important "liberal" guideposts —autonomy of individuals and groups, diversity, self-advocacy, public debate, competitive politics, and so on—but equally evident is the intention to subsume these vital, ineradicable aspects of a free society within a polity still attentive to the idea of an objective public good.[12]

The antifederalists accepted a similar duality but envisioned different accommodations within it. In the spirit of Paine's *Common Sense,* they believed earnestly in an independence and self-government as close as possible to the fabled model of the whole people "assembled . . . [under] some convenient tree [as] a State House, . . . to deliberate on public matters."[13] Intensely suspicious of federalist conceptions of a powerful, commercial nation able to project itself confidently into the world through taxes, conscriptions, officers, and compulsions, antifederalists instead saw mild, more local government, closer to the people, as a fulfillment of both Lockean contract government and classic civic republicanism. Public-spirited citizens and their closely attuned representatives would provide just government through the consent of the governed. Antifederal fears were not so much of the "violent passions, and . . . intemperate and pernicious resolutions" of the common people and their demagogue-ridden legislators so ill regarded by the federalists as of the greedy ambitions and corruption of those holding power and public office, especially in a national capital remote from the people. Conversely, they placed faith, not in the wisdom and useful ambition of the leaders (as Publius often did), but in the virtue of ordinary people, nourished by family, church, school, benign occupations, and town meeting experience, whose decency and public spirit would cherish individual rights and guide toward good government.

Thus, both sides in the ratification debate accepted "liberal" axioms of personal liberty, self-rule, and limitation on government, and each as well valued "enlightened policy, and attachment to the public good." One depended on indirectly elected leaders deliberating in small councils (as explained in Publius's defense of the Senate and the executive), the other on the virtue of ordinary people whose "respective callings" made them "more temperate, of better morals, and less ambition than the great."[14] The debate, then, did not find "moderns" or "liberals" on one side and "ancients" or "civic republicans" on the other. Rather, both sides accepted liberal and republican concepts, with difference over how best to protect individual rights and how best to educe the public spirit and virtue essential to good government. The federalists found the benign dynamic in the possibility of constructive deliberations among leaders, while the antifederalists found it most likely in "public talk" among responsible citizens and their closely attuned representatives.

The same ambiguity coursed through the apparently paradoxical initial opposition by Madison (and other federalists) to inclusion of a bill of rights in the Constitution and his later sponsorship of the Bill of Rights amendments in Congress in 1789–1791. Though Madison did not oppose substantially the provisions of a bill of rights, he thought those rights already sufficiently protected by state constitutions in 1787 and redundant in any case in a constitution of explicitly limited powers. Under urging from Jefferson and others, and responding to widespread concern over the lack of a bill of rights in the Constitution, Madison came to favor its addition as amendments. Its adoption and inclusion in paramount law (as Madison regarded the Constitution) would fix its provisions in the public mind as "fundamental maxims of free government," and it would thus "become incorporated with the national sentiment." It would also permit easier appeals under law should agencies of government attempt violation of fundamental rights. Madison revealed his civic republican understanding of rights and government, however, in the phrasing of his proposals to Congress in 1789 for what became the First Amendment:

> The civil rights of none shall be abridged on account of religious belief or worship, nor shall any national religion be established, nor shall the full and equal rights of conscience be in any manner, or on any pretext infringed.
>
> The people shall not be deprived or abridged of their right to speak, to write, or to publish their sentiments; and Freedom of the press, as one of the great bulwarks of liberty, shall be inviolable.
>
> The people shall not be restrained from peace fully assembling and consulting for their common good; nor from applying to the legislature by petitions, or remonstrances for redress of their grievances.

His understanding, that is, was that the five freedoms of the more felicitously phrased First Amendment as adopted had primarily *public* purpose: to prevent the dogmas of established churches from hindering reasoned *public* deliberation and to secure the *public* benefits of a free press and of free assembly in a self-governing polity. He approved the protection of individual rights but saw as even more important the place of such freedoms in fostering good republican government through reason and deliberation.[15]

The Jeffersonian Synthesis

The complexities of these political crosscurrents, however, were both most vividly revealed and most creatively resolved in the thought of Thomas Jefferson. The author of the Declaration of Independence and of the Virginia Statute of Religious Freedom, and the earnest defender of free trade and private enterprise, was certainly imbued with the "modern," "liberal," ideology of his "trinity of immortals," Bacon, Newton, and Locke. Yet Jefferson was also deeply classical—coauthor of the "republicanized" law code of the state of Virginia, a president of the United States who believed that the executive should "advance the notions of a whole people [slowly] to ideal right,"[16] and father of the University of Virginia—thus hearkening to civic republican conceptions still vigorous in the early American republic. In fact, we may say that Jefferson's standing as *the* fundamental theorist and practitioner of American democratic thought rests on his creative acceptance of both traditions.

Though Jefferson's articulation of the principles of government was always explicitly Lockean-"liberal," his assumptions about the underlying nature of government, its place in human society, and the proper mechanisms of participation and leadership were just as deeply civic republican. He would not have thought of himself as either Confucian or Aristotelian, but his attitude toward government nonetheless shared those traditions' rich sense of its importance and its potential. It is not that Jefferson was a student of Confucian thought or was in any direct way influenced by the Chinese sage, nor can Confucius be understood as a civic republican. Jefferson knew of Confucius, however, and had probably read the writings about China of Leibniz, Voltaire, Wolfius, and other eighteenth-century Sinophiles who idealized Qing China as having "beaten [the West] . . . in the principles of Ethics and Politics." This would have sustained Jefferson's general belief in good, rational, principled government, that, in the Chinese paradigm, "the polity bears a maximum responsibility as the moralizing agent of the society."[17] Thus, Jefferson in a way shared broadly premodern modes of thought that assumed the fundamentally social, deeply moral, uniquely constructive nature and potential of human government (see chapters 2 and 8).

Jefferson was more directly dependent on classical (ancient) thought, as he acknowledged in declaring Aristotle and Cicero authors of "elementary books of public right," as basic to the American founding as John Locke and Algernon Sidney.[18] He would have absorbed from the beginning of his education the ancient axioms in public philosophy of the Greek and Latin texts that he used— perhaps virtually memorized—in learning those languages. He believed that humans, indelibly social, lived together and formed governments, not merely to survive, but to seek the good life. With the Greeks, he had a rich sense of the uses of polity (what else can explain his intentions in the *commonwealth* of Virginia?). He believed that fulfilling the responsibilities of citizenship was an important part of one's human potential. Jefferson was, thus, a long way from Christian preoccupation with private spiritual life, from the laissez-faire tendency in political economy following Adam Smith, and from other depreciations of government in his day. He was even farther, of course, from the dogmatic antistatism of Herbert Spencer, William Graham Sumner, and other late-nineteenth-century social Darwinists (see chapter 6). These assumptions about the dimensions of the political, not often articulated or made explicit, nonetheless remained basic to his thought as long as he lived and reveal the ancient, civic republican strand that remained in American political thinking during the impact of the first modernity in Western thought.

Furthermore, though Jefferson would by no means have agreed with many Greek and Roman (to say nothing of Confucian) social norms and public policies and modes of leadership, he fully accepted that there was a substantial, rationally discernible idea of the public good, "the good society," that a polity ought to seek to understand and then work toward. The intention for him was not cultural conformity, or ideological purity, but rather acceptance that there were *res publica,* "things of the public," which any polity needed to deliberate about and pursue collectively. Jefferson also believed (following Aristotle closely) that governments were "good" or "bad," not according to how many ruled, but insofar as "rulers" (one, few, or many) paid attention to and sought the public good. He thus was in a basic part of his thinking about government deeply classical or, in terms of the debate of his day, still in some degree ancient as well as modern.

On this foundation, and without any sense of incongruity, he also accepted wholeheartedly the thought of English moderns from Bacon and Locke to Joseph Priestley and Thomas Paine. Most particularly, he added a much stronger emphasis on natural rights (what later ages would often call *human* or *universal* rights—the terminology changes, but the concept remains much the same) than ancient ideology set forth. Jefferson's stated purpose in his plan for common schools in newly independent Virginia, for example, combined the modern and classical themes: in those schools, citizens "would be qualified to understand their rights, to maintain them, and to exercise with intelligence their parts in self-government."[19]

Jefferson accepted as well further axioms of modern government that he learned from Locke, Sidney, Trenchard and Gordon ("the English Cato"), Priestley, and others. The conception of a natural, moral, civil society consisting of free and equal (qualified) parts, the model of government resting on a contract or compact among the individuals thus governed for their convenience, the acceptance of majority rule and emphasis on legislative lawmaking (including elections, representation, rule of law, and so on), balances in the exercising of power, and the right of revolution against tyranny were to the author of the Declaration of Independence and the victor in the presidential election of 1801 all canonical. These precepts, in Jefferson's thinking, derived from the foundation of modern thought in Baconian inductive reasoning—why else seek "input" from all the "parts," the members of the political community? (In the late eighteenth century, of course, this did not include slaves, women, nonproperty-holders, and others not then regarded as "qualified," or responsible, citizens.) The Newtonian understanding of a universe of ordered, lawful, and balanced forces and Locke's conception of a world made up of self-willed, diverse, reasonable, morally responsible, and educable (through the five senses) individuals were other axioms of modernity. Following his mentor Voltaire, then, who had explained (in his *Philosophical Letters* [1732]) how the three English "immortals" had fashioned a free, scientific, and productive worldview that opened up a novel future of progress and human fulfillment,[20] Jefferson was, thus, in a way thoroughly modern. He did not accept, or perhaps even confront, the powerful critiques of this first modernity being articulated in the eighteenth century by David Hume, Immanuel Kant, and others, to say nothing, of course, of the later assaults of Karl Marx, John Dewey, Harold Laski, Michel Foucault, and subsequent moderns and postmoderns.

Rather, though he welcomed and experienced the first modernity, Jefferson still lived in an intellectual universe agitated by the critique of the ancients (see chapter 4). He knew intimately and took seriously the arguments of Swift, Pope, Bolingbroke, and others even as he sided with his trinity of modern immortals. In understanding government, this meant that, however much he agreed with the moderns (what current study of political thought generally terms *liberal*) about individual (natural) rights, society as an aggregation of parts, majority rule, the sanctity of private property, and so on, he never understood these axioms as entirely supplanting either older modes of "essentialist" thinking or classical conceptions of the place of government in human affairs. This gave to his political ideology a kind of complexity that has often seemed to twentieth-century analysts to contain incompatibilities: How could Lockean "possessive individualism" be reconciled with Pericles' dictum that the merely private citizen (an oxymoron?) was "useless"? How could the liberal tradition and civic republicanism be joined consistently? How could Jefferson not have realized the strong tension between majority will and right reason? The answer, of course, is that, in experiencing only the "first" elaboration of modernity in the presence of a still basic ancientness in his thinking, Jefferson made different assumptions about the nature of government and asked different questions about it from those entertained by many modern political theorists.

Jefferson expressed the amalgam, laced with both tension and creativity, in his first inaugural address as president in 1801, a document that as much as anything conveys how the American polity fashioned in the preceding quarter century (1776–1801) was a response to the first modernity but still remained attentive to ancient precepts. The salutation "Friends and Fellow Citizens" itself echoes, perhaps self-consciously, Aristotle's long discourses in the *Politics* on the analogy between friendship and citizenship and on the commonality of rulers and citizens—the words to Jefferson had ancient linkages and connotations. His first theme is the need, after the election contest just concluded, to "unite in common efforts for the common good, . . . unite with one heart and one mind, . . . [and] restore to social intercourse that harmony and affection without which liberty and even life itself are but dreary things." The "difference of opinion" evident in the election was "not a difference in principle"; rather: "We have called by different names brethren of the same principle. We are all republicans —we are federalists."[21] Jefferson thus sought, deliberately, to change the factional, partisan terminology of party strife into *agreement* on the political principles that he saw as foundational to the polity. Republicanism, rule by the people on matters of common concern, and federalism, sustaining local and state as well as "general" (national) government, were, he alleged, canonical to all "parties." Though the language may seem trite and merely rhetorical, the very fact that the new president saw it as describing the understanding of his administration and that he believed it likely to resonate with the convictions of his audience reveals the residue of ancient thought in Washington, D.C., in 1801. Indeed, the address was translated into dozens of languages and reprinted hundreds of times in newspapers, journals, and broadsides around the world, as expressing the basic nature and purpose of the new American polity.

In a more direct effort to blend modern and ancient precepts, Jefferson denied that the toleration of different religions and of sharp differences of political opinion would lead to chaos, civil strife, or disunion. "Error of opinion," he insisted, "may be tolerated where reason is left free to combat it." On this ground, he argued that the minority could safely be afforded "equal rights, which equal laws must protect" (good "liberal" principles) because "the will of the majority, . . . in all cases to prevail, . . . to be rightful, must be reasonable." That is, instead of debate and political dispute leading to endless (though benign) strife in public life among competing and irreconcilable interests and parties (the coming "liberal" paradigm), the *reasoned* discussion would validate all the converging language that Jefferson had been using—*common good, harmony, unite, affection, sacred principle, brethren,* and so on—the ancient language of civic republicanism. Such a government, moreover, rather than being too weak to preserve itself, would be "the strongest government on earth" because "every man, at the call of the laws, would fly to the standard of the law, and would meet invasions of the public order as his own personal concern."[22]

Having laid this foundation in "federal and republican principles," the new president proceeded to explain how, nonetheless, the resulting government would respect "liberal" precepts. "A wise and frugal government which shall restrain men from injuring each other, which shall leave them otherwise free to regulate their own pursuits of industry and improvement, and shall not take from the mouth of labor the bread it has earned" was all that "was necessary to make us a happy and prosperous people," he declared, echoing Lockean, modern propositions about limited, individual-rights-oriented government. In passages stating the "creed" for his administration, Jefferson listed "the essential principles of our government": equal justice to all religious and political persuasions; peace and commerce with all nations, "entangling alliances with none"; support of the states for "domestic concerns and [as] the surest bulwarks against anti-republican tendencies"; "the preservation of the general [national] government in its whole constitutional vigor"; popular elections and majority rule; "the supremacy of the civil over the military authority"; economy in the public expense; encouragement of agriculture and commerce, payment of debts, and protection of the public credit; and faithful adherence to the Bill of Rights. Even these generally "liberal" precepts, however, were stated in ways that Jefferson understood to be entirely compatible with his civic republican orientation. Indeed, he signaled that especially in urging that his "creed" be "the text of civil instruction"—implying the responsible, deliberative, active role expected of the nation's citizens.[23]

Jefferson concluded his address modestly by claiming no comparison with "our first and great revolutionary character" (Washington) and admitting that he would "often go wrong through defect in judgment." Like his fellow citizens, he said, he was an "imperfect man." He pledged, simply, to "give firmness and effect to the legal administration of [public] affairs" and to seek to "command a view of the whole ground" in executing his office. The new president saw the legitimation and execution of his office depending, like that of the "fellow citizens" he addressed, on his intention to "unite in common efforts for the common good."[24] He thus grounded his avowedly modern, "liberal" precepts and policies on thoroughly classical, ancient ideas of the nature of government, the role of the leader, and the responsibilities of citizens.

Jefferson, then, fashioned an amalgam of democratic thought, resting on both ancient and modern precepts, that was foundational for the new United States and represented an effort to work out the political implications of the thought of Bacon, Locke, and others. The federal Constitution, as well as those of the state governments, rested on Lockean ideals of freedom and equality (humans are born free and equal and carry those rights with them when they form political societies), but those constitutions also sustained rich, ancient understandings of membership and citizenship. To be a citizen of a polity meant to be capable of responsible and reasoned participation. (Again, this excluded women and slaves, in the eighteenth century generally considered incapable, but also implied their inclusion should anthropological understanding of women and black slaves come to conceive their equal political capabilities with white, property-owning males.) To nourish that capability, Jefferson paid particular attention to means of livelihood conducive to good character, to public education, and to participation in state and local government and institutions of civil society. Thus, he believed that, since yeoman farmers would in their labor acquire essential civic qualities, agriculture should be encouraged, that states should provide all citizens with an education enabling them to "exercise with intelligence their parts in self-government," and that participation in state and local government would nourish the skills and attitudes of responsible citizenship.

Though in the federal Constitution these matters were implicitly left largely to the states, they were an assumed and vital part of the design that Franklin, Jefferson, Madison, and others had in mind for assuring that self-government would also be *good* government (the ancient sine qua non). The keystone was active, public-spirited citizenship, nourished at state and local levels and then exercised effectively in the nation at large. The intention was to sustain, as much as possible in a large, free, modern, increasingly commercial nation, classical ideals of citizen rulers seeking through a well-ordered polity to provide for the good life. Also sustained, even as competitive elections and majority rule were assured ("liberal" principles), were civic republican ideas of deliberative, harmonious decisions on public policy and leadership in accord with universal natural law and natural right. The idea of democracy, itself in part conceived in the seventeenth-century Battle of the Books between ancients and moderns, thus had its first modern articulation amid the moral and political ambiguities occasioned by the coexistence, in minds like Jefferson's, of regard for "facts submitted to a candid World" and for "the Laws of Nature." His resolution—that the parts (facts) converged reasonably toward natural law that provided universal guidelines for good government—would be challenged, elaborated, and denied in modernities to come.

6

The Second Modernity: From Bentham to Dewey

Even as government under the new constitution, and its Jeffersonian elaboration, implanted in the United States a political response to the "first modernity" inspired by Bacon, Descartes, Newton, and Locke, a second wave of further "modern" ideas took shape in Western, especially Anglo-American, thought. Jeremy Bentham, J. S. Mill, Charles Darwin, Herbert Spencer, John Dewey, and others fashioned a "second modernity," with its own implications for democratic government. Perhaps the difference in the modernities (beyond the obvious and important continuities) is best seen in the contrast between the associated scientific paradigms. The first modernity in its political dimension had Newtonian guidelines of order, balance, and harmony, while the second followed Darwinian guidelines of struggle, competition, and indeterminacy. Woodrow Wilson explained in 1908 how the paradigm shift was revealed in American government. The U.S. Constitution of 1787–1791, he said, "was . . . a sort of unconscious copy of the Newtonian theory of the universe. . . . The trouble with the theory is that government is not a machine, but a living thing [that should] fall . . . under the theory of organic life. It is accountable to Darwin, not to Newton. . . . Living political constitutions must be Darwinian in structure and in practice." We ought, he concluded, in an astonishing forecast of government in the twentieth century, to "think less of checks and balances, and more of coordinated power."[1]

Both the Newtonian and the Darwinian paradigms were in strong tension with "ancient" counterpoints (as traditionalists in the eras of both Alexander Pope and Matthew Arnold loudly proclaimed), but the Newtonian paradigm itself also possessed by the nineteenth century a kind of old-fashionedness revealed in its assertion of harmony and in its failure to follow through on the implications of its empirical foundations. This would be pointed out, in different ways, by David Hume in 1748 (*Enquiry concerning Human Understanding, Providence, and a Future State*), by Immanuel Kant in 1781 (*Critique of Pure Reason*), by Thorstein Veblen in 1897 ("Why Economics Is Not an Evolutionary Science"), and by late-twentieth-century postmodern critics of Enlightenment "universalism."

The flaw in the thinking of the first modernity, these critics point out, is its failure to see how its harmonizing, converging, orderly, universalizing tendency (as marked in Jefferson as in Newton) was not consistent with the empirical, inductive, reductionist, autonomous qualities of the thought of Bacon and Locke and the Royal Society's *Proceedings* (already lampooned, of course, by Swift in bk. 3 of *Gulliver's Travels* [1726] on "Laputa"). Hume showed how strict empiricism, though it could describe events in great detail and with sequential accuracy, could not establish anything about causation or necessity or universal laws. In the famous illustration, billiard balls could be described as moving in certain ways, but no conclusions could be drawn, ultimately, about why they moved as they did, and no assurance was possible, empirically speaking, beyond certain events generally following others. Nothing could be *explained;* events could only be observed and described. Noting this limitation, Kant explained how, even to come close to understanding humanity, the inadequacies of this *phenomenal* world required a priori the positing of a transcendent, or *noumenal,* realm where great primordial conceptions and universal values were not only real but essential.

An earnest Boston clergyman and social reformer, Theodore Parker (1810–1860), explained his unsatisfactory experience, as a college student, of the first modernity and his consequent move toward transcendentalism:

> I studied assiduously the metaphysics and psychology of religion.... Was [religious consciousness] natural to man, inseparable from his essence? ... The authority of Bibles and Churches was no answer to that question.... The common books of philosophy seemed quite insufficient; the sensational system, so ably presented by Locke in his masterly *Essay,* developed in various forms by Hobbes, Berkeley, Hume, Paley, and the French Materialists ... gave little help.... I found most help in the works of Immanuel Kant.... I found [in his thought] certain great primal intuitions of human nature, which depend on no logical progress of demonstration, but are rather facts of consciousness given by the instinctive action of human nature itself.[2]

Following Kant's Copernican Revolution, the placing of "essence" or intuition at the center of human nature (rather than the "center" or "essence" being the outside world as observed by the five senses), then, the transcendentalists, the

Romantics, the idealists, and others reacted against what they saw as the excessive materialism, reductionism, and empiricism of the first modernity. As the poet John Keats (1795–1821) asked: "Do not all charms fly at the mere touch of cold philosophy" (the "sensational system")?

> Philosophy will clip an Angel's wings,
> Conquer all mysteries by rule and line,
> Empty the haunted air, and gnomed mine—
> Unweave a rainbow.[3]

This critique, of course, spawned the immensely profound and creative Romantic era.

While this movement (itself often ancient or Gothic in its mood) turned some Western thought away from science and empiricism, thinkers persisting in the modern tradition of Bacon and Locke sought to construct what was to them a more sustainable, a less flawed or contradictory modernity. Within this intent, they fashioned a new rationale for self-government, reordered the institutions and processes of democracy, and altered understandings of citizenship and a just or good society.

Utilitarianism and Individuality in Bentham and J. S. Mill

Stepping back from the higher law, natural rights assumptions of "the heavenly city of the eighteenth-century philosophers," what for Carl Becker was "the bright spring time of the modern world,"[4] Jeremy Bentham (1748–1832) and his followers simply set aside political "universalisms" and attended instead to present and observable circumstances: the reasonable, self-oriented, and socially useful needs of the individuals in the polity. There was no rational or empirical basis for bringing in either divine providence or natural law. There was no whole, only parts. Politically, there was just social well-being calculated according to "the greatest good of the greatest number." Bentham thus agreed with Locke in repudiating ancient, hoary, and superstitious customs and traditions, in applying the methods of induction to human affairs, and in starting one's thinking with autonomous, rational individuals who sought "happiness," or to secure pleasure and avoid pain. Concepts of right and justice came, not from on high or in the guise of universal principles, but from the calculus of individual needs. Bentham insisted, however, that his system was the logical fulfillment of the ideas of Bacon, Newton, and Locke. He gave full force to the seventeenth-century worldview without any of the medieval heavenly city holdover notions that had flawed the first modernity. This second modernity, gathering force in the Western world, dominant in the Anglo-American world, and extending its reach even to East Asia, held sway for the century and a half between the intellectual milieus of Bentham and John Dewey—and had vast implications for the question of how democratic government should be understood and might (or might not) result in good government.

Rejecting a century of Western political thinking (and, indeed, millennia of Christian and classical thought before that), Bentham declared flatly: "There are no such things as natural rights—no such things as rights anterior to the establishment of government—no such things as natural rights opposed to, in contradistinction to legal . . . [rights]. *Natural rights* is simply nonsense. . . . As there is no *right,* which ought not to be maintained so long as it is on the whole advantageous to society, so there is no right which, when the abolition of it is advantageous to society, should not be abolished." Bentham reached this conclusion by positing that the human race consisted simply of individuals whose motivation was to secure pleasure and avoid pain. Thus, they strove to maximize happiness by having as much pleasure and as little pain as possible and existed in society to achieve this end. Since society, or the community, was, thus, only "a fictitious body composed of individual persons who are . . . its members, the interest of the community then is . . . the sum of the interests of the several members who compose it." The law ought to be formed by a calculus that sought the greatest happiness of the greatest number and as efficiently as possible put that into effect in any given polity.[5] Thus, less like Locke and his school, and more resolutely mundane in the way of Bacon, Hobbes, and Hume, Bentham eschewed all notions of universal moral principles (like those accepted by Jefferson) and insisted instead on a calculus of rational individuals seeking pleasure and avoiding pain. That is what defined what was "advantageous to society," and that is all there was to society, government, and legislation. The heavenly city was cast aside as literally non-sense and without a place in an empirical, scientific, modern understanding of humankind.

J. S. Mill (1806–1873) pursued the implications of Bentham's utilitarianism, which both men thought required democratic, representative government: How else could individual needs to maximize pleasure and minimize pain be registered in society and adjusted to the various other needs of other individuals? Though the resulting guidelines were often similar to those of Locke and Publius, the foundations differed. Freedom of expression, for example, Mill understood in *On Liberty* (1859) not so much as a natural right as a proposition of great social utility. The best, perhaps the only way of discovering the right (most true) ideas was to have all thought expressed and then contested in an open forum (marketplace?) of ideas. Foreshadowing Darwinian conceptions of evolution through struggle, Mill envisioned an open, ongoing public dialogue over social purposes and social policies that would sort out more or less "advantageous" proposals to achieve the greatest good of the greatest number. To exclude any opinion, then, was not so much an infringement on the natural right of the holder of the opinion as a restraint on the vital social process of searching for public policy of greatest utility to all.[6]

Representative government (the title of a landmark book published in 1861) was, in Mill's argument, the political frame within which this process could most logically and usefully go forward. It afforded access—as much as is possible in a populous industrial nation—for all the individualities in society and a means for sorting out and compromising their various pleasure-pain needs and conflicts. (As women were individuals in society as well as men, Mill argued that there were no grounds for their social subjugation or for their exclusion from the franchise and other public participations; note the absence of hierarchies of quality and the acceptance of unqualified inclusion.) Since government had as its main purpose the adjusting and facilitating of these needs, there was little reason, Mill thought, both following and extending Bentham, to be concerned primarily about higher purposes, divine right, natural law, the general will, or other abstractions that had befogged thinking about government since time immemorial. "The rights and interests of every or any person," Mill argued, "are only secure . . . when the person interested is himself able, and habitually disposed to stand up for them. . . . Government is a problem to be worked out like any other question of business." Its purpose consisted partly in "the degree in which [it] promoted the . . . advancement of the community . . . in intellect, in virtue, and in practical activity and efficiency; and partly of the degree of perfection with which it organizes the moral, intellectual and active worth already existing so as to operate with greatest effect in public affairs. A government is to be judged by its action upon men, and by its action upon things; by what it makes of citizens, and what it does with them."[7]

Since government thus had purpose only in relation to the needs and concerns of its individual citizens, it had generally, unless there was clear danger that pursuit of those needs might harm others, to leave individuals unfettered as much as possible: "Over himself, over his own body and mind, the individual is sovereign." This gave Mill's thinking about government a strong laissez-faire emphasis, especially in areas likely to benefit from the enterprise and creativity of individuals, but the utility principle also left it open to social action: the problem was "how to unite the greatest individual liberty of action, with a common ownership in the raw material of the globe and an equal participation of all in the benefits of combined labor."[8] Once again, the idea of good government, tied necessarily to representation, had set its sights on the needs (in a way materialized rights) of the individual parts, subject only to the restraints and benefits required and made possible by humankind's existence, often in large numbers, in close proximity. Though Mill distinguished between better and worse forms of happiness and sometimes assumed a version of higher law, he was also, like Bentham, thoroughly in the modern, empirical tradition of Bacon and Locke and, further, intent on following through with *all* its demystifying implications— so much so, and so much beyond the "eighteenth-century philosophers," that he foreshadowed a second modernity.

Comte, Positivism, and the Era of Science

At the same time, largely on the European continent, determinedly modern intellectuals did not follow the individualistic bias of Bentham and Mill but, rather, applied the precepts of induction and science to society at large. In so doing, they were at least as hostile to any kind of reverence for the ancients, or their Romantic or Gothic projections, as their British contemporaries were. They pursued a "science of society" that would attend to the mundane world in which people lived, attempt to understand its flaws, disutilities, misconceptions, and injustices, and then set forth programs to achieve a state of society, and forms of government, that would enhance human life. In this vein, Auguste Comte, Karl Marx, Friedrich Nietzsche, Émile Durkheim, and others (along with Anglo-American contemporaries such as Herbert Spencer, Beatrice and Sidney Webb, Lester Frank Ward, Thorstein Veblen, and William Graham Sumner) transformed social and political thought in thoroughly scientific, social, and earthbound ways—without, of course, agreeing on much more than *asking questions* about human society and government in those ways. All, for example, were more or less militant atheists and scornful of all ancient creeds, moral systems, natural law, and time-honored traditions of government. They were defining and extending modernity.

Comte (1798–1857) saw both the evolution of human thought and the progression of the sciences leading toward a "positive" understanding of human society that he called *social physics,* or sociology. Every branch of human knowledge passed, he thought, through three stages: the theological; the metaphysical (or philosophical); and the scientific (or positive). In the first, Comte argued, "Absolute knowledge" was sought, supposing "all phenomena to be produced by the immediate action of supernatural beings." Thus, the cause, nature, and meaning of all things human were to be found in the study and understanding of these supernatural actions and intentions: hence *theology,* or "god-study." In the second stage, "abstract forces, veritable entities," or natural law is seen as "the cause of all phenomena." Men thus studied philosophy to understand the world in which they lived. Just as the Middle Ages had been the great age of theology, the dawning of the Renaissance with its humanism and building of abstract systems began the era of metaphysics or philosophy. Then, although Comte saw the beginnings of the "Positive philosophy" in "the labours of Aristotle . . . and the introduction of natural science into the West of Europe by the Arabs," it emerged full-fledged only with "the precepts of Bacon, the conceptions of Descartes, and the discoveries of Galileo," precisely, of course, the foundations of the first modernity. In the next two centuries, the three stages competed with each other to achieve a "homogeneous doctrine" that would bring all "Social phenomena within its comprehension." By the nineteenth century, however, "positive knowledge" (science) had so triumphed over the "vague and mystical conceptions" (their doctrines "abundantly discredited," Comte thought) that it was clear that "the Positive Philosophy [was] the one destined to prevail."[9]

The positivism that Comte advocated, however, was not so much a lineal descendant of Bacon's inductive methodology (note Comte's quest of "a homogeneous doctrine") as it was a renewed effort to fashion a thoroughly scientific worldview that amounted to a religion of humanity. Comte classified the sciences, for example, according to their simplicity, or generality, "which comes to the same thing." That is, the sciences, in descending order of clear, logical, inclusive perfection of understanding, were mathematics, astronomy, physics, chemistry, biology, and "social physics" (or sociology, or social science). The logical perfection and comprehension of all relevant data according to universal laws he saw most complete in mathematics and astronomy, less so in physics and chemistry, and least of all in what he termed the *organic* sciences, biology and sociology. But there was in all the "lower" sciences a steady movement toward the completeness and the generality of the one above, all tending toward and capable of achieving the exquisite rationality and perfect predictability of mathematics and astronomy. Social science, Comte asserted, would be able over time to achieve the same "precision of knowledge" as the higher sciences, by "applying mathematical analysis" to all social phenomena. This would create a "science of society" and a "religion of humanity" resting on scientific principles and devoted, not to mystical or abstract ends, but to the needs and affairs of humans in the here-and-now world.

Though Comte's outlook was firmly in the tradition of the empirical, inductive, mundane thinkers whom he had acknowledged as the early founders of the positive, or scientific, era, he repudiated the "absolute individuality" that he found implicit in the idea common in the eighteenth century of individual rights derived from some higher theological or philosophical system (always "vague," "abstract," or "mystical" in Comte's writing). Instead, he placed at the center of social life (which human life always was) a "Positive spirit," where a complete synthesis "spontaneous and systematic in nature, . . . coherent and at the same time progressive," would produce "the generating influence of the worship of Humanity." The social sciences would rest on the same foundation as "the preliminary sciences, so that at last there would be *a unity of method in our conceptions*" (emphasis added). In social science, this unity of method was essentially a cooperative, fact-worshiping, inclusive pursuit of social improvement resting especially on three sources of strength. First, the "priests of Humanity" (prophet-intellectuals like Comte himself) would understand and explain this ultimate, "Positive" stage of human development. (The Leninist intellectual and political party shares this intent, of course.) Second, the life experience of women, whose "sympathetic influence . . . in the family" would provide a vast reservoir of nurturing and socially responsible sentiment, would help overcome the selfish, quarrelsome, militaristic, excluding tendencies of the earlier, male-dominated eras. And, finally, because "Society has now entered on its industrial phase" of previously unimaginable abundance (through the application of "positivism" in the "preliminary" sciences), time-immemorial strife and competition over scarce resources could finally be set aside in a comprehensive pacification of existence. These propitious circumstances and resources, all tending toward a "victory of Social Feeling over our innate Self-love," would make possible "the substitution of the Love of Humanity for Love of God," which had so long distracted and deluded humankind. As symbolized in his legendary encounter with the Jesuit father in Notre Dame Cathedral, Comte sought to retain the aura of faith and devotion found there but would replace the sanctified object on the altar, the mystery and otherworldliness of the cross, with the symbols of science, humanity, and progress.[10]

In seeking a religion of humanity, then, Comte was still in the grand, theorizing tradition of the eighteenth-century philosophers (as were, in a way, Condorcet, Rousseau, Saint-Simon, and Marx), even as he insisted so explicitly on his devotion to the inductive, scientific approach of Bacon, Galileo, and Descartes. He thus shared with British thinkers like Newton, Locke, and Adam Smith the conviction that the empirical method could, indeed, inevitably had to, result in the comprehensive conceptions that they called *natural laws*. "Our real business," Comte declared, "is to analyze accurately the system of phenomena, and to connect them by the natural relations of succession and resemblance."[11] On the other hand, like Bentham, Comte entirely repudiated the abstract, philosophical, even theological overtones of natural law thinking in his insistence on the here and now, on the facts of actual social existence, and on the determined application of the methods of science to human affairs. With this conviction, and in this spirit, Comte was the prophet of the new social science disciplines that achieved such prominence and influence in the years between the Franco-Prussian War (and the Civil War in the United States) and World War I—and contributed to the drastically revised intellectual foundations for democracy and self-government characteristic of the second modernity.

The actual nature and scope of the science that Comte so boldly heralded, however, received its full definition and impetus from the work of Charles Darwin. With the publication of his *Origin of Species* in 1859, the scientific methodology and evolutionary thinking that had been growing in Europe for decades (in the thought of, e.g., Bentham and Mill) achieved a spectacular impact on every branch of human thought. Darwinian thought and methodology set aside all notions of ultimate cause and final truth (the goals of both theology and philosophy) to concentrate instead on investigating all the finite and specific facts and circumstances of the actual observable world. Darwin's projection, then, of this scientific method beyond physics and chemistry to unravel the mysteries of biology impelled investigators to push it even further into psychology ("human science"), economics, politics ("political science"), ethics ("moral science"), and all other social sciences.

The understanding of man as an organism reacting to a complex environment (both natural and constructed) and subject to scientific study became axiomatic. The Darwinian emphases on complexity, change, and infinite variety weakened even more universal conceptions and ideas of natural or higher law guiding human affairs. Though a sort of Comtian enthusiasm for a religion of humanity continued to infuse some social thought, what was regarded as the more faithfully Darwinian approach, projecting only hypothetically and tentatively beyond the collection of data, came to characterize social science. The evolutionary paradigm and scientific method nonetheless favored the notions that human affairs could be understood and in some degree managed and that change and progress, as social processes, could lead step-by-step to an improvement of society and human life—thus foreshadowing a revised understanding of democratic government.

Darwinian thought led finally to a new set of values in which concepts of change, progression, and modernity, implicit in the evolutionary paradigm, replaced the eighteenth-century motifs of the rational, the orderly, and the lawful. Natural law itself, shorn of substantial, universal meaning, came to mean substantially nothing and was replaced by ideas of struggle and change, natural selection, and elimination of the unfit. The absolute truth sought and articulated by theologians and philosophers was meaningless in an evolving world— the *natural* of *natural selection* denoted, not guiding law, but unplanned, purposeless process with neither beginning nor end. The problem presented to Enlightenment ideas of natural law and to religious faiths was similar to that identified by Stephen Jay Gould in noticing continued belief that baseball was invented by Abner Doubleday rather than acceptance of the abundant evidence that the game as we know it represents a gradual evolution: "I do not know why we think so fuzzily [about the history of baseball], but one reason must reside in our social and psychic attraction to creation myths in preference to evolutionary stories—for creation myths . . . identify heroes and sacred places, while evolutionary stories provide no palpable, particular thing as a symbol for reverence, worship, or patriotism."[12] Soon combined with Freudian emphasis on the irrational and scientific attention to the unconscious, Darwinian science not so much disproved cherished systems and faiths, religious or secular, as simply set them aside as irrelevant to the modern world. In his famous debate with the traditionally orthodox Bishop Wilberforce, Thomas Huxley ("Darwin's Bulldog") not so much refuted him as simply refused to entertain his questions, asking literally, "What on earth are you talking about?" With Darwin and other scientists, Huxley bespoke a new modernity that pointed toward a new democracy.

Post-Darwin Social Science: Veblen, Sumner, and Dewey

Among the social scientists who most profoundly understood the implications of the new science was Thorstein Veblen (1857–1929). In a searching essay entitled "Why Is Economics Not an Evolutionary Science?" (1898), Veblen explained how the first modernity paradigm for economics, following Adam Smith and the classical nineteenth-century economics of Mill, Alfred Marshall, and others, violated the canons of modern science. The trouble with classical economists was that they were "content to occupy themselves with repairing a structure and doctrines and maxims resting on natural rights, utilitarianism, and administrative expediency." For "earlier natural scientists, as for the classical economists," Veblen explained, the "sense of truth . . . is not satisfied with a formulation of mechanical sequence. The ultimate term in their systematization of knowledge is a 'natural law,' . . . felt to exercise some sort of coercive surveillance over the sequence of events, [and] . . . apprehended in terms of a consistent propensity tending to some spiritually legitimate end." These economists, "scientists working under the guidance of this classical tradition," as Veblen satirically calls them, "formulate knowledge in terms of absolute truth, [which] . . . means a coincidence of facts with . . . an enlightened and deliberate common sense" — exact descriptions, Veblen implies, of Adam Smith's *Wealth of Nations,* J. S. Mill's *Political Economy,* Alfred Marshall's *The Economics of Industry* (1879), and all works of "classical economics" in between. This *taxonomy,* as Veblen terms it, retains something of "the elaborate discipline of faith and metaphysics [Comte's eras of theology and philosophy], over-ruling Providence, order of nature, natural rights, natural law, [and] underlying principles" of pre-Darwinian thought. In this kind of economic thinking, the observations of the facts of how a complex industrial economy worked were "reduced to a normalized scheme of relations" that were "spiritually binding," that is, made to fit within higher, abstract principles according to a "deductive method." Like Hume in the eighteenth century, Veblen accused many of the empiricists and social scientists of the nineteenth century of being unfaithful to the very methods of thought that they claimed to value.[13]

Instead, Veblen insisted that, "if economics is to follow the lead or the analogy of the other sciences that have to do with a life process" (Comte's "organic sciences," biology and sociology), it must consist basically, and simply, of "habitual methods of procedure." Within this understanding, "a given contrivance for effecting certain material ends becomes a circumstance which effects the further growth of habits of thought . . . and so becomes a point of departure for further development"—and so on ad infinitum. "In all this flux," Veblen explains, "there is no definitively adequate method of life and no definitive or absolutely worthy end of action." Though men may everywhere "seek to do something, what, in specific detail, they seek, is not to be answered except by a scrutiny of the details of their activity." (Veblen thus scorned simplistic absolutes such as "the hedonistic conception of man [as] a lightning calculator of pleasures and pains.") The evolutionary viewpoint, in economics as everywhere, "leaves no place for a formulation of natural laws in terms of definitive normality. . . . Neither does it leave room for that other question of normality, What should be the end of the developmental process under discussion?" In economics or any other social science, under the evolutionary paradigm (the second modernity), Veblen argued for a "habit of mind which seeks a comprehension of facts in terms of a cumulative sequence," but not one that implied "normality" or purpose. Under the stress of modern technological exigencies, he insisted, "knowledge which proceeds on a higher, more archaic plane is becoming alien and meaningless. . . . The social and political sciences must follow the drift" toward the methods of evolutionary science.[14]

In the late nineteenth century, and, indeed, through most of the twentieth century, social science sought to "follow the drift" that Veblen set forth down two rather different streams. The first, marked out in Britain by Herbert Spencer (1820–1903) and elaborated in the United States most notably by William Graham Sumner (1840–1910), stuck to a straightforward application of Darwinian guidelines to all aspects of human life. Both Spencer and Sumner wrote of "the science of society," meaning its understanding in secular terms (no divine, natural, or higher law) in accord with notions of struggle for existence, natural selection, elimination of the unfit, and so on. Human beings were understood as biological creatures struggling to survive in an often hostile environment and in competition with other life, within and without their own species. In this struggle, there were no special dispensations or guiding purposes for humankind, which, far from having a divine origin and destiny, was simply, in the historian Perry Miller's phrase, "the miserable and accidental consequence of a haphazard squabble."[15] Humans had potent survival abilities and remarkable capacities for adaptation and creative achievement that made life on earth arduous and even exciting, but there was no escape from the evolutionary struggle to live and prevail in a niggardly and hostile environment. The role of social science was to understand this struggle for survival as precisely as possible, to study the natural and social environments, and to propose such human adaptations and interventions as might facilitate evolutionary progression—but this did not include *state* intervention, which Spencer and Sumner regarded as futile and probably harmful interference with the only real source of progress, natural evolution. In the doctrine of three of Sumner's famous essays, social science must accept "The Challenge of the Facts" (1914) and give up "The Absurd Effort to Make the World Over" (1894) because the answer to the question of "What Social Classes Owe to Each Other" (1883) was nothing. He thus accepted the "dismal" implications of Malthus, Ricardo, and other classical economists, especially as far as government-sponsored social action was concerned, and agreed with their scorn for eighteenth-century notions of a higher, natural law. He retained, however, a steadfast faith in the scientific study of society according to the Darwinian methodology and hypothesis. The difference between science and religion, Sumner concluded, was in "the habits of thought which each encourages. No religion ever offers itself except as a complete and final answer to the problems of life. No religion ever offers itself as a tentative solution. A religion cannot say: I am the best solution yet found, but I may be superceded tomorrow by new discoveries. But that is exactly what every science must say."[16]

Another following of the Darwinian "drift," however, articulated in the United States by Lester Frank Ward (1841–1913), insisted that the evolutionary model could not be applied simplistically to *human* development. In fact, Ward argued, a full, scientific understanding of human evolution and anthropology required recognition of the distinctive attributes of Homo sapiens crucial to the growth of human society, especially intelligence and a capacity for social cooperation—the very abilities that allowed for the evolutionary progress of the species beyond the tooth-and-claw dynamic. Like Comte, Ward was intent to learn everything he could about the history of humankind ("the challenge of the facts"), and his writings are similarly filled with analyses of the "stages" of social development—Ward's went from autocracy to aristocracy, democracy, plutocracy, and, he hoped, sociocracy. A scientific understanding of human social evolution, then, in a way going parallel to and beyond biological evolution, took into account peculiar human adaptive qualities that provided special constraints and opportunities in the struggle to survive. The task of social science, guided by experts, was to usher in the stage of *sociocracy*, which was "the condition of positivity, this quantitative exactness of man's knowledge of observed phenomena, and his consequent ability to foresee future events by the light of invariable laws."[17]

Sidney Webb (1859–1947) and Beatrice Webb (1858–1943) would make the same point in their *Constitution for the Socialist Commonwealth of Great Britain* (1920), which would, they had earlier declared, "establish on a firm basis a Science of Society." This would "tell against Christianity as the one religion, against materialistic individualism, against autocracy, against luxury, in favor of organization, collective regulation, scientific education, physical and mental training—but on the whole not in favour of democracy." (This was in part a reflection on the Japanese victory over Russia in 1905.) A "select committee" of scientific experts would guide society and determine "the maximum working day, consistent in any particular industry with the health, existence, home life and citizenship of the average workman."[18] In a similar vein, Ward had no use for either the democracy of the presidency of Ulysses Grant or the plutocratic "rule of the fittest" exemplified by John D. Rockefeller and J. P. Morgan. "The strange truth comes up for our contemplation," he wrote, "that instead of having been impelled by intellect and reason throughout all the years of history, we have been ruled and swayed by the magnetic passions of epileptics and monomaniacs." The need was to understand that "the only ultimate object of human effort is the improvement of the human race on this planet." Thus, he hoped that evolutionary progress might lead to "the great panacea" (as he once thought to entitle his *Dynamic Sociology*) of a society guided and controlled by social scientists. To Ward, the second modernity, then, utterly set aside the foundations of democratic government fashioned in the first modernity. It also bypassed the reservations about human nature that made self-government complicated and problematic (as Publius, e.g., had understood). Beatrice Webb likewise scorned the U.S. Constitution because the "combination of efficiency with popular control . . . required by modern democracy . . . is exactly what cannot be brought about by the theory of checks and balances."[19] There was little place for ignorant, deluded, irrational democracy in the sociocracy toward which they believed society to be evolving.

More than Sumner or Ward or the Webbs, however, John Dewey worked out the implications of Darwinian science for every aspect of human society. Born in the year of the publication of *The Origin of Species* (1859), and trained in the new German-style philosophy and social science (Hegel, Marx, Tönnies) at Johns Hopkins University, Dewey explained why the publication "marked an epoch." For two thousand years, understanding "the fixed and the final" had been the goal of philosophers, but, by "treating the forms that had been regarded as types of fixity and perfection (e.g., religious dogma) as originating and passing away," post-Darwinian thinkers had "laid hands upon the sacred ark of absolute permanency." "The *Origin of Species,*" Dewey declared, "introduced a mode of thinking that in the end was bound to transform the logic of knowledge, and hence the treatment of morals, politics, and religion."[20]

Despite the popular clamor about the assault of the new science on religion that Darwinism provoked, however, Dewey insisted, as Veblen had done, that "the issue lay primarily within science itself." Science from Aristotle to Newton had sought to "observe order in flux and manifest constancy through change." This "unchanging pure and contemplative intelligence" of science saw nature as "one unbroken fulfillment of ends. . . . The conception of species, a fixed form and final cause, was the central principle of knowledge as well as of nature." Under this "logic of science, change as change is mere flux and lapse; it insults intelligence. Genuinely to know is to grasp a permanent end that realizes itself through changes, holding them thereby within the . . . bounds of fixed truth. Completely to know is to relate all special forms to their one single end and good: pure contemplative intelligence." Though Galileo and Descartes had taken important steps toward a different "logic of knowledge," all fields of human inquiry had continued to be subject to "the logic of the changeless, the final, and the transcendent."[21]

On the other hand, "the influence of Darwin on philosophy," Dewey declared, "resides in his having conquered the phenomena of life for *the principle of transition,* and thereby freed the new logic for application to mind and morals" (emphasis added) and social life. To Dewey, this meant, not a literal, simplistic transfer of the guidelines of evolutionary biology to human society (as Sumner had foolishly done, in Dewey's opinion), but instead the application of the Darwinian "logic" or method to the whole social realm, including politics. There, as everywhere, thinkers had to "foreswear inquiries after absolute origins and absolute finalities in order to explore specific values and the specific conditions that generate them." The "new logic" thus "outlaws, flanks, dismisses —what you will" —such outmoded conceptions as a state of nature, or natural law, or universal rights, or any notions of divinity or absolutes. Platonic ideals, Aristotelian set forms, Thomistic divine law, Lockean natural rights, Hegelian absolutes, Marxian dogmatics, and so on were viewed not so much as wrong as simply beside the point because they valued finality rather than transition, or process. Under "the Darwinian principle," Dewey explained, "if all organic adaptations are due simply to constant variation and the elimination of those variations which are harmful in the struggle for existence [that is brought about by excessive reproduction] . . . , there is no call for prior intelligent causal force to plan and preordain them." "Once admit that the sole verifiable or fruitful object of knowledge is the particular set of changes that generate the object of study together with the consequences that then flow from it," Dewey declared, encapsulating the scientific approach (also Darwinian or pragmatic in his vocabulary), "no intelligible question can be asked about what, by assumption, lies outside." Dewey's interest, along with that of other Darwinian thinkers, shifted from what or who made the world to "what kind of world it is anyway."[22] Why and where it started, and where it was going ultimately, were indeterminate and beside the point. (Though Dewey would in later life develop a more relational understanding of society, especially seeking a common or public interest, he never abandoned his emphasis on "specific values and . . . specific conditions" and his repudiation of "absolute origins and absolute finalities.")

Following Veblen, Sumner, Ward, Dewey, and their mentors, a host of philosophers, educators, and social scientists carried the Darwinian, "new science" approach into every field of study. They undertook in the United States what Morton White has called *the revolt against formalism* in philosophy, history, law, economics, government (termed, revealingly, *political science*), education, psychology, anthropology, and sociology. Universities from Harvard and Chicago to Wisconsin and California organized themselves in strict disciplinary departments, and their faculties founded the academic associations (the American Political Science Association, etc.) that would guide scholarly inquiry throughout the twentieth century. Though some debate remained within the associations between varieties of classical and natural law thinking (formalism or abstractionism), on the one hand, and the new Darwinian, largely positivist social science, on the other, the trend ran strongly toward the latter. (The establishment in Great Britain by the Webbs and others of the London School of Economics and Political Science, as a counterweight to "genteel" Oxford and Cambridge, made the same point there.) These academic associations, of prime importance to scholars in all fields, were a key element in the second modernity that was hostile, not only to the more conventional aspects of what George Santayana scorned as "the genteel tradition" (orthodox Christianity, Romanticism, Hegelianism, natural law—all "exquisite moonshine"), but also to the abstracting, universalizing tendency so strong in the allegedly scientific first modernity. It was time, the Darwinian worldview insisted, to be thoroughly and consistently empirical, scientific, mundane—or, in words used variously by Dewey to describe the new outlook, experimental, instrumental, and pragmatic. Dewey also explained how this required new understandings of "liberalism" and democracy.

Dewey and the other second moderns provoked, of course, vigorous responses from the ancients of their day, just as Bacon, Descartes, and Locke had provoked Temple, Swift, Pope, and Bolingbroke (see chapter 4). Though the lines were not drawn as explicitly in the last half of the nineteenth century as they had been between ancients and moderns in the first quarter of the eighteenth century, the tension was, nonetheless, pervasive in the world of thought between those who heralded the new methods and assumptions of (Darwinian) science as the path toward knowledge and progress in all fields and those who still asked traditional questions and who, at least outside the natural sciences, still saw wisdom and virtue and purpose in time-honored study and inquiry. The struggle was again, so to speak, between those who emphasized the wisdom of the age and those who emphasized the wisdom of the ages. Those traditionally minded writers who responded to T. H. Huxley's question to Bishop Wilberforce, "What on earth are you talking about?" insisted that they were talking about the most profound and important matters facing humankind and that the new science, technology, and industry created a need, not for new human values and cosmologies, but rather, simply, for the projection and application of ancient wisdoms to new circumstances.

William Blake, William Wordsworth, and many other Romantics, of course, had reacted against both the ancient and the modern versions of the Enlightenment (as American transcendentalists did in the next generation [see above]) and, thus, critiqued reductionist, scientific thought and the Industrial Revolution from the "outside" long before publication of *The Origin of Species.* Thinkers such as Bentham and Veblen, however, thoroughly mundane and uncosmological, undertook a different critique from the "inside," arguing that luminaries of modernity such as John Locke and Adam Smith were not modern or scientific enough. They insisted that the inductive methodology of Francis Bacon needed, not abstracting and universalizing in the manner of Newton and Locke, but rather ever more rigorous empirical application.

Reading such rigorously modern ideas in the writings of Bentham and others, however, Thomas Carlyle (1795–1881) was appalled at what he saw as their shallowness. How was it, Carlyle asked in 1834, when "man's whole life and environment have been laid open and elucidated; scarcely a fragment or fibre of his Soul, Body, and Possessions, but has been probed, dissected, distilled, desiccated, and scientifically decomposed," that "the grand Tissues, the only real Tissue, should have been quite overlooked by Science?" What about "the vestural Tissue [covering garment] . . . which Man's Soul wears as its utmost wrappage and overall; wherein his whole other Tissues are included and screened, his whole Faculties work, his whole Self lives, moves, and has its being?" Logic choppers, practitioners of the "dismal science" (economics), utilitarian reformers, even "mere justice-loving men" (Benthamites) were, Carlyle thought, "inexpressibly wearisome." "The man who cannot wonder, who does not habitually wonder, were he President of innumerable Royal Societies, and carried . . . the epitome of all Laboratories and Observatories with their results, in his single mind,—is but a Pair of Spectacles behind which there is no Eye. Let those who have Eyes, look through him, then he may be useful."[23] He then took aim at the critical, "philosophical" (i.e., analytic) history of Hume, William Robertson, and their followers, who "sacrilegiously mishandled; effaced, and what is worse, defaced!" the past, calling the "Norman conquerors . . . vulturous, irrational tyrants, [and] Becket . . . a noisy egoist and hypocrite." Carlyle called instead for a reverence for the past and an understanding of the larger, deeper, even mystical themes that had guided and ennobled human life. "All great Peoples," he declared, "are conservative; slow to believe in novelties; . . . deeply and forever certain of the greatness that is in LAW, in Custom once solemnly established, and now recognized as just and final."[24]

Equally attached to ancient wisdom, and representative of the academic establishment, Professor John Grote (1813–1866) of Trinity College, Cambridge, attacked especially the "new" doctrine of J. S. Mill's 1861 *Utilitarianism* but also the larger patterns of "scientific" thought articulated by Bentham and Comte. "We must have . . . an idea of what *ought to be,* or what it is desirable *should be,* as well as a power of observing, recording, and analyzing what *is,*" Grote declared. He complained of "a way of thinking about morals . . . called by the name *Positivism* . . . which endeavors to construct a system of morals . . . from observation and experience of fact alone. . . . This, we are told, is the course which has been pursued with other sciences, and which now ought to be pursued in moral science, if it is to exist as a science at all." Such a view, which Grote saw as pervasive both in what he understood as Bentham-Mill utilitarianism and in Comtian positivism, was insufficient in that "it leaves unnoticed much that we actually see in human nature. Every part of our nature—feeling, reason, imagination alike," Grote said, "suggests to us that we are made not only for self-enjoyment but for . . . a range of thought and feeling going beyond ourselves." This larger view of human nature and the loftier goals to which human beings could aspire ("shoulds") could be acquired through "a general advance of moral knowledge." By studying Aristotle ("the greatest of philosophers"), the Stoics, medieval writers, and, especially (though not necessarily), the doctrines of Christianity, Grote thought that humankind could discern and understand the "shoulds" and "oughts" that would frame a moral vision of the good society and of which Bentham and Comte and Mill were simply bereft[25]—in Carlyle's image, they were "Spectacles behind which there is no Eye."

Although Grote did not press the point particularly, he scorned the individualistic pursuit of material well-being and happiness that he saw at the foundation of utilitarian thought as a hopelessly deficient concept of human motivation. Virtue, he declared, far from being defined in terms of even enlightened self-interest, was, rather, "noble self-will . . . , a self-forgetfulness and regard for the happiness of others . . . [without which] social feelings are merely weak and ineffective."[26] In social morality, and, by implication, in the whole idea of civil society, then, Grote insisted on profound, time-honored ideals as guides rather than any calculus of the greatest happiness of the greatest number or any mere projection of scientific method to the whole range of human nature and human affairs.

In a more sophisticated way, and in the presence of the arguments of Thomas Huxley and other Darwinian enthusiasts for science, Matthew Arnold (1822–1888) declared for "the wisdom of the ages" over the emphasis on "machines" and the faith in material progress. Condemning alike aristocrats, whom he considered "Barbarians," ordinary people, who were, scornfully, "the Populace," and the dominant middle-class "Philistines," Arnold called instead for a devotion to "culture, the best that has been known and thought in the world." Arnold drew his definition of culture self-consciously from the *Battle of the Books* (1704), in which, he noted, Swift held up "*sweetness and light* [as] the two noblest of things," the things that made human life meaningful and deeply moral. Echoing what he called the "Hellenic" strain in human history, Arnold took the essence of culture to be both an "expansion of human nature, . . . an aptitude for seeing more than one side of a thing" (sweetness), and a capacity "to see things as they really are . . . harmonious perfection" (light). Both these qualities were, of course, nourished by the broadest possible study and understanding of history, literature, science, religion, and philosophy, not just in the Western tradition, but, as Arnold emphasized against his fundamentalist, chauvinist, and reductionist critics, from around the world and throughout time. Arnold repudiated "all that was harsh, uncouth, difficult, abstract, professional, exclusive," in order to find the great, unifying, humanizing themes in history and society—which he repeatedly said was the way "to make reason and the will of God prevail."[27] (Arnold thus accepted the dictum of Plutarch that "to follow God and obey Reason is the same thing.")

This view of culture, drawn from the reservoir of the human wisdom of the ages, condemned, not only all the limited, class-bound "wisdoms" of nineteenth-century Britain (Barbarians, Philistines, the Populace, etc.), but also the politics of both "middle-class liberalism and the world of democracy." "Having a vote, like having a large family, or a large business, or large muscles," Arnold observed, would not in itself have an "edifying and perfecting effect upon human nature." Nor was much to be expected from "some Bentham or Comte . . . elaborating down to the very smallest details a rational society for the future." Rather, with the spread of culture, "sweetness and light," to *every* part of society, there might develop "a *national* glow of life and thought when the whole of society is in the fullest measure permeated by thought, sensible to beauty, intelligent and alive."[28] Arnold obviously had something in mind other than the social science–guided, process-focused approach of the heirs of Darwin. To Arnold, as always with ancients, there were qualitative, time-honored standards for the good life and for good (perhaps, but not necessarily, democratic) government.

Arnold's poetic lament of the problematic, indeterminate, unglowing nature of the second modernity echoed the "dread Empire, CHAOS . . . uncreating word . . . [and] universal Darkness" of Pope's 1729 curse of the first modernity:

> Ah, love, let us be true
> To one another! for the world, which seems
> To lie before us like a sea of dreams,
> So various, so beautiful, so new,
> Hath neither joy, nor love, nor light,
> Nor certitude, nor peace, nor help for pain;
> And we are here as on a darkling plain
> Swept with confused alarms of struggle and flight,
> Where ignorant armies clash by night.[29]

In the United States, generations later than Carlyle and Arnold, Lewis Mumford laid similar strictures on the rising tide of evolutionary science and philosophy, especially against what he regarded as "the pragmatic acquiescence" of John Dewey and others. "Unchecked, unmodified, industrialism controlled the mind" of the country after the Civil War, Mumford charged, as the great universities dedicated themselves "to the practical application of science in the arts, agriculture, manufacture and commerce." Leading intellectuals seemed transfixed by a narrow and reductionist group of writers. Dewey, for example, wrote "eulogies of Bacon . . . but none of Shakespeare; . . . of Locke but not of Milton; of Bentham, but not of Shelley and Keats and Wordsworth and Blake." Dewey, Mumford charged, "seemed to believe that the 'ends' or 'ideals' will come into existence of themselves, if only we pay careful heed to the means, [but] . . . the means necessary to the fulfillment of ends or ideals were inevitably scientific or mechanical means." This meant that his pragmatism, or instrumentalism, simply tinkered with "improvements" while implicitly acquiescing in existing values and institutions. "Without vision," Mumford concluded, echoing the Book of Proverbs, "the pragmatists perish." He called for a philosophy and an education where, instead of acquiescing in existing culture and values and "learning by doing," young people would study, in Arnold's terms, "the best that has been known and thought in the world" so that they might glimpse, profoundly, integratively, and even radically, what the deeper and wider dimensions of human life and society might be.[30] For democracy and citizenship and good government this analysis had clear implications: only citizens with the broader, more liberal education and understandings that Mumford extolled (and not self-interested avoiders of pain and seekers of pleasure) would be able to deepen and enrich the democratic process in a way that would result in wise and good government.

The most searching critique of the whole post-Darwinian (and post-Marxian and post-Freudian) second modernity, however, came from the American theologian and social critic Reinhold Niebuhr (1892–1971). Beginning with a critique of the British first modernity empiricists Hobbes, Locke, and Hume, Niebuhr saw their scientific, naturalistic (words virtually synonymous for him) outlook as hopelessly deterministic and incomplete (Swift's scorn of Laputa in *Gulliver's Travels* again comes to mind). "In Hobbes' sensationalistic psychology and materialistic metaphysics," Niebuhr observed, "there is no place for human individuality," while Lockean (and Cartesian) explanation of the "existence of the self is hardly an adequate description of the whole dimension and uniqueness of human self-consciousness." Hume's "interpretation of the empirical ego as a stream of impressions" still had to confront, in Niebuhr's view, the human capacity to in some degree stand outside, and in some measure transcend, the empirical, "scientific" understanding of the first modernity.[31]

Subsequent "psychological systems which remain within the naturalistic tradition," Niebuhr concluded, "never got beyond the varying interpretations of Hobbes, Locke and Hume." Behavioristic psychology ("an elaboration of Hobbes"), "psychologists who emphasize the initiative of the ego" (Lockean), and the rejection of "both the unity of consciousness and the transcendent ego" (William James and other "followers" of Hume) were all reductionist in that they denied or ignored "the real profundities of self-consciousness, [and] the complex problems of personality, in the breadth of its relation to the world of nature and history . . . and in the depth of its dimension as self-conscious ego." Seeing nineteenth-century thought (the second modernity) as more an extension than a critique of the ideas of Hobbes-Locke-Hume, Niebuhr notes that empiricism "is actually more certain of the complete irrelevance" of traditional doctrines than of their falsity.[32]

This continuing preoccupation with the mundane and with the progress of science left much of modern thought both naive and too optimistic. "Modern man," Niebuhr declared, "considers himself the victim of corrupting institutions which he is about to destroy or reconstruct [Marx], or of the confusions of ignorance which an adequate education is about to overcome." This latter shortcoming Niebuhr laid especially on John Dewey, "a typical naturalist philosopher of the twentieth century," who was even "less conscious of the social perils of self love [capitalism] than either Locke or Hume." Dewey hoped to achieve "a vantage point which transcends the corruptions of self-interest . . . [by] trusting the 'scientific method.'" He had "a touching faith," Niebuhr noted, "in achieving the same results in the field of social relations which intelligence achieved in the mastery of science." But the idea that "the procedure of organized co-operative inquiry" (Dewey's phrase), applied to both education and the handling of social and political problems, could achieve wise and disinterested solutions quite apart from any transcendent standpoint was, to Niebuhr, "an incredibly naïve answer" for dealing with "the worst injustices and conflicts of history."[33] Using Dewey's "one-dimensional presuppositions of naturalism," political scientists, sociologists, and psychologists (of the 1930s, 1940s, and 1950s) had "covered the field of political analysis with sentimentality and confusion, probably because they are so intent on being as scientific as the natural sciences, and so foolishly hopeful that a technical age will be able to master the vast realm of historical vitality by the same methods which it used to 'manage' nature."[34]

Instead of this faith in projecting the methods of science to all fields of social inquiry and supposing that "the procedure of organized, co-operative inquiry" could in itself discern principles of justice, Niebuhr insisted that "every society needs [transcendent] working principles of justice, as criteria for its positive law and system of restraints." Thus, he understood the doctrines of natural law to be, not "exquisite moonshine" or the rationalizations of dominant power, as Santayana, Justice Oliver Wendell Holmes, and other Darwinists asserted, but rather transcending principles, "fixed and immutable," even though "every historical statement of them is [contingent and] subject to amendment." Each generation, therefore, was not in a hopeless position of naïveté, flux, relativity, and nihilism but, rather, in need of discerning as best it could what the higher law meant for it—even if its own place in history would limit and taint its understanding and result in some degree in its own self-interested rationalizations.[35] It was not that natural, universal, immutable law did not exist but, rather, that humans would never fully grasp it—though it was essential to (full) human nature to keep it in view and to seek to understand it. Though Niebuhr's own place to stand somewhat apart from the "miserable and accidental squabbles" of existence in history was the biblical faith of Christianity, his critique of the second modernity was not dependent on that standpoint, nor did he rule out the validity of other versions of higher law. He stood with the ancients of his and earlier times, however, in insisting on bringing to bear on human life more than the (scientific, mundane, reductionist) approach of the contemporary age—always the counterpoint to modernity.

The ancients of the nineteenth century and the early twentieth, then (the five here discussed, though perhaps particularly searching in their critiques, are merely representative of a legion of intellectuals in the Western world), brought similar, though updated, counterviews to the modernity of their day. They also saw that the world of scientific thought that they found around them had implications for every area of inquiry. Their most fundamental critique was that the moderns misunderstood human nature itself and the nature of the moral, social, and political world in which they lived. Human beings were not the blank slates entirely fashioned by the sense impressions that the new science and philosophy supposed, nor was the society in which they lived merely the accumulated summation of the individual intentions and actions composing it. This view missed, the ancients maintained, the deeply important moral and spiritual dimensions of human nature (capacities that gave breadth and meaning to life) and a social and political indelibility that opened up for humanity an array of fulfilling public opportunities—as well as opportunities for chaos and degradation. Ancients were, thus, inclined to look to the cultural and moral and civilized experience of the human race to understand how to fulfill these wider dimensions and aspirations—even to learn what those dimensions and aspirations might be. They saw various modernities as often exciting and progressive in the natural sciences but as "Spectacles behind which there is no Eye" or "pragmatic acquiescence[s]" in other realms. They objected especially, therefore, to what they insisted was a misguided and febrile projection of inductive, analytic, quantitative techniques of science and technology into all dimensions of human experience—indeed, to the very idea of *social science.* Politically, this meant that they hearkened to time-honored and universal themes in understandings of justice and the good society and modes of government while tending to scorn the talk of contracts and conveniences and calculuses and individuality and majoritarianism and instrumentalism that seemed to go along with modernity. In somber self-reflection, George Santayana caught the mood:

> My heart rebels against my generation,
> That talks of freedom and is slave to riches,
> And, toiling 'neath each day's ignoble burden,
> Boasts of the morrow. . . .
> What would you gain, ye seekers, with your striving,
> Or what vast Babel raise you on your shoulders?

You multiply distresses, and your children
Surely will curse you. . . .
Nature hath made us . . .
That we might, half knowing, worship
The deathless beauty of her guiding vision,
And learn to love, in all things mortal, only
What is eternal.

(In the same mood, Santayana once termed pragmatism "a sort of acoustic illusion," supposing that the voice of mundane scientific analysis "reverberates from the heavens.")[36]

Second Modernity Law and Politics: Oliver Wendell Holmes and Harold Laski

Nonetheless, the new modernity continued to flourish during much of the twentieth century and to project itself powerfully into politics and the understanding of government. In the correspondence, for example, between Justice Oliver Wendell Holmes, who was refashioning American jurisprudence to accord with "experience" rather than "logic," and the immensely learned British philosopher and political scientist Harold Laski, its themes received brilliant projection and illumination. Laski was in full revolt against the formalism of both British politics and British academe, while Holmes had nothing but scorn for those who thought in universal or absolutist or moralistic ways about anything, especially the law, as was dominant in the 1910s among Holmes's colleagues on the Supreme Court. During World War I, as Holmes was writing often dissenting opinions condemning natural law and upholding the power of governments (state and federal) to enact social legislation (designed in part following "Brandeis briefs," according to the new social science), he visited and corresponded with Laski, then beginning a stint as a junior instructor at Harvard. Holmes was seventy-five and Laski twenty-three, the older man long steeped in the Darwinian thought and science of society that he had studied with Chauncey Wright and William James in the 1860s, the younger keenly attuned to the latest social and political thought of Europe, to which he eagerly introduced the intellectually avaricious justice.

Laski began by declaring himself a Darwinian and, hence, dissatisfied with Herbert Croly, Walter Lippmann, and other Progressive intellectuals who were really still "theologians" with their "belief either in goodness or in sin as original." Generally agreeing, Holmes replied: "All my life I have sneered at the natural rights of man." Criticizing along with Laski various efforts to use Darwin to sustain a "discreetly religious belief in the upward and onward," Holmes insisted on a "humbler battle cry" acknowledging "the progress of the last 2000 years, [but without] convictions as to its infinite continuance." "Philosophy," he added, "is only cataloguing the universe and the universe is simply an arbitrary fact." In response to Holmes's acquiring of a Rembrandt painting, Laski said that he preferred to collect books and to "crowd his study" with portraits: "Darwin, Thomas Huxley, Descartes, Newton, Laplace, and even J. S. Mill and Jeremy Bentham." Holmes had agreed earlier on a preference for the new scientific spirit in finding that Edward Gibbon, with his stories of saints and "wanderings of tribes" and "superceded accounts of the Roman law," did not say "a thing that I cared a damn to hear." "There are few books more than 25 years old, except sources," the justice concluded, "that I much enjoy." Turning his own phrase against him, Holmes said of Matthew Arnold that his ideas were "a philistine dogmatism which I don't care for."[37]

Though Laski and Holmes thus entirely bespoke Dewey's (and Comte's and Veblen's) scorn for theological absolutes and natural law, they had no more use for the allegedly Darwinian dogma of Spencer and others that created new natural laws of struggle and evolution forbidding intervention by government in social affairs—like Veblen, they believed that this was not evolutionary science. In one of his most famous dissents (a 1905 case finding unconstitutional a New York State law regulating hours and working conditions in bakeries), Holmes declared: "The Fourteenth Amendment does not enact Mr. Herbert Spencer's *Social Statics*.... [The Constitution is] not intended to embody a particular economic theory, whether of paternalism and the organic relation of the citizen to the State or of *laissez faire*." "It is made for people of fundamentally differing views," he added, so judges, acting under the Constitution, should allow legislative bodies to enact whatever economic and social policies the majority willed. Furthermore, even Bill of Rights provisions, such as the protection of freedom of speech, were not absolute but were affected by questions of "proximity and degree" and could be limited should the speech "create a clear and present danger" to the enactment and execution of powers granted to Congress.[38]

The Constitution, Holmes said in another opinion, "is an experiment as all life is an experiment," and "the best test of truth is the power of the thought to get itself accepted in the competition of the market." Hence, freedom of expression was not so much a natural right as a pragmatic way to assure that a Darwinian "competition of ideas" went on as part of social evolution. "What proximate test of excellence can be found," he asked, "except correspondence to the actual equilibrium of force in the community [a Darwinian resultant]—that is conformity to the wishes of the dominant power? ... The proximate test of a good is that the dominant power has its way." Thus, to Holmes, democratic government, which he saw as a framework for the human struggle for existence, meant majority rule ("dominant power") and nothing else, beyond preservation of processes (like freedom of expression) to let the struggle go on. Thinking of Chief Justice John Marshall's insistence on the Constitution as "paramount law" (natural law) controlling all legislation, a legal scholar has observed that, what "Marshall had raised, Holmes sought to destroy." Holmes himself, in a halfhearted, ritualistic tribute to Marshall, could muster praise only for Marshall's strong federal union "for which Hamilton argued, and he decided, and Webster spoke, and Grant [and Holmes] fought, and Lincoln died."[39] In law and jurisprudence, Holmes bespoke the second modernity of post-Darwin as much as Marshall bespoke the first modernity of post-Newton.

Laski's own views on law and on constitutions and on democratic government were equally Darwinian and equally hostile to what he saw as Louis Brandeis's and Woodrow Wilson's "romanticising the simple beauty of the masses," which reminded him "painfully" of how "Jeremy Bentham and John Mill thought they could bring about the millennium with a mechanic's institute." Rather, it was necessary "to restate all our ideas of representative government" in ways consistent with the new science that repudiated what Laski saw as Wilson's "Jeffersonian verities" resting on natural law. (Sixteen days after Wilson's 1917 war message, Laski wished that statesmen "generally did not promise us a heaven after peace.") Instead, Laski sought "a revival of 'natural law' . . . [as] the purely inductive statement [monographs of social scientists] of certain minimum conditions we can't do without if life is to be decent." As there was a "transference of economic and political power from the mercantile to the working classes" (through the democratic process), "the things the crowd will die for, . . . democratic control of industry, the control of prices and profits, a graduated income tax and the like, . . . [would move] towards the inductive realization of these 'natural' rights into a generalized social scheme."[40] Laski rejected in Mill and Wilson, thought of as modern, a tendency to seek "verities" and promises of "heaven," a rejection similar to that by Hume, Bentham, and others of tendencies toward systems and natural law of their modern predecessors; they were not modern enough. Or was Laski himself simply (and inconsistently) redefining natural law as a "purely inductive statement of certain minimal conditions" or a "generalized social scheme," as the next cycle of modernism (postmodern) would charge?

Laski explained systematically his understanding of democratic government in *A Grammar of Politics* (1925). The "starting-point of every political philosophy," Laski's Darwinian voice insisted, "is the inexpungable variety of human wills." (Contrast the Locke/Jefferson beginning with self-evident truths.) The "most distinguishing feature . . . of modern life," that is, was "a multiplicity of wills which have no common purposes." The only "unity" possible politically was, "not of object, but of subject," when there is a recognition "of the way in which the wills [that any one person] shall encounter are related to each other."

As history thus evolved in any particular society, Laski observed as a social scientist, "customs, institutions, beliefs, grow up in haphazard, semi-conscious fashion" (the "folkways" described by anthropologists and sociologists). "He would be an optimist indeed," Laski added, "who could discover any system of governing principles applied to civilization." Within this "haphazard, semi-conscious" social development, Laski accepted the "individualist doctrine" that each "adult member" sought as much as possible "unbarred . . . access to self-expression," and the state was, thus, "a fellowship of men aiming at the enrichment of the common life," acknowledging that "the average man is, in fact, a political animal." A citizen had "a claim upon society to realize [his] best self in common with others." Rights were, thus, "functional," "inherent as a member of society," and present, "not that we may receive, but that we may do."[41]

"Democracy . . . if it is to work," Laski concluded, must enable its citizens to "grow to their full stature . . . in the environment of responsibility. . . . To realize life [citizens] must control life; to control it, they must make articulate to their fellow-citizens what intuition they have of the experience they have enjoyed. It is the largest task before civilization to train men to the coherent statement of what their experience implies." The guiding "values," the sense of purpose of any polity, then, came, not from any idea of providence or natural law (*theology* or *philosophy* in Comte's language, *exquisite moonshine* in Santayana's), but from life experiences, from the will toward self-expression, and from the capacity for "coherent statement" of what was "decent." (How "coherent statement" of what was "decent" differed from eighteenth-century "reason" divulging "natural law" neither Laski nor Holmes explained.) The democratic state was, thus, simply "a place where . . . a multiplicity of wills . . . encounter and relate to each other . . . [and where] an inductive realization . . . of the enrichment of common life" could happen. Though Holmes went no further than supposing that, in the industrial era, limitation of working hours, regulation of child labor, and other social measures of the day were constitutionally permissible (if they were "the wish of the dominant power," i.e., a legislative majority), Laski supposed that, in the Britain of the 1920s, "control of industry, . . . of prices and profits, a graduated income tax and the like" were the obvious (though not necessarily universally valid) means toward "the enrichment of common life"—and, he thought, the will of the majority. This was the "new political philosophy . . . necessary to a new world."[42]

Social Science and the Democratic Process: Dewey, the Webbs, and Arthur Bentley

It was John Dewey, however, who most comprehensively regrounded thinking about democratic government according to scientific, Darwinian, second modernity thought. Following from his general projection of these precepts to philosophical questions, and in the fashion of Veblen's repudiation of classical economics as un-Darwinian, Dewey argued that it was time for a "new individualism," a "new liberalism," and a new understanding of democratic citizenship suited to the new paradigm. Continued adherence to the "old individualism" derived from Protestant emphasis on personal faith, capitalist dogma about private property, frontier self-reliance, and the philosophy of natural (individual) rights was, Dewey wrote in 1930, evidence that in "thought, feeling, and language . . . we are living in some bygone century, anywhere from the thirteenth to the eighteenth, although physically and externally we belong to the twentieth century." The essential circumstance that required a redefinition of values and social purposes was that "the United States has steadily moved from an earlier frontier individualism to a condition of dominant corporateness." In business, social, and public life, "associations . . . more and more define the choices and the actions of individuals" so that "collective wholes" (most notably huge corporations and trusts), not "personal capacity, effort and work," were the dominant forces. "A mentality that is congruous with the new social corporateness," Dewey noted, led many to "believe that socialism of some form is needed to realize individual initiative and security on a wide scale." It was necessary, he insisted, to "cease opposing the socially corporate to the individual" and, instead, develop "an intelligently planned approach" to social and political matters—"for that is what science is."[43] And it is that to which *social science* faculties of universities throughout the industrial world should turn their attention.

Dewey worked out the new political understandings suited to the corporate age and to evolutionary science in calling for a "new liberalism." The "old liberalism" of John Locke and Adam Smith, he said, was designed "to protect the rights that belong to individuals prior to political organization" and held that "the activity of individuals, freed as far as possible from political restriction," is the chief source of social welfare. It further argued that social welfare was "the cumulative, but the undesigned and unplanned, effect of the convergence of a multitude of individual efforts"—as Spencer, Sumner, and other social Darwinists insisted. But the "corporateness" of the new industrial age, and the social methodology of the new science (the true Darwinian approach, Veblen and Dewey argued), simply made that liberalism passé. Though Dewey acknowledged that Bentham, in "assaulting the conception of inherent natural rights" and allowing for "the power of government to create, constructively and positively, new institutions," and Mill, in questioning the benignness of the capitalistic ethic, had taken important steps to redefine liberalism, they still operated from atomistic bases: "the greatest good of the greatest number [of individuals]" and the fact that "human beings in society have no properties but those which are derived from . . . the laws of individual men."[44]

It was not until the latter part of the nineteenth century, however, under the twin pressures of industrial organization and the methods of Darwinian science, Dewey observed, that there was a "reaction against the basic philosophy of individualistic liberalism and individualistic empiricism." "The crisis of liberalism," Dewey asserted, was its "failure to develop . . . an adequate conception of intelligence integrated with social movements as a factor in giving them direction." "Mere precedent and custom or . . . the happy intuitions of individual minds" were immature and inadequate guides for social action in an age when the "experimental method in science demands a control by comprehensive ideas [Laski's 'inductive realization(s)'], projected in possibilities to be realized in action"—that is, *social* science. The only effective path toward "the cultural liberation and growth of individuals," he concluded, would be a method of "organized social planning [wherein] . . . industry and finance are socially directed." This would define the new liberalism and a process of self-government appropriate to a Darwinian age. Echoing Bacon and Comte, but deeply at odds with Carlyle and Niebuhr, Dewey insisted that social progress could come only from applying "the method of experimental and cooperative intelligence" to all aspects of human life, in a way analogous to what "has already been accomplished in subduing to potential human use the energies of physical nature." Not to do this, he concluded, "would be to revert to savagery." Using the new method, however, could create a "vital and courageous democratic liberalism" able to transcend the notion that the future (in 1935) was destined to be a bipolar "struggle between Fascism and Communism."[45]

Dewey's call, then, was for a regrounded and a recast understanding of self-government suited to the modern, corporate era and utilizing a scientific, cooperative idea of intelligence that would define individual fulfillment and social progress. Though some post-Darwinian intellectuals, including Veblen, Ward, the Webbs, and Laski, conceived of a sort of elite of social scientists guiding toward and, perhaps, directing this progress and scorned the capacity of ordinary people (*the democracy,* as some termed it) to take part according to the new scientific paradigm, Dewey insisted on the capacity of all to take part if "the first object of renascent liberalism is education." "The task," he said, "is to aid in the producing of habits of mind and character, the intellectual and moral patterns" that would be the foundation of a citizenship able to think scientifically and, thus, to make self-government good government. This would require, of course, profound changes in many institutions and economic practices. Thus, for half a century, Dewey focused on such questions (reflected in his titles) as *The School and Society* (1899), *Democracy and Education* (1916), and *Freedom and Culture*

(1939) as the keys to a "renascent liberalism," a new understanding of democratic government. New methods of teaching, from the earliest grades onward, would make classrooms into "laboratories of democracy" where teachers and pupils together would not only master "the three R's" but also study experimentally and instrumentally the society in which they lived. Teachers would not so much transmit and demonstrate the truths of the past (the traditional approach, akin to Matthew Arnold's) as discover and apply (scientifically) so much of the "truth" (hypotheses) of the present as they could in discussion with their pupils, who would "learn by doing" as much as possible. This kind of education, Dewey believed, would nourish a "procedure of organized cooperative inquiry [similar to that] which has won the triumphs of science in the field of physical nature"— and would, thus, properly train democratic citizens able to become a true "public."[46] Though Dewey later explained this process, in works like *The Public and Its Problems* (1927) and *A Common Faith* (1934), using terms similar to those used by late-twentieth-century communitarians, he understood it as a "new liberalism" retaining the emphasis on individual enhancement of the "old liberals" Locke, Adam Smith, and Mill but suited to a more intricately social but still Darwinian time.

As this method and approach became more characteristic of institutions and practice (which Dewey promoted in his support of hundreds of reform movements in his long lifetime), and as the schools (Dewey always emphasized *public* schools) produced more appropriately educated citizens, Dewey envisioned a materially, socially, and morally progressive society guided throughout, from lowest to highest levels of government, by a scientific, instrumental intelligence, mundane and socially responsible, understood and applied by rulers and ruled alike. Indeed, in his formulations, there was no clear or lasting distinction between the two categories; all were part of the democratic process. As Holmes and Laski (and, in a way, Bentham) had explained, however, this "process" had no foundation in natural law or higher principles (as Locke or Jefferson supposed) but was simply a way of making social decisions that gave weight to (a majority of) the political community. With institutions (especially the great corporations) reformed or regulated in accord with the new science, and with citizens trained in the processes of self-government, Dewey argued that a new conception and practice of democracy, suited to post-Darwinian modernity, could come into existence.

The thought of Bentham, Mill, and Comte, the post-Darwinians Spencer, Sumner, Ward, and Veblen, and, finally, the largely twentieth-century figures Holmes, Laski, and Dewey, then, defined a new paradigm, a second modernity that not only recast Western thought generally, but required a radically different foundation for thinking about democratic government. At the same time, the new modernity provoked, somewhat in the mood of Pope and Swift, a further traditionalism among a host of ancients who urged attention to dimensions of human nature and to wisdom from the past that, in its view, considered the human condition much more profoundly—and more effectively for the future—than a reductionist outlook. The new moderns, however, insisted, not only that their approach and method repudiated the various strands of what Santayana called *the genteel tradition,* but that it followed through to their logical conclusion the only partially consistent empiricism and induction of the thought and science of the first modernity. In the understanding of government, undertaken with special intensity in the United States, the ground shifted abruptly as post-Darwinian thinkers tried to work out what democracy could mean if the eighteenth-century natural law thinking of Locke and Paine and Publius and Jefferson and Marshall was repudiated: Why did Justice Holmes have to "destroy" what Chief Justice Marshall had "raised" if the U.S. Constitution was to be a basis for self-government in the twentieth century? Did natural law have to give way to "inductive realization[s]" and "dominant power"? Indeed, did there need to be a "second founding," a reconceiving of the nation's polity, if it was to be suited to the new circumstances and the new thought of a new age?

In effect, the second moderns faced the questions that Aristotle and Confucius asked about good government, and Jefferson asked about good *self-* government, with three pathways before them. Those most enthralled by the new science and most contemptuous of existing governments, such as Comte, Veblen, the Webbs, and Ward, argued simply that government and other social decisionmaking should be put in the hands of *social* scientists. Ward, for example, said that legislators should be "thoroughly versed in the whole theory and practice of 'social physics'" (Comte's term). Their work should be done largely in committees that would "investigate questions, . . . hear testimony, . . . weigh evidence, . . . and discover the truly scientific principles involved." They should use "the statistical method . . . [to discern] the facts that underlie the science of government." These were "the inductions of political science" on which all the laws and administration of the state should rest. Ward believed that the application of this method might usher in a fifth stage of government. Roughly following a century or more of history in the United States, Ward saw first autocracy (under George III), then aristocracy (the age of the founders), then democracy (the Jacksonian era), and then plutocracy (the Robber Barons), but the pathological results of all these stages (not one exhibited understanding of the science of society) made clear that a fifth stage, sociocracy, was needed to bring the benefits of modern science to the social and political realm.

"All democratic governments," Ward declared, "are largely party governments" where a "puerile gaming spirit . . . [and a] factious excitement of parti-san struggles" are managed by "professional politicians and demagogues." Societies thus "in the hands of mere politicians" soon found themselves "easily managed by the shrewd representatives of wealth," ushering in a plutocracy like that evident, Ward thought, in the post–Civil War United States. "The prevail-ing democracies of the world," he concluded, "are incompetent to deal with the problems of social welfare." Good government, then, can come only when the investigations, values, and knowledge of social scientists are the foundation of social decisions and political life. Though Ward had no use for democratic politics as he had seen it in the United States (or anywhere else), he thought that evolution into the stage of sociocracy was possible through the gradual dissemination, under the leadership of civil service experts and academic social scientists, of the spirit of the new science throughout society, first to an elite leadership, then more generally to a population willing to "defer to the superior judgment" of the sociocrats. Although he scorned the word *democracy* (using it much as Aris-totle had twenty-three hundred years earlier and Henry Adams had in *Democ-racy* in 1880), Ward did not see his view as hostile to government by consent; at least it was government for the people—on their behalf and according to "the true interests and improvement of the people."[47]

The Webbs, too, saw "democratic" decisions as best disconnected from union officials who were "ignorant, if not incapable, of understanding . . . complica-tions . . . [and] one-sided in their opinion" and from the foolish and ignorant voice of "the average sensual man." Instead, decisions should be based on science, which meant "measurement, . . . the objective testing of persons and policies." They would derive, not from "spontaneous promptings" from politi-cians or even the people, but rather from "a stream of reports from independent and disinterested experts, retained expressly for this professional service." Parlia-ments would not make decisions by majority vote but be facilitators of discus-sion between the experts, with their "stream of reports," and the people, creating a "consciousness of consent" that would constitute a new democracy suited to the age of science and industry. This echoed Platonic or Confucian concepts of philosopher-kings or sage counselors, of course, but Ward and the Webbs had made a critical turn by defining these "measures needful for the prosperity of the people"[48] (they did not speak of justice, inalienable rights, or natural law) in quan-titative, inductive terms. They did not use the idealistic, universal, or tradition-laden language commonly used in political discourse by Plato and Confucius—and by Moses, Thomas Aquinas, and Muhammad, too, of course. For those espe-cially concerned about government of and by the people, Ward and the Webbs proposed a mundaneness, a scientific method, and an expert specialization that, in the second modernity, permeated thinking about democracy.

A second approach pictured a data-driven, pragmatic public life of competitive interaction among groups in the political arena. This view was less inclined toward comprehensive systems and the idea of scientific "truth" than Comte's and Ward's and more attuned to a Spencer-Sumner view of the political-social world as an unpremeditated, indeterminate Darwinian struggle, firmly scientific, statistical, and behavioral. Though sometimes resolutely laissez-faire about government, and sometimes open to Holmes's willingness for majorities in legislative bodies to be a changing "dominant force" in society, social scientists increasingly worked within a corporatized model of a polity where economic, social, racial, religious, regional, and other groups, parties, and organizations struggled with each other for survival and power. As Arthur Bentley put it in *The Process of Government* (1908), "human society is always a mass of men, and nothing else," and "political phenomena" were to be understood as simply the actions of people "in the masses in which they are found aggregated." Furthermore, Bentley asserted, "there is no group without its interest"; thus, in the "world we can . . . actually . . . observe and study, . . . there are interested men, nothing more and nothing less." There might be a "beyond-scientific question" of the "reasonings" of the groups, but these reasonings were notable only "as indicating where to look for the facts" (i.e., they were merely obfuscating rationalizations); of them, Bentley said, "I do not know or care."[49] Though human beings might be parts of many different groups that interacted in complex ways, this did not change the basic dynamic, nor did it alter the task of the political scientist to examine and analyze the behaviors, the pressures, and the outcomes.

In a starkly Darwinian (and Hobbesian) model, Bentley asserted: "All phenomena of government are phenomena of groups pressing one another, forming one another, and pushing out new groups and group representatives (the organs or agencies of government) to mediate adjustments." In democracies as well as despotisms, a group might at one time manipulate the government and work through it and at another time see it as its "deadly enemy," but the process of struggle to dominate is always the same, "however it might be phrased in public opinion or clamor." In democratic legislatures, in societies "with classes broken down into freer and more changeable group interests," Bentley noted, "the more difficult becomes the analysis of the group components, [and] . . . the more adroitly the group forces mask themselves in morals, ideals, and phrases," but the basic process is unchanged. Thus, "log-rolling, or give and take, appears as the very nature of the process. It is compromise, not in the abstract moral form, which philosophers can sagely discuss, but in the practical form. . . . It is trading. It is the adjustment of interests. . . . It is a battle of strength, along lines of barter." In the United States, then, Bentley defined a political party as "an organization of voters, brought together to act as a representative of the underlying interest groups in which these voters, and to some lesser extent, other citizens, present themselves." There was, to be sure, "a formally differentiated discussion phase" in which party platforms were offered, but, "as every schoolboy knows," this was "most of the time a hollow mockery" in which "the underlying groups are not accurately represented." Groups that "are exerting themselves in the political field," perhaps initially through regional "machines," had, "to secure results," to approach these "quasi-corporate organizations."[50]

Bentley thus outlined what was to become the leading understanding of the democratic political process throughout most of the twentieth century and, implicitly, the chief function of the political scientist. As in the Comte-Ward-Webb model, the main task was the reductionist one of collecting facts (meaning, largely, the wants and behavior of interest groups), the statistical manipulation of them, and rigorous analysis in order to better understand and perhaps foresee the workings of the system. Since the "morals, ideals, and phrases" were merely masks, the political scientist would be obliged to expose them for what they were and, thus, enable more precise, less befogged attention to social facts and to the real process of struggling groups—in Harold Lasswell's famous title, *Politics: Who Gets What, When, How,* or conflict-of-interest politics. In Paul Appleby's formulation in *Big Democracy* (1945), the enlarged bureaucratic (post–New Deal) state simply allowed more places within the administrative structure where citizens and groups could exert pressure—and, in an effectively democratic state, get significant response.[51]

As a mainstream understanding of democratic government for the twentieth century, this science-grounded, group-oriented, conflict-of-interest model of politics had implications for all participants. Legislators were representatives of (various) special interests delegated to pursue and compromise them as the process (in Congress and elsewhere) made necessary. Legislative, executive, and party leaders were mainly to be brokers who studied society, identified pressure groupings, facilitated compromises, and managed to produce some resultants in public policy that were the only possible definition of the public interest; there was no higher understanding of that term. Administrative officials ("bureaucrats") should be trained social scientists sensitive to these pressures and skilled at analyzing, accommodating, and compromising them. Citizenship consisted of gaining a realistic knowledge of how "the system" worked; finding, acknowledging, or organizing groups that accorded with one's understanding and interests; and then, if it seemed "cost effective," becoming active, as an advocate, functionary, or voter. "A scientific frame of mind," Karl Pearson wrote in 1892, consisting of "the classification of facts, the recognition of their sequence and relative significance, . . . and forming a judgment upon these facts, . . . seems to me an essential of good citizenship. . . . Modern science, as training the mind to an exact and impartial analysis of facts, is an education specifically fitted to promote sound citizenship."[52] Along with the political scientist analysts and the brokering leaders, of "beyond-scientific questions" and "reasonings" citizens could also say, "I do not know or care." In Carlyle's image, attention was on the "Spectacles," not the "Eye" behind them.

Less deterministically, and sustaining a more complex understanding of a democracy, John Dewey's thinking about government and education sought a model of political culture still suited to the new Darwinian age but somehow avoiding what seemed the "new dogmatisms" of the elite social science and group-conflict models. He had full enthusiasm for the growth of the social science disciplines where scholars studied every aspect of modern society, but his resolutely "instrumental" approach required that they be efficient agents working directly to improve society in ways useful to the public at large. He also had full sympathy for the emphasis, in the twentieth century, on corporateness, on groups, and on politics as interaction and struggle for power among them, but he posited beyond the conflict of self-interested groups the possibility of there being a genuine "public." Though he shared Bentley's scorn for natural or higher law, Dewey always supposed that, in an open and democratic society, a public could form that was capable, as it went along, of discerning useful social "ends" from the open deliberative process itself. Indeed, ends arose from the means and were in no way transcendent or universal. The vital need was to somehow and in every way nourish that process so that it could be an effective, even decisive factor in the polity. This echoed in a way, as Dewey acknowledged, a Jeffersonian faith in the efficacy of reason in a self-governing polity, but he rejected Jefferson's natural law foundation for this efficacy. It simply happened, Darwinian fashion, without foreordained substance. Social science could help at both ends, so to speak, first by devising and carrying out an instrumental system and method of public education. This would train children in the inductive social approach to community and school problems within their experience, training that they would take with them to their standing as adult citizens. Then, in the larger political world, social scientists would study, analyze, and communicate to the public understandings of the real, corporatized world around them. Through thoroughly inclusive and responsive democratic processes, the pragmatically trained citizens would then understand and use the data made available to respond to "felt needs" and, hence, further social improvement. It was possible, in a quasi-communitarian but not transcendental way, both to create a "public" and to achieve its useful, "instrumental" attention to "problems."[53] Like Bentham and Ward and Laski, Dewey was entirely open to using government (at any level) in seeking social progress, but he refused to be dogmatic about it. He always rejected Marxism as well as laissez-faire "old" liberalism (and, of course, fascism and communism) and had only limited enthusiasm for thoroughgoing socialism on the British, Fabian model.

Thus, though the intellectual design of the second modernity evolved over at least the nearly two centuries between Bentham's earliest writings (1776) and Dewey's last (1951), it had reached its mature political configuration by the early decades of the twentieth century. It had by then profoundly criticized the politics of the first modernity for its only partly scientific, still natural law foundations (witness, e.g., Veblen's scorn for Adam Smith, Holmes's for John Marshall's absolutist "obiter dicta," and Charles Beard's formulation of an economic interpretation of the Constitution).[54] It had, thus, replaced the structure and theory of democracy of the first American founding with a "second founding" that shifted fundamentally the rationale for self-government: from the Declaration of Independence to the dissents of the *Lochner* (1905) and *Abrams* (1919) cases; from self-evident truths, inalienable rights, and just government derived from the consent of the governed to government under a constitution that, like all of life, was an experiment, that was made for people of fundamentally differing views and enacted no particular theories either of paternalism or laissez-faire, and endorsed majority rule as simply the dominant force in society. Though this second modernity formulation with its three contending emphases faced many critical arguments from both those who thought it too modern and those who thought it not modern enough, its general perspective and theory of what self-government could and should be like was dominant in much of the world (and especially in the United States) through much of the twentieth century. And it raised for the rest of the world and for the future questions of how this idea of democracy would fit with other profound conceptions of government, especially in East Asia, perhaps yielding a "third modernity" foundation of self-government, and of how yet another extending of modern thought (a "fourth modernity") might engender still other ideas of democracy.

7

Liberal Democracy in the Twentieth Century

By the turn of the twentieth century, the new understandings of democracy, along with rapidly changing industrial society, had begun to spawn in various parts of the world revised versions of self-government. In the years before World War I, in the United States and Great Britain, for example, reforms in the idea and practice of democracy began what would amount to a virtual refounding of their polities. The fulfilling and consolidating of these reforms, largely in the years following World War II, resulted in a pervasive reconfiguring of democratic polity into what is perhaps best termed the *liberal corporate state*. (The *welfare state, social democracy,* and the *new liberalism* are other terms sometimes applied to this phenomenon.) In accord with guidelines set forth by Harold Laski, John Dewey, Arthur Bentley, and other second modernity thinkers, democratic governments moved to broaden the mechanisms of participation by the people, to be responsive to the various needs of all elements of society, to accept an enlargement and bureaucratization of government appropriate to the new industrial and corporate world, and to apply the methods of science and technology in the public sphere. Following Holmes, the new democracy repudiated ideas of natural law, and adopted neither a laissez-faire nor any other particular economic theory, but intended, as Laski argued, to accept the indelible diversity of human intentions and achieve through government, inductively, minimum standards for decent existence.

Progressivism, the New Deal, and the Liberal Corporate State

In the United States, this "second founding" had roots in the Populist movement of the 1890s, saw enlargement in the Progressive era of the first two decades of the twentieth century—including the "New Nationalism" and "New Freedom" programs of Theodore Roosevelt and Woodrow Wilson—and achieved fulfillment in Franklin Roosevelt's New Deal. By 1945, American government bore little resemblance to that which Theodore Roosevelt had inherited from William McKinley in 1901 and had been set on intellectual foundations foreign to Thomas Jefferson and to the authors of the *Federalist Papers* alike. A chorus of publicists and political leaders in the generation before World War I proclaimed that American democracy needed a rebirth to suit the new conditions and new thinking of the twentieth century. As Herbert Croly put it in *The Promise of American Life* (1909), contrasting the Jeffersonian and Hamiltonian legacies, modern America needed less of the "extreme individualism," the emphasis on personal rights, the dependence on "local authorities," and the "old fatal policy of drift" of the nineteenth-century Jeffersonian model. Rather, it needed more of a policy of "energetic and intelligent assertion of the national good . . . by persistently willing that it should prevail and by the adoption of intelligent means to that end." Science and the efficiencies of corporate organization, as well as effective majority rule, not abstract rights and natural law, should provide the guidelines for democratic government.[1]

As the origin of the Populist movement among farmers in the West and South revealed, the basic thrust was toward more popular control of government (federal, state, and local) in order to assure that the national needs of ordinary people, rather than those of various plutocratic forces, would direct the polity. This demand for broadened participation resulted most immediately in the forming or taking over of many local and state organizations, the infiltration of the existing political parties, and even the founding of a national third party, the Populists. The movement (increasingly incorporated into the major parties) also stimulated constitutionally broadened participation in the form of amendments for the direct election of U.S. senators and for the enfranchisement of women. The argument for these enlargements was not only that they were fair and just but, even more, that they would ensure that the special concerns of the previously neglected and the newly enfranchised would receive proper attention —Prohibition, for example, to protect female homemakers from the evil influences of the saloon. Responsiveness to these interests (*all* the interests in society) was a further intention of the Populists. That, after all, was increasingly seen as the point of democratic government.

Progressives, concentrated in the burgeoning native middle class of towns and cities, as well as Populists supported these reforms and also generally backed the democratizing notions of initiative, referendum, and recall. By popular vote, legislation could be initiated by the people, laws could be enacted only after being referred directly to the people to be voted up or down, and public officials could be recalled from office by popular vote before the end of their term or appointment. Though the use of these devices occurred formally at state and local levels of government and, hence, varied greatly in detailed provisions, the underlying idea was to assure that the majority would be, as Holmes argued, the dominant force and prevail. In many states, these devices were used to make constitutional changes, thus further underscoring the insistence that at issue was not so much sustaining fundamentals or "paramount law" (John Marshall's phrase) as meeting the immediate needs of the majority. More generally, much of the emphasis on the meaning of democracy focused on the questions of inclusiveness, full participation, and direct access in order that all groups and interests be effectively part of the process, as Arthur Bentley had explained. Later federal amendments to eliminate lame-duck congresses, to restrain entrenched interests by limiting the president to two terms, to outlaw poll taxes, and to lower the voting age to eighteen, as well as the broad civil rights movement, all had populist, inclusive implications. Lyndon Johnson and Thurgood Marshall, heirs to Franklin Roosevelt and Walter White, agreed.

The Progressives also led efforts that, as they saw it, would update the organization of government at all levels to suit the vastly altered circumstances and understandings of the twentieth century. To Theodore Roosevelt in 1912, the problem of the huge transportation, industrial, and financial trusts spawned by modern technology and business organization required appropriate government response. Laissez-faire nostrums (Adam Smith's "natural laws" of economics) and Jeffersonian dicta about "governing least" were, in the presence of the reach and power of Standard Oil and U.S. Steel, simply irrelevant. Roosevelt's in-house intellectual, Herbert Croly, insisted that "the Jeffersonian principle of non-interference be abandoned [because] . . . the automatic harmony of the individual and the public interest [the benign 'invisible hand'] . . . has proved to be an illusion."[2] Roosevelt proposed the regulation of the trusts by government boards or bureaus to protect workers, women, consumers, and other interests in society. Though the Progressive Party did not prevail in the election of 1912, it received a sort of partial enactment in the Wilson administration (the Federal Trade Commission, the Federal Reserve system, and many boards created to mobilize for World War I), and then, during the New Deal and World War II, the liberal corporate state envisioned by the Progressives took nearly full form in the United States. Under the New Deal, the bureaucratization of the federal government continued to become more and more a means to protect the interests of large groups in the society: the National Labor Relations Board for labor unions; the Agricultural Adjustment Administration for farmers; the Social Security Administration for the elderly; the Tennessee Valley Authority for the Tennessee Valley region; even the Securities and

Exchange Commission for Wall Street financiers; and so on. This conformed, of course, to what Lester Frank Ward and Harold Laski said was the nature and purpose of democratic government.

These new purposes and mechanisms were undergirded and worked out in detail according to the data and methods of social scientists in academe and government research bureaus. Though these experts remained for the most part advisers and civil servants rather than becoming top executive officers themselves (Franklin Roosevelt's "Brain Trust" of adviser-colleagues would be a leading example), their work, focused on the immediate, material needs of all groups of people in the society, set forth Laski's "purely inductive statement of certain minimum conditions" to guide the policymakers. They collected and made available the information about social conditions, economic forces, political possibilities, and so on that could be the basis for legislation and administrative decisions thus attuned to the diverse "felt needs" (Dewey's phrase) of the people. Furthermore, the enlarged and much more complex operation of government itself (at all levels) became the subject of scientific study—institutes of municipal research and schools of public administration came into existence to infuse the processes of government with the methods and guidelines of the second modernity.

Perhaps Franklin Roosevelt best captured the spirit of the new democracy when he claimed that he "sought Jeffersonian ends using Hamiltonian means." That is, he understood himself as seeking the same ideals of genuine self-government, human rights, and "the pursuit of happiness" for all that Jefferson had declared 150 years before the New Deal. In the industrial era of massive technological and social change, however, Jeffersonian nostrums about pastoral self-reliance and the primacy of local (and state) government seemed simply beside the point and, in fact, stood in the way of effective response to social needs—discoverable through "inductive statement" resulting from social science research and leading to organized response. On the other hand, Alexander Hamilton's rational (and effective) plans for managing the public debt, his research on the American economy undergirding the (not enacted) Report on Manufactures, and his positive use of federal power to implement his plans in a way foreshadowed the approach of the Roosevelts and their adviser-intellectuals. Yet the basic distance remained between the heavenly city of the eighteenth-century philosophers (see chapters 4 and 5) and the welfare society of the social scientists of the twentieth century. The first was intent on rights and purposes and programs in accord with natural law and the second on efficient response to the felt needs of diverse interests and groups in a complex economy and society. (This assumes, of course, that the eighteenth-century thinkers were earnest and serious about natural law and universal rights, rather than cynical and hypocritical about them, as twentieth-century, second modernity social scientists have often argued.)

As Jefferson probably understood more deeply than Franklin Roosevelt, however, the means themselves, the approach to government implicit in Hamilton's financial plans and in the New Deal, had and would always have a tendency to overwhelm the ends. As the New Deal matured and pursued implementation of its "Jeffersonian ends," the scope and nature of government itself came to have at least as much impact on the reality of democracy as the declared ends. As the Agricultural Adjustment Administration carried out policies to enhance the welfare of farmers (e.g., crop limitation), it often seemed that regulation meant heavy interference with farmer freedom and self-reliance. Had the means overwhelmed the ends? More generally, did the entire bureaucracy created by the New Deal ("alphabet agencies") really enhance the sense of a citizen's control over his or her life ("pursuit of happiness")—or diminish it? That is, the procedures and organizations of the industrial era, embodying as they did the scientific approach of the experts and administrators, created a democratic government that worked and felt much different from that associated with Locke and Jefferson. The Liberty League of the 1930s and other opponents of the New Deal loudly proclaimed and condemned that contrast. This reconceiving and reunderstanding of self-government, both cause and effect of the new era, was characteristic of the liberal corporate state that became dominant in most of the twentieth century.

British Socialism, the Great Society, and the Vital Center

The British move toward the liberal corporate state took a different route but, by the 1960s, had reached much the same place. Moving ahead from the foundations laid in the second and third Reform Acts and the social programs of "Tory democracy," the Liberal government of 1906 undertook explicitly to remake Britain along the lines of the "social democracies" being proclaimed and tried out around the world. (Experiments in Australia and especially in New Zealand in the 1890s in welfare and labor legislation, e.g., attracted attention in Britain and even in the United States.)[3] Liberal Party dogma about the "natural" laissez-faire laws of economics gradually gave way to the evidence of social scientists about their harmful effects on people's lives. Charles Booth's *Life and Labour of the People of London* (1889–1891), for example, portrayed in stark terms the degraded life of Britain's poor. The "Lloyd George Budgets" of 1907, 1908, and 1909 extended such social reforms as expansion of education, old-age pensions, workmen's compensation, a beginning of national health insurance, and new taxes on the wealthy. The rise of the Labour Party rested on the ideas of second modernity intellectuals and called explicitly for responsiveness to special interests in society, the virtual elimination of the power of the House of

Lords (1911), and the enfranchisement of all adult Britons (including women). The United Kingdom had moved a long way from the "natural order" of Peel and Gladstone, as George Bernard Shaw, Sidney and Beatrice Webb, Harold Laski, and others bespoke the revised foundations of British democracy.

The triumph of the Labour Party in the election of 1945 entrenched social democracy securely. Under Clement Attlee, the Labour Party enacted broad socialist (Fabian, not Marxist) legislation nationalizing coal, transport, steel, and other enterprises, establishing a national health service, strengthening old-age and unemployment compensation, funding education for all, and abdicating empire, transforming Britain into a corporate welfare state. The Conservative victory in 1951, rather than reversing Labour's accomplishments, generally endorsed them and merely halted or at least slowed down the growth of the welfare state. The programs of the Conservative chancellor of the exchequer, R. A. B. Butler, and the new leader of Labour, Hugh Gaitskell, were in the 1950s so close that *Butskellism* became the descriptive term for British government. In the 1960s and 1970s, whether led by the Conservatives Harold Macmillan and Edward Heath or the Labourites Harold Wilson and James Callaghan, Britain became a model liberal corporate state: assured health and welfare services; protection of civil liberties; pragmatic adjustment of nationalizations; education expansion; liberalization of international trade; retention of a market economy; and insistence on fair and accessible political processes. British democracy existed, all proclaimed, to meet the needs of all segments of the population, to assure a decent standard of living for all, and to meet, as they came along, the economic and social problems of the modern world—the inductive realization of social policy. John Locke and J. S. Mill were not so much repudiated as decidedly re-dressed for a twentieth-century modernity.

Two books by vintage second modernity intellectuals, Karl Popper in Britain and Arthur Schlesinger Jr. in the United States, elaborated these midcentury versions of the democratic state. Popper's *The Open Society and Its Enemies* (1950) identified two patterns of political thinking that had coursed down through Western thought. One, from Plato and Hegel and Marx to Lenin, Hitler, Mussolini, and Stalin, argued for "closed societies" where one idealized model state was set forth as absolutely right, justifying its forced imposition on society and excluding all others. The state was then organized to implant and maintain that perfection or ideal and was closed to change and to all other models. Oppositely, from Aristotle, Bacon, and Locke to Bentham, Dewey, and the Fabian socialists, political theorists had outlined "open" societies where absolutes were not envisioned or imposed but, rather, various forms and ends of government were set forth and tried and were always open to revision or repudiation as circumstances and needs changed. Thinking about the political realm was tentative, experimental, and critical, ready to try anything and attached to no dogma (contrast Plato's *Republic* with Aristotle's *Politics*), laissez-faire or totalitarian. This seemed to be both the lesson to be learned from the twentieth-century assaults on democracy, in writing and warfare, and the clear implication of second modernity thinking.[4]

Drawing on the same lessons of history and the same intellectual worldview, Schlesinger insisted, in a 1949 book of the same name, on the importance of what he termed *the vital center*,[5] that part of the political spectrum excluding fascism and communism but including right-of-center and left-of-center from Herbert Hoover to Norman Thomas or from Winston Churchill to "Nye" Bevin. Within this broad range, there was ample room for democratic polities to explore many degrees of socialism, many configurations of a market economy, many devices of welfare and justice for all, and many adjustments to the processes themselves. Forbidden were only the closing of any (democratic) alternatives and the ending of the cycles of change. Though Popper and Schlesinger themselves favored "leftist" directions such as Labour Party socialism and the New Deal and argued vehemently for their legitimacy as open societies, they just as fervently insisted on the legitimacy (if not the wisdom) of the Churchill-Eden and Eisenhower "adjustments" of the 1950s, for example. The tags in the titles of both books became commonplaces in explaining the nature of liberal corporate state politics after World War II. (George Soros, e.g., deliberately chose "The Open Society" as the title for his foundation devoted to spreading liberal corporate state ideas and institutions in Stalin's former empire.)

The pattern in the United States also endorsed the open society and vital center arguments, though that doctrinal emphasis proclaimed, different from Britain, was more capitalist than socialist. Under President Dwight Eisenhower, the programs of the New Deal remained largely in place (and, in some instances, even extended) as "turn-back-the-clock" rhetoric harking back to the first modernity lost force. For thirty years, a dominant coalition of "centrists," both Republicans and Democrats, controlled Congress. A succession of presidents, some Republican and some Democrat, gained office by persuading the public that they stood for the modern democratic welfare state. Neither party (at least the dominant wings) opposed the broadening of participation entailed in the civil rights campaign and in the student and women's movements—the goal was to include all the increasingly diverse elements in society in the political process. (The vociferous oppositions to these movements, though sometimes effective, were in the long run overcome by the "mainstream.") The pervasive institutions of the liberal corporate state implanted under Franklin Roosevelt and Harry Truman, and accepted by Eisenhower, found elaboration and extension in Lyndon Johnson's Great Society programs and, no less markedly, in such Nixon initiatives as the Occupational Safety and Health Administration, the Environmental Protection Agency, and the Handicapped Americans Act. Further programs to meet the needs of all individuals and groups in society brought the essentials of the liberal corporate state to other levels of government under governors such as Democrat Edmund Brown of California and Republican Nelson Rockefeller of New York and mayors such as William Hartsfield of Atlanta and John Lindsay of New York City. Though intense partisan struggles went on within and between the major parties, the basic movement at all levels was to realize a model of democracy consistent with the understandings and proposals of the post-Darwinian, social science–oriented thinkers of the second modernity.

Liberal Democracy as Twentieth-Century Orthodoxy

Democracies throughout the developed world took more or less similar directions after World War II. From Australasia to Scandinavia, nations with stable traditions of self-government moved from strong tendencies toward either socialism or laissez-faire capitalism to a more centrist combining of the social welfare state with a free enterprise economy. The forcibly democratized governments of (West) Germany and Japan soon acquired all the earmarks of the liberal corporate state (indeed, their predemocratic corporatized institutions often provided useful models for such a state) and, with surprising speed and effectiveness, helped define the quintessential polity of the second modernity. By the 1970s, worldwide organizations such as the Organization for Economic Cooperation and Development and the Tri-Lateral Commission (Western Europe, North America, and Japan) and a sophisticated idea of a world capitalist economy gave shape and definition to the paradigm of liberal, corporate democracy. The reigning design of politics was to gather, again in Laski's words, "the multiplicity of wills" present in society in order to achieve the "inductive realization . . . of the enrichment of common life." Though the diversity and complexity of modern society was, thus, acknowledged, the "new liberalism" of the corporate state did not suppose, as the "old liberalism" had, that, in Dewey's words, an "undesigned and unplanned . . . convergence of a multitude of individual efforts" would provide sufficient direction for society. Rather, in some degree, as Dewey had urged, the "experimental method in science" would project "comprehensive ideas, . . . possibilities to be realized in action" wherein, again in some degree, "industry and finance are socially directed" (see chapter 6).

Good government would come from an elaborate structure that sought, in the style of Franklin Roosevelt, Clement Attlee, and a host of their "successors" around the world, to be both responsive to the "multiplicity of wills" in their complex, modern societies and attuned to constructive hypotheses provided by social science—as Bentham, Veblen, and others had been proposing since their condemnation of natural law and universal rights a century or more earlier. This meant, at the top, legislative, executive, and judicial institutions all in some fashion responsive to "the people." Legislatures, given ultimate lawmaking power, were to be truly representative of and responsive to the needs and intentions of the various interests, groups, and factions in the society. Political parties served importantly as organizers and conduits of these forces in all branches of government, and the media provided channels of information in all directions and with a variety of motivations, from greedy and devious, to public-spirited and profound. The executive responded to these same forces (indeed, was chosen in some manner by them) but was intended as well to provide the nation with a guidance in the public interest—though that concept itself generally had no more than a brokering definition arising from the clash of groups and interests, akin to Bentham's calculus of the "greatest good of the greatest number" or Bentley's "compromise, not in the abstract moral form, . . . but in the practical form . . . trading . . . adjustment of interests . . . battle of strength . . . barter."[6] One thinks at once of the dynamics of Lyndon Johnson's Great Society. The ever-enlarging administrative apparatus ("bureaucracy") became a place where these various forces could help define, deflect, and otherwise impinge on policies of all kinds. Social science insights ("facts") provided by civil service specialists, think-tank researchers, and academics would interact with special-interest input to produce the hybrid of popular access and scientific expertise that Dewey and Laski proposed as the essence of twentieth-century democracy. By the 1960s and 1970s, it was *the* model in the trilateral world as well as the recommended and widely attractive way for the Third World—and even the design toward which the misguided Second World of communism would have eventually to move.

In fact, the cold war itself, supposedly a contest between the free and the Communist worlds, helped define the nature of the liberal corporate state. The military-industrial demands of the cold war required elaborate national defense bureaucracies while at the same time needing popular support to sustain, man, and pay for the whole "complex." A powerful free world ideology kept First World nations busy constructing, tending, and defending the apparatus of the liberal corporate state in order that democracy prove effective at home and attractive abroad. Political scientists supported this state with behavioral and statistical studies showing that it best fulfilled the "revolution of rising expectations" girdling the globe after World War II. Though still resting on a Locke-Jefferson ideology of natural rights and self-determination (attractive, so they said at least, to Nehru, Ho Chi Minh, Sukarno, and other postcolonial leaders), the post-1945 liberal corporate state was in practice the pragmatic, gross national product–oriented, bureaucratic government presided over by the likes of Harold Wilson, Ludwig Ehrhardt, Robert Menzies, and Lyndon Johnson. It was democratic because it rested on and sought to improve access to government for all its interests and people; it was liberal because it defended substantive and procedural rights, private property, and free trade; and it was corporate because it accepted the complex organization, rationalizing procedures, and productivity emphasis of modern capitalism. It thus claimed to be the legitimate, practical fulfillment of the "evolutionary science," the "new liberalism," and the "grammar of politics" that Veblen, Dewey, Laski, and others had insisted should replace the old liberalism of natural law and universal rights, or at least recast those laws and rights in evolutionary or "situational" terms. It was what second modernity guidelines made of self-government, in rationale and practice, just as the American Constitution and Jeffersonian democracy were the fruits of first modernity thinking.

In an odd sort of way, thought and practice in the Communist Second World seemed also to endorse some of the essentials of the liberal corporate state. Analysts propounded a "convergence theory" when they saw, not only that Western (and Japanese) governments had developed administrative bureaucracies not unlike those of the Soviet Union (apparatchiks = bureaucrats, etc.), but also that the Soviet Union and its satellites had found that they had to move back from centralized command economies to some market-like policies. When Khrushchev proclaimed "coexistence" with capitalism, he had in mind, not only geopolitics, but also allowing some flexibility and decentralization in the Soviet economy itself. Even under Brezhnev, a certain backhanded pragmatism kept that tendency alive in an effort to overcome the manifest inefficiencies of the Soviet system. Gorbachev vastly accelerated such moves and declared explicitly that the Soviet Union would have to adopt many liberal corporate guidelines and institutions if communism was to survive and prosper in the modern world. Gomułka's post-1956 reforms in Poland, János Kádár's "goulash communism" in Hungary (1957–1988), and other "undogmatizings" in the satellite countries (similar moves took place in Tito's Communist Yugoslavia) made the same point: there was something profoundly right about the liberal corporate state model of the post-1945 West. Even Mao Zedong's China gave some endorsement to convergence theory with Liu Shaoqi's moderately liberalizing reforms of 1960–1966—an endorsement vastly magnified by Deng Xiaoping after 1978. (Deng's adage was, "It doesn't matter what color [i.e., ideology] a cat is, as long as it catches mice"—a sentiment that he might have shared with John Dewey during the latter's famous lecture tour of China in 1919–1921 [see chapter 9 below].)

Even with all this dispersal, endorsement, and convergence, however, by the 1960s and 1970s, a chorus of critics was proclaiming "the end of liberalism," "the collapse of liberal empire," and so on. Part of the critique had to do with "failures" such as the Vietnam War, the nuclear arms race, the growth of an underclass, and oppression of minorities, which many commentators thought could be corrected and avoided by a more complete and consistent application of liberal guidelines. The failures were not of corporate liberalism itself but of its inadequate fulfillment. The theory was good, the practice flawed. The politics of Britain, the United States, and other trilateral nations revolved around these issues for two or three decades, but always within the liberal corporate paradigm: should there be more or less of this or that? should something be speeded up or slowed down? how could a program or intention that had gotten off the track be reclaimed? and so on. Lyndon Johnson and Richard Nixon were the paradigmatic practitioners in the United States, as were Harold Macmillan and Harold Wilson in Great Britain. Theodore Lowi and the end-of-liberalism critics, however, asserted that the paradigm of countervailing power and interest group liberalism itself was incapable of achieving justice or any other higher goal; its characteristic product was the "stagflation" of the 1970s.[7]

Even more fundamental critics of the corporate state and its liberal democratic ideology, however, made the further charge that the system, its dynamic, and its implicit direction were themselves deeply flawed. Even if the R. A. B. Butlers and the Ludwig Erhardts and the Eisaku Satos, John Kennedys, and Nelson Rockefellers of the world could have their way, the result would be far from satisfactory. In the United States in the 1960s, the broadside assaults on "the Establishment" and on the nation's most prestigious universities reached beyond the immediate civil rights and anti–Vietnam War objectives (though these matters were seen as deeply complicit in, the natural fruit of, the established system) to question the totality of the existing polity and society. Rather than an "American Golden Age" that seemed to have been promised after the exertions and triumphs of World War II, a group of "Students for a Democratic Society" (SDS) charged in the Port Huron Statement (1962) that paradoxes, failures, and unfulfillments abounded. Peaceful intentions were contradicted by the "economic and military investments in the Cold War," creating what C. Wright Mills termed a *power elite* that made a mockery of democracy and what Dwight Eisenhower warned of as a dangerous *military-industrial complex*. Meaningless work and idleness "characterized the lives of many Americans." "Two-thirds of mankind suffered from undernourishment" as the rich reveled in "superfluous abundance." "Uncontrolled exploitation governed the sapping of the earth's physical resources," and anarchy was "the major principle of international conduct." Young people felt powerless before the "enormity of events," "separated" and "isolated" without influence, and caught in a "democratic system apathetic and manipulated rather than 'of, by, and for the people.'" Liberal, corporate democracy, as understood and practiced in 1962, was a grotesque betrayal of the hopes and promises of 1945.[8]

Even more revealing of underlying shortcomings was the attack on the very universities that SDS members attended, widely considered the best in the world. Their experience at those institutions, they said, brought no "moral enlightenment." Professors and administrators "sacrificed controversy to public relations," and "passion was called unscholastic." All around there was "astute grasp of method, technique," but all this expertise and sophistication was "incompetent to explain its implicit ideal," which was the defense of the Establishment. "The specialization of human activity" characteristic of the great research universities seemed to forget (or deny) that "the search for orienting theories and the creation of human values is complex but worthwhile." The result was "the rise of a democracy without publics [where] . . . the great mass of people [were] structurally remote and psychologically hesitant." Hence, as democratic institutions attenuated, they became "progressively less accessible to those few who aspire to serious participation in social affairs."[9] The theory of democracy as articulated in the second modernity, as well as its practice so far in the twentieth century, was to these young dissidents deeply problematic. They were, in fact, part of what has been called a "New Romanticism," envisioners of a "New Age" where the whole worldview of the second modernity was challenged and found wanting, just as Wordsworth and Carlyle and Emerson and Arnold had found earlier modernities neglectful of vast realms of human life and aspiration.

Many scholars, academics, and journalistic commentators, generally unsympathetic to the student critics and themselves often settled firmly in a second modernity mind-set, also, like Bentham, took a hard look at the state of democratic theory and practice. As the war in Vietnam dragged on, as the cold war seemed grotesque, as the war on poverty remained unwon, and as racial tensions festered in American cities, something surely was wrong. Budget deficits, energy shortages, and stagflation frustrated efforts in liberal corporate democracies to meet the needs of the diverse peoples and groups that they professed to serve. Critics turned to question whether there was something amiss in the structure and intent and dynamics of the paradigm itself. Since, according to the orthodox model, its effectiveness and fairness depended on input from all parts of the system, much attention centered on making sure "access" was as open and easy as possible. In the United States, poll taxes were eliminated, voting rights were assured for formerly segregated Southern blacks, and eighteen-year-olds were enfranchised. More direct primaries (especially in party nominations for the presidency), political acceptance of non-English languages, and assuring participation for women and minorities in the political process shared the intent to make every person and every group part of the process. Only then could the sorting out of interests and the compromises that second modernity democracy saw as of the essence go on properly.

Political scientists and political consultants conducted elaborate studies of political behavior, devised scientific polls to register public opinion, examined legislative, executive, and judicial processes, probed the workings of political parties, and researched pressure groups and the connections between "money power" and politics, all in the interest of understanding how politics worked. They conducted their studies generally within the implicit assumption that democracy meant, fundamentally, as full, fair, and equitable an access to its procedures as possible. In the same spirit, political theorists developed sophisticated arguments about how or why such access was or was not possible and, indeed, whether it was or was not the essence of democracy. The result was analyses, hypotheses, theorems, and estimates that often came to the conclusion that Jeffersonian standards of meaningful self-government were an illusion in modern society. The effort nonetheless persisted to describe the myriad forces and procedures as fully as possible because to understand the political was to understand, in the manner of Arthur Bentley, the conflict of interests in any modern society. The difficulty, however, as Herbert Marcuse pointed out, was that, while "the given form of society [the liberal corporate state] . . . remains the ultimate frame of reference for theory and practice, there is nothing wrong with . . . methodology placed into the service of exploring and improving the existing social conditions—in industrial sociology, motivational research, marketing, and public opinion studies." But, if there is a need to challenge the very structure, values, and purpose of society, then the "ideological and political" complicity of "the fallacious concreteness of positivist empiricism" became apparent. The social scientists became "tools" of the Establishment.[10] Set aside was anything like an idealist, Platonic search for justice.

Increasingly, it seemed neither that the institutions of the liberal corporate state, and the second modernity understanding of democracy that undergirded scholarly efforts, were conducive to a very just, happy, or even equitably prosperous society nor that they particularly fulfill aspirations for meaningful self-government. Though in the oldest democracies, Britain and the United States, for example, devotion to representative institutions remained unchallenged, the societies presided over by Richard Nixon and Jimmy Carter, Edward Heath and James Callaghan, were widely discontented, frustrated, unfulfilled. Economies stagnated, social problems persisted, politics foundered in corruption, and citizen alienation grew apace. In one critique, Robert Wolff pointed out that, among other flaws, modern interest group theory worked well for those already in the arena, already politically organized on the "plateau" of conflict, but at the same time worked powerfully against groups struggling to enter the arena, to climb onto the plateau where the struggle was under way. Entrenched interests had inherent advantages, that is, that mocked rationales of equitable access and participation. The forms and dynamics of the liberal corporate state, Wolff argued, were not and could never be meaningfully and inclusively democratic. Instead, he called for the nation to "give up the image of society as a battleground of competing groups and formulate an ideal of society more exalted than the mere acceptance of opposed interests and diverse customs, . . . a new philosophy of community beyond pluralism and beyond tolerance."[11] Were the liberal corporate state and the sort of society that it sustained deeply flawed, afflicted with "malaise," as Jimmy Carter asserted in a famous 1979 pronouncement? And was the whole second modernity ethos of democracy at "the end of its tether," as another analysis averred?[12]

Democratic Stagflation and the Thatcher-Reagan Challenge

As politicians and scholars pondered these paradoxes and shortfalls, however, others turned the critique in a different direction. Keynoted by Margaret Thatcher's ringing first campaign (1979) slogan to "roll back the frontiers of the state," politicians and theorists moved to amend the liberal corporate state, not by entrenching or extending it according to the guidelines of Dewey's new liberalism, but rather by reclaiming some of the axioms of the old liberalism. Milton Friedman and other leading economists attacked the compulsions and inefficiencies of state-operated enterprises from schools and welfare systems to transport and post offices. They scorned government regulation of almost any kind as an interference with *freedom to choose* (as Milton and Rose Friedman titled their well-known book) in ways that merely substituted a democratically imposed control for a fascist or Communist one. By creating a collusion between powerful economic forces and "big government," Friedman and others argued, the new liberalism denied to enterprising people trying to make something of their lives an essential openness and freedom. Capitalism, the market economy made as pervasive as possible, was an indispensable foundation to democracy as well as freedom because only its competitive dispersal of power could nourish the variety of associations and points of leverage required for meaningful self-government.[13] Far from government being a means for enhancing and spreading opportunities for enterprise, prosperity, and creativity and for giving scope to the voice of the people, as Lester Ward, Harold Laski, and other new liberalism theorists had supposed, it was condemned as the great enemy of those things, as the way, not to fulfill democracy, but actually to stifle it. Hence the call to "roll back the frontiers of the state"—echoing, of course, old liberal Herbert Spencer's classic *Man vs. the State* (1884).

When Mrs. Thatcher's remarkable success both at the polls and in significantly remodeling the British state was mimicked in some degree by Ronald Reagan in the United States, Helmut Kohl in West Germany, Yasuhiro Nakasone in Japan, Brian Mulroney in Canada, Roger Douglas in New Zealand, and others elsewhere around the world, it was clear that, though the liberal corporate state was by no means to be dismantled, it had at least been repositioned. From being seen as the proactive center of the thrust of meaningful democracy in the modern world (surely what Dewey, Laski, and others had argued), the liberal corporate state was viewed with suspicion, as capable of doing more harm than good, and as in need of restraint lest it impinge on the freedom to choose essential to self-determination. When Mrs. Thatcher proclaimed famously that she could "do business" with the Mikhail Gorbachev whose "perestroika" and "glasnost" sought to liberalize the massive, centralized Soviet state, and when Deng Xiaoping set Mao's China, slowly but deliberately, on the path toward a more market-oriented economy, it seemed that, rather than there being a global "convergence" toward bureaucratized institutions, there was an irresistible move toward old liberal laissez-faire. Though neither Kohl nor Deng, not even Thatcher or Reagan, could in the 1980s do anything like uproot the institutions of the modern state, they did endorse and stimulate, from radically different starting places, a revised sense of where the tendency of good government was: against state-enlarging policies and institutions and in favor of state-diminishing and market-enhancing ones.

The ideology and practice of this new orthodoxy, however, did not really repudiate the politics of the second modernity. Rather, they were simply another version of it, one that also harked back self-consciously to the old liberal outlook of William Graham Sumner and William E. Gladstone—and even (though less authentically) to Adam Smith and Thomas Jefferson. It was thoroughly modern in its emphasis on individualism and reduction to the parts, in its endorsement of competitive energies, in its devotion to the facts and to material well-being, and in its sense of natural law as struggling diversity rather than harmonizing universality. The dynamic political interaction in the multifaceted arena of modernizing society remained much the same. Only the nature of the players and the kind of cards that they held changed. Emphasis remained on conflict of interest among individuals and groups, on giving voice to all elements of an increasingly diverse society by some party or leader or "political action" association, and on the use of sophisticated polls and surveys and statistical studies and focus groups to measure public opinion and to determine appropriate policy objectives—notice, for example, both the Republican and the Democratic Conventions in 2000.

In a curious way, earnest defenders of individual rights and of the "rights" of minorities and other "marginalized" groups, though generally opposed politically to Thatcher-Reaganism, also seemed to hark back to first modernity language of inalienable rights and justice for all. The Warren and Burger Supreme Courts (1953–1969, 1969–1987), in upholding personal rights, in broadly defining the First Amendment, and in insisting on equal protection or even affirmative action for unfairly treated groups, seemed often to appeal to timeless concepts of liberty and justice. The idea of a rights-based polity defined largely in courts of law, often in repudiation of the acts of democratically elected legislatures and executives, for many liberals (new and old) became the grounds for resisting the bureaucratic compulsions of the in-practice-not-so-liberal corporate state. Yet the various rights, openings, and accesses thus upheld were, in fact, generally understood, not as natural or universal, to be defended for everyone, but rather as fitting and appropriate and "just" for the particular individual or group before the Court. Though Ronald Dworkin and others claimed more absolute grounds, Justice William Brennan's assertion in 1987 that the protection of rights "has been transformed over time in response to both transformations of social conditions and evolution of our concepts of human dignity" became a dominant understanding. "The anachronistic view of long-gone generations" could not "cope with current problems and current needs," Brennan added.[14] After a century of second modernity assaults on the idea of natural, universal law, even rights had to be understood in pragmatic, ad hoc terms.

Emphasis and degrees of success among groups changed, and their rights as defined by the courts were, in many respects, better established, but the political realm remained a place where multinational corporations, labor unions, minority interests, the elderly and handicapped, religions, media and entertainment empires, farmers, main street merchants, environmental groups, regional interests, and on and on contested with each other. In the United States, these various groups sought influence in and control over political parties, state and local governments, bureaucracies, Congress, the White House, political consultants, media outlets, sources of funds, and all the other elements and places of influence and power—Arthur Bentley's 1908 "phenomena of groups pressing one another, forming one another, and pushing out new groups and group representatives (the organs or agencies of government) to mediate adjustments" (see chapter 6). Indeed, one of the underlying arguments of "Thatcher-Reagan-Friedmanism" was to make the interaction among all parts of society fairer, more dynamic, and more inclusive by limiting the inefficient, stifling, and coercive hand of government—"roll[ing] back . . . the state"—hence the urge to privatize, for example. This was the modern model of democracy and the definition of good government—or at least the best obtainable in a diverse, evolving, imperfect world bereft of higher law.

The Problematic Liberal Corporate State in 2000

The elections of Bill Clinton, Tony Blair, Gerhard Schröder, and their counterparts in other nations in the 1990s again left the same ethos and dynamic of politics in place, though there were further turnings of the cycles of policy—as the second modernity theory of democracy validates. Means, the political process itself, willy-nilly surface new ends that themselves, when implemented, become means in a further cycle. Thus, though the Thatcher-Reagan and Clinton-Blair eras postdated and, in some fashion, softened the flogging of the liberal corporate state by the end-of-liberalism critics of the 1960s and 1970s, the theory and practice of second modernity democracy still faced profound challenge from many directions. Though heralded as "the end of history" in the First World and as the obvious antidote to the flaws, failures, and dilemmas of both Second World totalitarianism and Third World underdevelopment, *liberalism, neoliberalism,* or *postliberalism* (name it what you will) mocked and shortchanged much human aspiration and much of what George Bush I, in vintage second modernity bewilderment, had called "the vision thing." Critics and dissenters in Los Angeles, Berlin, or Tokyo, Kiev or Guangzhou, São Paulo, Cairo, or Djakarta, see with the alleged triumph of liberal democracy, not a just, attractive, and prosperous society for all the earth's billions, but rather a drab, materialistic, alienating, purposeless world not at all fulfilling of human potential and aspiration. End-of-history theorist Francis Fukuyama mused (1989) that, with "daring, courage, imagination, and idealism . . . replaced by economic calculation, the endless solving of technical problems, environmental concerns, and the satisfaction of sophisticated consumer demands, . . . centuries of boredom" might ensue that would provoke "a powerful nostalgia" for a more exciting and morally creative era.[15] People might yearn for a time when, in Aristotle's terms, "a state exists for the sake of a good life [morally, aesthetically, etc.], and not for the sake of life only" or, in Carlyle's terms, when concern is for the "vestural Tissue . . . [of] Man's Soul" rather than for the "inexpressibly wearisome," "dissected, distilled, desiccated" calculations of the "dismal science economics."[16]

In any case, the liberal corporate state of the mid-twentieth century, the "rolled-back" state of Thatcher-Reagan, and the pragmatic populism of Bill Clinton and Tony Blair were all twentieth-century versions of second modernity democracy—and George W. Bush's "compassionate conservatism" is but yet another, perhaps even more hyped and cynical version. They fulfilled the guidelines of which John Dewey and Harold Laski had written with such assurance in the century's opening decades. (Though each would have denied that he was an "idealist," just as Locke and Jefferson would have resisted the notion of a heavenly city, Dewey and Laski were nonetheless caught in the same paradox of speaking in idealist terms within a modernism that generally repudiated such elevations.) Their model of democracy was intent on the fairness of its processes—the inclusion of diverse people and groups, the fine-tuning of the mechanisms of consent, and the leveling of the playing field for all. It had become at least the proclaimed pattern for political life, in Britain and the United States, and in most other parts of the world. Largely realized, too, were the evolutionary, undogmatic guidelines and the devotion to the accumulation of data and the scientific method characteristic of second modernity intellectuals. Though first in one way by Justices Hugo Black and William O. Douglas and then in another by Justices William Rehnquist and Antonin Scalia the language of rights remained strong in the U.S. Supreme Court, the parlance of the law was often the pragmatic, judicially restrained, majority-attuned language of Justices Oliver Wendell Holmes and Felix Frankfurter. Courts were not so much upholders of natural law as they were overseers of the processes of self-government, especially openness to the changing will of the majority and to "changing times."[17]

The end-of-liberalism critiques, however, still focused on the unfulfilling, minimal, lowest-common-denominator nature of the states and societies that subscribed to the democratic guidelines. Instead of drawing forth the sort of leadership toward "ideal right" envisioned by Jefferson, for example, leaders became merely brokers among interest groups. Though presidential candidates presented themselves to the public as concerned for the common good, in practice this meant ordinarily that they had assembled a coalition that could, by adjusting and compromising interests, provide a government for the nation. *Competence, fairness, a kinder, gentler America, compassion,* and *inclusiveness* became campaign keynotes for the George Bushes and Michael Dukakis, Bill Clinton and Bob Dole, and even Jesse Jackson and Ross Perot. Leadership in Congress, on both sides of the aisle, in the manner of Lyndon Johnson, Sam Rayburn, Everett Dirksen, Howard Baker, Robert Byrd, Bob Dole, Dennis Hastert, and many others, intent on compromise, brokering of interests, and getting a bill through Congress, had the same hallmarks and valued the same traits: managing the "clash of factions," in the language of the often-quoted *Federalist* no. 10. A similar style and intention of leadership, much reduced in ideology or "vision," developed in nearly all the liberal corporate states.

This brand of leadership was both cause and effect of the dynamic of decisionmaking that had become standard in twentieth-century democracies.

The conflict-of-interest model, heralded by Bentley and elaborated by legions of political scientists, was defended as supremely democratic. It accepted persons, interests, and groups where they were, attended to their particular needs and goals, and brought them seriously into the political process, where they contended with other interests, factions, and groups. The assumption that there was no whole, no common good or natural law, but rather only parts (and that all parts were legitimate) made the aggregation and compromise of interests the essence of politics. The rhetoric of the public interest remained as part of the claim of most groups (though, increasingly, its existence was simply denied), but the reality was the bringing of the various interests to the public arena, there to be advocated and contested, with the further assumption that the public interest was merely the resultant of that process. After all, if one assumed at the start, in a modern society, only a complex variety of groups and interests all more or less equally entitled to voice, then their interaction defines the public. To claim anything beyond or above that was to sideline the essential parts (Laski's "inexpungable variety of human wills") and to start down the road to a command or closed society, toward, as Popper pointed out, some form of Plato's "gentle persuasion." As this process gained validation and momentum, accepted as the bedrock of public life, ideas of the good life as values in some measure generally shared, even common understandings of justice, disappeared from view. For second modernity thinking, in politics as in mathematics, the axiom was "the whole equals the sum of the parts." Period.

Perhaps most problematic of all was the understanding of citizenship that accompanied the liberal corporate model of politics. Citizenship came to be understood as "optional," "minimal," self-interested, or occasional. In a free society, the argument went, attending to public affairs was a matter of choice. If it suited one's inclinations or interests, then various kinds of attention or advocacy or organizing were permissible, proper, and even responsible, that is, a fulfillment of citizenship. Choosing not to take part, however, was equally validated, and even responsible, if that suited one's inclinations and interests. The motivation behind either choice was assumed to be self-interested—if active, in pursuit of personal or group needs and interests; if inactive, content that those needs and interests had nothing to gain, practically or effectively, from politics. Hence, citizens might enter or leave the public realm as self-interest required. It was their right, if they chose, to vote, advocate, organize, or demonstrate, and it was the obligation of democratic government to pay attention and respond. Minimal citizenship and active, advocacy citizenship alike suited the conflict-of-interest corporate state. Ronald Reagan's predilection "against government" and Lyndon Johnson's inclination "for government" equally fulfilled the model—and their supporters were equally good citizens. The media often treated politics in this way (watching the "horse race" as parties competed), and politicians approached the (potential) voters as though they so understood their role. In 2000, both George W. Bush and Al Gore listened to focus groups, raised money from special interests, practiced "niche politics," and incorporated the various pleas and needs into their party platforms. Schools and universities often taught "citizenship" or "participation in government" validating the same dynamic.

Even the idea of natural rights, inalienable, due to every citizen of a democracy, and the essential means of individual advancement, though valued in a way under second modernity thinking and honored by the liberal corporate state, had in its late-twentieth-century garb come to be seen as problematic. As early as 1922, the Chinese philosopher and reformist Liang Qichao had observed that the Western habit of "reckoning life in terms of material value" possessed by individuals was deeply flawed. "The sum total of the efficiency of mankind," he said, "is not measured either by the addition or the multiplication of the efficiencies of individuals." This understanding, combined with "the standard of rights upon which is based all the political thinking of Europe and America," resulted in "feelings of antagonism [that by] its very nature is acquisitive and insatiable." "It is evident," he concluded, "that the expression of rights can only be conflict and murder. That a society built on such foundations will ever be safe is inconceivable. No wonder men of vision in Europe should predict the collapse of civilization" (see chapter 8).[18] The very concept of natural rights, so embedded in the eighteenth century in doctrines of higher law and public good, had, under the pressure of the thought of Bentham and Laski, Holmes and Dewey, and their followers, become individual attributes and power points vital to the drive to survive, prosper, and prevail in the modern world. Carried more directly into politics, "rights thinking" fashioned defenses of the rights of various groups and set forth openings and legal strategies for engaging in the give-and-take of conflict-of-interest politics. But the emphasis was more on what Liang had in mind with words like *antagonism, acquisitiveness, insatiability,* and *conflict* than on the quality and responsibilities of public life (note, e.g., Madison's original wording of the First Amendment [see chapter 5]). In any case, the preoccupation with individual and group rights in legal and political circles in the United States, Britain, and other countries, far from "harmonizing" and dignifying public life, seemed often merely to exacerbate the claims and quarrels of various groups—that is, become part of the pervasive dynamic of second modernity democracy and the liberal corporate state.

Altogether, then, both the theory and the practice of liberal democracy had by the end of the twentieth century reached a sort of festering crisis. Though still generally dominant and attractive to many around the world (Fukuyama's "end of history"), there was as well a powerful feeling that, both as idea and as fact, liberal democracy was exhausted and uncreative, even mean-spirited ("daring, courage, imagination, and idealism" were all lacking in Fukuyama's scenario). It was certainly unfulfilling of the claims made for it, not only by Locke and Jefferson, but also by Woodrow Wilson and Winston Churchill and Franklin Roosevelt, and even by the confident leaders of the liberal corporate states who congratulated themselves on their 1989–1991 victory in the cold war. The restructured and refocused democratic government undergirded by second modernity thought (from Bentham to Dewey) had had a century-long trial amid vast technological and social changes. What was cause and what was effect mattered less than the result: an ideology and form of democracy ruling over increasingly large and diverse populations, intent on devices of majority rule, responsive to the felt needs of interests and groups within society, protective of civil rights, committed to market economies at home and abroad, pragmatic about the powers of government and the uses of bureaucracy, and convinced of the benefit of competitive/conflict/adversarial models in economics, politics, and intellectual life. All this seemed faithful to the ideas and structures of self-government implanted in Great Britain, France, the United States, and elsewhere in the eighteenth and nineteenth centuries. But the practice was so different, the purpose so altered, the intellectual defense so shifted, and the sense of satisfaction and fulfillment so problematic that it seemed that a new paradigm was needed. An intriguing and portentous hybrid, a "third modernity" in a way, grew with amazing vitality as East Asia modernized, while, in the West, intellectuals, driving Baconian and Darwinian modernities ahead yet another cycle, struggled to fashion out of sophisticated critical and deconstruction studies of "discourse" a "fourth modernity" understanding of democracy and good government.[19]

8

Second Modernity Thought in Japan and China

Even as second modernity thinking undergirded and fashioned the peculiar brand of democracy dominant in the Western world in the twentieth century, it led as well to the development of a kind of hybrid, or "third modernity," in the Confucian-based cultures and nations of East Asia—China, Japan, and Korea. Major second modernity intellectuals, at their prime when Western thought most influenced East Asia, had the greatest impact on the development of a hybrid third modernity between the opening of Japan in 1854 and the May Fourth (1919) movement in China. J. S. Mill and Herbert Spencer, T. H. Huxley, Bertrand Russell, and John Dewey were the writers whose vigorous, new thought was most in vogue when Fukuzawa Yukichi (1835–1901), Yan Fu (1854–1921), and other traditionally trained scholars contended so eagerly and so creatively with Western learning. The result, a century or more in the making, has been a configuration of democratic ideas, Western affected largely by second modernity thought, but still so deeply East Asian–Confucian as to amount to a third modernity.

China and the First Modernity

East Asia, of course, had experienced the impact of the first as well as the second modernity. In the sixteenth century, as first Portuguese and Spanish and then French, Dutch, and English mariners, warships, and missionaries ventured past the East Indies and into the South and East China Seas, they brought with them to China and Japan, not only the science, firearms, seamanship, and technologies that were to prove so awesome and invasive, but also the modes and patterns of thought intertwined with them. Often tutored by Jesuit missionaries, who became both curiosities and oddly influential in the ruling circles of both China and Japan toward the end of the sixteenth century, the ancient and sophisticated cultures of East Asia learned something of the learning and worldview of the European Renaissance and Enlightenment. Though the Romans had traded along the silk road, Nestorian Christianity had reached China at least by the seventh century C.E. and had remained there through the centuries, and Marco Polo had been at the court of Kublai Khan in the thirteenth century, the impact of the West on a culture already more than two millennia old had been minimal. Seaborne Arab and Western traders and even the great expeditions of the Ming admiral Zheng He in the early fifteenth century to India, Africa, and Arabia also had little effect on the Middle Kingdom, the center of the world as the Chinese fashioned themselves. (Showing only faint interest in the return of Zheng He's last "treasure fleet" expedition in 1433, the Chinese Xuande Emperor said, "I do not care for foreign things," and turned, following his Confucian advisers, to the encouragement of China's internal trade, agriculture, and culture.)[1] The coming of powerful and self-confident Europeans, then, extending their systematic intrusion eastward following the epic exploration of the Portuguese Vasco da Gama in 1498, began an unprecedented cultural exchange and confrontation.

The arrival of the Italian Jesuit father Matteo Ricci in the "new" (since 1420) Ming capital Peking (Beijing) in 1600 marked a wider impact of the first European modernity on the Far East. (The work of Jesuits led by Francis Xavier and the presence of William Adams in the retinue of Tokugawa Ieyasu, also about 1600, resulted in a parallel but perhaps less lasting impact in Japan.) Ricci mastered the Chinese language, adopted an open attitude toward Chinese learning and philosophy, and became an adviser and teacher to Chinese officials, including, indirectly, even the emperor himself. Learned in mathematics, astronomy, and geography, Ricci enormously expanded Chinese understanding in these fields. His teachings and improvements included remarkably accurate clocks, predictions of eclipses, measuring instruments, and the first detailed, relatively accurate world map the Chinese had ever seen, resting on coordinates of latitude and longitude. The pattern, however, was one of viewing Western thought and artifacts as curiosities and exotic opinions that had no real significance or importance for the ancient, officially promulgated philosophy and worldview of the Middle Kingdom. Orthodox scholars, moreover, obliged to follow the official line, scorned any implication that Western thought might replace or improve Chinese wisdom or practice, especially in ethics, government, or social customs (Leibniz and Voltaire, a century later, would agree). In fact, Ricci himself was much changed by his experience of China, learning from its scholars and accepting some of its ways of life.[2]

For nearly two centuries, Jesuit successors to Ricci remained in Peking, earnest in their efforts to gain converts to Christianity (with some modest success), engaging with Chinese scholars, and even holding important posts at the Bureau of Mathematics and Astronomy with the title *most profound doctor*. Some high Chinese officials, most notably "Paul" Hsu (Hsu Kuang-ch'i), converted to a sort of Christianity, and Jesuit missionaries spread Western learning to some provincial centers. They carefully respected Confucian customs and beliefs, especially ancestor worship, as civil and social rituals and not religious ceremonies, so they were not seen as incompatible with Christian doctrine and practice. The Western (largely Jesuit) presence remained generally strong during the long reign of the sympathetic Qing K'ang Hsi (Kangxi) Emperor (1661–1722). It suffered a serious setback, however, when in 1715, after the so-called Rites Controversy, Pope Clement XI decreed that Confucianism was, indeed, a religious doctrine and, hence, forbade Chinese Christians to use Chinese words for God, make sacrifices to Confucius, offer prayers to ancestors, and otherwise engage in "heathen" rites. The K'ang Hsi Emperor returned the pope's contempt by accepting the continuation of the more tolerant practices of the early Jesuit fathers and blocking the work and doctrines of the Holy See. (Scorning the appearance before him of an emissary from the pope who required a Chinese interpreter, the K'ang Hsi Emperor wrote: "A man in this empire who should show such ignorance would move the hearers to laughter.")[3] Thus, the hope of the early Jesuit missionaries that first modernity learning might be a vehicle for the (partial?) Christianizing (and Westernizing) of China was aborted by papal decree, a form of premodern Western dogma.

At the same time, the Jesuit reports back to Europe about Chinese learning and culture provoked an outpouring of praise and admiration. Leibniz enthused in his *Novissima Sinica* (1699) that, whatever the Western achievements in logic, science, and technology, they were "beaten by [the Chinese] . . . in the principles of Ethics and Politics," which emphasized "public tranquility . . . [and] good order in the relations of men to one another." In the famous article "De la Chine" in the *Dictionnaire philosophique* (1764), Voltaire asserted that Chinese principles of "wise and tolerant government concerned only with morals and public order" were so superior to those of Europe that "in these matters we ought to be their disciples." "Thomas Aquinas, Scotus, Bonaventure, Francis, Dominic, Luther, Calvin, canons of Westminster," the French philosophe declared, had nothing better to offer than the ancient Chinese philosophy. Sir William Temple in England wrote in 1683 that Chinese conceptions of government had so "reached the utmost force and reach of human wisdom, reason, and contrivance" that they "excelled even the Western ideals of Xenophon, the Republic of Plato, the Utopias and Oceanas of our modern writers." The Chinese learning explained by the Jesuits thus reinforced the mundane, orderly, carefully reasoned precepts of neoclassical, Enlightenment Europe and, in a way, took part in patterns of thought linked to the first modernity there. The vitality of European Sinophilia and the *rêve chinois* in architecture, painting, and other arts lasted through much of the eighteenth century.[4]

Despite this rather remarkable convergence of Western and Eastern thought, and despite the continuance of the Jesuit presence at the Chinese court during the long reign of the Qianlong Emperor (1736–1796), Chinese thought and culture seemed less penetrable by the West at the end of Qianlong's reign than at the beginning. Western traders were carefully regulated in south China ports, and, in his famous rebuke to the British embassy of Lord Macartney to Beijing in 1793, Qianlong wrote that China had not "the slightest need of your country's manufactures" and that British requests for "normal" (by Western standards) trade and diplomatic relations were "not in harmony with the regulations of the Celestial Empire." Returning empty-handed to Britain, Macartney condemned China as like an "old, crazy, first rate man-o-war . . . kept afloat . . . merely by her bulk and appearance." It would be impossible in the long run, however, for China "to attempt arresting the progress of human knowledge."[5] The same sense of contentment with its ancient culture, and the need to protect it from "barbarian" intrusions, was fostered during the long period of Tokugawa expulsion of Western influence (save a small Dutch trading post in Nagasaki harbor) from Japan, 1638–1854.

When Western power thrust its way back into China following Great Britain's victory in the Opium Wars (1840–1842) and into Japan following the arrival of American warships in Tokyo Bay in 1853, some people in both nations began to realize their inability to defend themselves against Western intrusion without acquiring at least some of the technology and material sophistication of the West. Guns and warships, industrialization, and training in Western modes of military and commercial organization, at least, seemed indispensable to self-defense and survival as independent nations. Intellectuals in both nations, however, saw that Western technological and industrial prowess rested on patterns of thought and a worldview very different from that of their generally Confucian-based cultures. Indeed, it seemed that it would be impossible to gain the critically needed technological advantages without absorbing, at least in some degree, the thought and values on which they seemed to be based. Hence, the Japanese slogans of the Meiji Restoration of 1868 to "revere the emperor and expel the barbarians" and to have "Eastern morals and Western science" seemed problematic or contradictory even from the beginning. Chinese tendencies in the same direction seemed similarly quixotic.

Fukuzawa Yukichi, Nishi Amane, and Western Thought in Meiji Japan

Because of Japan's much more forthright opening to the West after its first "treaty" with the United States in 1854, its encounter with Western thought was generally earlier and more pervasive than was China's. (The Korean encounter was later and even more ambiguous.) Especially after the Meiji Restoration, as Japanese missions went to Europe and North America seeking to learn Western ways and Western experts and advisers came to Japan, Japanese intellectuals encountered the astonishing—exciting and appalling—second modernity worldview of J. S. Mill, Charles Darwin, Karl Marx, and Herbert Spencer. In almost every case, the Japanese who first read these Western thinkers were already learned in their own Confucian-grounded worldview and were engaged vigorously in its development and criticism. Though, by the mid-nineteenth century, the dominant schools of Japanese political thinking emphasized the unique and historically grounded nature of the Japanese state (*kokutai,* "national polity"), as opposed to the neo-Confucian (Zhu Xi) emphasis on universal principles dominant early in the Tokugawa era, understandings of the political realm were still entirely within the Confucian "mode of thought."[6] Hence, it was assumed that the precepts of good government were to be found in the Confucian classic Four Books and their accounts of the legendary rulers Yao and Shun, that scholars had a duty to understand and expound on these precepts as applied to contemporary affairs of state, and that rulers, whether Tokugawa shoguns or Meiji era oligarchs, were bound to consult and abide by such precepts. It was further assumed that the state represented "the highest embodiment of civilization" (see chapter 2) and that wise and active rulership was essential to this fulfillment.

When, in the years following the Meiji Restoration, Fukuzawa Yukichi planned the educational program for Keio Gijuku, his new university, he found that "the education of the East, so often saturated with Confucian teaching," lacked two things: "studies in number and reason in material culture [scientific method]" and "the idea of independence [individualism] in spiritual culture." "Japan could not assert herself among the nations of the world," he declared, "without full recognition and practice of these two principles. . . . Chinese philosophy as the root of education was responsible for our obvious shortcomings." As he founded and taught at Keio, he also sent incessant memoranda to the Meiji oligarchs (as had been the obligation of scholars in East Asia for centuries) of Westernizing advice and wrote a series of immensely popular works based on the Western books that he had been reading and translating since he had learned Dutch and English in the 1850s. In his most important work, *An Encouragement of Learning* (1872–1876), which went through seventeen printings (3.4 million copies) in his lifetime, he explained Western ideas of society, education, and government. By this time, Fukuzawa had read some Japanese and Chinese books about the West and perhaps read or translated Adam Smith, J. S. Mill, Herbert Spencer, and many other Western thinkers unknown in Japan before the opening to the West had begun in 1854. He also collected (especially on a trip to the United States in 1867) many American and British textbooks, themselves reflecting Western second modernity thinking, that he used in his translating, writing, and teaching.[7] Hence, his Westernizing advice was an amalgam of the classical Confucian studies that he had grown up on and the ideas in the exciting new thought of the second modernity.

Fukuzawa began his *Encouragement of Learning* with a basic liberal democratic precept that he might have drawn from J. S. Mill (though expressed in somewhat "Confucianized" terms): "When men are born from heaven they are all equal [more literally, 'heaven did not create person above person']. . . . Men can freely and independently use the myriad things of the world to satisfy their daily needs, . . . and as long as they do not infringe upon the rights of others, may pass their days in happiness." Furthermore, Fukuzawa declared: "There are no innate bonds around men. They are born free and unrestricted, and become free adult men and women." Still following Mill and working out the implications of government for free and equal individuals, Fukuzawa asserted: "The government represents the people. It conducts its affairs in accordance with the wishes of the people. . . . [I]t protects [them]." In return, fulfilling an idea of "contract" newly familiar from his reading of John Locke and his followers as well as Mill and others, Fukuzawa explained that the people were duty bound to obey the government and support its officials and services. This meant, however, not the centuries-old obligation to obey an immemorial or divinely ordained power, but rather "obedience to laws enacted by [the people] themselves."[8] Thus, Fukuzawa outlined the basic values and foundation of liberal, representative, self-government, phrased in words faintly familiar to his Confucian-oriented audience but, on the whole, far distant from their traditional conceptions of government.

In calling for the Japanese people to become "free adult men and women," however, Fukuzawa did not mean to endorse the Western ideal of individuality for its own sake. In the lengthy treatise "Theory of Civilization" (1876), he pointed out that "those who exert themselves to extend the right of their own nation, to enrich their own nation, to improve the wisdom and virtue of their own nation and to glorify the honor of their own nation are called people faithful to their country" (i.e., patriots or citizens). As Fukuzawa would later do in emphasizing the new science of political economy at Keio Gijuku, his theme was not simply that his students be trained in Western, competitive economics in order that they might become rich but, rather, that they be empowered and motivated to make Japan a rich, powerful, and virtuous nation through the contribution of their individual productivity and creativity to the good of the whole. In making "political economy" (in addition to art and law) one of the three founding departments at Keio, rather than speaking simply of "economics," Fukuzawa endorsed the East Asian presumptions that economic matters rested on and derived from the political and that individual pursuits had always to be considered and evaluated within a context of national goals.[9]

In turning to the idea of citizenship and the role of "free and equal" people in liberal democratic government, Fukuzawa broached a topic entirely foreign in East Asia. As the Chinese scholar and reformer Liang Qichao would observe of the Confucian tradition: "Government by the people is a thought left untouched. . . . Neither the method nor the theory . . . [of self-government] has been studied." Fukuzawa recognized at once, both in his role as an adviser on government and in his role as a teacher at a new university, that the most profound obstacle to bringing self-government to Japan was the ill-preparedness of the Japanese people to fulfill the responsibilities of democratic citizenship. Japan, he said, had traditionally been a "nation divided into masters and guests," where the masters were, at least ideally, "intelligent persons who direct the affairs of state," while the guests "relied entirely on their masters without taking any initiative themselves." The people thus lacked "the spirit of personal independence" (individualism), and it was supposed that "the wise [would] control the masses from above [and] the masses [would] obey the will of their superiors." It was as though, Fukuzawa explained, using a familiar Confucian metaphor, shepherds of talent, virtue, and wisdom "would love [the people] as children or tend them as sheep." "Under the rigid administration of the Tokugawa shogunate," Fukuzawa observed, "the people were spiritless [and were] faces of brass . . . like hungry dogs raised in a house. . . . Fear and subordination became habitual, [and people] do not speak out on questions which call for discussion." All initiative was in the hands of the few who "bound the majority to their will and bore the burdens of government alone." In this situation, everything "from military defense, literature, to industry and commerce, every significant affair of the people has been under governmental jurisdiction."[10]

To bring self-government to Japan, then, Fukuzawa thought it necessary to explain the startlingly new idea of "the duties of the citizens of the nation." "Each citizen," he insisted, "has a double office." The first, as of old, was to sustain the role of guest and follow the rules and customs (laws) of the land. The second, however, required each person (free and equal) "to join together with the other citizens of the nation to form a company, as it were, that is called the nation, to enact and implement the laws of the nation." Under this idea, "the citizens of the nation are at the same time the government itself." The chosen "higher" officials were simply the "representative and manager" of the people, who were "the real masters and bosses." The "managers" of government thus "receive the mandate of the people, must seek to promote the rights of all, . . . and must not exhibit even one degree of injustice or selfishness in its correct application of the law and the punishment of crime."[11] This model, of course, required that citizens possess "the spirit of independence," be willing to attend to public affairs, speak up on matters of public concern, and even take part, as voters, speakers, organizers, and officials, in the public business. In order to enable the people to fulfill this "second office," Fukuzawa noted, he made it his goal at Keio Gijuku "to train the students to acquire good judgment."[12]

"Acquiring good judgment," of course, had been the ancient, millennia-old ideal in what Fukuzawa termed the *Chinese sphere* as wise advisers steeped in Confucian learning had counseled the rulers (shoguns, kings, or emperors) and administered their realms. Fukuzawa sought, in his idea of the second, "governing" office of the citizen, to bring this quality—indeed, from his background, this prerequisite—to the function of governing even as he shifted the base from an elite few to a much larger body. To this end, Fukuzawa counseled his students at Keio to "maintain an interest in the administration of the nation and the morality of society." Keio itself was to be "a model for the people to look up to" in public-spiritedness, a "guide" for moral and social behavior for all. Noting the progress toward a more "civilized" society since the Meiji Restoration—"permission for commoners to assume family names," "encouragement of learning," "beginning of railways and telegraphy," and Western-style printing—Fukuzawa urged his students to achieve the ethical and civic standards intrinsic to that progress. "Establish your personal independence and that of your households, . . . start a new enterprise, . . . plan with confidence an undertaking for the benefit of the nation, . . . write about and circulate your ideas to the public, . . . [and] be eager to work for your country." He thus prepared a sort of ideal of civil society for Japan in urging students to "find a sphere of thought and activity outside the world of law and politics" where they could organize and learn to "stand firm as the backbone of the nation."[13] Here, in a way, Fukuzawa outlined a public-spirited "republican" model of citizenship more attuned to first modernity ideas of polity (see chapter 5) than to the more minimal, special-interest-oriented conceptions that emerged only gradually through second modernity thinking and practice in the twentieth century. When Fukuzawa learned second modernity thought, he also absorbed its foundation in first modernity conceptions and paid more attention in some ways to the continuities than to the underlying divergences. Thus, for example, Adam Smith's emphasis on the competitive energy of the parts and even Locke's extolling of individual diversity, part of the first modernity worldview, fit easily with second modernity thought. What in Japan was termed its *Enlightenment* in the early Meiji era, then, was, in fact, a blending of ideas basic both to the Western Enlightenment (first modernity) and to post-

Darwinian second modernity.[14] (A similar thing happened in the Chinese Enlightenment of the early decades of the twentieth century [see below].)

Even in offering these propositions about self-government and citizenship, obviously depending on the new Western writings of democracy that he had been reading, Fukuzawa could not avoid phrasing questions and approaching government in ways still bound to the "Chinese education" that he had had in the late Tokugawa era. Although he reported that, as early as the 1850s, he and his fellow students of Western thought had "the general opinion . . . we should rid our country of the influences of the Chinese altogether,"[15] they themselves remained entirely within the traditional pattern of studying under the control of their clans in order that they be able to use their learning on behalf of the health, prosperity, and good government of the clan and, eventually, the nation. It would not have occurred to them to pursue their studies and careers apart from this pervasive public consciousness of and need for the wise guidance of public affairs. They would, moreover, always adapt their Western learning to that underlying assumption about the nature and purpose of the polity—and, thus, emerge with a revised version of the second modernity understanding that undergirded democratic government.

Another early Japanese student of Western thought, Nishi Amane (1829–1897), after thorough training in traditional learning, studied Dutch and English and, in the 1850s, became enamored of Western learning. The Tokugawa government then sent him to the University of Leiden in Holland from 1862 to 1866 to study European social science. Like the monks and scholars who had gone to China in the seventh century to bring back to Japan Tang dynasty learning, religion, and practices of government, Nishi and others went to the West to bring back to Japan, not only the military and industrial technology that might save Japan from conquest and physical domination, but also the ideas and practices that would more fundamentally transform Japan, as they saw it, into a modern nation. The slogan "Eastern morality, Western technology" retained a powerful hold, but it was also clear that Japan was, nonetheless, to experience vast changes in its cultural and intellectual landscape. As Nishi wrote when he left for the West, he hoped that Japan would not "duplicate the mistakes of the Ch'ing emperor, Qianlong." "The explanations of life's principles [in the West] . . . are superior even to Sung Confucianism [the official doctrine of Tokugawa Japan]," he wrote, while "the civilizations and institutions of the United States and England . . . surpassed Yao and Shun . . . and the Chou system" of ancient China, which had for centuries been held up as moral and social ideals.[16]

At Leiden, long a center of advanced scientific learning, Nishi studied statistics, law, economics, politics, and diplomacy as well as reading Descartes, Locke, Hegel, and Kant, whose thought he expected to be different from the older religious doctrines (i.e., those of Christianity) prohibited in Japan during the Tokugawa era. (Nishi already thought that Socrates was "comparable to our Confucius.") He was assigned to Professor Simon Vissering and listened twice weekly to lectures on natural law, international law, constitutional law, economics, and statistics. He was even more excited by the philosophy lectures of Professor C. W. Opzoomer, who introduced him to Anglo-French positivism, especially the works of August Comte (1798–1857) and J. S. Mill (1806–1873). When Nishi returned to Japan, he brought back his notes on Vissering's lectures, which became the basis for published works in the social sciences that Nishi used in his own teaching and advisory work. More important, however, was Nishi's wholehearted adoption of the empiricism, logic, economics, ethics, and politics of the philosophy that he studied with Opzoomer.[17]

The key to the superiority of modern European philosophy, Nishi thought, was its rational, practical search for knowledge, using the inductive method to investigate evidence. "Since antiquity" in both East and West, Nishi proclaimed, "all logic has been deductive, but logic reached its pinnacle with the system of logic developed by Mill. Here we have the highest stage of science. Scholars by all means must rely on the inductive method."[18] The adoption of this mode of thinking, Nishi believed, would bring to Japan *keimo*, an enlightenment, resting on European values of rationality, practicality, awareness of individual rights, and legitimizing of the profit motive. Following Mill's *Utilitarianism* (which, he recognized, differed importantly from eighteenth-century natural rights ideas), Nishi explained that the greatest happiness in human life came from the possession of three "treasures"—health, knowledge, and wealth (cf. Benjamin Franklin's "healthy, wealthy, and wise"). The unashamed pursuit of these treasures, Nishi noted, required the abandonment of the traditional, Confucian "virtues of docility, naïveté, humility, deference, unselfishness, and freedom from avarice." Furthermore, if the Japanese people were to have a modern state capable of progress and able to defend itself, they would have to overcome the "servility" of centuries of quasi-military rule and the pervasive, "asinine" hierarchies imposed by official Tokugawa Confucianism. Instead, Nishi insisted that the "inborn moral nature" of humankind propelled it to possess the good health vital to a full life, to acquire the "individual mental power" necessary to "surpass others," and to "seek all sorts of wealth" in order to assure individual as well as national prosperity.[19] Only the acquisition of this new morality would create among the Japanese people the outlook and habits essential for them to be constructive parts of a modern society.

Turning more directly to government, Nishi noted that the "three treasures" morality assumed that "each individual has a free nature" and that "those who participate in national government should treat all men equally." The people, therefore, Nishi insisted, "should be governed with clemency, and we must develop industry, encourage all sorts of learning, nourish men of talent, and enrich the nation by not needlessly wasting wealth." Since, however, some people might "take selfish advantage of . . . individual liberties," it was, Nishi insisted, necessary that all be required equally to obey the laws and "respect the ruler," who was, after all, "selected . . . from among the people" and, thus, attuned to their needs and happiness. Government, that is, was to be utilitarian, practical, and attentive to the needs of its citizens to have as much scope as possible for their particular paths to fulfillment and happiness.[20] This emphasis on treating all equally directly contradicted, of course, the legally enforced hierarchy of samurai-farmer-artisan-merchant of the Tokugawa era, and the emphasis on private pursuit of health, knowledge, and wealth contradicted the self-effacing, group-centered norms of Confucian society.

Nishi's determination to spread liberal, utilitarian thought centered for a time (1874–1875) in his membership in the so-called Meiji Six Society, a group of Western-oriented intellectuals (including Fukuzawa) committed to spreading "enlightenment and civilization" in Japan. At the height of the reforms of the Meiji Restoration (the systematic replacement in 1868 of the feudal Tokugawa *bakufu* with a more centralized national rule nominally under the emperor) and of the halting efforts even toward some democratic government, Nishi and his colleagues applied Western learning to current issues. Their intention, as intellectuals, was to replace the "empty learning" (*kyogaku*, 虚学) of Buddhism and Confucianism with the "practical learning" (*jitsugaku*, 実学) that they had understood from the West, especially what they saw as a progressive, scientific positivism culled from Comte as well as Mill and Spencer. They advised Japan to abandon deriving its public policies, foreign and domestic, from time-honored general principles (in accord with the advice of Confucian counselors) and instead to understand each specific issue in the light of current needs and circumstances and of practical consequences—a distinction that Nishi explained as the difference between deductive and inductive thinking, as he had learned from his Dutch professors. In the same spirit, Nishi hoped that, "by broadening human wisdom, such things as folly, coarseness, and obscene beliefs are eliminated."[21]

In addressing the issue of a popularly elected assembly (*minsen giin*, 民選議院), the Meiji Six Society revealed the complex mixture of traditional East Asian thought, Anglo-American utilitarianism, and European state positivism that its outlook had come to embody as its members labored to understand intellectual currents. Though Fukuzawa and others supported an 1874 petition to establish a parliamentary assembly, Nishi thought that the people were not yet enlightened enough to elect members of a legislative body properly. He feared that "politics would become like a theatrical production" if officials were popularly elected.

Instead, he proposed an assembly to be appointed by the existing governing officials surrounding the Meiji throne that would "represent" people throughout the nation. The assembly would also have delegates from various government agencies and include intellectuals of "great learning and moral influence." Though it would have no specific powers and might even be dissolved by the Meiji oligarchs, Nishi thought that the assembly would be useful to gather public opinion, to stimulate interest in public affairs, to create respect and support for the government, to bring intellectuals more into the public sphere, and to prepare the people eventually for full participation in government.[22] An 1875 imperial proclamation, responding to the petition to establish a *minkai* (people's assembly, 民会), virtually placed Nishi's views in the emerging Meiji constitution: "We now establish the *Genro-in* [Council of Elders] to enact laws for the Empire. . . . By also assembling representatives from the various provinces of the Empire, the public mind will be best known, and the public interest best consulted, and in this manner the wisest system of administration will be determined."[23]

Another member of the Meiji Six Society, Kato Hiroyuki (1836–1916), also believed that the Japanese people were not yet ready for true parliamentary government. Instead, he favored an assembly of intellectuals, wealthy merchants, and industrialists who would guide and rule the nation in its modernizing endeavors. "If the government wishes to excite in the people the spirit of activity and to teach them to take a share in the conduct of the business of the empire," he wrote, "this object is not to be obtained simply by the establishment of a deliberative assembly. The only method of obtaining it is the establishing of schools and thus nourishing the nation's intellect." Kato simply could not relinquish the centuries-old East Asian concept (present in Buddhist as well as Confucian thought) that good government rested on great learning whether those who ruled were one or a few—or, by extension to an idea unconsidered there, the masses. Kato, heavily influenced by his reading and translation of German nationalist writers, became president of Tokyo Imperial University and a prominent middle- and late-Meiji official intent on imposing a "German-style" regime in Japan. Somewhat like Nishi Amane, he was more impressed with Comtian, Continental thinking about a positive, scientific, "top-down" state than with Anglo-American liberalism and limited government. In fact, he represented a mode of thinking much more influential in the actual frame and system of government adopted in Meiji Japan after the imposition of the German-inspired imperial constitution in Japan in 1889.[24] This system of government was simply far more congenial to traditional modes of government in East Asia (for Liang Qichao's absorption of this view from Kato, see below) than the liberal, democratic ideas of Fukuzawa and others more impressed with Anglo-American second modernity liberalism. Such thinkers retained some influence in developing ideas of more democratic government in Japan, but, for generations after the 1880s, the actual regime moved strongly in other directions.

The imperial constitution of 1889, drafted by Ito Hirobumi and based on German, not Anglo-American, constitutional precepts, embodied in reality almost none of the essential provisions of liberal democratic government—although liberal critics of the constitution urged further inclusion of them and there was some formal acknowledgment of them in the document. "Japanese subjects" (never referred to as *citizens*), for example, were given "freedom of religious belief," but only "within limits not prejudicial to peace and order, and not antagonistic to their duties as subjects," and freedom of "speech, writing, publication, public meetings, and association" had to remain "within the limits of the law." This latter proviso was the more significant because real legislative power was firmly in the hands of the nonelected Privy Council, the Genro-in, and other oligarchs around the emperor, with the result that "the limits of the law" were set, not by the Diet (itself of severely limited franchise), but by above-the-people officials. As Ito explained it, "the consent of that assembly which represents the people [the lower house, the Diet] must be obtained," but, nonetheless, "the legislative power is ultimately under the control of the Emperor, while the duty of the Diet is to give advice and consent."[25] A memorandum prepared for the emperor and his advisers stated bluntly: "Cabinet ministers shall be responsible to the Emperor and not to parliament."[26] Some of the proposals, and even some of the terminology, were like those of Fukuzawa, Okuma Shigenobu, and other liberals, but the practice was more in accord with, not only the ideas that Ito brought back from Germany, but also the reservations about government by the people that arose from ancient precepts of polity in East Asia.

Even more telling, and scornful of the rising celebration of party conflict as the essence of second modernity democracy in the West, was the careful insulation of political parties from real power in the state. "It cannot be helped," Ito noted as the constitution went into effect, that, "as the people acquire advanced political ideas, [and] political parties grow, . . . there will be conflicts in the Diet." But, rather than welcoming this, Ito declared it "absolutely necessary for the government to have no connections whatever with any political party. . . . The sovereign power . . . resides in the Emperor. . . . If the Ministers of State who assist the Emperor and conduct the government . . . have any relation to political parties, it is impossible for them to maintain . . . impartiality."[27] Parties meant "partiality" and "conflict," which, however much validated in the era of Disraeli and Gladstone (and of Cleveland and McKinley), were in the reverberations of *kokutai* and Confucian statecraft anathema, the antithesis of good government. Though the Japanese oligarchs sought a kind of acceptance of the ethos of constitutional government, it was clear as well that, if there was ever to be anything like a genuine, democratic ethos and practice in Japan (sixty years would pass before that would happen), it probably would not be the same as the emerging second modernity model of the West.

The difficulty in Japan of moving toward ideas and forms of self-government more attuned to Anglo-American modes is illustrated in countless, often subtle interactions between such modes and traditional ideas of government and public affairs. In his role as an adviser in Western learning to government officials, for example, Fukuzawa Yukichi was asked to translate an English-language economics textbook. When he submitted the translation, an official focused on *kyōsō* (競争), a word meaning "race-fight" that Fukuzawa had made up of two Chinese characters to translate the key English word *competition,* for which there was no existing Japanese equivalent with the right connotations. Seeing the character for "fight," the official complained: "Here is the word 'fight': What does it mean? It is such an unpeaceful word." Fukuzawa explained that his new word meant simply what Japanese merchants did all the time: seek to provide better and more attractive goods at lower prices than other merchants in order to increase their sales and profits. This was *kyoso,* or "competition," a key concept that, in Western economics, set prices and provided for efficient exchange of goods in the marketplace. The official said that he understood that, but still, he asked, was there not "too much effort," too much selfish striving and struggle, in Western affairs? He could not, he said, show a paper with the character for "fight" on it to his superior. Fukuzawa responded that he supposed that the official wanted a paper covered with characters bearing traditional connotations such as "kindness," "loyalty," "generosity," and "harmony" conducive to anciently admired canons of exchange and government—perhaps phrases like, "Harmony is most precious," an adage of Prince Shotoku (ca. 600 C.E.) still memorized by Japanese schoolchildren. But such characters could not possibly convey the central concept of the Western idea of competition, Fukuzawa replied, so he would have to leave out the idea altogether.[28] There was simply too great a chasm between conventional Confucian discourse on economics and government and the new Western concepts for there to be any way really to translate ideas or even words.

Similar problems arose when, in 1866, Fukuzawa sought to translate the American Declaration of Independence. In the first sentences of the famous second paragraph, for example, Fukuzawa's translation, rendered literally back into English, reads: "Heaven [*ten,* Chinese *tian,* 天] created all persons [*hito,* 人] in the same rut [*tetsu,* 轍] endowed them with unremovable rights [*tsūgi,* 通義]. These rights are, for instance, rights to preserve one's own life, to seek liberty [*jiyū,* 自由], and to enjoy happiness [*kōfuku,* 幸福], and they cannot be taken away from one by others." Though all the Japanese words flagged in this retranslation were problematic and carried connotations somewhat different from the English words for which they stood, Fukuzawa nonetheless managed a largely faithful rendering. In the next sentence, however, he lost a vital meaning: "The reason to institute governments among persons was to make their rights secure, and government can truly claim its legitimacy *only when it satisfies its subjects*" — the italicized (added) words standing for the English "the Consent of the Governed."[29] Here, Fukuzawa shifts the active role from those being governed, whose consent legitimates rule, to the government, which must "satisfy" the governed in order to be legitimate. A vital dynamic of Western democracy, first and second modernity, an active, consenting citizenry, had been left out and replaced by a hallowed Confucian ideal of government acting to satisfy the people. We do not know whether Fukuzawa (*a*) understood the problem and did the best he could given the languages with which he was dealing, (*b*) did not realize that he had made an important change in meaning, (*c*) did not think the change important, or (*d*) deliberately changed the meaning to make the idea more intelligible or acceptable to his Japanese audience. In any case, the episode again revealed both the complexities and the opportunities of conveying the meaning of Western democratic thought to the cultures of East Asia.

Fukuzawa and his Westernizing colleagues had, in fact, to create virtually a new language to convey the new ideas—a vernacular that would so much depart from traditional usages as to make classical learning and literature virtually unintelligible to people educated only in the modern way. (At least twice in the twentieth century Chinese scholars and officials have undertaken to do the same thing: after the 1911 Revolution, when Lu Xun, Hu Shi, and other intellectuals sought new language usage intelligible to ordinary people, and in the reforms of simplified character writing and pinyin romanization in Mao Zedong's China.) Second modernity Western thought, it seemed, was so foreign in its concerns and connotations that even writing and words and meanings in East Asia had virtually to be reinvented.

In 1877, in another incident full of implication for the reception of Western thought about government in East Asia, Motoda Eifu, a Confucian scholar who was official reader-tutor to the Meiji Emperor, was asked to write a memorandum on the topic "creating public opinion." Motoda began, conventionally, with a quotation from a Confucian classic (the *Book of History*): "Throw open the doors [of communication between the court and the people of the empire].... See with the eyes and hear with the ears of all." He went on to interpret the passage for the emperor as sages had done for East Asian rulers for millennia: "When avenues of expression are closed, the feelings of those below are blocked off.... The government should weigh the good and bad proposals, select the best discussions and the most reasonable opinions, subject them to discussion in the cabinet, and have the decision made by the emperor himself." Motoda proceeded to distinguish between "mass opinion" (*shūron,* 衆論), a common, ill-informed, "opinion poll" idea of public sentiment that should by no means be regarded as authoritative, and "correct, impartial opinion" (*seiron,* 正論), which was understood as "public" in the sense of what was good for the nation as a whole and could be known only through a process of study and deliberation among wise counselors and rulers.[30] In effect, Motoda explained the only meaning that the idea of public opinion could have in a Confucian context: "mass opinion" should be sought and taken into account but could be regarded as relevant to government only when subordinated to understandings of "correct . . . opinion." The same point was made in the first of the Five Articles sworn to by the Meiji Emperor in 1868: "Promote discussions widely and decide everything in accordance with 'fair [public] opinion [*seiron,* 正論].'" In another memorandum, Motoda condemned "the mad outpourings of mistaken Western ideas, growing worse daily," and insisted instead that, in Japan, "the Emperor wields the power of government and education for the entire nation" and that the "principles [be] benevolence, duty, propriety, deference, loyalty, filial piety, uprightness, and honesty. Sovereign and people, high and low, constitution and laws, none can depart from these principles."[31] Motoda understood, at least superficially, the point of the task assigned to him in writing the memoranda, but, nonetheless, he could respond only within a Confucian framework of thought that gave very different significations to the issues. To him, there was simply no valid relation between "mass opinion," or the will of the people at large, and achieving good government, which had to rest on the ancient wisdom of the Confucian classics as explained by scholar-advisers. In seeing "correct" opinion as a sort of articulated higher law ("the mandate of heaven" in Confucian thought), of course Motoda placed himself at odds with the second modernity thought then coming into Japan from the West.

The ideas of democratic government, it seems, would have different foundations and assumptions in East Asia from those developing in the worldviews of J. S. Mill and Herbert Spencer. Such basic concepts as competitive energies, active citizenship, and attentiveness to public opinion, for example, either found no resonance at all in East Asian thought or required such drastic reunderstanding that they bore little resemblance to their supposed analogues in the West. Even as intellectuals such as Fukuzawa and Nishi took great strides toward understanding and absorbing liberal, positivist, and evolutionary thought, that is, and worked diligently to adapt Western learning to Japanese circumstances, they achieved not so much a transplanting as a grafting, looking toward a third modernity version of representative government that also remained attuned to traditional assumptions and practices. Though generally overwhelmed by, and often even suppressed by, antidemocratic thought and practice from the 1880s to 1945, the Japanese encounter with second modernity versions and validations of democratic thought remained, as part of losing struggles for democratic government before 1945, and ready to surface after that in justifications and practices significantly different from those common in North America and Europe.

Yan Fu and Social Darwinism in China

After the crumbling and chaos that followed its defeat by Great Britain in the Opium Wars, China too, more fitfully than Japan, began more seriously to seek to understand and benefit from some of the learning and outlook of the West that intruded so powerfully on the country. Though since at least the 1830s Chinese officials had paid attention to Western, intrusive ideas, their impact came more strongly to China through the opening of "treaty ports" along the coast and the gradual spread of Christian missions. Chinese emissaries also began to travel to Europe and the United States to study and gather information and technology, especially about weapons and warships, to help China cope with the now inevitable confrontation with the West. It was not until the 1890s, however, when Chinese intellectuals increasingly contended with official resistance to Western influence, that the currents of second modernity thought began seriously to circulate in China and to have more influence on political thought and practice.[32]

The most direct and profound impact of Western learning on China came through the translations by Yan Fu (1854–1921) of the writings of Thomas Huxley, J. S. Mill, Montesquieu, Adam Smith, Herbert Spencer, and other European thinkers. Even before Yan undertook his most influential translations (1895–1908), however, he was thoroughly acquainted with European (especially English) thought and the European worldview and had adopted earnestly as his own outlook the social Darwinism of Herbert Spencer. After a traditional Confucian education, Yan gained admission as a fourteen-year-old to a "school of navigation" in coastal Foochow where instruction was in English. For several years, he studied mathematics, science, and navigation. His brilliant performance earned him sponsorship for two years' study of naval science in England, where he absorbed, not only the subjects taught at school, but also an intense awe and admiration for the vigorous, competitive, forward-looking way of life that he thought was responsible for making Victorian Britain the wealthiest and most powerful nation in the world. Yan returned to China in 1879 and spent most of the next twenty years at a naval academy in

Tianjin, where, somewhat in the circle of the powerful Qing bureaucrat Li Hongzhang, he taught English and technical subjects. Most of his intellectual energies, however, went into extending his own command of Western learning and devising his own evolutionary philosophy—under the spell of second modernity thinkers. (Notably, he did not study in Japan, nor did he learn Western thought, as many Chinese intellectuals did, through Japanese translations, which were easier for Chinese to read than the Western originals.)[33]

Yan's foundational preceptor in Western thought was Herbert Spencer, whose writings Yan had become generally familiar with in England, and whose *Study of Sociology* (1872) he read with great seriousness and absorption in the 1880s and would translate in 1903. In a series of essays in 1895, Yan espoused his own Spencerian philosophy, which would then undergird all his landmark translations and commentaries of the next dozen or so years—years of trauma in China as it experienced defeat in the war with Japan, frustrated reform, the Boxer Rebellion, foreign occupation of Beijing, and the last spasms of the Qing dynasty. Yan's turn to Spencer arose, as did all his thinking, from a persistent drive to understand how China could achieve the wealth and power (exemplified by Great Britain) to survive and flourish in a technologically advanced, heavily armed, dangerous, competitive world. Like all Chinese intellectuals, he was deeply distressed by and obsessed with the stagnant, impoverished, backward, impotent condition of China in the nineteenth century compared to the powerful, thriving, aggressive nations of the West. As Chinese thinking about the state since before the time of Confucius had generally assumed, Yan believed that the sources of this preeminence rested basically in the realm of ideas and values (the legalist tradition, e.g., would be an exception). The wealth and power of the state, that is, derived from the thought and outlook guiding its rulers and intellectuals. From this flowed the energy, the creativity, the public spirit, the prosperity, and the strength of the nation.[34]

Yan was, thus, impressed with Spencer's argument that the key to British wealth and power was the skill, the education, the energy, and the dynamism of its people as, experiencing the freedom of the British state, they strove to prosper and to improve their lives. They thus exemplified the Darwinian paradigm of surviving amid a flux of competitive forces, ever improving their circumstances and generating the complexities and adaptations that characterized human evolution toward higher stages of social progress. Yan insisted, however, that this progress, so evident in late-nineteenth-century Britain, was neither accidental nor inevitable but, rather, rested on "the teachings of Mr. Darwin[, which] have done more to renew the eyes and ears" of the modern West and, thus, sustain its progress than anything else. China needed to understand the evolutionary outlook of Darwin that Spencer applied to human society and understand the inductive, scientific approach implicit in all the Western books that Yan read and translated. Yan appreciated especially, for example, the comprehensively scientific approach to human society, sustaining Comte, found in Spencer's *Study of Sociology.* The commitment to objectivity and the earnest search for truth were, to Yan, modern analogues to ancient Chinese precepts of the "sincere" (誠) pursuit of truth and right principle that was the highest duty of the scholar. "Spencer," Yan wrote in 1895, "applies the methods of evolution to explain human relations and the ordering of society. He also uses the most recent principles of science to illuminate [the principles] of self-cultivation, to regulate the family, to govern the state, and set the world at peace."[35] Yan thus offered a Spencerian version of the ancient, endlessly invoked and honored wisdom of the Confucian classic the *Great Learning,* looking toward an orderly (but active) state and a peaceful world (see chapter 2).

Curiously, however, Yan did not see, or at least chose not to acknowledge or emphasize, the antistate aspect of Spencer's outlook. To Yan, the idea of laissez-faire, to let alone, keep hands off, as a precept for the conduct of the state was simply unconceived. It was absent from the whole millennia-long, much-elaborated Chinese consideration of the role and purpose of government; it was a proposition unsubmitted and, hence, one that Yan would not have entertained, pro or con. Instead, he moved directly to the idea, implicit, he thought, in the dominant position of the British state in the world in the late nineteenth century, that it was the release of the entrepreneurial energy of the British people and its organization into the practices and institutions of an industrial society that were the foundation, not of a minimal state, but of a manifestly powerful one—what Yan envied for China. He simply missed (probably, rather than bypassed) Spencer's distinction between the efficient, complex, and highly organized structures of the private sphere and the pathological, evolution-interfering institutions of the state—a basic proposition of the classic liberal, limited-government ideology of the West, upheld, for example, by Spencer in Britain and William Graham Sumner in the United States. Yan read Spencer as propounding an evolutionary view of the release, enhancement, and projection of human energy that created the goods and (private) institutions that made Britain a rich and powerful nation. But Yan saw a crucial, constructive relation, not an antithesis, between the fostering in Britain, by the government, of the ideas and values of science, industry, and entrepreneurship and the fostering there of the institutions that were vital to Britain's economic growth and led to national greatness.[36]

Yan was impressed with Spencer's theory, moreover, not so much for its contribution to the lives of striving individuals as for its mobilization of the energies, and even the self-interest, of the people, which resulted in the good of the nation as a whole. Yan saw this as a manifestation of public spirit, energy that enhanced the common good, that contrasted sharply with a fatalism, passivity, and stagnation that he saw as all too common in China. He drew the same lesson from his translation of Adam Smith's *Wealth of Nations,* which he termed the *Book of Smith* written by the sage of Britain, analogous to, say, the *Book of Mencius* written by the ancient Chinese sage. Perhaps because Smith addressed ultimately the old mercantilist question of the wealth of the nation and focused less on the social Darwinian question of the struggle and prosperity of individuals, Yan ascribed Britain's greatness to its adherence to Smith's wisdom.

"The policies which account for England's growth in wealth and power since Smith are innumerable," Yan wrote in his commentary on *The Wealth of Nations.* "The growth of scientific knowledge, the effectiveness of her steam and electric powered engines, [and] *the enlightenment and knowledge of her sovereign*" (emphasis added) were the foundations of Britain's dominance—which Yan envied for China and which contrasted so sharply with its nineteenth-century circumstances.[37] (In fact, in the very next book on his translating agenda, Mill's *On Liberty,* Yan found Western agreement: China, Mill said, was "a warning example [of] a nation of much talent, and in some respects even wisdom, . . . provided at an early period with a particularly good set of customs," but its people had "become stationary—have remained [so] for thousands of years; and if they are ever to be further improved, it must be by foreigners.")[38] Yan valued *The Wealth of Nations,* then, not so much as a theory of laissez-faire for its own sake as an explanation of how the "invisible hand" of competitive economics could sustain national wealth and power. It is, perhaps, no accident that Yan, assuming the traditional Confucian view of the state as "the highest embodiment of civilization" (see chapter 2), resting on the mandate of heaven, was more impressed by Smith's Enlightenment imagery of an invisible hand guiding toward national power than by second modernity images of indeterminate struggle for survival. Yan thus was redirecting a conventionality of second modernity thought in a way that at once harked back to first modernity ideas and looked ahead to a reformulation amounting to a third modernity that mingled with the Confucian tradition of China—much as Fukuzawa had done in Japan (see above).

Yan nonetheless had to confront head-on the ethic of self-interest, even enlightened self-interest, which Smith placed prominently among the values essential to achieving the wealth of nations. Aware that Smith was a moral philosopher as well as an economist and that the tension between "righteousness" and "interest," between "benevolence" (Chinese *jen*) and "self-centeredness," was a key moral issue in the West as well as in China, Yan sought to explain Smith's exaltation of one's own self-interest in economic affairs as a matter of practical evolution. Yan thought that the "new" ethic of "private vice public benefit," public good coming from individual pursuits of self-interest (see chapter 4), could be taught and applied in China just as Bernard Mandeville and others had seen it as the basis of the spectacular growth of wealth and power in the West. China, Yan insisted, needed to experience this just as Smith, Bentham, Spencer and others had heralded and encouraged it in the West. Economics, like other sciences, Yan commented, "concerns itself with questions of truth and falsehood and not whether its findings coincide with benevolence and righteousness." Thus, Yan saw himself as explaining to China the habits and values of "calculating gains and losses . . . [in] the realm of economics" that were essential to material prosperity and that did not in other realms require the repudiation of Confucian moral principles.[39] Even in advocating Smith's modern ethic that far, however, Yan recognized that he was urging startlingly different values on his countrymen—just as Fukuzawa had done in his encounter with Japanese officials over economic textbooks (see above).

The basic tension between benevolence and self-centeredness emerged even more sharply in Yan's translation of Mill's *On Liberty,* completed in 1903. Mill argued, Yan explained, that "freedom of opinion is nothing more than to speak the truth plainly" and that this plain speaking required the vigorous exchange of ideas. Yan noted further, however, that Mill's faith in the free market of ideas required a startling reversal of ancient Chinese precepts: "One is not deceived by the ancients or cowed by those in authority. . . . Accept facts as facts even if they proceed from an enemy, and falsehoods as errors even if they proceed from one's lord or father." Yan then expressed Mill's point about the good effect of ideas rubbing against each other in his own now habitual social Darwinian terms: "Without liberty, . . . [truth and] the people's virtue would not evolve. It is only when people are granted liberty that natural selection can be applied and that the good of society can ultimately be achieved."[40]

In translating Mill's famous chapter "Of Individuality, as One of the Elements of Well-Being," however, which most eloquently celebrates individual creativity and eccentricity for its own sake, Yan shifts the emphasis even in the title, which he translates as "Explaining the Principle of Freedom of Action and Individuality as the Basis of the People's Virtue." (In yet another effort to capture Mill's argument while lacking adequate Chinese translations for the connotations that Mill gave to *liberty,* Yan used *On the Boundaries of the Rights of Society and the Individual* in place of *On Liberty,* once again keeping the needs of the state clearly in view.)[41] When Mill begins to acknowledge social benefit because "it is through the cultivation of these personal impulses, vivid and powerful, that society both does its duty and protects its interests," Yan continues to translate in a Chinese way: "Statesmen must realize that it is only by fostering superior people [*chüntzu,* 君子] of this type [i.e., creative, eccentric geniuses] that they can be said to have fulfilled their heaven-imposed duty. . . . The strength of the state can only be achieved thus."[42] The purpose of nourishing personal creativity is, for Yan, not to exalt the individual person, "the end of man" in itself, as Mill was emphasizing, but rather to enhance the power of the state—the collectivity of the empowered individuals. Japanese authorities made the same point in 1904 in proposing Confucian-based, moral texts for elementary schools: "The advances in a country's civilization and increases in its wealth and power are dictated largely by the educational level of its citizens."[43]

Yan revealed his own particular blending of Mill, Spencer, and the Chinese tradition in translating the political summary of *On Liberty*: "In the present world of struggle for existence [note Yan's Darwinian language], the capacities of the state are in direct proportion to the capacities of the people. By consolidating the freedom of the individuals in order to achieve the freedom of the state as a whole, *the prestige of the state is raised to insuperable heights*" (emphasis added).[44] Mill's point, however, had been to warn against the growth of state bureaucracy, at the expense of individuality, and to emphasize instead the more fundamental advancement that came through releasing the capacities of individuals.[45] Yan's choice of words regarding the "heaven-imposed duty" of statesmen and the state raised "to insuperable heights" reveals his own preoccupations much more than Mill's own reservations about state bureaucracy. Yan accepted the competitive, evolutionary concept of truth and social progress in Mill's essay, but his deep-seated Confucian assumption of the state as "the highest embodiment of civilization" and his preoccupation with the wealth and power of the Chinese state as it faced the challenge of the West (and, increasingly, Westernized Japan) in 1903 prevented him from accepting either Spencer's vigorous anti-statism or even Mill's utilitarian cautions about too much state bureaucracy.

In translating Montesquieu's *Spirit of the Laws* (1748) (from its English edition), Yan moved closer to considering social and political questions as he resumed interlacing the translation with long commentaries of his own—written in an elegant Chinese designed to attract and impress China's sophisticated intellectuals, yet embodying his own adopted Spencerianism. Yan admired Montesquieu as a proponent of the universalism of the Western rule of law (an analogue to the omnipresent Chinese idea of the mandate of heaven). He saw this, however, as consistent with the nineteenth-century social science of Auguste Comte, Herbert Spencer, and others who sought to discern generalizations, universal principles, and even cosmologies in the inductive aggregations of data. Indeed, Yan, then, saw Montesquieu's comparative study of political systems as a precursor of the scientific approach of Émile Durkheim and other second modernity scholars.[46] (This distanced Yan, of course, from the self-proclaimed more faithful adherents of "evolutionary science" such as Thorstein Veblen who insisted that there was "no place for a formulation of natural laws," even like those of Adam Smith's classical economics [see chapter 6].)[47] For Yan, as for Montesquieu, the experience of history, the data of social scientists, and the comparative study of political systems were oracles of truth, guides to universal principles that he hoped to apply in China. This understanding of the natural law basis of Montesquieu's thought, however, along with similar approval of Adam Smith, reveals both the affinities of such thought to the universalizing nature of Confucian thought and the tendency in the developing third modernity rationales for democracy in East Asia to look back past second modernity to first modernity higher laws.

Following Montesquieu's idealization of Great Britain's balanced, aristocratic, and active government, his condemnation of China as the epitome of despotism, and his observations on other systems in between, Yan used the survey, in evolutionary fashion, to endorse the nineteenth-century commonplace that democracy was "the very highest point of human development . . . [that] will one day bring about good government on all five continents." The fact, however, that China was so far, in evolutionary terms, from being ready for even the type of self-government that Montesquieu saw in eighteenth-century Britain made Yan consider, for China, preliminary stages. Historically in China, since "only the sovereign and officials can concern themselves with the affairs of society," as Montesquieu had explained, the people as a whole did not develop the public spirit necessary for their useful participation. As long as this was so (and Yan entirely agreed), China could not hope to use representative institutions effectively. It would have to wait until its people were qualified to thus take part.[48]

At this point, Yan seized on Spencerian precepts of the improvability of human individuals to suggest a way out of the passivity and fatalism that had for so long justified Chinese paternalism and tyranny. Local bodies, perhaps resting on ancient customs of village deliberation and headmen, could consult with ministers of state and, thus, furnish energy from below. Most important for Yan, this would encourage the evolution of the Chinese people: "If the people can be made to concern themselves with the strength of the race and the survival of the state, their enlightenment will proceed rapidly." This connection would nourish the earnest public spirit that Yan saw as essential to self-government in Britain and the United States and begin to move China in the same direction. Again, however, Yan's emphasis for China, not entirely faithful to Montesquieu's argument, was that the freedom of the nation-society is more urgent than "the liberty of the individual." (For *individual*, Yan uses the depreciatory *hsiao-chi*, 小己, lit. "small self.")[49] The freedom of the state, its ability to become independent, wealthy, and powerful, depended finally on the energy, public spirit, and sense of duty of the people, which would ultimately validate democracy, but, at China's stage in 1900,

Yan hinted, the need was for sage (or perhaps elite party?) guidance, to educate the people and bring them out of their lethargy and backwardness.[50]

To show China a more evolutionary view of politics (beyond Montesquieu), in 1904 Yan translated Edward Jenks's *History of Politics* (1900). Following Comte, Marx, Spencer, and others who saw human history as evolving through stages, Jenks presented political systems as part of an organic social evolution. Thus, Yan could interpret Chinese history as having passed through various intellectual, feudal, and military eras but not having reached the scientific and industrial stages of the West. Yan did not, however, see this evolutionary development as inevitable or tied to economic or social forces beyond human control or intervention. China's backwardness, for example, resulted from the intention by its governments over millennia to encourage passivity in its people in order to achieve harmony and stability in society. Conversely, it was the encouragement of enterprise, self-assertiveness, and struggle by governments in the West that had led to their nineteenth-century dominance. Chinese patriots needed, then, as Western intrusion increasingly undermined Qing authority, not to revolt against the faltering empire, thus further weakening the state, but rather to foster "the creation of a healthy sense of economic self-interest, the technical and scientific education of the masses, and, above all, the creation of the organs of a rationalized national state."[51] This was an evolution that would ultimately bring democracy to China, but Yan had learned nothing from his study and translation of second modernity thinkers that led him to suppose that the Chinese people were ready, at their evolutionary stage, for self-government.

This preoccupation with the Chinese state of mind that seemed to block the way to the wealth and power of the nation led Yan to his final major translation effort, J. S. Mill's *Logic*. Mill there explained that all the advances of Western science and technology rested on the use of inductive reasoning, which, Yan noted, "Bacon had called the law of all laws and the science of all sciences"—the very part of Bacon, of course, that Veblen and other second modernity intellectuals insisted they merely fulfilled in their scientific, inductive approach in following Darwin (see chapter 6). The trouble with older Chinese learning, Yan noted, was that "its deductions were based on theories spun from the mind." The elaborate deductions of Chinese numerology and astrology, for example, were "based on nothing but trumped up fantasies and not on generalizations inferred from facts," as inductive logic, the only true source of knowledge, required. Politics itself was a science that required one to study the practices of various countries at various times around the world in order to discern, inductively, what trends and guidelines and generalizations might be applicable in making China a wealthy and powerful nation. Though Yan endorsed Mill's insistence on induction as the road to knowledge, wealth, and power, he as well bypassed Mill's "studied indifference to the realm of the 'mysterious noumenous.'" Yan remained closer to Spencer's concept of a realm of "the inconceivable" that existed beyond the "sensations . . . of the ten thousand things" attended to by Mill's inductive logic.[52]

In fact, as Yan completed his vastly influential translating efforts, he began to pull back from some of the more strictly empirical and democratic implications of second modernity thought. In commentaries on *The Way* of Lao-tsu, published as he concluded his translation of Mill's *Logic,* Yan found congruities among what "Lao-tsu calls . . . the Way, what the [Confucian] *Book of Changes* calls . . . the Great Ultimate, what the Buddhists call . . . the Self-existent, what the Western philosophers call . . . the First Cause"—and what Spencer had called "the Inconceivable." "The Ten Thousand Things are all relative . . . and are in flux, . . . [but the Way] neither comes into being nor perishes, neither increases nor decreases. It stands alone. . . . It does not change." Yan expressly distanced himself from "the methods of the Confucianists [that] serve as a tool for authoritarian rule," however, when he declared that "only the views of Lao-tsu are compatible with the views of Darwin, Montesquieu, and Spencer."[53] Yan was, thus, like Western critics of second modernity thought (see chapter 5), seeking to avoid the merely empirical, narrowly scientific, relativistic aspects of the works that he had been translating—perhaps in response to deeply felt conceptions of the Way, or the mandate of heaven, in traditional Chinese culture. In the same way, he sustained his devotion to Spencer's more cosmological evolutionism as he set aside the strictly inductive preoccupations of second modernity thought.

This tendency, together with the failed efforts at governing by Sun Yatsen and other republicans after the fall of the Qing dynasty in 1911, the disasters suffered by Western democracies even as they "won" World War I, and the neglect of Chinese interests by the victors at Versailles, led Yan in his last years to grave reservations about democracy, at least as it was understood and practiced in the West. Yan's concern for the wealth and power and, hence, the stability and authority of the state prevented his enthusiastic support of the 1911 Revolution (better, he thought, to liberalize the Qing dynasty while preserving its authority) and even led to his mild backing of Yuan Shikai in his 1912–1916 bid to reestablish the empire. Appalled at China's weakness in the face of Japan's Twenty-one Demands in 1915 and in being forced to accept Western dictates of Versailles in 1919, Yan found it increasingly difficult to maintain his Spencerian conviction that evolutionary science, liberalism, and democracy were the wave of the future and could, ultimately, bring China to wealth and power.

In his 1914 "Critique of *The Social Contract,*" Yan scorned Rousseau's view that people were born free and equal and could, thus, anywhere, anytime, once old, enchaining institutions had been swept away, rest government on the general will of the people. This contradicted Yan's Spencerian ideas about the need for peoples to struggle through stages of development and their unfitness for institutions and practices for which they were not yet evolutionarily suited. It also ran counter to the ancient Chinese conviction that wisdom and public spirit had to be learned and that good government depended on the steady growth of firm and effective state power. Yan wrote a young disciple about 1916 that "I regret you are unable to read the books of Machiavelli and the modern writer [Heinrich von] Treitschke," to learn about the means necessary to sustain state power (exactly the sort of books that Kato Hiroyuki and other "Germanized Confucians" in Japan extolled). "It is my personal opinion," Yan said, "that China must continue to be guided by a despotic government. Otherwise it will be impossible to restore order, let alone attain wealth and power." He admired Ito Hirobumi's 1889 constitution in Japan, with its severely restricted democracy, because it was "based on the people's degree of advancement." It was wise, he thought, for Japan to emulate German institutions because, had it copied British or French governments, "it would have been difficult to achieve national power." In fact, as Yan reflected in 1918 both on seven years of republican government in China and on three hundred years of "civilization and science" in the West, culminating in the horror of World War I, he saw nothing but selfish degradation in the trend toward democracy.[54]

Though this mood of discouragement caused Yan to "look back on the way of Confucius and Mencius . . . [as] truly the equivalent of heaven and earth [that] have profoundly benefited the realm" and led him to value traditional family-oriented precepts and the principle of authority in general, he did not abandon his conviction as well that understanding evolutionary progress, benefiting from the inductive methods of science, and mobilizing the energy and patriotism of the people were essential to China's survival in the competitive twentieth-century world. In fact, ever since his experience of the prosperous and powerful society of Victorian Britain and his awed understanding, in the 1870s and 1880s, of the Darwinian worldview undergirding it, Yan had sought to formulate a Chinese version of the intellectual world of second modernity thinkers, especially of the role and purpose of government and of citizenship. He accepted wholeheartedly the assumption of Mill, Spencer, Adam Smith, and others that genuine wealth and power in any state rested on the capacities of the people composing it. Therefore, it was necessary to draw forth, release, and mobilize their energy if the state was to be strong. Yan also accepted the democratic corollary that this fulfillment required some degree or manner of participation of the people in public affairs, to direct their energy into the wider concerns of the nation. (Yan had in mind how people in Western democracies submitted to conscription, paid taxes, and took part in local government.) He generally bypassed, however, the implication that this release of energy of individuals required laissez-faire or the diminishment of government. Rather, he saw it as a responsibility of the state to guide this fulfillment and empowerment, especially through expanding education and nourishing the infrastructure, technology, and competitiveness of the nation in ways that would enhance people's talents, capacities, and opportunities and, thus, China's standing in the world. President Jiang Zemin would make the same point in 1999: "Competitiveness in our overall national strength is an increasingly decisive factor in shaping a country's fate. Only by unceasingly enhancing our economic strength, defensive strength and national cohesiveness can we establish an unbeatable position in international competition that grows more intense each day, and effectively protect our national sovereignty and national dignity."[55] Yan and Jiang were, thus, closer to Adam Smith's idea of free trade to promote the wealth of the nation than to the later focus on what Mill termed *individuality* and Spencer saw as the fulfillment of striving and achieving persons.

Though Yan was faithful enough to the message of the seminal works that he translated to believe in the equitable rule of law and in the need for government for and even of the people, he backed off from the fuller, democratic implications of government *by* the people. He rested this decision partly on his pervasive sense of the evolutionary backwardness of the Chinese people, but he also reflected persistently the ancient Confucian precept that the common weal required elite guidance. Yan was willing, therefore, to seek and listen to what the Japanese called *shūron,* or "mass opinion," but the policies of the state needed to be guided by *seiron,* or "correct, impartial opinion" attuned to the common weal (see above). All but the most radical Japanese proponents of Western thought agreed with this precept that undergirded the Ito/Meiji constitution of 1889—which Yan admired. In both Japan and China, second modernity ideas of government in accord with the aggregated felt needs of the people, whatever diversities and special interests this might include, too much offended ancient assumptions about the guiding role of the state for Yan and most of those with similar training to accept. All the Western notions of evolving human needs, of competitive economics, of the science of society, and of the sovereignty of the people could not by any means banish traditional Chinese concepts of the enlightened ruler, of sage advisers, and of an elite administration (or, in some sense, party) necessary to good government. "In three centuries of progress [modernity], the peoples of the West," Yan said sarcastically in 1923, "have achieved four principles: to be selfish, to kill others, to have little integrity, and to feel little shame."[56] The need, it seemed, was to somehow so understand the profound and progressive ideas of the Western second modernity, and so attune them to traditional Confucian precepts, as to fashion a third modernity rationale for democratic government.

Twenty years younger than Yan Fu, Liang Qichao (Ch"i-ch'ao) (1873–1929), as thoroughly steeped in traditional studies as Yan and just as enthusiastic in his absorption of the new Western learning, also played a key role in refashioning Chinese ideas of government. The son of a village schoolteacher, Liang proved to be a prodigy. By age sixteen, he had completed study of the Confucian Four Books and Five Classics, passed the second-level official examination (making him a *chü-jen*, 舉人), and was betrothed to the chief examiner's daughter, thus giving him the twin keys to prestige in China, status and connections. Too curious to stay within the narrow bounds of conventional learning (as most Chinese intellectuals had done for centuries), Liang undertook study with Kang Youwei (1858–1927), a brilliant scholar and teacher who was conversant with Western thought and committed to moving beyond the "useless old learning" but who nonetheless still thought within basic Confucian paradigms. Under Kang's influence, Liang studied Chinese philosophy, paying particular attention to Mencian texts upholding the concept of *min-pen* (民貴), or "the primacy of the people," in which rulers and their sage counselors are urged to listen to the people and rule in their best interest, which in turn meant in accord with ancient wisdom and the mandate of heaven. Liang also continued his Western studies, though he knew no foreign languages. As part of his involvement with Kang in the reform movements in Beijing of 1895–1898, Liang compiled "A Catalogue of Books on Western Learning," listing some Chinese books on Western applied science, medicine, and military matters but almost nothing on modern history or Western political thought. When the reform movement was suppressed by the dowager empress and her advisers in 1898, Liang was forced to flee to Japan, where he lived until the demise of the Qing Empire in 1912.[57]

In going to Japan, Liang became part of two highly significant aspects of the impact of Western thought in East Asia. First, because of its eager and systematic pursuit of Western science and technology, Japan became by far the most effectively and powerfully modern nation in Asia, able easily to defeat China in 1895 and Russia in 1905 in wars humiliating and disastrous to those countries. Then, as Zhang Zhidong, a key Chinese official, observed in 1898: "Since Chinese and Japanese conditions and customs are similar, it is easy to imitate Japan, reaping twice the results with half the effort." "The Japanese language," Zhang noted, "is close to Chinese and easy to master, . . . [and] the Japanese have already expunged the parts [of Western books] not essential to Western learning and modified these [books]."[58] Thus, in a movement encouraged by both the Japanese government (in order to gain influence over young men whom it expected would lead China after the fall of the moribund Qing Empire) and the Chinese government (in order to gain the benefits of Western thought and science inexpensively and in culturally sympathetic ways), thousands of Chinese students took up residence in Japan. In 1905 and 1906, there were more than 8,000 Chinese students in Japan, compared, for example, to only 130 in the United States.[59] Many Western books, and books about the West, were, largely through these students, translated into Chinese from Japanese. Liang and his fellow students, then, came to Western learning through a screen of Japanese words and concepts and of the interpretations of Fukuzawa, Nishi, Kato, and other Westernized Japanese intellectuals. Liang himself, though a brilliant student and writer, never learned English or any other Western language well enough to get beyond his dependence on Japanese (and Chinese, of course) translations of Western books.

Liang's immersion in Japanese writing and culture led him to share the Japanese ambivalence toward the West. Liang called the impact of the West "debasing, barbarizing, enslaving, and animalizing," and he even espoused at times a Japanese "Pan-Asianism" hostile to the West and emphasizing the cultural and racial hegemony and superiority of East Asia.[60] He also saw, however, as Fukuzawa had a generation earlier, that the much-envied Western "wealth and power" rested on ideas, concepts, and a worldview as well as on physical science and technology. In making this turn, he came, as was so common among East Asian intellectuals, to espouse a variety of evolutionism and social Darwinism derived from Herbert Spencer and others and from their Japanese interpreters.

As Liang pursued his studies and writing in Japan, then, he more and more made use of the phrases and interpretations of the Japanese students of Western thought. His understanding of social Darwinism, for example, came largely through his reading of editions of Kato Hiroyuki's *Essays on the Laws of Evolution* (1899) and *Competition and the Rights of the Strongest* (1893), works taken directly from Kato's study of Comte, Spencer, and other European writers. Liang followed Kato in deemphasizing Spencer's individualistic argument, but, like Yan Fu, he understood the law of evolution and the rights of the strong to apply especially to states. Since Kato and many other Japanese scholar-statesmen of the 1880s and 1890s had also been reading and translating German theorists such as J. K. Bluntschli (*Allegemeines Staatrecht* [Public law], 1872) preoccupied with the theory and power of the state as an organic, evolutionary entity, they tended to see social Darwinism as national rather than personal survival and the right of the strong. Though Liang did not follow Kato all the way in the latter's imperialistic projection of state power ("Germanized Confucianism"), Liang emphasized the need for China to "organize well-equipped government for public welfare and national defense" in order to survive in a world of competitive states.[61] Thus, Liang's idea of the role and purpose of the state grew from a curious mixture of German (sometimes already translated into English) state theory, English evolutionism, and Japanese translation and commentary. The result was a political ideology that Liang saw as urgently needed by China in her desperate, vulnerable situation.

In considering *how* China could achieve the power necessary to the modern nation-state, Liang came to emphasize, as Yan Fu had (and as Fukuzawa had for Japan), the capacities and energy of the parts; what he termed *the new citizen*. The key, they all thought, was to nourish through independence the spirit and initiative and accomplishments of the people that would lead, cumulatively, to the wealth and power of the nation. Liang, for example, used a Japanese translation of Samuel Smiles's *Self-Help* (1859), revealingly entitled in Japanese *Success Stories in the Western Nations*. Rather than the personally fulfilling Horatio Alger theme of Ragged Dick makes good that characterized Smiles's original work, the Japanese version stated its intent to explain how the power of Western nations came "from their peoples' sincere belief in Providence, from their possession of the right of self-determination, and from the justice of their government and laws." Liang further followed his Japanese mentors to emphasize the moral strength of individuals, moving toward self-reliance, self-respect, and motivation, to achieve results rather than to "just rely on the ancients [and be] . . . but a mechanical and soulless wooden figure."[62]

Liang's "new citizen," then, was actually to be "a new Chinese" with new habits, values, and intentions. (The Chinese *hsin-min* [新民] for *new citizen* more literally means "common people" or "subject." Liang could make his point only by creating a new meaning. There was no Chinese character having the connotations of the English *citizen*.) No longer "the slave to custom" or the passive subject, the new citizen would have personal energy, take initiatives, and become prosperous but would, more particularly, exhibit the qualities of the active, responsible citizen. He would seek to understand public affairs, to see the place of his country in the world, to strive for public rather than merely personal good, to willingly pay taxes and submit to conscription, and otherwise to sustain national power. Liang noted Chinese precedents in the doctrine of the *Great Learning* that, "from the emperor down to the people, all, without exception, consider cultivation of individual character as the root" (see chapter 2) and in Mencius's observation that "every man can become a Yao or a Shun." He also saw, however, that these ancient sources overwhelmingly were cast as instruction and advice for rulers and officials. For Liang, every Chinese citizen would have to be among the "fittest" in the world (Anglo-Saxons had, in Liang's opinion, most proved themselves in the "struggle for existence") if China was to achieve the wealth and power to survive.[63]

Though the new citizen argument—that both national power and self-government required, at bottom, enlightened, empowered people—remained firm in his thinking, Liang became increasingly troubled and perplexed about the application of this liberal democratic idea to the pressing needs of the Chinese state. He read and absorbed (first through Japanese translation) Mill's *On Liberty* and accepted its argument that, in the progress of mankind, there is nothing more important than freedom of expression. He admired and tried to emulate Mill's openness to new ideas and his earnest commitment to criticism and deliberation, but, like Yan, he could never quite grasp the notion of individuality, the value of freedom in enhancing unique personality for its own sake. He was most interested, he said, in national or political liberty, which meant primarily popular participation in government and national independence, that is, the contribution that personal liberty could make to government. He furthermore paid little attention to Mill's (and, through him, Tocqueville's) worries about "the tyranny of the majority" but, instead, was inclined to emphasize the utility of the majority principle in discerning a Benthamite idea of the greatest good of the greatest number. Liang used this concept, linked to the Chinese idea of *jen,* "benevolence" (see chapter 2), as a guide for government. He understood Mill's desire to limit the pressure of a conformist society on the freedom of the individual, but he generally cast this as a tension between "government" and "people," reflecting his preoccupation with national or political needs rather than social or personal concerns.[64] In fact, Liang virtually transformed *On Liberty* from a tract about limiting government to achieve individuality into one about using liberty to achieve good (effective, powerful) government—Mill and Spencer turned upside down.

Liang's efforts to project the views of Spencer, Mill, and Bentham into proposals for a form of democracy relevant to China, however, increasingly foundered on his acute awareness of how far the people of China were from possessing the attributes of the new citizen essential to making democracy work. On a trip to the United States in 1903, he was awed at how the practices of openness and activeness in public life were so woven into the fabric of society, and he was appalled at how the residents of San Francisco's Chinatown, behaving like Chinese subjects—corrupt, boss ridden, and inefficient—were, he thought, "simply not ready for democracy." In the 1908 essay "Enlightened Despotism," Liang made explicit his conviction that, at least in the circumstances that China faced as the Qing dynasty crumbled, a strong state, able to sustain independence and viability in a predatory world, was better than a democratic one resting on ill-prepared citizens. Extolling Frederick II and Napoléon I as "enlightened despots," Liang believed that a consultative assembly, perhaps preparatory to full representative government, was as far as China could go toward democracy in the early twentieth century[65]—exactly the position that Nishi Amane had taken contemplating the needs of governing Japan as the Meiji Restoration began (see above). Both Liang and Nishi were responding to nineteenth-century Western ideas of positivism and the organic state, but they were also echoing ancient Confucian ideas of paternalistic leadership and government for the people in the national interest.

This led Liang to oppose the more revolutionary programs of Sun Yatsen and others for the overthrow of the Qing dynasty. Instead, he backed proposals to reform the empire while retaining its authority. Both in Japan before the 1911 Revolution and after that for a few years in government posts in China, Liang wrote, agitated, and organized on behalf of various reform plans, generally seeking a constitutional monarchy for China. Without a power base, and often caught between Sun's Guomindang and the ambitions of would-be emperor Yuan Shikai, Liang thrashed ineffectually, in and out of impotent offices and assemblies, amid the crosscurrents of a disintegrating China made the more chaotic and vulnerable by the imperatives of World War I in East Asia. Liang had a good chance to extend his thinking about democracy, human rights, and government in China, however, when he was made part of a Chinese delegation to Europe in 1919. There, he experienced the exhaustion and bitterness of the victors in the terrible war just ended and saw very little that encouraged him to think of liberal democracy as the benign wave of the future or even as a morally desirable form of government at all. Even those who "praised the omnipotence of science" had, following World War I, seen that "science gives us catastrophes," and Europeans, he wrote from Paris in 1919, "decry its bankruptcy."[66]

The "standard of rights upon which is based all the political thinking of Europe and America," Liang wrote in a study of Chinese political thought after his return to China, is "founded on the feeling of antagonism; its very nature is acquisitive and insatiable." The notion of one's own rights, upheld against both other individuals and society, Liang noted, injected feelings of separateness and conflict where there should be feelings of fellowship, affection, and good will. Preoccupation with "individual rights, municipal rights, institutional rights, class rights, and even state rights," he observed, simply obliterated the cardinal Chinese principle of *jen* ("benevolence"). (The richness and centrality of the Chinese concept, filled with positive and multifaceted connotations from its use and elaboration in centuries of Chinese philosophy and literature, cannot be conveyed in any one English word—goodwill, humaneness, affection, kindness, and benevolence are all involved [see chapter 2].) "It is evident," Liang concluded, "that the expression of rights can only be conflict and murder. That a society built on such foundations will ever be safe is inconceivable. No wonder the men of vision in Europe [i.e., Spengler and others] should predict the collapse of civilization."[67] Liang saw, too, that the self-preoccupation of emphasizing individual or group rights applied as well to the whole liberal democratic paradigm of politics understood as mundane conflict of interest. He thus not so much gave up the liberalism that he had learned from Mill and Spencer as came to see the need to temper its more individualistic and conflictual motifs with traditional Chinese "harmony-seeking" guidelines for public life.

Democracy in Japan and China

Liang had gone through the same deep engagement with second modernity Western thought as had Fukuzawa, Nishi, Yan, and other East Asian intellectuals. Also like them, he had undertaken this engagement after having had, largely before Western thought was known in the region, a thorough traditional education. In each case, an urgency and desire to learn the ideas and ways of the West seemed the only way to save China from domination and, perhaps, conquest by the industrially and militarily more advanced and powerful West. All these thinkers came to see as well, however, that the West's wealth and power rested, not only on the material and technological prowess so evident in its ships, weapons, and factories, but also on a spirit and philosophy and worldview that shaped the physical manifestations. In accepting the basic outlook of Mill, Darwin, Spencer, Comte, Huxley, and other second modernity thinkers, they became, more or less, second modernity intellectuals themselves in their own habits of thought. They saw Montesquieu and Adam Smith as moderns on the way to the late-nineteenth-century worldview, and they acknowledged Bacon and Descartes as founders of modernity. The Japanese and Chinese scholars sought earnestly to convey to their countrymen the essentials of the second modernity thought that they regarded as crucial to a mentality able to survive in a competitive, predatory world.

None of the four, however, could entirely abandon or discredit the entirety of the Confucian (usually termed *Chinese* in Japan) outlook that they had studied and absorbed before encountering Western learning. In varying degrees, they both retained traditional ways and values in their careers and private lives (relations with their families, schools, etc.) and returned to some traditional emphases and modes of thought in their writing. They concurred in the inductive, scientific approach of the Darwinian era and accepted the projection of its evolutionary, progressive, competitive dynamic to all areas of thought. They at least countenanced its application in ethics, sociology (a word that they learned from Comte and Spencer), and politics in ways that had profoundly wrenching implications. In fact, they refashioned Western second modernity thought in a way that, while remaining fundamentally modern, was also being turned into what can be called a *third modernity* as it came to terms with Confucian precepts still deeply embedded in the minds of the East Asian scholars.

The four thinkers who so fundamentally encountered Western thought, then, absorbed and refashioned basic ideas of polity and government. They all accepted, as Fukuzawa did in the first sentences of his *Encouragement of Learning*, that people were equal and should be able "freely and independently [to] use the myriad things of the world to satisfy their daily needs." This swept away ancient harmonies and hierarchies and privileges and statuses and, instead, in the manner of Locke, Bentham, and Mill, required response to and, perhaps, even participation by the people. This shift required consideration of representative institutions, freedom of thought and expression, partisan politics, the rule of law, expanded economic opportunity, the application of social science, and other essentials of Western polities, that is, some form of what was becoming the liberal democratic orthodoxy of the twentieth century. Undertaken with a powerful sense of the evolutionary and progressive nature of human society and institutions, this left East Asian theorists with an exciting and daunting task: none of the liberal democratic precepts had any currency in either the theory or the practice of the centuries-old Tokugawa shogunate or Qing Empire or, indeed, in the millennia-old traditions of government in either China or Japan (or Korea). As Liang put it, Chinese thinking honored government "of the people and for the people," but government "by the people is a thought left untouched. . . . Neither the method nor the theory . . . [of self-government] has been studied."[68]

This chasm of difference in background and tradition caused the East Asian thinkers to draw back from, indeed, scarcely even be able to hear, three basic propositions of their Western mentors: to give priority to personal fulfillment; to limit government in order to protect individual rights and opportunity; and to facilitate direct participation of citizens in government. Thus, all the Millian or Spencerian (and generally American) enthusiasm for developing individuality for its own sake and for allowing personal evolutionary growth was shifted into arguments for the need to strengthen individual capacities so that they could be somehow aggregated to enhance the wealth and power of the state. The arguments of Mill, Spencer, and others about the dangers that enlarged government might pose to individual liberty and about the likely pathological "interference" of government in natural evolutionary processes simply did not register on minds conditioned to think of the state as "the highest embodiment of civilization."[69] Rather, attention remained on the constructive use of the authority and agencies of the state to foster education, opportunity, and fulfillment among the people so that they might in turn strengthen the state. Finally, the idea that citizens (the concept and word themselves were unknown and unconceived; persons living in a polity were spoken of as *subjects* or simply, en masse, as *the people*) might—indeed, *had* to—take part in governing themselves ran afoul of the Confucian dictum that good government rested on deep learning and wisdom. How could that be the case, Nishi, Yan, and others asked, if the people, ignorant, small-minded, and passive, at least in their present stage, were given active roles in the direction of the state? Without, often, scarcely sensing the depth of their challenge to a Western second modernity increasingly throwing off its own elitisms and moving toward one-person-one-vote dogma, the East Asian scholars were fashioning an understanding of, and a rationale for, a democracy notably different from that in the West.

To a remarkable degree, for example, responding in part to the ancient Confucian emphasis on the importance of the upright moral character of people (see chapter 2), both Japanese and Chinese scholars saw the need to nourish in their countries the development of a new citizen, indeed, to bring the very connotations of the word into East Asian languages for the first time. Fukuzawa noted that "each citizen has a double office," to be a "guest" who obeys the laws and to have the mentality of a "master" who "enact[s] and implement[s] the laws of the nation." East Asian languages required that two conceptions of human nature, always understood as functionally quite separate, be literally joined in one person to create the Western idea *citizen*. Liang wrote elaborately of the need for China to have new citizens capable of taking part in government. Each regarded their people, however, as being exceedingly distant from this demanding ideal, so each was inclined to postpone the granting of full citizenship rights. It was then, urgently and massively, the duty of the state to educate the people to be up to the task—in the manner of both Thomas Jefferson and John Dewey in the United States, but also in accord with millennia-old precepts in China requiring the elaborate education of those who would take part in government. The East Asian version of democracy, then, was strongly inclined toward insisting on the "training" of citizens before they were empowered to take part in government, not with any long-term sense of the incapacity of the people, but in acknowledgment, as Confucian thought had long held, of human malleability under the guidance of good teaching. (The practice in Mao's China of sending millions of people "to the countryside" where they might be "educated" by the populace, though undertaken for generally Communist purposes—so that they would lose their bourgeois mentality and, thus, become good comrades—shares the intent of preparing the people for their "public" role. The early insistence on universal public education in Meiji Japan also manifested the same idea.) This accorded, too, with the evolutionary notion of societies and people at different stages of progress toward the viability of citizens for self-government: Britain and the United States in the vanguard, China and Japan far behind but capable, with the proper education, of catching up.

In the meantime, however, East Asian scholars—Nishi and Yan, for example —had to refashion the Western idea of representation. To move directly and immediately to legislative assemblies elected by the people to make the laws, in the palpable absence of new citizens up to the task of choosing qualified representatives, seemed the height of foolishness. Instead, both men at one time proposed consultative assemblies that would meet and bring the views of the people to the government and deliberate with them but would have no power actually to make or execute the laws. In Nishi's case, the assembly would even be chosen by already empowered officials (formally servants of the emperor, but actually a self-perpetuating oligarchy) from among the people and groups in provinces throughout the country, and the officials would have the power to dissolve the assembly. Any idea that good government might come from "below," from the common people, was simply absent, inconceivable to Confucian-trained scholars. On the other hand, in accord with the "see with the eyes and hear with the ears of all" guideline, leaders of all kinds, emperors and mandarins, oligarchs and shoguns, were obliged to consult from "the bottom up" and, in the long run, could lead and rule only if they maintained consensus with the will of the group. Perhaps even more important than the advice given to the government was the education provided to the people as they learned from their representatives and came to understand something of the business of government, thus improving the quality of the consensus. Though Nishi, Yan, and others stated their long-term acceptance of truly representative government (they had, e.g., read or knew of and admired Mill's work of that name), they could not square it with either their sense of the "backwardness" of the Japanese and Chinese people or their assumption that good government came from a learned, wise, and public-spirited center—operating under the mandate of heaven. The East Asian version of representation, then, was and would continue to be biased against the growing Western second modernity concept of delegates from "the parts" conflicting at the center over their various special interests to hammer out policy (à la, e.g., Arthur Bentley and even John Dewey [see chapter 6]) and biased in favor of the idea of knowledge, needs, and advice drawn from the parts to assist, but not control, the center of authority. The ancient practices of administrators from Chinese districts reporting to the capital and of Japanese daimyos making required semiannual visits to the shogun in Tokyo, of course, were, in some fashion, reflected in those biases.

None of the startlingly innovative yet earnest attention of the Western-oriented scholars to a new citizenry or to the idea of representation, however, drew them very far away from the ancient notion of enlightened, authoritative leadership. Indeed, the ideas that the new citizen would have to understand and be in harmonious consultation with officers of the state and their problems and that representation involved advice and consent more than making laws were both, in a way, required by the exalted conception of guidance and direction from the center both explicit and implicit in East Asian modes of government.

In fact, the ideas of the new citizen, the continued emphasis on wise leadership, and the disdain for partisanship in representation all resonated with the ancient, much admired Chinese conception of the *chüntzu* (君子), the exemplary or noble person. As described in the *Analects*,

> Junzi [chüntzu] seek harmony not sameness; petty persons, then, are the opposite.
> Junzi are self-possessed but not contentious; they gather together with others but do not form cliques. . . .
> Junzi understand what is appropriate; petty persons what is of personal advantage.[70]

Whether officials, representatives, or citizens, participants in East Asian versions of self-government would have a powerful, even hallowed model of moral exemplariness as a constant guide and presence.

In the Japanese case, for example, though the emperor (both before and after the Meiji Restoration), seen as the divinely descended father and guide of the people, did not actually rule, the power surrounding the court of the shogun before 1868 and the tightly held power of the emperor's advisers (including the self-perpetuating Genro-in of elder statesmen) after 1868 kept in place the ancient Confucian idea that the highest authority came from above and had to be exercised by the wise and the good. Though this might eventually come to involve *all* citizens and significantly refashion the idea of representation so that input came in some degree from below, it was exceedingly difficult, at least early on in responding to Western thought and practice, to denigrate leadership or to reorient it toward the "brokering" model (see chapter 7) implicit in the Western second modernity understanding of democracy. (A practice akin to brokering might, in effect, have gone on in the formal and elaborate sessions of advice and discussion conducted before the king, emperor, or shogun by scholars and officials, but the tenor of the sessions, and their explicit purpose, was to transcend partisan, special interests and to enlighten the leader on understanding the public good, "the Way of heaven," which it was his duty to discern and to carry out.) The question became how strong leadership by one or a very small number, up front or behind the scenes, would be accommodated to more democratic practices—*the* problem, for example, of the democratic mode in Japan from the implementing of the Meiji constitution in 1889 throughout the twentieth century.

In responding so earnestly and profoundly to Western second modernity thought, then, Confucian-trained scholars in East Asia propelled the theory and rationale of democracy into a different and potentially fruitful context. Like the participants in the May Fourth movement in their enthusiasm for science and democracy, they were convinced that their nations had to reground their thinking to accord with Western precepts of inductive reasoning, of scientific advancement, of democratic government, of the beneficence of competitive energy, of evolutionary progress, and so on if they were to survive and prosper in the modern world. Yet they all saw and appreciated the fact that there was, nonetheless, deep wisdom and value in their traditional understanding of the nature of polity that required, not simplistic adoption of Western ideas and practices, but rather a refashioning of them into a third modernity related to, but significantly different from, the second. This rethinking by the first generation of scholars to know Western thought (yet still thoroughly trained in the traditional Confucian way) set the questions and the guidelines for the theorists, politicians, generals, and statesmen who, in the twentieth century, through many ups and downs, gradually moved the ancient polities of China, Japan, and Korea toward their own modernity.

9

An Asian Third Modernity

In China, the effort to fashion a polity attuned to modernity went on almost frantically in the decades following the fall of the last imperial dynasty in 1911. The turmoil of the warlord era (1912–1928), the twenty-year struggle with Japan and between the Guomindang and the Communists, and then the Communist era of Mao Zedong (until 1976) and the paramountcy of Deng Xiaoping afterward led to continued debate over the meaning and nature of democracy for China—constitutional democracy, people's republic, guided democracy, the role of parties, socialism with Chinese characteristics, and so on. Sun Yatsen (1866–1925) was accepted after 1911 by Nationalists and Communists alike as the father of the Chinese Revolution, which overthrew the Qing dynasty (actually, the dynasty more simply collapsed or sunk under its own moribundity than was overthrown). He both led and followed chaotic movements by mixtures of radicals, moderate reformers, Communists, constitutional monarchists, Qing restorationists, and regional warlords toward a new government for China. Sun and his colleagues sought to fulfill in China versions of democracy that Yan Fu, Liang Qichao, and other intellectuals had fashioned from their study of second modernity Western thought.

Sun Yatsen and "Nationalism, Democracy, and Livelihood" in China

In a broad theory of government articulated in the 1920s, Sun outlined (in a phrase taught in China throughout the Communist era) *san min chu i* (三民主義), "the three principles of the people"—nationalism, democracy, and livelihood. After emphasizing under the principle of nationalism, as all Chinese intellectuals did, China's need to be strong enough to survive in the modern world of powerful, predatory nations, Sun turned to the second principle, democracy. "China has now the idea of democracy," he wrote in 1924, but it did not yet know how to "build the machine . . . to make use of it." Those of "vision and foresight," he said, would have to take the lead in this process. He distinguished between "sovereignty," which rested with the people, and "government," which needed to possess the power and means "to transact business . . . [and] work on behalf of the people." Through the four devices of suffrage (the election of representatives), recall, initiative, and referendum (Sun was well acquainted with Progressive era reforms in the United States), the people would control the ultimate direction of the polity: "the political power of the people." On the other hand, the "Administrative Power of the Government" would carry out the people's work through five organs or departments: the customary legislative, executive, and judicial branches familiar from Western models but also two additional functions, civil service examinations and censorship. These "two new features in our quintuple-power constitution," Sun noted, "come from old China," where, for centuries, the government had conducted examinations to select the learned, wise, and public-spirited advisers and administrators needed to carry out the governing of China. Furthermore, a "bureau" and function of censorship had long existed, meant to be an internal, somewhat independent check on corruption, malfeasance, and factionalism in the conduct of government.[1]

Sun seemed to envision rather conventional versions of the American separation of the legislative, executive, and judicial powers, and his designation of the four powers of the people, whereby they exercised surveillance and control over the government (and thus expressed their sovereignty), also followed the guidelines of J. S. Mill, John Dewey, and other second modernity theorists of democracy whose writings were by the 1920s well-known in China. The civil service examination system and the explicit function of censorship, however, though not alien to Western thought, were, for Sun, important additions to the idea of self-government derived from ancient Chinese practices. Government had to be conducted by highly qualified officials (learned, morally grounded, and devoted to the public good) if it was to be good government, and there had to be a surveillance or judgment, from a standpoint of superior principle and ritual, to assure that the conduct of government accorded with a higher law, universal precepts understood in China as "the mandate of heaven." These four powers of the people ("sovereignty") and the five powers of administration ("forms or directions of work"), Sun thought, would "manifest great dignity and authority and become [the] all-powerful government" that China so desperately needed.[2]

Popular sovereignty (democracy) was assured since the people could "at any time command the government to move or to stop." Also, with the civil service examinations and the censorship function acting as "checks" on the active branches, the people did not need to fear government becoming "uncontrollable." Sun was especially pleased that this idea of government might "develop tremendous horse-power." Its prestige would grow and the power of the people increase. It would be "an all-powerful government seeking the welfare of the people—and blaze the way for the building of a new world." By adding the traditional Chinese "power of censorship" and "the selection of real talent and ability through examinations" to the Western idea of balanced legislative, executive, and judicial branches, Sun proposed to combine "the best from China and the best from other countries . . . [into] a government . . . the most complete and finest in the world, . . . a government . . . indeed . . . of the people, by the people, and for the people."[3] Though, by the time Sun outlined this theory of democracy, affairs in China moved powerfully in different directions, notions and ideals of a Sinicized version of Western second modernity self-government were, nonetheless, coming into view for reference and guidance throughout East Asia.

Sun's third principle, livelihood, meant essentially "the achievement of a minimum standard of living for the Chinese peasantry" by applying the ideas of science and technology and the structures of socialism in post–Qing dynasty China. This idea, expressed poignantly and with increased frustration and desperation as living conditions in many ways worsened after the fall of the empire, led Sun and the May Fourth generation to countenance both pragmatic, Western models of "Mr. Democracy" and "Mr. Science" and socialist ideas, including Marxist-Leninist models brought back to China from Europe and supported in China by Soviet agents of the Comintern. The inclusion of livelihood among the three people's principles had the effect of turning Sun (and many others) to include socialist ideas in their proposals for Chinese revival and modernization and to mirror Leninist contempt for "bourgeois democracy" and support for an elite "party of the people."

Crosscurrents: Hu Shi, Chiang Kaishek, Liu Shaoqi, Mao Zedong,
Deng Xiaoping, and Tiananmen

Foremost among the Chinese intellectuals in promoting Western, especially Anglo-American, themes of science and democracy, and in insisting that these themes required the modernization of the Chinese language and of the whole philosophical basis of Chinese culture, was Hu Shi (1891–1962). After receiving a thorough Confucian education in the Four Books and the Five Classics, he studied for seven years (1910–1917) in the United States, where, while completing a doctorate at Columbia University, he became a disciple of John Dewey. In completing his dissertation, titled "The Development of the Logical Method in Ancient China," he both deeply absorbed the scientific methodology of Dewey, Mill, Bertrand Russell, and second modernity Darwinianism and worked out its relation to traditional Chinese philosophy. A leader of the New Culture movement, which advocated using colloquial rather than classical Chinese in newspapers, magazines, and literature, a participant in the May Fourth movement, and a professor at and president of Beijing National University (1917–1926), Hu was at the center of efforts to formulate a Chinese modernity and make it manifest in public life.[4]

Already regarding himself as a pragmatist, Hu was the main host for John Dewey's long visit to China, 1919–1921. Dewey spent days on end with Hu and lectured all over China in what amounted to a reenactment of the ancient custom of welcoming sages and monks and scholars to China to learn from their wisdom. In these lectures, often to huge audiences, Dewey summarized his epistemology and ethics, gave particular attention to his second modernity theory of democracy (emphasizing Mill much more than John Locke or Thomas Jefferson, e.g.), and then sought most especially to influence the theory and practice of education by speaking at teachers colleges throughout China. (At one conference in Changsha in 1920, considering a more democratic "constitution" for Hunan Province, both Dewey and Bertrand Russell spoke to an audience including Mao Zedong—a few months before Mao became a Marxist.) Thus, what Hu heard Dewey say in China (a synopsis of what he had been writing and teaching for thirty years) reinforced his already strongly pragmatic views and turned him more directly to their application to the tumultuous political and intellectual life of China in the era of the May Fourth movement.[5]

Hu followed Dewey in emphasizing that the industrial, engineering, and technological accomplishments of the West rested on a worldview and pattern of thought that had to be understood and, in some measure, adopted if China was to gain the material benefits known in the West. As Dewey explained to his Chinese audiences in a lecture entitled "The Authority of Science": "Modern science . . . [in the West] produced the knowledge which produced the machines which produced the industrial revolution."[6] Hu believed that China must, thus, first learn to think in a rigorously scientific way to gain the real knowledge on which progress depended. He exhorted the Chinese, "do not imitate the ancients," "speak your own words; do not repeat what others say," "do not use ancient allusions or quotations" or otherwise adhere to the deductive, abstract conventions of Chinese scholarship, especially the neo-Confucianism of Zhu Xi. Instead, in a manifesto that hostile Christian missionaries termed *Hu Shi's New Decalogue,* Hu set forth thoroughly scientific, mundane, bluntly atheistic guidelines that would undergird a deep-seated modernity for China. (He said very little, of course, that Comte, Marx, Veblen, Dewey himself, and many other second modernity thinkers had not asserted for a half century or more.) Modern astronomy, physics, and geology taught that the universe was virtually infinite in time and space and not "in need of a concept of a supernatural Ruler or Creator." Anthropology, sociology, and biology taught that human society was evolving and that "morality and religion were subject to change . . . [and could] be scientifically studied." Hu ended his "Decalogue," however, with an assertion as deeply mundane and Confucian as it was scientific and pragmatic, as deeply relational as it was individualist: "The individual self is subject to death and decay, but the sum total of individual achievement, for better or for worse, lives on in the immortality of the Larger Self; that to live for the sake of the species and posterity is religion of the highest kind; and that those religions which seek a future life either in Heaven [Christianity] or in the Pure Land [Buddhism] are selfish religions."[7]

Hu also followed Dewey in insisting that the advancement and modernization of society was much more a matter of study and responding to "problems" than of endorsing and applying "isms." He condemned alike Marxism-Leninism and nationalist theories reflecting Hegelian ideas of the state and looking forward to fascism. In the real world, Hu asserted, "there are no abstractions that can fully comprehend the concrete proposals of a particular person or party. . . . The great danger is a fondness for theories on paper, and a refusal to engage in factual examination." The need was to look at "problems" such as the working conditions of ricksha coolies, foot-binding and other social abuses of women, standards of public health, and school curricula and then to devise means of solving or at least ameliorating them.[8] Hu thus sought to work steadily at the task of reforming Chinese thought and the Chinese worldview to accommodate them to the scientific method and to the pragmatic solution of social problems. "It is certainly not good to be led by Confucius and by Chu Hsi [Zhu Xi] by the nose," he wrote in 1930, but "to be led by Marx, Lenin, and Stalin by the nose is not a great man either." In emphasizing science and pragmatism, Hu said, "I am . . . only teaching people a method by which they will not be deluded."[9]

Though, like Yan Fu, Hu was in his philosophical orientation thoroughly Western (he was as deeply Deweyan as Yan was Spencerian), he was also profoundly aware of the echoes of traditional Chinese thought in his pragmatism and traditional in his long career as a public intellectual. He acknowledged "the democratic spirit of classical Confucianism" in its Mencian concepts of a "good" human nature and of basic human equality and in its emphasis on educability, attention to practical problems, and government in the public interest. Dewey himself had noted, in an essay written shortly after his arrival in China in May 1919, that a "democratic spirit" was manifest in China "in the absence of classes, the prevalence of social and civil equality, [and] the control of individuals and groups by moral rather than physical force—that is, by instruction, advice, and public opinion."[10] Hu saw this "democratic spirit," however, as reinforcing the ideas of science and democracy that he had learned from John Dewey; he had scant inclination to turn to China's past for guidance in the future. Though there was in Dewey's later thought some turn toward more "communitarian" as opposed to "liberal" ideas, for Hu and his other Chinese followers Dewey bespoke the Darwinian, scientific, conflict-of-interest idea of politics that he brought to China in 1919–1921, a pattern of thought deeply out of sync with traditional thought as well as with other powerful currents in post–May Fourth China. Thus, Hu left his students and fellow intellectuals with little effective guidance toward democratic government between 1917 and 1949, when he was active in Chinese public life. He opposed both communism and fascism, but his intrepid insistence on a step-by-step, modern, scientific approach to the problems of the people of China, without a clear idea of democratic processes and political institutions appropriate for China, left his an increasingly lonely voice amid the more purposeful isms offering solutions and programs for China's future.[11]

In fact, in the light of the acquiescence of the Western democracies to Japanese aggression against China in Shandong, Manchuria, and elsewhere and the many failures of democracy throughout the world in the 1920s and 1930s, the idea that democracy might be suitable for China lost credence. Chiang Kaishek, the self-proclaimed heir to Sun Yatsen and his revolutionary Guomindang, or Nationalist Party, declared in 1930, for example, that, of the three reigning political theories in the world, communism "does not apply to China with its undeveloped state of industry and its inherent morality" and that liberal theory was ill suited because it "proposes parliamentary debate [and] allows questions and difficulties to develop among the popular masses." Fascist theory, however, could undergird "the most effective governing power." Claiming to follow the three people's principles of Sun Yatsen, nationalism, democracy, and livelihood, Chiang insisted that the state was "an entity of spirit and morality" that would "organize the social consciousness" of the people and direct it toward the common good. To fulfill this good, only the Guomindang, the party led by Chiang himself, could be allowed to exist; otherwise, the three people's principles would be debated, factionalized, and otherwise lost in the strife of competing parties. From the standpoint of both ancient Chinese theories of despotic leadership and contemporary fascists around the world, democracy as understood by Mill and Dewey was a futile and pathological idea, especially for a threatened, underdeveloped nation like China. Instead, a people-based, elite-led party was needed to provide strong leadership in the public and national interest—that would be "demo-cracy," "people's government," in its only effective, modern understanding.[12] One is reminded of the remark: "If democracy means only giving the people what they want, then it is scarcely distinguishable from fascism."

The move in China toward both fascist- and Communist-oriented political practice in the 1920s, 1930s, and 1940s provoked ideological attention to concepts of leadership and political parties and to the place of "the people" (*min*, 民) in the polity. At the same time that Chiang Kaishek was forming his nationalist people's movement (*Guo-min-dang; Kuo-min-tang*) into a single party requiring authoritarian leadership "for the people," the Chinese Communist movement was conceiving and organizing itself along similar Leninist lines. The leading Communist theoretician of party, Liu Shaoqi (1899–1969), understood the Chinese Communist Party (CCP) as "a unified organic whole," embodying the outlook and interests of the people—in Marxist terms, "the masses" or "the proletariat." The CCP, like any Marxist-Leninist party, was, thus, "the highest and concentrated expression of the character of the proletariat," a party in which, however, "generally speaking, the whole determines the parts," that is, in accord with the Leninist principle of "democratic centralism" where leadership is enforced from the top down.[13]

This leadership was to be understood, not in terms of obedience and loyalty to a party leader as person, or even in terms of obedience conditioned on correct principle, but rather in terms of the fulfillment or culmination of the very nature of the party as an organization. "Collective leadership," Liu insisted, "is the gathering together of the experience and intellectual power of the whole Party. It collects the best opinions and plans of the whole Party, and turns them into one resolution and one programme," to be obeyed unconditionally by all members of the party. "Only a few wise, talented and far-sighted people," he added, "can discern the development of the objective matters and the far progress of history." (One is reminded, of course, of the endlessly repeated ritual, at least formally, of Chinese, Korean, and Japanese emperors gathering the "opinions and plans" of their Confucian-oriented counselors—"See with the eyes and hear with the ears of all"—but then making the decisions themselves, decisions to be obeyed and enforced throughout the empire by administrative officers.) The faithfulness of party members to the decisions of the leaders, however, should not be "mechanical" or merely a matter of compulsion but, rather, rest on such effective education and self-criticism that there would be "true uniformity in the Party in ideology and principle and the consciousness of Party members." In thus explaining leadership in the CCP, Liu explicitly repudiated both "individual centralism" or "dictatorship" (having in mind, probably, Western, fascist models) and such traditional Chinese practices as *jiazhangzhi* (家長制, "patriarchism" or family headship) and *guanxi* (圈系 , or favoring personal relation-ships): everything was to be subordinated to the leaders of the party as the embodiment of the consciousness of the people and the discerners of "the objec-tive . . . progress of history."[14]

In emphasizing the elite nature of CCP leadership, however, Liu was careful to explain the leaders' relation to "the masses." The masses were more con-cerned with immediate economic needs and, thus, not inclined to attend to the larger *political* matters necessarily left (by them) in the hands of the party. This created a difference between leaders and led and resulted in a different treat-ment of people according to their position in society (a salient feature in China for two millennia or more, of course). Ignoring these differences, Liu declared, resulted in an "ultra-democracy," an "egalitarianism [that] negates any differ-ence in authority and in treatment." Nonetheless, Liu insisted that a "demo-cratic spirit" should prevail where those in "higher" positions did not regard themselves as above others; differences were temporary or contingent because "mankind is basically equal" (again, as Mencius had taught).[15] Here, as else-where, Liu accepted a Marxist-Leninist outlook and applied it to a political concept, the party, in a way that is at once faithful to the Western ideology and in accord with ancient Chinese guidelines of polity.

Mao Zedong himself made much the same points about the people and the party in explaining his understanding of the concepts *freedom* and *democracy*. "Freedom and democracy," Mao insisted (following dialectical materialism, i.e., second modernity scientific Marxism), "do not exist in the abstract, only in the concrete. In a society rent by class struggle, if there is freedom for the exploiting classes to exploit the working people, there is no freedom for the working people not to be exploited, and if there is democracy for the bourgeoisie, there is no democracy for the proletariat and other working people." Even when freedom and democracy did exist for the people, however (after the destruction of the exploiting classes), freedom could not exist without "discipline" (obedience to law), and, most pointedly, democracy could not exist without "centralism" (party rule). "Freedom is freedom with leadership," Mao said, and "democracy is democracy under centralized guidance, not anarchy." He repudiated the idea that there was "more freedom under Western parliamentary democracy. . . . The so-called two-party system is nothing but a device for maintaining the dic-tatorship of the bourgeoisie. . . . [This] democracy . . . in the last analysis . . . serves the economic base." The unity of freedom and democracy in "a people's democratic dictatorship," Mao explained, "constitutes our democratic central-ism" and defines the "civil rights" of the people in "concrete" terms rather than in the bogus terms of parliamentary democracies.[16]

In a fashion that might have pleased Yan Fu, Hu Shi, and even J. S. Mill himself, however, Mao insisted: "The only way to settle questions of an ideological nature or controversial issues among the people is by the democratic method, the method of discussion, of criticism, of persuasion and education, and not by the method of coercion or repression." This process required, as Mao wrote, a "formula of 'unity, criticism, unity,'" where the people (having eliminated the exploitative classes) "start from the desire for unity [proper class consciousness], distinguish between right and wrong through criticism or struggle and arriving at a new unity on a new basis." This "new unity," moreover, would be in accord with the desire of the people "to carry on their production and studies effectively and to arrange their lives properly." "The people," Mao added, "want their government and those in charge of production and of cultural and educational organizations to issue appropriate orders of an obligatory nature." These "administrative regulations," however, would not work without "persuasion and education"; rather, the whole system of internal criticism and persuasion combined with obligatory regulations was necessary to "resolve contradictions among the people."[17] Within this pattern, intellectuals had the responsibility of instructing the people in a proper class consciousness embodying their interest, while the CCP had the obligation to lead and provide the administrative direction necessary to achieve the broad economic, cultural, and ideological goals of the state, the People's Republic of China. Again, the echo of long-standing precepts of the role and purpose of government in China is powerful, as is the evidence of the methods and language of second modernity science and democracy as well as Marxism-Leninism. Equally evident, however, is the repudiation of many of the standard guidelines of Western liberal democracy—freedom of expression beyond the limits of "centralism" and "discipline," a multi- or two-party system "with one party in office and the other out of office" (Mao's phrase), the definition of policy not from the top down but in some measure from the bottom up, and so on. The dominance of Marxism-Leninism in Chinese political thought for most of the twentieth century, however, did not so much divert thinking from second modernity modes as it provided an altered slant and rhetoric for the continuing consideration of how China might govern itself in the modern world.

Though Liu Shaoqi himself fell afoul of Mao Zedong and was a victim of the "Great Cultural Revolution," his Leninist idea of party supremacy as the embodiment of the people's republic remained firmly entrenched both in the last years of Mao's life (d. 1976) and in the paramountcy of Liu's protégé, Deng Xiaoping (1978–1997). Deng insisted on four basic principles: "Upholding the Socialist Road, dictatorship of the proletariat, leadership of the Communist Party, and Marxism-Leninism–Mao Zedong thought." Then China might follow the path of "socialism with Chinese characteristics" in pursuing the "four modernizations" of industry, agriculture, science and technology, and national defense. At the same time, Deng encouraged openness to the West, expanded (though still limited) freedom of information within China, and stimulated development toward a market, semicapitalist economy, both internally and in China's trade with the rest of the world. In thus moving cautiously toward some of the precepts and organization of second modernity liberal democracy, Deng moved Chinese communism, itself a form of second modernity ideology, toward the same sort of convergence with world capitalist institutions—globalization—going on elsewhere.[18]

In encouraging economic liberalization, Deng largely resisted, as might have been expected after the reservations earlier expressed by Yan Fu, Liang Qichao, and other Western-oriented reformers (see chapter 8), moves to democratize the Chinese polity. In line with the ancient Chinese emphasis on elite, "harmonious" leadership (as well as Leninist party supremacy), attentive to the people but not obliged to respond to or follow their immediate opinion or demands, Deng had little patience with elections, representative institutions, or, as Tiananmen (1989) revealed, mass demonstrations of students and others. To him, *democracy* (a word that he and other Communist theorists readily invoked) still meant, as both Communist and traditional Chinese thought and practice required, rule "for the people," not "by the people." In a way, then, the half-century-long Communist paramountcy of Mao Zedong and Deng Xiaoping (1940s–1990s), when the ideas and arguments of China's first half century of Western influence (1890s–1940s) seemed overwhelmed by "Marxism-Leninism-Mao Zedong thought," the earnest, searching efforts of Chinese intellectuals to absorb and work out an East Asian version of science and democracy remained on the agenda and help in understanding efforts still under way, formally and informally, in that direction.

Foremost among the Chinese intellectuals experiencing the less repressive atmosphere of the Deng Xiaoping era was a "network" gathered around Hu Yaobang (1915–1989) that was encouraged to revive the spirit of the May Fourth movement of open inquiry as it might bear on Deng's four modernizations campaign. The *People's Daily,* only a few months after the fall of the Gang of Four (1977), turned toward a less dogmatic second modernity mode of thought when it declared that "Marxist philosophy cannot replace natural science"—a sentiment that both Hu Shi and John Dewey (and Yan Fu and Herbert Spencer, too) would have welcomed, of course. Other official pronouncements found "the scientific spirit and the democratic spirit inseparable" and insisted that "differences of opinion and . . . clash of ideas" were as important in "philosophy and social science" as in the natural sciences. Hu Yaobang's associates even declared that "without democracy [meaning mainly open discussion] there can be no modernizations" and that "the four modernizations must be accompanied by political modernization."[19] Thus, even though Deng remained committed to the essentials of a Communist polity (the socialist road, the dictatorship of the proletariat, the leadership of the CCP, and Marxism-Leninism–Mao Zedong thought), he also allowed redirection of the debate over "the people's republic" away from Marxist-Leninist dogma to once again consider the broader implications of second modernity impact in China.

A so-called theory conference, held January–April 1979 and supported by Deng Xiaoping, pursued forthrightly in some of its working groups the political implications of what might be termed Deng's *Chinese glasnost.* One paper insisted that "socialist democracy" meant that "the people must have the right to express their opinions extensively on all kinds of political issues." The concept that "all men are endowed by their creator with certain inalienable rights," it continued, though advanced "by the bourgeoisie," was nonetheless a "step forward for man in history." Another paper pointed out that, since the "rights of the leaders and cadres" were "given by the people" and not "dropped from the sky," the term of office for political leaders should be limited—and, most radical of all, leaders should somehow be made responsible to the people. Moreover, study of the fields of political science, jurisprudence, history, and philosophy should be made relevant to the political system and processes of the nation. The *People's Daily,* in an editorial entitled "Strengthen the Legal System, Develop Democracy, Accelerate the Four Modernizations," expressed the overall view of Hu Yaobang's circle of "reformist" intellectuals: "Democracy and the legal system [independent courts and the rule of law], like food and clothing, are things that people of a socialist country cannot do without. Without [them] . . . there is no socialism and there is no powerful country and happy people." Hu's democratic elite, that is, called for the adoption of some of the Western (philosophical) essence (*ti,* 体), which was inseparable from the avidly sought for Western science and technology (*yong,* 用).[20]

Though the theory conference thus opened up and introduced into the Chinese political debate ideas of liberal democracy, CCP elders challenged Hu's reformists and, often with Deng's support, kept the official line close to the canonized Marxist-Leninist–Mao Zedong thought. Axioms of the Communist ideology present in China since at least the 1920s and imposed as dogma during the Maoist era (1949–1976) as well as the continuing presence of the top-down practices of traditional Chinese government meant that Western liberal democratic ideas and modes were still deeply suspect and strongly resisted during the Deng era (1978–1997). The "anti–spiritual pollution" and "anti–bourgeois liberalization" campaigns of the 1980s, directed against Hu Yaobang, Zhao Ziyang, and other reformers, sustained the century-long tension in China between defenders of the authoritarian state and admirers of the liberal democratic state associated with second modernity thinking in the Western world. The mode of selection of the members of the theory conference, for example, though the process was undertaken by Hu and his associates, reflected the ancient idea of hierarchy and choice from the top and the neglect of liberal concepts of choice by the people. Hu appointed the chairmen of the five discussion groups, who then chose ten further participants, who in turn each chose fifteen more participants. The more than two hundred discussants thus assembled represented not so much the people themselves as a putting together of views likely to produce harmonious and constructive deliberations.[21] Though this method of selecting conference members is not unlike that sometimes used in the West, its top-down character and emphasis on like-mindedness are nonetheless indicative of understandings different from those of Mill or Dewey. Perhaps the tension echoes that at the 1920 conference where Mao listened to Bertrand Russell and Dewey. If China was moving toward more open and democratic government, as Deng himself proclaimed and in some ways supported, it was moving there in accord with restraints and guidelines that might make democracy in China look different, and rest on a different rationale, than democracy in the West.

The background, the manifestos, and the negotiations incident to the Tiananmen demonstrations and the massacre of April–June 1989 reveal further strong connections with the century-long effort to modernize China, especially its political practice and culture. The year 1989 was the seventieth anniversary of the May Fourth movement and the fortieth anniversary of the establishing of the People's Republic of China; the tens of thousands of students in Tiananmen Square during the seven weeks of demonstrations and argument were well aware of those signal events. The initial cause, memorials to the death of Hu Yaobang, who had been removed from office for his cautious treatment of earlier student demonstrations in 1986–1987, made clear the intention of the students to seek further progress toward the socialist democracy and the political, social, and cultural democratization discussed at a recent national people's congress. The student demonstrators saw themselves as in the centuries-old Confucian tradition of bringing criticism and moral enlightenment to bear on rulers turned corrupt and oppressive, as extenders of the efforts of the reformers of 1898, 1911, and 1919 to bring to China the science and democracy of the modern world, and as correctors of party leaders gone astray. They hoped as well that China's leaders might be persuaded to endorse some of the political and intellectual freedoms that the visiting Soviet leader, Mikhail Gorbachev, was introducing with the perestroika and glasnost programs in his own rapidly reforming Communist state—modernizations and opening to the West.

In addition to the demand to be allowed to speak, publish, and meet freely in order to be part of the public life of the nation and to extend the small movements toward open elections of local officials already approved by the CCP, the students sought in particular "sincere," significant conversations with top government and party officials. Setting aside, as conceptions of self-government in East Asia had tended to do for more than a century, any call for a representative assembly, an elected president, or a limited government of separated powers, the students instead wanted the government to listen to them, to take criticism, and, generally, to open the public councils to the views and advice of the people. They were incensed when the hard-line premier Li Peng was haughty and dismissive in the brief audience that he permitted but pleased and grateful when Zhao Ziyang, the more sympathetic CCP leader, listened respectfully to them and indicated that the government might in some measure be responsive to their ideas and proposals. Zhao reported on May 13 to Deng Xiaoping himself: "The student slogans all support the Constitution; they favor democracy and oppose corruption, . . . demands basically in line with the Party and government, . . . so we cannot reject them out of hand." He also reported that the demonstrators included a "majority . . . of people from all parts of society."[22] The key thing was not that the students wanted to take over the government or even seriously upset it, though, after harsh speeches by Li and Deng condemning the students as "counterrevolutionaries," they called for their resignations. What the students actually wanted was to be heard and taken seriously. (One is reminded of the Japanese Confucian Motoda Eifu explaining to the Meiji Emperor, when considering public opinion, that he should "see with the eyes and hear with the ears of all" but make the decisions himself—a procedure from which Chairman Mao himself would not have dissented.[23]) The "goddess of democracy" held high by the students (and crushed by the authorities) was clearly an import from the West but just as clearly had a special, and amended, meaning for its makers and celebrants—two hands on the torch, for example, to show the difficulty of bringing democracy to China.

Understanding the arguments and actions of both the authorities and the students during the Tiananmen events reveals the difficulty and ambiguity, however, of assimilating East Asian concepts of the state to democratic guidelines. Fundamental for both students and authorities was a paternalistic assumption of the state resting on the basic Confucian idea of filial piety. The son was to revere and obey the father, and the father was to have affection and care for the son. Then these sentiments were to be generalized into similar feelings (*jen*) and guidelines (*li*) applicable to all "upper-lower" relationships: husband and wife; master and servant; elder brother and younger brother; teacher and pupil; ruler and subject; and so on (see chapter 2). The hard-liner Li Peng insisted that the government had only "loving care for the masses of youth and students" and, thus, acted slowly in seeking to correct their misguided, disobedient movement. The students, on the other hand, insisted that they sought only to expose and resist corrupt, self-indulgent, and oppressive officials in order to restore rectitude and harmony to the state; "Mama, we're not wrong," one of their big character banners proclaimed. Sustaining the parental analogy, however, when the students refused to heed the state's advice and command, the authorities, like angry parents, condemned them. They were the "dregs of society," Deng Xiaoping declared, who "subvert our country and subvert our party" and deserved stern punishment. "Of course we want to build socialist democracy," Deng told his ruling colleagues as martial law was imposed, "but we can't possibly do it in a hurry, and still less do we want that Western-style stuff. If our one billion people jumped into multi party elections, we'd get chaos like the 'all-out Civil War' we saw during the Cultural Revolution."[24] The students, for their part, asserted that they sought merely to restore China's "ancient, thousand year civilization," where loyal children rendered honor and obedience to caring parents even as they sought earnestly to be heard and to expose wrongdoing. The appeals for democracy and liberalization sought to bring to the Chinese state some of the guidelines of (the second) modernity. But the reformers of 1898 and 1919, as well as those of 1989 (and even of 1945–1949, if one takes Communist anti-Guomindang rhetoric at face value), also shared the need to adjust to ancient ideas and practices of government. On both sides in Beijing in 1989, the need was to restore stability and preserve the state—to crack down to prevent "turmoil," as Deng Xiaoping and Li Peng saw it, or, "to pursue multilevel, multichannel dialogue" between leaders and the people, to get "things to settle down quickly," before they get "nasty," as, according to Zhao Ziyang, the students sought.[25]

Modern Democracy in Japan and East Asia

In many important ways, the Japanese response to second modernity thought and to ideas of democracy in the Meiji era was very different from the pattern in China, especially in the governing circles. Under the influence of Ito Hirobumi, Yamagata Aritomo, Inoue Tetsujiro, Kato Hiroyuki, and other intellectuals and Meiji oligarchs, the form, theory, and operation of Japanese government, after the proclamation of the imperial constitution (1889) and the imperial rescript on education (1890), turned increasingly toward an authoritarian nationalism attuned to both Japanese *kokutai* (national essence) concepts and German state supremacy doctrines. Some forms and ideas of democracy, of the sort urged by Fukuzawa Yukichi, Okuma Shigenobu, and others, remained in place and, in the 1920s, even gained some influence in the Japanese state—

witness the enactment of universal manhood suffrage in 1925. But what has been termed "the Confucianist state nationalism of the Meiji leaders"[26] was dominant in Japan and achieved especially vigorous and militarist manifestation during the long East Asian and Pacific War, 1931–1945. In fact, by the 1930s and 1940s, Japan was part of a worldwide pattern of both the theory and the practice of liberal democracy being overwhelmed by an authoritarian regime echoing ancient practices of tyranny. Under militarist, fascist, or Communist ideologies, nations responded only to the technological, populist, and scientific dimensions of modernity. Japanese *kokutai* thought and the "emperor system" were emphatic evidence, furthermore, that, in East Asia, ancient patterns of government contained potent elements that, if they did not entirely push aside notions of liberal democracy, would at least require substantial modification of them. As both Japanese and Chinese intellectuals had been demonstrating for nearly a century, the idea of democracy in East Asia was not likely to achieve a simple transplanting but might require an alternate third modernity manifestation if it was to survive at all.

Under attack from American occupation authorities and from Marxist intellectuals, much of the formal defense and structure of the emperor system in Japan disappeared after 1945. In 1947, Japan adopted (at American insistence) a democratic constitution that made government in Japan, in form at least, much like that of the second modernity liberal corporate states of the West (see chapter 7). The understandings of self-government, borrowed from the West, set forth with such a sense of awe and reform by Fukuzawa and others in the 1870s, and only very incompletely incorporated into Meiji government, seemed after 1945 to be the way and wave of the future. The 1947 constitution provided for a constitutional monarchy and parliamentary system similar to those of Great Britain and for courts and a somewhat federated electoral mechanism partly along American lines—though the role of law and the administrative organization was more in accord with such centralized practices as those of France than with Anglo-American ones. Political parties assumed important, publicly prominent roles, and the media freely and vociferously brought public affairs to a large and attentive citizenry. Indeed, it seemed, especially since, for half a century, Japan had had universal education and literacy, that the fears of Nishi and others that the Japanese people were "unsuited" to the demands of representative self-government could finally be laid to rest. The acceptance of a democratic and capitalist Japan in the United Nations, in world trade organizations, and in such sophisticated interdependencies of the developed world as the Trilateral Commission (North America, Western Europe, and Japan) seemed to establish the country's place as a functioning liberal corporate democracy. The earnest acceptance of largely democratic forms both by the citizenry and by leading circles and the performance of the astonishingly successful economy under-scored the same point.

Yet, much as it seemed that Japan had become a democracy in accord with second modernity guidelines, in practice, and in underlying rationale, things remained somehow very different. Yoshida Shigeru, Japan's leading postwar statesman, made the point most basically when he observed in 1950: "For abstract theorizing we must learn from the West. But I feel where our daily lives are concerned, and in matters of intercourse among men, there is nothing that we cannot find in the Chinese classics and Chinese poetry."[27] The Japanese assumption of the unity of the nation, and the general prevalence of a state theory that accepted "the whole Chinese, or East Asian, emphasis on the central-ized state as the highest embodiment of civilization,"[28] for example, severely restrained Western liberal concern for limiting the powers of the state. This near reverence for the state carried with it at its best, moreover, a powerful sense of the moral basis of government and relatively high standards of honesty and efficiency in public administration. Officials at all levels of government were trained to be "absolutely loyal to their superiors, scrupulously honest, meticu-lous in the performance of their duties, and efficient."[29] Though these ideals were, of course, not always lived up to (and were mixed with pervasive but somehow less corrupting practices of gift giving and favoritism), they provided for an effectiveness of administration seldom matched elsewhere in the world. The centuries-long practice of bureaucratized government under the Tokugawa (*bakufu*), the even older tradition of merit selection of officials (national exami-nations were not used in Japan as they were in China, but similar standards of wise and skilled service obtained), and the custom of group rather than person-alized leadership further distanced Japan from minimalist ideas of democratic government. These attitudes and practices all tended, as Fukuzawa and Nishi had recognized from the beginning of the Western impact on Japan, to implant a top-down, elitist emphasis in democratic concepts while at the same time deemphasizing the "by and of the people" element of Anglo-American democ-racy. This is every day evident in the powerful position held by the officials and functionaries of the various ministries in Tokyo, both in the operating of the leg-islative branch and in the carrying out of the laws throughout the nation.

Furthermore, though since 1945 Japan has had such familiar elements of dem-ocratic practice as openly contested elections, campaign oratory, party rivalry, and debate in legislatures, the way the elements work is different and not deliber-ately and positively aimed at majority decisions or at sustained, principled oppo-sition. In his 1960 novel *After the Banquet,* for example, Yukio Mishima described a true-to-life election in Tokyo where there were nominating caucuses, noisy, elaborately planned campaigns, enormous expenditures of money, strenuous exertions by dedicated workers, deals of all sorts to gain support, intraparty struggles, and other similarities to American political contests, but the whole affair is presented as both unfamiliar and distasteful to thoughtful Japanese. At one point, after some ineffectual campaign speeches, a high-minded candidate nonetheless seems to gather public support among elderly voters. This is because there was, traditionally, a "peculiar Japanese trust in inept talkers."[30] In Japan, that is, rather than clear, logical expression, as might sustain democratic public life, being valued, it is thought rude and insensitive because it neglects the nuanced indirection essential to Japanese modes of discussion appropriate for the hierarchical yet emotionally attuned interactions of omnipresent group life. Western democratic politics was, simply, too blunt and confrontational for a culture that valued above everything emotional, moral, and respectfully hierarchical relationships among people. (Partly for this reason, "politicians" connected with the faction-driven, speech-giving national legislature, whatever their formal importance, are widely scorned as being counterproductive, as impeding good government.) Similarly, the valuing of sustained opposition after majority-based decisions have been made, in order to keep honing the quality of decisions, seems needlessly enervating within an idea of group process that values above everything sincere, heartfelt agreement on and commitment to the purposes and program of the group. Hence, far more respectful attention is paid to the intragroup meetings of the numerous personally led "factions" in the Diet than to such contentious speechmaking and debate as take place in the public assembly. The whole ethos of second modernity conflict-of-interest politics, in a deep way, as Yoshida Shigeru had implied, seems antithetical to the moral conducting of human relationships, personal, private, or public.

This tension reflects a skepticism, already evident in the earliest responses of Fukuzawa, Nishi, and others to the practices of representative government, about laws made and administered by the people or their delegates. Instead, as is in a way implicit in traditional prescriptions that emperors (or shoguns) should be attentive to the needs of the people, there should be "a change in the direction of the motion of energy," from top-down to bottom-up. "What the Japanese mean by 'democracy,'" Nakane Chie wrote in 1970, "is a system that should take the side of, or give consideration to, the weaker or lower; in practice any decision should be made on the basis of a consensus which includes those located lower in the hierarchy." The goal overall is "unanimous decision-making on the basis of maximum consultation." A "bad" decision, on the other hand, is one "influenced by top members or a dominant clique and governed by the principle of majority rule, with scope for the effective use of hierarchical power relationships." Majority decisionmaking, within this understanding, feels like either a decision forced on a leader, supposed to be taking the interests of all into account, by perhaps more narrow-visioned "lowers" or a divisive way of imposing the will of "one-half plus one" on everyone else, likely to produce endless quarreling, deal-making, and manipulation. Nakane suggests, then, that, ideally, "Japanese 'democracy' is a kind of community sentiment, with, as a major premise, a high degree of cohesion and consensus within the group." Within this idea, freedom of expression is favored to allow "the lower or the underprivileged the freedom to speak out." There is, however, no endorsement of the liberal idea, expressed classically by Mill, that continued criticism even after decisions are made is a constructive part of democratic practice and even an obligation on the part, in the British phrase, of "Her Majesty's loyal opposition." Instead, the admired posture for dissenters, after great effort within a group to find agreement among at least two-thirds of its members, is to say that, since so many have agreed and we have been able to have our say, we will cease opposition and are ready to cooperate fully for the good of the group.[31] Thus, though Japanese democratic thinking and practice accept the basic premise to take the needs and views of all into account, and especially to "take the side of, and give consideration to, the weaker or lower," they have serious reservations about the dynamics of majority rule, the role of opposition, and even the idea of finding a public-spirited "general will" among the people that might serve as a guide for government.

Though other countries or regions in East Asia, in general within the Confucian cultural sphere—particularly Korea, Taiwan, Singapore, and Hong Kong — have had political histories very different from that of Japan (and China, too, of course), they have all had encounters with the second modernity democracy of the West that have resulted in varieties of what is best understood as looking toward a third modernity understanding of democracy. Since 1945, all these polities have begun by favoring decidedly authoritarian, top-down regimes intent on creating or ensuring a government in accord with the East Asian emphasis on the centralized state and accepting, one way or another, a paramount leader. The names of Park Chung Hee in Korea, Chiang Ching-kuo and Lee Teng Hui in Taiwan, Lee Kuan Yew in Singapore, and even Tung Chee-hwa in Hong Kong, by no means "democrats" in either Western eyes or those of "liberals" in their own countries, all were (are) vigorous pursuers, as they saw it, of government "for the people." (In rather different ways, Deng Xiaoping and Jiang Zemin fit somewhat the same pattern in the People's Republic of China, as does Mahathir Mohamad in Malaysia.) They have all insisted that they governed "for the people" and for the prosperity and economic development of the country as a whole and that they welcomed in some fashion the "advice and consent" of the people. There might be elections of a sort, at least consultative assemblies, and perhaps progressing involvement of an increasingly educated and attentive public.

In fact, all six polities (Korea, Taiwan, Singapore, and Hong Kong as well as the People's Republic of China and Japan), in various stages of movement (sometimes stalled or retrograde) toward more genuine (by Western standards) democracy, are reacting more or less in accord with the interpretations and reservations present in the East Asian response to Western thought and prescriptions since the mid-nineteenth century. (There are, of course, important differences, too, among these polities.) There is, most fundamentally, a profound, indelible conviction that proper government, essential to the well-being and improvement of all the people, must be somehow paternalistic, in accord with higher, time-honored precepts best understood and carried out by a father, a guide, or sage counselors, by someone who "knows best." Along with this, a deep skepticism about the capacity of the people, at least in their existing stage of ignorance and public uninterest, prevented ready endorsement of truly representative government. Finally, just as did Fukuzawa and Yan Fu, the twentieth-century leaders of these countries found something distasteful and even demeaning about the ceaseless bickering and controversy that seemed to surround Western ideas and practices of democracy. Judging from the way in which representative assemblies and popular party politics worked in "new democracies" and often even in long-established ones, there was little that was attractive in that process for national leaders intent on active government in the interest of the whole. Mao Zedong himself had in 1937 proclaimed that the spirit of liberalism was "a corrosive which eats away at unity, undermines solidarity, induces inactivity, and creates dissension."[32] Non-Communist East Asians might not have accepted Mao's prescription in response, but they would have understood and agreed with much of his analysis of the flaw at the heart of liberal democracy: it seemed to rest on dissension and special interests rather than on common interest and harmony. Deng Xiaoping wrote President George Bush in February 1989 that, "if we were to run elections among China's one billion people now, chaos . . . would certainly ensue. . . . Democracy is our goal, but the state must maintain stability."[33] The need, then, was to find a mode of democracy at once faithful to the ancient precepts of good government but also accepting of the openness, the freedom of political activity, and even the participation by citizens that seemed so essential and forward-looking in the new Western ways.

Japanese and Chinese Reactions to Rabindranath Tagore

The reservations about Western-style democracy and its compatibility with traditional East Asian values had been highlighted in dramatic, emotional tours that the Indian Nobel laureate Rabindranath Tagore (1861–1941) had made in Japan in 1916 and in China in 1924. One of his followers, Okakura Kakuzo, had in

1903, after twenty-five years of study of philosophy and of Asian art and religion (begun in Tokyo as a student of the American art critic Ernest Fenollosa), written *The Ideals of the East,* emphasizing both an overall unity of Asian culture and important contrasts. "Asia is one," he proclaimed. On both sides of the Himalayas, its "two mighty civilizations" shared a "broad expanse of love for the Ultimate and Universal." The West, on the other hand, "loved to dwell upon the Particular, and to search out the means, not the end, of life." Calling especially to "revivify the dormant life of the old Asiatic unity," he sought to restrain the spread of Western science and technology and, instead, "seek a higher solution in Indian religion and Chinese ethics."[34] By this time, Okakura had absorbed both Western thought about the supposed contrast of the "spiritual East" (including Islam and Persia plus South and East Asia) with the "materialist West" as well as Tagore's Pan-Asiatic ideas. At Tagore's retreat community and study center in Bengal, Santiniketan, Okakura and other scholars and mystics from around the world studied and practiced a pantheistic combination of Hindu and Buddhist mysticism and Western-, Jewish-, and Christian-tinged religious and romantic idealism. They sought to rescue the world from the "strife, exploitation, restless change, discontent, and destruction" that Bertrand Russell told Chinese audiences characterized the West at the end of World War I.[35] Tagore had as part of his lifelong mission, then, to "wake up" Asia to its spiritual greatness as a way of resisting Western political and intellectual intrusion. Just as for intellectuals in the West (Coleridge and Emerson come to mind) who had come on the ancient books of "the Orient" (mostly Hindu and Buddhist at first), the great task for Tagore seemed to be, depending especially on the inspiration of Hindu and Buddhist texts, to put together a universal religion and morality of love, peace, harmony, and spiritual richness that could unite the world and resist the pall of materialistic modernity emanating from the West— a mood still potent in various ways from Cairo to Kyoto.

Tagore's speeches and their reception in East Asia, however, not only reveal his misunderstanding of Japanese and Chinese intellectual worlds, but also shed a broad light on the impact of Western thought in East Asia—including ideas about government and democracy. With little knowledge, apparently, of indigenous East Asian thought beyond a book of Lao-tsu's aphorisms, which he thought "thoroughly Indian . . . [like] our own Upanishads," Tagore understood both Japan and China as basically Buddhist and supposed that intellectuals there would, thus, share much of his own South Asian cultural heritage. In Japan in 1916, Tagore was greeted by Buddhist-oriented art and religion scholars as anxious as he was to find an antidote to the Western aggression and material culture that seemed as omnipresent in Tokyo as in Calcutta. He sought at once an eclectic middle ground: he praised European "ideals of the public good and liberty of thought and action" but condemned the West as "scientific, not human," and called for a renewal of the common spiritual heritage of India, Japan, and China. He also asked Japan to take the lead in resisting Western political and cultural imperialism in East Asia and, altogether, saw a fundamental "Asian unity," as he put it later, in the "Vedic, Buddhist, Semitic, Zoroastrian . . . and other cultural currents . . . from Judea to Japan" (note that Confucianism is not listed).[36]

At no time, however, did Tagore seem either to know anything himself of the Confucian underlay of East Asian culture or to realize that it altered profoundly how his Japanese audiences would hear him. He began to see something of the difference, however, when he observed that the Japanese "acquired a perfect sense of the form at some cost of the sense of the spirit." They possessed "a sense of decorum and deftness of mind and fingers . . . [but not a] sense of the infinite in man. . . . Their nature is solely aesthetic and not spiritual."[37] Tagore sensed a gulf between the Indian tradition of the separation, into different castes, of the Brahman priest and the Kshatriya warrior-administrator, the latter conducting the government and attending to mundane matters, the Brahman holy men and intellectuals pursuing the (higher) life of the mind and the spirit. In the Japanese (East Asian/Confucian) tradition, however, thinkers, the scholar-intellectuals, were obliged themselves to advise government and to take up its reins. Political thinking and practice, moreover, were in East Asia, not lower, but higher orders of business, so Japanese scholars heard Tagore's appeals to revive ancient spiritual preoccupations (which he mistakenly thought his audience shared) and to push aside nationalistic and materialistic aping of the West as thoroughly misguided and opposite to what the "message of India to Japan" ought to be. In fact, one Japanese intellectual wrote, "he should learn from us rather than we from him"—Tagore was "a patriot in a ruined country" (Britain ruled India in 1916) who should be heard as a poet, not a philosopher, that is, as a dreamy literatus rather than as one with useful things to say about government and public affairs or even ethics and culture.[38]

Philosophers reflecting Japanese *kokutai* (national essence) and neo-Confucian thought, as well as the growing number of Japanese intellectuals already deeply Westernized in their thinking, joined in criticizing Tagore's spiritual Pan-Asianism. Inoue Tetsujiro (1855–1944), a "Germanized Confucianist" and member of the select Imperial Academy, did not find in Tagore's thought "any ideas which promote the welfare of society or of the nation." He agreed with Tagore only in seeing that, though "science is necessary in order to reach human goals, . . . science is not the goal itself." Nonetheless, Inoue thought that Japan still needed more Western science, in order to continue its pursuit of wealth and power, and less of the "negative attitude . . . and pessimism" coming from Tagore's British-ruled India that, Inoue said, was "the song of a ruined country."³⁹

Waseda University professor Tanaka Odo, who had studied in the United States from 1890 to 1899 with John Dewey and others, attacked Tagore by combining a Deweyan scientific social pragmatism with a traditional Confucian emphasis on good government in the public interest. "From the standpoint of modern civilization or modern life," Tanaka wrote, meaning the Westernized yet still strongly traditional society coming into existence in Japan, the nation possessed a culture "based on deeper [human] needs than in Tagore's." "When I compare the civilization based on science with the civilization based on religion and art," Tanaka continued, "it seems to me that the former is more spiritual than the latter; I cannot believe that the former is more materialistic." "When discussing our country's past," Tanaka charged, Tagore "overestimated the influence of Buddhism" and too much criticized Western scientific thought for its influence in Japan. Tanaka's view was reflected in a newspaper article written on Tagore's departure from Japan: "Japan's mission is to amalgamate the civilizations of the Occident and the Orient, but a moral civilization not built on material foundations can only lead a country to ruin. . . . [Tagore's] words are like jewels, and his sentences sparkle like stars, but he offers no statistics, no figures to support his theories. . . . We must not let him discourage us in the pursuit of science and wealth."⁴⁰ To Japanese intellectuals, then, Tagore entirely misunderstood both Japan's cultural heritage and its progress in "amalgamat[ing]" that heritage with modern thought from the West and preached a romantic, politically naive worldview that certainly was not Pan-Asian and would, in fact, be a disaster for any nation seeking to survive and prosper in the modern world. Tagore left Japan puzzled, frustrated, and discouraged.

In going to China eight years later (1924), Tagore was the last of four distinguished foreigners to be invited there by the Society for Lectures on the New Learning, a group of "new thought" intellectuals, sponsored by Liang Qichao and including Hu Shi, Chen Duxiu, and Zhang Junmai, eager to bring to China the modern thought of the rest of the world. The earlier lecturers had been John Dewey, Bertrand Russell, and the German idealist Hans Driesch, so the society saw Tagore as bringing the latest from India to the intense intellectual ferment going on in China.⁴¹ Tagore, for his part, hoped to "reestablish the cultural and spiritual connections between India and China." "My general idea," he told his welcomers when he landed in Shanghai in April 1924, "is to advocate Eastern thought, the revival of traditional Asian culture, and the unity of the peoples of Asia." Perhaps unpropitiously for him, he also came to China when his most immediate hosts and intellectual compatriots, Zhang Junmai and the poet Xu Zhimo, enamored of a sort of Germanized romantic idealism, had recently largely "lost" their challenge to the Dewey-Russell-oriented advocates of science and democracy and to Marxist advocates of scientific socialism as well. So, when Xu told Tagore at the welcoming ceremony that he hoped that "the radiant personality, the profound philosophy and the irresistible poetry of the Great Messenger from India would dissipate . . . the prevailing spirit of scepticism . . . and revitalize the spiritual thoughts of China,"[42] he thrust Tagore ambiguously into an already heated and often hostile intellectual landscape. Where would his call for a revived Asian spirituality, which in any case profoundly misunderstood the place of the Confucian tradition in China, fit in the intense debate over the adaptation of Anglo-American scientific empiricism, of Marxist socialism, and of romantic idealism to the intellectual, moral, and political needs of modern China?

Tagore found a sympathetic audience among many Chinese Buddhists and among Chinese intellectuals such as Xu Zhimo who reveled in the same European poets and idealists admired by Orientalists East and West. Others, however, more and more backed away from his message. Liang Qichao graciously acknowledged the debt of China to "elder brother" India in philosophy, religion, music, and the visual arts and even medicine, astronomy, and education, but, perhaps pointedly, he omitted reference to government or politics, topics that Tagore either explicitly set aside or seemed not to understand in their Chinese context. In Beijing, leaflets more directly hostile to Tagore were distributed after in his lectures he condemned the "iron monster" of industry, "cloven-footed commerce," and other "servitudes [to] the fetish of hugeness, the nonhuman," that characterized materialistic Western modernity.[43] Tagore, the leaflets proclaimed, was dead wrong in appealing for a revival of a Chinese civilization that, instead of being characterized by beauty and harmony, "crushed the people and enriched the prince, subjected women and exalted men, . . . [had] streets which are latrines, . . . shameless prostitution, rapacious mandarins devouring the people, . . . and women making their beauty consist in the mutilation of their feet." If this was the "ancient Chinese civilization which Mr. Tagore calls spiritual," "[w]e . . . protest, Mr. Tagore." In fact, the leaflet continued, China's "present ills have been caused in large part by the indifference to public matters of too great a number of our fellow citizens," so Tagore's ideas that "we torment our souls too much by worrying about such things" and that "there is no further need for nations or for governments" were entirely misguided. Tagore's hope that Chinese poets, "capturing on their instruments the secret stir of life in the air and giving it voice in the music of prophecy," might lead China to salvation was to most May Fourth intellectuals simply nonsense. This was a "doctrine of hypnotism" that would "hand us over paralyzed to our enemies." Allied with "our ancient theory of Yin and Yang, our Taoism and

Confucianism, ... [with] the foreign doctrine of Christianity," and with the Western-tuned idealistic literati, Tagore's thought would obscure China's desperate need for a philosophy and a practice that would revive and rescue the polity and the nation.[44] Marxist critics attacked Tagore even more bluntly as one whose ideas were nothing but "the morphine and coconut wine of those with property and leisure" and whose advice was like Chinese "literati of long ago, [who] tried to destroy bandits by chanting Confucian classics at them."[45]

Hu Shi and other intellectuals oriented toward Western science and pragmatism tried (ineffectually and in terms with which Tagore himself would not have agreed) to explain that Tagore's call for a sort of universal spirituality was consistent with the "highly idealistic and spiritual" science and evolutionism of John Dewey. It "makes the fullest possible use," Hu explained, "of human ingenuity and intelligence in the search for truth in order to control nature, ... to liberate the human spirit from ignorance, superstition, and slavery to the forces of nature, and to reform social and political institutions for the benefit of the greatest number." Hu would even claim later that this "scientific and democratic civilization" of the modern West was consistent with and might "resurrect ... the humanistic and rationalistic [Confucian] China" that was its genuine and valuable heritage, rather than the mystical Buddhism and Taoism from which Tagore had tried to fashion his alleged Pan-Asian spirituality.[46]

Other Chinese scholars commented more comprehensively on the large and complex intellectual currents that coursed through Tagore's lectures. Placing China in broader patterns of world cultures, the philosopher Gu Hongming (1857–1928), at once Western educated and deeply Confucian in his outlook (Hu Shi called him a true *chüntzu*, or "Chinese gentleman"), explained that China's was "not an Oriental civilization like the civilization of India and Persia" at all. Rather, in its deepest guise, Gu insisted, China's was "a civilization of rationalism and science." Buddhism, "a product of the Oriental civilization of India," he explained, had, more than a millennium earlier, "nearly destroyed ... the true ancient Chinese civilization ... of the Han dynasty" and had then produced the "Puritanism of the Sung dynasty ... which had made the real civilization of China become stagnant and unprogressive." Gu drew a parallel between this Buddhist influence in China and the submersion of Greco-Roman civilizations by Christianity in the European Middle Ages. Just as what the West had needed to revive its classical culture of "rationalism and science" was to overcome "Mediaevalism," what China needed was, not more of Tagore's mystical Pan-Asianism, but rather to reclaim its ancient Confucian culture, which had more in common with the premedieval and post-Renaissance (modern) West than it did with South Asian Buddhism. "In Chinese civilization," Gu concluded, "there are neither mysteries nor darkness."[47]

The most intellectually influential corrective to Tagore's misunderstanding of Chinese thought, however, came from Liang Shuming (1893–1981), whose widely read *Cultures of East and West* (1922) had already proclaimed the need for a combining of traditional Confucian thought with "the spirit of science and democracy[, which] is entirely appropriate to our circumstances." (He agreed with the synthesis implied in Bertrand Russell's remark: "The distinctive merit of our civilization, I should say, is the scientific method; the distinctive merit of the Chinese a just conception of the ends of life.") Liang understood that Indian civilization and Chinese civilization had evolved along different lines, Indian (at least in the spiritual formulations of Tagore) in the desire to withdraw from the world, Chinese in the search for harmony within it. This latter, he thought, emphasizing a down-to-earth, rational approach, paid necessary attention to the social and political aspects of human life. It was as though, Lin Yutang has observed, "India produced too much religion, China too little." Thus, Liang recommended that "the Indian attitude must be rejected": "Western civilization must be accepted, but . . . its underlying attitude must be transformed, [and] the original Chinese attitude must be reevaluated and presented anew."[48] Westerners, Liang said, had a "concept of self" that led to human relations of a "cold, indifferent, hostile, and calculating kind," that "relied on intellect," while "Chinese do not want the Self" and "rely on intuition and emotion" to develop relationships that "nourish human life." (Is this why, as Russell had noted, the Chinese had a "remarkable . . . power of securing the affection of strangers"?)[49]

Unfortunately often in practice in Chinese history, in misapplications, this attitude had been distorted to result in "only a few ancient ceremonial regulations, lifeless precepts that created a tomb-like oppression and caused no little suffering." Liang urged, then, as a corrective, a combining of the Western emphasis on the scientific approach and its application to social problems with the ancient, deeply held Confucian idea of a morally based community bound together by the central concept of *jen,* "benevolence" or "human-heartedness." Liang was glad that Dewey and Russell had come to China, but he was happy that Henri Bergson had stayed home—just as he obviously had little use for Tagore's message. Although Liang did not address the point directly, he was suggesting a kind of polity, basically democratic as he understood the term, that embodied Western empiricism without its selfish calculating. He favored a "Chinese just conception of the ends of life," resting on "a psychology of happiness and tranquility," without the lifeless ceremonialism and endemic oppression that had so often dominated Chinese history, a view that he continued to uphold through denunciations from Mao himself and into the Deng Xiaoping era.[50]

The reaction of Japanese and Chinese intellectuals to Tagore's visits to their countries, then, begun in celebratory welcoming to the poet and sage from their Buddhist motherland, turned out to reveal the nature of their own deepest intellectual traditions, the chasm between them and Tagore's South Asian mysticism, and the direction that their accommodation with Western thought might take. Except in centers of deep Buddhist conviction, though East Asian intellectuals admired the elegant poetry and striking presence of their guest, they listened in puzzlement and disbelief. Finally, they repudiated his Pan-Asian assumptions, his championing of the spiritual over the mundane, and his unconcern and distaste for the political. They further came to believe, often with scorn and indignation, that this representative of a "ruined country," under the heel of British imperialism, had nothing to offer, that, in fact, he brought a dangerous message to their nations in need, as they saw it, of, not less, but more of the Western science and modernity that they hoped would bring them wealth and power. In fact, the response of the Japanese and especially the Chinese intellectuals to Tagore emphasized, not only "the primacy of the political order" in their own tradition (as Benjamin Schwartz put it),[51] but the way in which they might partake most fruitfully of Western modernity. Though the questions of government and democracy were not much on Tagore's agenda and were little spoken of in his exchanges in Japan and China, the way in which democratic government might become manifest, and, even more, the rationale, the intellectual placing of it, and the tension that it faced with other ideas of polity, had been clarified.

A Third Modernity Rationale for Democracy in East Asia

In the half century or more between the first efforts of Fukuzawa Yukichi and others to explain Western learning in Japan (begun in the 1860s and 1870s) and the "new citizen" and "new thought" movements of the early twentieth century in China (ca. 1900–1930), then, the intellectual foundations for another understanding, a third modernity rationale for democracy, were set in place. These conceptions have provided the guidelines for the forms of democracy that, more or less, and with steps backward as well as forward, came into existence in East Asia during the twentieth century. It was as though the thought undergirding second modernity democratic theorizing in the West, from its beginnings under Bentham and Mill to its post-Darwinian flowering in Bertrand Russell, Harold Laski, John Dewey, and others, had found a new and enriched life through its consideration by East Asian thinkers. These thinkers absorbed it earnestly and then worked out its implications within their own Confucian tradition. It is not that the Western patterns of thought *caused* the tumultuous changes in government that followed Western intrusion from the mid-nineteenth century on—there were many economic, military, political, technological, and other reasons for that. Rather, East Asian intellectuals, first in their efforts to understand the new thought, then in their pursuit of its implications for government, developed often very different conceptions of what government of and for (and by?) the people might amount to—and different rationales for its purpose and conduct. Hence, there emerged a third modernity understanding of democracy that, though derived from the explanations of Western second modernity thinkers and akin to the practices of the liberal democratic state pervasive in the West during much of the twentieth century, was, nonetheless, interestingly and significantly different.

Most fundamentally, East Asian students of democracy had even graver reservations about what government *by* the people might mean than did many Western thinkers. It was not that Confucian-based thought had a kind of Machiavellian cynicism and contempt for the lives and needs of ordinary people. In fact, the dicta in the *Book of Mencius* that "benevolence, righteousness, propriety, and knowledge are not fused into us from without; they naturally belong to us" and that "if allowed to follow their nature [people] will be good" injected into much Japanese and Chinese political thinking a sense that, at least originally and ultimately, people had good moral and intellectual capabilities basic to the well-being of society.[52] Always allied with this, however, was the assumption that rulers and their sage advisers and administrators would have superior wisdom and a better understanding of the good of the polity than would the common (ignorant, provincial, uneducated) people. The needs and aspirations of the people were to be sought out and made known to the rulers ("see with the eyes and hear with the ears of all"), and they were to be considered in consultations, but the decisions, the actual governing, if it was to be wise and in accord with the mandate of heaven, would have to be by the wholly qualified, that is, those who understood the ancient wisdom and had studied its application to contemporary affairs. When the Western idea of democracy, people governing, came to East Asia, then, it could not seem to mean that they would actually rule through elected representatives who would make the laws; rather, it would have to mean that, somehow, their needs and views would be more than ever taken into account.

Thus, in Japan, the first proposals for "legislative assemblies" called, not for elected representatives to make laws, but for "representatives" to be sought (by officials already qualified and in place) from among the people who would then repair to the capital to be consulted by and to present concerns to those who would then declare and administer the laws. All this was to be done conscientiously and in good faith to bring the views and needs of the people into the process of government. There would be earnest deliberations in which the people would be present through those selected to "represent" them. Similarly, Yan Fu, impressed with the evolutionary unfitness of the Chinese people to take part in government, had little use for Rousseauistic ideas of resting government on the general will of the people. Instead, he preferred the severely limited role for representative assemblies provided for in Japan's 1889 imperial constitution and even gave some support to the restoration of the Chinese Empire in 1914–1916. He presumed that its reconstitution could be in accord with social Darwinian ideas of releasing the energies of the people in order to enhance the wealth and power of the state.

One can see some evidence of the different East Asian concept of representation in the reversion of Hong Kong to Chinese rule in 1997. The British tradition, in which Chinese subjects and associates had been long tutored, had in mind Western-style representative government with an elected parliamentary body responsible to the people. The framework designed by the British and agreed to by the Peoples' Republic of China, however, embodied ancient East Asian precepts of government and arrangements to uphold the power and ideology of the CCP and the mainland regime as well as Western ideas of representation. The Legislative Council was to be only partially elected by the people under rules designed to assure that the "real" needs of groups and interests in Hong Kong ("functional constituencies"), as well as those in China as a whole, would be taken into account. The chief official, moreover, Tung Chee-hwa, though *of* Hong Kong, was as well a senior, important person fully in tune with the presumably omniscient and properly omnipotent mainland authorities who ruled for the good of all. At one level, this was sheer power play by the Communist authorities, but it was as well eerily in accord with the century-and-a-half-long effort to give the "new" idea of democracy an East Asian configuration. A cornerstone concept of second modernity democracy, a fully representative, equitably proportioned legislature, had been refashioned (indeed, nearly subverted) to accord with East Asian ideas of good government, in this instance agreed to, perhaps tactically, by the British negotiators. In another example, Lee Kuan Yew of Singapore once proposed that "every man over the age of 40 who has a family" have two votes because he would likely be more "cautious" and "serious" in using them "than a capricious young man under 30." Lee was not "intellectually convinced," he said, "that one man, one vote is the best."[53]

The reluctance to accept fully elected and representative legislatures was also part of a Confucian distaste for factious assemblies and open party strife. For decades, even Japanese and Chinese reformers, eager for Western technology, science, and democracy, deliberately drew back from modernizing proposals if they seemed to entail factious, self-interested contention—"effort," as the traditionally minded officials whom Fukuzawa faced put it. The factious, partisan spirit that Arthur Bentley and other second modernity democrats had validated and even celebrated (see chapter 6) seemed sure to bring to the state councils all the selfish, narrow-visioned energy that Confucian guidelines had always seen as fatal to good government. The very low standing in modern Japan and Korea, for example, of "the politicians," the sense that their bickering, their alliances with various special interests, and their attention to particular regions were inimical to the good of the nation as a whole, has placed what is generally understood in the West as the necessary give-and-take of politics in a much less favorable light. In commenting on a recent scandal of Diet members ("politicians") seeking, on behalf of constituents, to influence "the bureaucracy," for example, the *Asahi shimbun* noted that, "when bureaucrats tie up with specific legislators to benefit specific groups, fairness is compromised." These "undisciplined relations between politicians and the bureaucracy," the report concluded, damaged the standing of democratic government in Japan. If Western-style democracy meant, as Arthur Balfour once said of the British constitution, a form of government wherein people "can safely afford to bicker," then it would seem deeply problematic to a tradition of political thinking that valued harmony above everything.[54] Though contemporary Japanese and Korean politics are bitterly strife torn and faction ridden in their own styles, they are in a way both more intense and more submerged than is generally the case in the West. When opposing forces or interests, nourished by the idea of self-government, do quarrel openly, the result is often unseemly, even violent, in ways that violate liberal, democratic, second modernity guidelines (note, e.g., the recent political history of Taiwan). On the other hand, factions operate more behind the scenes and according to East Asian group behavior modes than unashamedly in public view, as is acceptable and even required in Western-style politics. In any case, the notion that sustained contention, quarreling, and opposition constitute a constructive part of public life has less standing in East Asian democracy than is generally true in the West and makes it work differently.

This distaste for openly factional politics is tied closely to the Confucian tradition of firm, paternalistic government, from the top down, in accord with a "Japanese essence," or the mandate of heaven, or some other version of higher law. From the earliest stories of the legendary sage-kings Yao and Shun, who themselves were attuned to ancient wisdom and consulted earnestly with the wise men of their day, the intent was to establish in China (ca. 2000–3000 B.C.E.) a unified polity that was the highest embodiment of civilization, a fulfillment of the moral order, the enactment of the mandate of heaven. This always meant the focusing of authority in the hands of those most steeped in the ancient wisdom, best embodying a sense of the state's moral foundations (mandate of heaven), and best positioned to understand and carry out the system of government. In China, Korea, and Japan, this resulted in a paternalistic mythology of rule descending from a legendary progenitor of the people who is seen as their father and whose family successors inherit the mantle of guidance, care, and rule of the parental figure. Always associated in some form are sage counselors whose deliberation and advice the king or emperor (the father of his people) is in some fashion bound to heed—even though the monarch himself at least formally rules, makes the decisions. This basic way of conceiving, framing, and conducting government has lasted for millennia, far longer, of course, than any other articulated, in-place, and sustained understanding of polity anywhere in the world—and this even though, in all three countries, there have been substantial challenges to reigning Confucian orthodoxies (e.g., Legalist thought in third-century-B.C.E. China, Song neo-Confucianism, and eighteenth-century *kokutai* thought in Japan). The understanding of the ruler's responsibility remained much the same.

The result, over millennia, has been repeated manifestations of top-down, theoretically sage-guided government in East Asia. For centuries in China, a system of nationwide examinations based on knowledge of the Four Books and the Five Classics "recruited" the wisest and most learned to fill the councils and offices around the emperor and throughout the land. In Korea, the first kings of the Yi dynasty (1392–1910 C.E.) instituted daily "royal lectures" where scholars expounded the principles of Confucian statecraft to the monarch and then discussed with the king and his counselors the implications for public philosophy and policy.[55] Furthermore, an academy of Confucian scholars (akin to the Hanlin Academy in Beijing) was established officially, near the palace in Seoul, to educate officials and counselors for the monarch but also to provide a perhaps critical voice to keep the ancient precepts before the rulers. Even in the twentieth century, student protestors, moving from their universities into the streets of the capital, sought generally, not to destroy or take over the government, but to condemn its corruption, to bring it to principles of righteousness, and to insist that their views (as earnest students and acolytes in the wisdom essential to good government) be listened to seriously[56]—just as had the demonstrators in Tiananmen Square in 1989. The intention, theoretically at least, was to put the reins of government in firm hands that would rule justly and wisely—and the conviction that the student proposals would provide neither firm nor wise government was in Beijing as well as Seoul the grounds for brutal suppression. This shows, of course, that East Asian governments have often betrayed the idealism of Confucian guidelines (in fact, defaults have been grievous and severe), but the guidelines have remained for regimes to be called back to or for new ones to rally around for support.

A similar idealistic rationale often undergirded various Japanese governments. During the Tokugawa era, Confucianism (specifically Sung neo-Confucianism) was set forth as the official ideology of the nation, and scholars of that school were installed near the shogun to assure that he would know how to rule righteously. "A ruler of the Empire ought to know the Four Books of Confucius," Tokugawa Ieyasu (1542–1616) observed, "and if he cannot be versed in them all he should certainly know [the *Book of*] *Mencius*. How can one who is ignorant of the way of learning rule the Empire properly? And the only road to this knowledge is through books. So the publication of books is the first principle of good government." Furthermore, as promulgated in the "Code of Keicho" (1615), provincial lords (daimyo) "must select men of ability for official positions under them. The art of government lies in obtaining the right men." "The clear admonition of the ancient sages," the order concluded, was that benevolent rule by the right men would lead to "prosperity," foolish, greedy rule to "ruin."[57] The same principle was present in the early Meiji era practice of attaching a Confucian adviser to the imperial court and persisted in a different form in the large but loosely defined powers of the Genro-in, or Council of Elders, which existed more or less formally until the 1930s and, indeed, has never disappeared as a concept in Japanese political thinking. Before the Pacific War, for example, the last survivor of the original Genro-in, Prince Saionji Kinmochi (1849–1940), was always consulted about important decisions. And it was said that, from Yoshida Shigeru's "retirement" in 1954 to his death in 1967, little of importance was decided in Japan until government emissaries had traveled to his country estate in Oiso for consultation—even though he had endured political defeat. The conviction was that considerable powers of government had to derive from the ancient wisdom and right principles of scholars and from the counsel of public-spirited elders. In fact, the Genro-in was a reversion back to more traditional practices after brief experiments in the early Meiji with a Kō-gisho (Public Deliberation Chamber) selected from the provinces and a Shūgi-in (Assembly Chamber), a sort of petitioning and questioning organ supposed to reflect public opinion. The idea that the people, even in limited ways, might take part in actually governing was simply too remote and inconceivable to push aside the central, ancient proposition that only firm rule in accord with right principle could result in good government.[58]

Higher law was understood as right opinion in accord with the public good (*seiron*) rather than "mass" opinion coming from the general populus (*shūron*) (see chapter 8). Closely allied with this reverence for higher law was a difficulty in seeing either the meaning of or the virtue in the idea of sacred individual rights. If democracy meant *beginning* with the innate dignity and rights and fulfillment of each individual and supposed that society and the state existed to protect and enhance those rights and that individuality, then minds nourished in traditional Confucian concepts would raise serious questions. In its baldest form, as Liang Qichao noted (again, see chapter 8), the idea of rights and individual aggrandizement seemed simply to endorse greed, selfishness, and, consequently, strife. This was the polar opposite of the Confucian ideal of social harmony resting, not on the rights of individuals as over against other individuals or society as a whole, but rather on correct and morally grounded relationships with other people. Hence, insofar as democracy exalted a sort of rights-defending individualism or a kind of social Darwinian struggle for survival and enhancement by individuals and even various private groups (conflict-of-interest politics), it would have little appeal in traditional East Asia. Rather, the need would be to refashion the notion of individual dignity so that it operated between people and within groups, finding fulfillment, not in private rights, but rather in social contribution—eventually as useful citizens enhancing the wealth and power needed for national survival, and eventually sustaining the moral correctness that was the ideal of all human life. Again, a third modernity approach, anxious to absorb the good in second modernity thinking to be sure, but also attuning itself to East Asian culture, came into view in a way requiring the recasting of democratic axioms (recall again Bertrand Russell's remark: "The distinctive merit of our civilization, I should say, is the scientific method; the distinctive merit of the Chinese a just conception of the ends of life"). As Dewey explained to Chinese and other audiences, the political manifestation of the scientific method was (second modernity) democracy, while for China "the just conception of the ends of life" could be realized only through a government of wise and public-spirited counselors and leaders.

A final, and perhaps most basic, reorientation seemed necessary from the very beginning of the contact of East Asian scholars with second modernity thought—encountering the notions of laissez-faire and "man versus the state." Politics as conflict of interest, minimal citizenship, and "roll[ing] back . . . the state" all had the effect of diminishing, trivializing, or corrupting the idea of the centrality and usefulness of the state and were again and again "read out" of East Asian perceptions of second modernity rationales for democracy. The point is seen most clearly, perhaps, in Yan Fu's version of Herbert Spencer's antistatism. To Yan, Spencer's explanation of how the limited British state had released the energies of its people, leading to its wealth and power, was still a theory of what the state ought to do—foster education, encourage trade, maintain law and order, and so on—in order to create the manifestly grand and prosperous nation and empire that Great Britain was in 1895. The state took the lead, in Yan's understanding; only then did wealth and power ensue. Yan, moreover, read Spencer's Darwinian emphases on struggle and survival of the fittest as applying especially to *states* competing, sometimes fighting, in a danger-filled world. Seeing things in these terms, Yan assumed that China needed, not less or limited government overall (such would surely lead to her destruction by powerful aggressor nations), but rather an active government empowered by an energized people benefiting from the scientific method and technological prowess brought in (by the government) from the West. This led Yan to condemn the ancient stagnation and autocracy of the Chinese state, but, at the same time, he did not see how the other half of the celebrated Western model of science and democracy, democracy, could be of use to China in its orthodox Western form as explained by Mill, Dewey, and others and as practiced in Great Britain and the United States. So what could *democracy* mean in an East Asian nation intent on modernization yet steeped in an understanding of government at odds with political precepts and practices—representative, "quarrelsome" democracy—thought to be part and parcel of modernity?

The answer is that the Confucian-based polities of East Asia accepted a commitment to (the second) modernity as earnest as that of Fukuzawa Yukichi and Liang Qichao in their first, enthusiastic acquaintance with Western learning. The scientific approach, the technological sophistication, and the social pragmatism of the West were especially and awesomely transformative. East Asia, that is, was to be part of the modern world, not only in trade and international relations, but also in many of the undergirding ways of thought. But, in the realm of government (an area, recall, where Leibniz had declared in 1699 that Western achievements were "beaten by the Chinese" and where Voltaire had said that "we ought to be their disciples"),[59] East Asian thinkers have had grave, even profound reservations that have led, through a multitude of twentieth-century revolutions, reforms, trials, and transformations in half a dozen or more polities, to rationales and practices of democracy often different from those in the West. Some of these rationales and practices have been (from an Anglo-American perspective at least) decidedly undemocratic. Others have significantly altered even nominally democratic guidelines. Yet it may also be true that there are evolving ideas and modes of government in some broad sense democratic ("energy from below," e.g.) that might even be usefully corrective to some of the very Western theories and practices of democracy that provoked the East Asian reservations about second modernity democracy in the first place. Organizing forums as part of legislative proceedings that listen to and take seriously the views of ordinary people might enhance the public perspective of those who then make the laws. Attending more to the *quality,* and not only to the *quantity,* of citizen participation might help overcome the mindless, circus-like aspects of democratic public life. And firm, vigorous, less partisan leadership, something like the model of a "patriot king," though elected and supported by the people, might help provide what Jefferson termed "the strongest government on earth" (see chapters 4 and 5). But, as these third modernity democratic alternatives came more into view, second modernity ideas were receiving more direct challenge from postmodernism in the West.

10

Postmodernism and a Fourth Modernity Democracy

Nietzsche, Heidegger, Foucault: "Supermodernism"

"The will to a system is a lack of integrity," Friedrich Nietzsche (1844–1900) wrote in *Twilight of the Idols* (1888), expressing what would become the central theme of postmodern thought, traced from Nietzsche through Martin Heidegger to Michel Foucault, Jean-François Lyotard, and Jacques Derrida. The pattern of thought assumes, Allan Megill has observed, "cultural crisis, a derelict present, [and] a nothing out of which everything must be created."[1] It thus reflects in some measure the critical, antiuniversalist mood of the first and second modernities that had caused first Alexander Pope to lament in 1729 of a "CHAOS! . . . [a] universal Darkness [that] buries All" (see chapter 4), and then Matthew Arnold to mourn in 1867 a world that "Hath neither joy, nor love, nor light, / Nor certitude, . . . / Where ignorant armies clash by night" (see chapter 6), and W. B. Yeats to cry out in 1920 that "Things fall apart; the centre cannot hold; / Mere anarchy is loosed upon the world."[2] This further turn of the wheel of modernity, a "fourth modernity," in the last third of the twentieth century, moreover, soon set forth its own version of and rationale for democratic government that both sustained the analytic, reductionist tenor of the earlier modernities and repudiated the "universalisms" that it saw as having developed in them. It contested, that is, the Enlightenment universalism spawned by the first modernity and the liberal orthodoxy of the second modernity as well as, though less explicitly, the from-on-high predilections of the third modernity. In thus rejecting what it took to be inconsistent tendencies of a "will to a system" in other modernities, however, and in stoutly insisting on difference, "otherness," and deconstruction, postmodernism is, in fact, itself a fourth or *super*modernism, skilled in critical analysis, and intent on parts (differentness) more than the whole. It is, one scholar observes, "the Cartesian critical intellect [at] its further-est point of development, . . . applying a systematic skepticism to every possible meaning."[3]

While questioning the entire Apollonian, Socratic, and post-Socratic tenor of Greek thought exalting the conscious, the logical, the scientific, the reasonable in human life and experience, Nietzsche emphasized instead the instinctual, the mythic, the subconscious, and the artistic dimensions. Socrates' flaw, Nietzsche declared, was to uphold "theoretical man" and to sustain the "profound *illusion* . . . that thought, using the thread of causality, can penetrate the deepest abysses of being," that one could "correct the world by knowledge, guide life by science, and actually confine the individual within the limited sphere of solvable problems." He argued further that the post-Darwinian, "scientific" thought of his day (sec-ond modernity) had, inconsistently, spawned "systems" of its own that proposed to "guide life by science" and otherwise impose orthodoxies and universalisms[4]— what postmodernists would later term *metanarratives*. Nietzsche's protest thus paralleled Bacon's first modernity strictures on "ancient" Aristotelian and Aquin-ist deductive systems and Thorstein Veblen's second modernity complaints that Adam Smith had abandoned first modernity empiricism by attempting to fashion "natural laws" of economics. To Nietzsche, the determined, rational system building of Comte and Marx and Spencer, and even the liberal "system" of J. S. Mill, re-created the "profound illusion" of rationalists from the time of Socrates that one could discern a "thread of causality" that encompassed human life and that set forth universal guidelines for its conduct. In the hands of those in power in modern, efficient states, these guidelines resulted in multiple oppressions built into all laws, institutions, rationales, and patterns of thought. Thus, even as main-stream, second modernity thinkers pursued their critical analysis of bourgeois rigidities and the genteel tradition, and traditionalists (and romantics) sought to "journey back to wholeness," Nietzsche saw that, nonetheless, the (second) mod-ernist tendency, after "the death of God," was to "unfold, unravel, or unweave" and to "awaken the idea of primal difference or differentiation" that anticipates "twentieth century uncertainty."[5]

In *On the Genealogy of Morals*, outlining the emphasis in Western thought on themes of dominance and of will to "systems" and power, Nietzsche noted that "even with good old Kant: the categorical imperative smells of cruelty." In *The Antichrist*, Nietzsche observed further: "A virtù arising purely from respect for the concept 'virtue,' as Kant desired it is noxious. . . . '[V]irtue,' 'duty' . . . with the character of . . . universal validity . . . are . . . but phantasms. . . . Exactly the opposite principle is required if life is to expand and develop: that each man should find his own virtue, his own categorical imperative."[6] Kant's injunction to "act only . . . to will universal law"[7] was merely another prescription and intervention impelled by an ideological and cultural will to universal behavior. The very words *categorical* and *imperative* reeked of dominion and authority—and the fact, furthermore, that they moved from German to English (and French) essentially without translation revealed the hegemony of Western thought and language. Martin Heidegger (1889–1976), the other forerunner, with Nietzsche, of late-twentieth-century postmodernism, bespoke a similar distaste for all forms of dominion and universalism that thus tended to suppress, ignore, or marginalize otherness, or "difference." Heidegger's thought can be understood only if one sees his preoccupation, as one student explains, with the "ubiquity of the finite" or, as another puts it, with "exploring how we should respond to otherness."[8] The essence, if one can use that term in discussing postmodern thought, is not in any core or central or universal meaning or cosmology or even ethic but, rather, in all the difference and diversity that infuse human discourse and experience. Of course, then, God is dead, Kant's categorical imperative is a "cruel" hegemony, and all metaphysics is "exquisite moonshine," as George Santayana once remarked. Even the apparently open-ended and tolerant empiricisms of the "old liberal" John Locke and the "new liberal" John Dewey were merely more subtle (some would say insidious) impositions of enclosing worldviews that neglected or marginalized difference and otherness while seeming to welcome them. Their rationales for democracy, by seeming to enfold them in a system, were in fact as dogmatic, and as hostile to difference, as the "closed societies" of Plato and Marx themselves (see chapter 7).

Heidegger challenges what he terms *Gestell,* a broad aspect of Western thought that "has always envisioned action as being guided by reason . . . and sustained by will, . . . [a] narrow, essentially teleocratic conception . . . within which action is identified with the production of effects guided by strategic reason." This mode of thought, dominant in the West since Aristotle, has permeated, not only traditional or ancient understandings, but also the various modernities that have done no more than rearrange the universalisms and the categorized and excluded others. (Various oppressions and tyrannies and hegemonic states are the political analogue.) Heidegger urges instead a posture of *Nähe,* or "nearness," in which humans, profoundly aware of their own finitude, are simply "present" to others and aware of their differentness, where the "everyday chatter of willing and wanting subsides and we really become open to hearing one another." This requires "unlearning" the modes and discourses of "modernity: the increasingly one-sided cognitive-instrumental orientation to the world expressing itself in the pressures for societal rationalization."[9] In this way, Heidegger's repudiation of the "mathematical conception of things," Manfred Stanley has noted, opposes a tradition in modern Western thought that includes Max Weber's history of "rationalization," the idea of "reification" in Marxist literature, and "instrumental reason" as discussed by the Frankfurt school. Oppositely, according to Stephen White, in Heidegger's thinking, "the genuineness of community rests upon a radical willingness to hear and experience the difference of the other."[10]

Heidegger's deep alienation from ubiquitous modern thought and culture, and his compulsion toward particularity and presentness, led him briefly to countenance Hitlerism as an alternative to universalizing, depersonal democratic liberalism (evoked brilliantly in, e.g., Herman Hesse's *Steppenwolf*), but, in the long run, the political implications of his thought were no more than suggestive. His "other thinking," basically "plural, unstable, motile, and unhierarchical," led him away from any of the modern forms of the state, whether fascist, Communist, or democratic. Rather, his "political theory" seemed to require an elimination of all the processes and discourses of modern governments with their "teleocratic, technocratic disposition over words, deeds, and things."[11] In fact, he scorned all major twentieth-century tendencies and repudiated any sense of universal purpose or direction. "The darkening of the world, the flight of the gods, the destruction of the earth, the transformation of men into a mass, the hatred and suspicion of everything free and creative," he said in 1935, "have assumed such proportions throughout the earth that such categories as pessimism and optimism have long since become absurd."[12] If there were no grounds for establishing preferable (to say nothing of universal) categories and not even any way, in being present to the "difference" that one faced on all sides, of distinguishing better from worse or a good direction from a bad, then it would seem that the whole realm of the political necessarily becomes at least problematic, if not overbearing, dangerous, and pathological.

If, as Heidegger once said, "in the most hidden ground of his essence, man is like a rose—without why,"[13] then there is no need to compel acceptance or to legitimize, no responsibility to act, and no implication for collective action. Room is left for little more than a predilection for a devolved, small, radical democratic politics. Heidegger thus shares with Thomas Jefferson (first modernity), John Dewey (second modernity), and Fukuzawa Yukichi (third modernity) a sense of human equality and a defiance of privilege and hierarchy, but he repudiates their assumptions that reason, analysis, and criticism tend toward convergence ("will to a system") and that societies can, thus, recognize common social purposes and move toward them politically—at least in any compulsive or elaborately organized way. Instead, Heidegger points (hesitantly and vaguely) toward "a small, radical democratic politics" that, by privileging "notions such as plurality, difference, motility, instability, dissemination, and lack of hierarchy, . . . does not become entangled within new discourses about legitimacy or justice." He thus seeks "a politics attuned to presencing . . . [that does] not initiate a new principal regime."[14]

Michel Foucault (1926–1984) in 1976, then well established as the successor to Jean-Paul Sartre and Claude Lévi-Strauss at the apex of Parisian intellectual life, picked up Heidegger's theme of alienation from "dominant modes of discourse" by noting that, since about 1960, there had emerged "a sense of the increasing vulnerability to criticism of things, institutions, practices, discourses." This pervasive vulnerability, Foucault declared, gave an "amazing efficacy [to] discontinuous, particular, and local criticism" (Heidegger's difference and plurality) but, at the same time, encountered the powerful "inhibiting effect of global, *totalitarian theories*," that is, the whole structure of Western thought, especially Enlightenment universalism. Foucault explains the Enlightenment (from Kant; *Aufklärung*) as "a singular event inaugurating European modernity and as a permanent process manifested in the history of reason, in the development and establishment of forms of rationality and technology, [and] the autonomy and authority of knowledge." "The Enlightenment's promise of attaining freedom through the exercise of reason," Foucault asserted, had, in its "will to a system," "been turned upside down, resulting in a domination by reason itself, which increasingly usurps the place of freedom." He explained that the tendency toward "established forms of rationality" and "totalitarian theories" was also powerfully present in such more modern movements as Marxism and psychoanalysis (Freudianism) and had, as a result, "proved a hindrance to research . . . [of the] autonomous, noncentralized kind"—necessary if Heidegger's emphasis on "plurality, difference, motility, instability, dissemination, and lack of hierarchy" was to achieve the presencing that contemporary circumstances required for it. A veritable "*insurrection of subjugated knowledges*" was needed, a surfacing from centuries of repression of the localized "historical contents," "the ruptured effects of conflict and struggle, that the order imposed by functionalist or systematized thought is designed to mask."[15]

Foucault insists on setting aside all the formal, "juridical" studies of the past that use the language and techniques and assumptions and integrations of orthodox scholars and that, thus, form a "discourse" that is itself complicit in the dominant forces in society. Instead, there must be a search for "a particular, local, regional knowledge, a differential knowledge incapable of unanimity and which owes its force ONLY to the harshness with which it is opposed by everything surrounding it." It is "these local popular knowledges, these disqualified knowledges" (at least to conventional scholarship), Foucault declares, that must be reclaimed if human history is to be understood. This is not to formulate a new "unitary discourse" (which would simply institute another "functionalist theory" of domination) but, rather, to "just go on, in a cumulative fashion," to set forth a "genealogy" where, "on the basis of the descriptions of . . . local discursivities, subjected knowledges . . . would be released . . . [and] brought into play."[16] Foucault thus undertook searching studies of prisons, institutions for the "insane," the control of human sexuality, and even schools, clinics, and psychiatric hospitals to reveal "lately liberated fragments" of how the increasingly pervasive institutions of the modern state (particularly since the sixteenth- and seventeenth-century rise of capitalism) actually impinged on, disciplined, and oppressed ordinary people. The "genealogies" of prisons and insane asylums, for example, examined from the standpoint of their effect on and categorization of the "inmates," show the institutions to be instruments of control and discipline serving the needs of the dominant economic forces and political sovereignties. Schools, clinics, hospitals, and customs and laws regulating sexual behavior are no less oppressive, if more subtle, means of controlling deviations or differences subversive to dominant forces. The theories and ideologies, all tending more or less toward general, universal, "scientific" expression, that rationalized and justified and even criticized (from within) these institutions and practices were a "dominant discourse" that implicated social science and all other dimensions of modern, Enlightenment thought. (In this way, Foucault's argument is a sort of follow-up on 1960s broadside attacks on the Establishment, paralleling his own sympathy for the radical politics of 1968 in France.) Not only did he condemn the pervasive bourgeois liberal thought of the West, but he saved particular scorn for Marxism and psychoanalysis, to him both prototypical universalisms. That "Soviet psychiatry is indeed the best in the world," he observed in 1976, "is precisely that which one would hold against it."[17]

Instead, reflecting Heidegger's profound alienation from what he took to be the systematizing, intrusive, controlling nature of the whole Western intellectual tradition from Plato onward, Foucault saw that tradition, and the institutions that it rationalized, as in complex relation to the power of dominant forces. One had to be wary especially of a "descending type of analysis" that sought to see causation go from the needs of the dominant bourgeois, capitalist forces to the pervasive mechanisms of discipline and control in modern society. (For example, reasoning that went from the need for an orderly, submissive workforce to justifying institutionalizing the "insane.") Instead, "what needs to be done is something quite different," Foucault insisted. One needed to investigate, historically, locally, and "at the lowest level, how mechanisms of power have been able to function." "Families, parents, doctors, etc." had to be studied "in precise conjuncture" to see "the mechanisms of exclusion that are necessary, the apparatuses of surveillance, the medicalization of sexuality, of madness, of delinquency, all the micromechanisms of power, that came, from a certain moment in time, to represent the interests of the bourgeoisie." At this "certain moment in time," the reasons for which Foucault said needed to be studied, these mechanisms of exclusion and control (applied, e.g., to madness and "deviant sexuality") began "to reveal their political usefulness and to lend themselves to economic profit . . . [so that] they came to be colonized and maintained by global mechanisms" embodied in "the entire state system" of the world. This dominant worldwide hegemony (the liberal corporate state of the twentieth century [see chapter 7]), Foucault explained, was interested, not in madness or infantile sexuality in order to "treat" or "cure" them or even to understand their "differentness," but rather in the power that is exercised by "the complex of mechanisms with which delinquency [of various kinds] is controlled, pursued, punished, and reformed, etc."[18]

In pursuing this focus on the actual, pervasive exercise of power in modern society and the modern state, Foucault accorded fundamental importance to "the production of effective instruments for the formation and accumulation of knowledge—methods of observation, techniques of registration, procedures for investigation and research, apparatuses of control." Power came to be "exercised through these subtle mechanisms" of thought, which become part of "the techniques and tactics of domination." These "mechanisms" and approaches to study were, Foucault pointed out, the assumptions and the methods of second modernity social scientists. Their research, theories, and policy analysis ("discourse") provided the undergirding and compulsive (universalizing) rationale for the observations, investigations, and registrations that, bureaucratized, became the means of power and control by the dominant social forces. Conventional languages of rights and formal "juridical" power were used and incorporated (or, rather, co-opted), but, as the techniques and discourses of the social sciences exert their authority, there comes into play, Foucault asserts, "the global functioning of what I would call *a society of normalization.*" These "procedures of normalization," given authority by the "dominant discourse" of social science (or liberalism, or structuralism, or Marxism), moreover, increasingly invade and supersede the formal meaning of rights and of "welfare"; in Foucault's language, they "engage in the colonization of [the precepts] of law." The result is a pervasive system that controls and oppresses any "nonnormal," different, "other" element in society. This happens, not only through the institutions and procedures of the modern corporate state, but more fundamentally through the "discourse," the psychology and social data and theories of the orthodox (second modernity) intellectuals, that rationalizes and authorizes, in the form of allegedly objective and universal guidelines, the interests and institutions of dominant power.[19]

In critiquing this pervasive and "colonizing" style of thinking, Foucault complains that it engages in only "the illusion of autonomous discourse."[20] For him, there is simply no such thing as research, analysis, or theory that is in any way either objective or "free" from the subjugating influence or perspective of the narrator. In fact, any claim of objectivity is alienating because, by bringing the allegedly unbiased state of mind of the narrator into the discourse, it also excludes by not simply presencing the subject and not allowing for its difference—thus engaging in profound oppression of Heidegger's otherness. The very claims for neutrality and scientific objectivity, that is, serve only to require "others" to accept intellectual foundations that assume that universally valid, unparticularized concepts can exist. Foucault sees the history of Europe since the sixteenth century, and especially since the eighteenth, as a series of events where the need for universalizing (creating "sameness") has, in a kind of Hegelian dialectic, repeatedly also created "the Other." Hence, for example, the elimination by modern science of one excluded Other, leprosy, required the creation of another, madness, which then had to be defined, enclosed, and "treated" with the allegedly objective but actually alienated and alienating techniques of modern psychiatry —in effect, exclusion and oppression. The emergence of clinical medicine subjected bodily illness to the same sort of "objectifying gaze" from the "expert" physician, while the modern prison, on Bentham's model of the "panoptic" (all-seeing) penitentiary, similarly subjected the "inmates" to the observation and corrective measures of the dominant ideology. In all cases, there was a "political technology" at work, one that "serves to reform prisoners, ... treat patients, instruct school children, confine the insane, supervise workers, [and] put beggars and idlers to work" and is applied "whenever one is dealing with a multiplicity of individuals on whom a task or a particular form of behavior must be imposed."[21] In no case were the "others" seen or even present in their own terms; instead, they were classified and objectified in ways that enhanced the controlling ideologies and institutions of the dominant power. Everything—institutions, bureaucracies, ideologies, and especially language and methods of research, explanation, and categorization ("discourse")—was implicated in the "will to power" of the dominant class. Again, in Heideggerian terms, rather than encountering difference as difference, there was always the attempt "to enclose it within identity" as defined by the (objective, universal) paradigms of the ruling order.[22]

In his *Madness and Civilization* (1961), Foucault tried to recapture "the experience of madness" before its "objective" categorization in the late eighteenth century through the "invention" of psychology and psychiatry, which "thrust into oblivion all those stammered, imperfect words without fixed syntax in which the exchange between madness and reason was made." The claim of the social and medical scientists to be observing with "a trained and neutral eye" was utterly false and had the effect both of concealing the "undifferentiated experience" of madness and of subjugating the constructed (by the psychologists) experience to the canons of the dominant order. The developing disciplines of psychology and psychiatry, then, were rife with a "scientific pretension and theoretical blindness, . . . committed to a positivistic methodology in which measuring, counting, and calculating took a pride of place" that made them worthless, misleading, and dangerous.[23] The result was a deeply flawed, self-aggrandizing, totalitarian ideology masquerading as "science." (One is reminded of Veblen's attack on the classical economics of Adam Smith, supposedly drawn from the enlightened knowledge and scientific understanding of the eighteenth century. Smith and his successors were "not satisfied with a formulation of mechanical sequence" [*narrative* in postmodern terms], Veblen pointed out, but had to exercise "some sort of coercive surveillance over the sequence of events, . . . to formulate knowledge in terms of absolute truth . . . [and] natural law." Instead, Veblen called for a "habit of mind which seeks a comprehension of facts in terms of cumulative sequence . . . that leaves no place for a formulation of natural laws in terms of definitive normality" [see chapter 6]. That is, this second modernity charge against Enlightenment compulsion toward natural law clearly parallels Foucault's fourth modernity condemnation of Enlightenment and even of second modernity universalism.)

Foucault argues that the development of Western thought and society in the nineteenth and twentieth centuries (i.e., since the Enlightenment and the Industrial Revolution) has followed a twofold course. On the one hand, a "heterogeneous" path exists between a "superimposed" ideology of rights and a "democratization of sovereignty," that is, the idealized view of the liberal corporate state. On the other hand, a "closely linked grid of disciplinary coercions also exists whose purpose is in fact to assure the cohesion" of a society that otherwise, through its "rights" and "democratic sovereignty" aspects, tends toward disorder and autonomy. But it is this "grid of disciplinary coercions," this "polymorphous disciplinary mechanism," that actually exercises power in a modern polity and enforces a "normalization" according to universal guidelines that sustain the dominant (oppressive, privileged) forces. These disciplinary forces, moreover, "engender . . . apparatuses of knowledge," a "discourse of the human sciences" that "invades" the realm, or discourse, of rights and popular sovereignty in a way that "colonizes" it, renders it subservient to the needs of the "normalizing" dominant power. It is this invading, colonizing, "scientific" way of thinking, this "will to a system," dominant in the West especially since the Enlightenment, that enfolds and categorizes all difference and otherness (in its own terms) and, thus, constitutes "the general mechanism of power in our society."[24]

Foucault declares, however, that it is a "blind alley" to attempt to oppose or struggle against the controlling, disciplinary, oppressive mechanisms of power in the modern state by appealing to the rights and sovereignty of the people. Their constitutive institutions and patterns of thought (schools, "correctional" institutions, corporate capitalism, political theory, judicial system, etc.) have been so co-opted that they have become "absolutely integral" parts of the dominant discourse. It is no good, that is, to use the language of rights and democratic sovereignty to oppose the dominion and oppression since that language (discourse) accepts and "thinks within" the very paradigms that also undergird the "normalizing mechanism," the universalizing social scientific "apparatuses of knowledge" of both the first and the second modernities. There is no point, for example, in trying to improve treatment of prisoners and those accused of crimes by appealing to their "rights" because the very concept of rights assumes and accepts the existence of a state that must somehow "protect" the rights but that is, actually, always at the disposal of oppressive forces. Instead, Foucault suggests, "if one wants to look for a non-disciplinary form of power, or rather, to struggle against disciplines and disciplinary power, it is not towards the ancient right of sovereignty (even popular sovereignty) that one should turn, but towards the possibility of a new form of right, one which must indeed be anti-disciplinarian, but at the same time liberated from the principle of sovereignty" — and, perhaps more profoundly, liberated from "a system of psychological reference points borrowed from the human sciences." Following Nietzsche, Bonnie Honig finds the answer in the fact that "politics," in the grand sense of a people in struggle and conflict finding their way to fulfillment, "is one of the casualties of modernity, and its preoccupation with acquisition, safety, and salvation. . . . Human beings have changed. . . . Politics in modernity [the liberal corporate state] has been all too successful in its project of containment, control, and disempowerment," especially of the Other.[25] The path, then, that postmodern liberating government must take (if, indeed, it can in justice "govern" at all) is toward some "new form of right," some new understanding of what justice means, and away from the very idea of sovereignty, the principle that there should be an ultimate, controlling power, a "state" at all, in 2000 and beyond — Locke, Jefferson, Mill, and Dewey invalidated, as are, of course, East Asian ideas of the state as the highest embodiment of civilization.

Antifoundationalism and Deconstruction: Lyotard and Derrida

Jean-François Lyotard (1925–1998) sustains Foucault's search for (nonhegemonic) "new forms of right" and reformulations of the idea of sovereignty by emphasizing the ad hoc, the contextual, and the local. He scorns particularly the modern "mythologies" of Enlightenment "liberation" of humanity from political constraints and triumph over physical ones and of post-Hegelian quest for the speculative unity of all knowledge. By their very intellectual methodology ("discourse style"), these mythologies enfold and co-opt, or exclude, marginalize, stigmatize, and oppress difference and otherness by attempting to bring everything within allegedly universal guidelines and paradigms. Hence, Lyotard summarizes, "I define *postmodern* as incredulity toward metanarratives," the latter his term for all the "hegemonic" philosophizing and theorizing of the Western intellectual tradition, up to and including both the Marxist-Leninist and the liberal democratic ideologies current in the twentieth century. Lyotard rejects "Newtonian anthropology," including such modern constructs as systems theory and structuralism that "follow a logic which implies . . . that the whole is determinable . . . [and that] allocate our lives for the growth of power." So, Lyotard asks, after the exposure ("deconstruction") of these metanarratives, "Where can legitimacy reside?" "Consensus obtained through discussion" (e.g., à la Jürgen Habermas) is out because it "does violence to the heterogeneity of language games," that is, to the necessarily subjective and partial nature of all theories, explanations, conclusions, and rationales. Rather, "postmodern knowledge, . . . not simply a tool of the authorities, refines our sensitivity to differences and reinforces our ability to tolerate the incommensurable."[26] (The affinity to Heidegger is evident here.)

Applied to social and political understanding, emphasis is turned toward the plural, the local, and "a justice of multiplicities." "The discourse of law and that of the State," all political inquiry in the Western tradition, Lyotard asserts, is based on a "presupposition which guarantees that there is meaning to know and thus confers legitimacy upon history." All political "statements" have their own "speculative language" derived from a supposed meaningfulness that excludes other discourses—all sustained by "The University, [which] as its name indicates, is its exclusive institution." That is, the self-proclaimed higher learning is itself deeply complicit in the "language game" of validating the dominant power and marginalizing all others. The "crisis," however, "accumulating since the end of the nineteenth century" and related to the "progress in technology and the expansion of capitalism," rests most fundamentally on "an internal erosion of the legitimate principle of knowledge [itself] . . . , an erosion at work inside the speculative game." Thus, "disciplines disappear; . . . the speculative hierarchy of learning gives way to an immanent, . . . 'flat' network of areas of inquiry."[27] The political dimension of this is the disappearance of any single, overarching theory of justice or even a legitimate foundation for the state at all—what Bonnie Honig sees as the inadmissibility of "the would-be perfect closures of god, self-evidence, law, identity, or community." Instead, as another scholar explains it, there is a needed sense of "a decentralized plurality of democratic, self-managing groups and institutions whose members problematize the norms of their practice and take responsibility for modifying them as situations require."[28] Though Lyotard is hesitant about pursuing or systematizing political "knowledges," there is, nonetheless, a strong affinity between the delegitimizing of the whole Western "speculative game" and a tendency politically toward a decentralized "justice of multiplicities." In another hint of how to escape a mere morass of "multiplicities," Lyotard states that "what brings us out of capital and out of 'art' [modern conceptions] . . . is not criticism, which is language bound, nihilistic, but a deployment of libidinal investment"—presumably, the emotional and egotistical (*Dionysian* in Nietzsche's categories) rather than the rational.[29]

Moving in a way that he regards as more fundamentally postmodern, more deeply repudiating of Apollonian "logocentrism" (the emphasis on reason, light, and system in Western thought since Socrates), Jacques Derrida (b. 1930) explains: "The concept of centered structure is in fact the concept of a play [of words] based on a fundamental ground, on . . . a reassuring certitude, which itself is beyond the reach of [such] play." All the notions, even the slightest hints, including those in a generally postmodern mode, that suggest anything like the "centered structure" typical of traditional inquiry (including political) reflect a proclivity for "reassuring certitude" and "fundamental ground" that is simply out of place, inherently inadmissible and illegitimate, in postmodernity. Derrida thus insists, for example, that Foucault's claim to have written a history of "madness itself . . . before being captured by knowledge," that is, to have set forth a genealogy, a narrative, of the actual experience of madness before its scientific "discovery" and (mis)explanation by scholars during and since the Enlightenment, is itself a complicit manifestation of the language of reason. "All our European languages, the language of everything that has participated, from near or far, in the adventure of Western reason," Derrida explains, "nothing within this language can escape the historical guilt" of logocentrism. Even all the critique and condemnation that "the postmodern condition" directs at the Enlightenment and modernity, supposedly from outside the dominant tradition, is not a repudiation but actually a further, if highly sophisticated, engagement in the language game of objectifying universal reason—logocentrism.[30] Thus, Derrida concedes that a reasoned critique of modernity, in the mode of Foucault, Lyotard, and others, is meaningless and impossible (as well as complicit) because it accepts the language games, the social science methodology, of the dominant power.

Allan Megill points out that, if, following Nietzsche, "God is dead, then we all live in secondariness." Derrida names this secondariness *writing*. That is, all that remains after the demise of universal and final meaning, and after all the multitudes of logocentrisms and language games that in Western thought have elaborated and legitimized them, are the words themselves. "Texts" are simply "there," to be deconstructed, but not with the idea of, "through the manipulation of words and letters, to find a path back . . . to God" and to meaning. Rather, "Derrida takes the manipulation of words and letters as something close to an end in itself; for Derrida there is nothing beyond the letter, no primal voice speaking a long-concealed truth." By attacking the messenger, the language and text itself, so to speak, Derrida in effect renders the message (the theory, the universal idea) nonexistent. Deconstruction is, then, not a method of manipulation, or criticism, finding meaning, or a progressive evolution, or a dialectic of thesis, antithesis, and synthesis (logocentrisms), but rather a way "to make a given text mean anything at all"—or nothing—thus denying "the priority of text over interpretation." "Text was reduced to pretext" where all that was left was the deconstruction itself, the text having been "nullified." "The text to be interpreted becomes . . . the product of its own supposed exegesis. Interpretation . . . becomes an end in itself, no longer seeking justification in its attempt to reveal the meaning hidden in an 'original text'"—because there is no (larger?) meaning in the text and, in any case, there is no language game (discourse) capable of elaborating meanings even if they existed.[31]

Thus, in repudiating the whole logocentric tradition of Western thought, its dominating expression in the Enlightenment, and even its critique by postmodern thinkers (especially Foucault, who, Derrida asserts, fell into the very logocentric trap that he faulted in others), Derrida in a sense brings postmodern thought full circle—one might say to its logical conclusion (though Derrida, of course, would deny the very ideas of *logical* or of *conclusion*). The words, the "texts" of the Western tradition (and, presumably, of other logocentric traditions such as Islam and Confucianism), are deconstructed to have no rational or objective meaning(s), thus losing their significance and their "priority" over the words of the deconstructing critic. But these words, like all other "word games," are without communicability except as manifestations of the subjective existence of the deconstructor. The American Declaration of Independence is, for Derrida, no more than a "fabulous retroactivity" where the signers have "invented" themselves, as founders, by adding, after the fact really, a "constantive," the "Laws of Nature and of Nature's God," to the "performative utterance" "We hold," which they had seemed to declare, as the grounds for what they had done—simply what had happened. That is, the "self-evident truths" were there because they were "held" by "we," that is, the signers; that's all. The Declaration, thus, was essentially a word game, without meaning, until deconstructed by another "subjectivity" such as Derrida himself. In any case, the notion that the Declaration and the Constitution, which claimed to rest on it for ultimate authority, were somehow legitimately foundational, resting on universal, natural law, was a mere fable of some self-appointed "signers."[32] Again, criticism has been "prioritized" over text in a way that leaves the text itself without meaning. Hence, courses studying any allegedly canonical text, for example, will ordinarily read much more criticism than text itself because all there is to understand is not in the text itself but in the situation and method of the criticism that has engaged in the deconstruction. The impact on political inquiry of any kind is even more destabilizing and disorienting than was the case for the "earlier postmodernists" whom Derrida challenges (he repudiates the enterprise of postmodernism and the label *postmodern* often designated to him). For him, there is simply no way to entertain intelligibly the traditional questions of political inquiry or to evaluate the nature of political regimes—except to negate (deconstruct) all previous commentaries and all existing regimes.

The result is a language of "politics" and an understanding of "democracy" (the words themselves lose customary connotations in postmodern discourse) that deny foundationalism in theories of reality, in concepts of human nature, and in ideas of history, resting, instead, on contingency, pluralism, and difference. The world is a place of "agglomerate possibilities" without necessary order where what has happened and what might happen form no pattern and are finally indeterminate anyhow. Hence, the realm of political thinking is understood as one of acceptance and invention where being open to and creating new possibilities are much more in order than understanding or applying any existing ideology or practice. In looking at the world, one sees a "plurality of heterogeneous spaces" that spawn a "plurality of cultures and discourses."[33] Thus, there is no possible master plan for the world, no political ideal (such as democracy) to which all societies might or should aspire, and no universal concepts of justice. All that can be hoped for, even facing death, is a "few rules that can help us move about our existence in a non-chaotic and undisorganized way while knowing that we are not headed anywhere."[34]

The role of the political theorist, contra Plato, Locke, or Marx, is not to evaluate and set forth ideals of justice or other political conceptions but, rather, to interpret texts with complex analyses open to challenge and to facilitate communication across diverse and autonomous traditions, that is, to acknowledge and respect difference. The result is both a politics of identity and a politics of difference where any (heterogeneous) identity is at once defined and undermined by its difference. That is, any group finds part of its own particular identity through its various contacts (migration, conquest, secession, oppression, etc.) with other groups and is, at the same time, made aware of how its identity is not special (a chosen people), or universal, but simply different. Since this vital process of differentiation always takes place within an interplay of dominant and subordinated groups and forces, however, politics in some degree must be

more than cognizant of differences. It must as well encourage and foster differentness rather than hegemony, especially among the myriad oppressed (marginalized) groups, in ways that nourish multiculturalism—*democratic cosmopolitanism*,
as Bonnie Honig terms it (see below). Apart from this differentiated group identity, which is understood both to separate groups and to provide important bonds
among individuals within them, postmodern political thought resists any conception of a self-willed, rational, autonomous person. Rather, it speaks of "subjects"
who are "regarded as complex combinations of relatively random components . . .
patched together out of a variety of different bits of values, identities, and beliefs;
dispersed or decentred . . . creative . . . inventive in ways unknown to the modernist subject."[35]

Oppression, Marginality, and the Politics of Identity

Though this critical, deconstructive approach to the political realm, with its
opposition to theory and systems and universals (metanarratives), tends powerfully to repel any broad understanding, or reformulation, or refounding of democratic government, political conceptions can be expressed in a postmodern
way. The whole, postmodern political commentary, moreover, though expressed
originally by German and, recently, especially French thinkers, has had major
reference to the mainly Anglo-American "liberal" ideology (second modernity).
In *Justice and the Politics of Difference* (1990), for example, the American theorist
Iris Young elaborates "a positive sense of group difference and a politics that
attends to rather than represses difference," which, she declares, "owes much
to . . . such postmodern writers as Derrida, Lyotard, Foucault, and Kristeva."
She thus "appropriates a critique of unifying discourse to analyze and criticize
such concepts as impartiality, the general good, and community." "What are the
implications for political philosophy," she asks, "of postmodern philosophy's
challenge to the tradition of Western reason?"[36] (Many other challenges, with
often similar arguments, could be cited, of course.)

Young focuses this "challenge" on the idea of "distributive justice" as it had
come to be rationalized and practiced in the liberal corporate state (what Young
terms the *welfare corporate society*) of the twentieth century. Questions of participation and of justice, or fairness, were there resolved "in a context of interest-group
pluralism where each group competes for its share of public resources"—precisely
the notion of conflict-of-interest politics explained by Arthur Bentley in 1908
(see chapter 6) and embodied in the practice and theory of democratic government in most of the world during the twentieth century (see chapter 7). For
Young, this model of self-government has two "normative defects." First, its
"privatized [self-interested] form of representation and decisionmaking" does

not require any "appeal to justice" and, thus, tends to see all expressions of interest as equally worthy in pursuit of particular goals. Second, inequalities in the "resources, organization, and power" of the various (all legitimated) interest groups allowed some to dominate while others had little or no voice, thus undermining the principle of equal access to political power in an allegedly democratic system.[37]

Hence, Young proposes a different understanding of justice that, while responsive to postmodern ideas of otherness and differentiation, nonetheless retains grounds for distinguishing among claims for influence: "Justice [is] the institutionalized conditions that make it possible for all to learn and use satisfying skills in socially recognized settings, to participate in decisionmaking, and to express their feelings, experience, and perspective on social life in contexts where others can listen." Thus, Young moves toward a politics where justice is understood in terms of "institutionalized conditions" or "socially recognized settings," that is, in terms of groups. These groups, moreover, have been formed by social and cultural circumstances, by response to dominating values, and by institutions that at once oppress and differentiate and internally solidify the group. Thus, race and gender and sexual orientation, for example, are understood, not as hereditary or biological "facts," but rather as social constructs flowing from the history (narrative) and experience of the group. This narrative and experience, though much varied among and between groups, nonetheless produces five general categories of oppression: "exploitation, marginalization, powerlessness, cultural imperialism, and violence." (These were the experiences, of course, of the "insane," the imprisoned, the "sexually deviant," and the other oppressed groups whose "genealogies" Foucault had narrated.) The disadvantages and oppressions that these groups have felt and continue to feel, moreover, in the United States and other "democratic" countries, at least, come, "not because a tyrannical power coerces them, but because of the everyday practices of a well-intentioned liberal society."[38] Justice, that is, is not something to be "established" to accord with universal norms (as, e.g., the U.S. Constitution implies) but, rather, something that is understood as a response to the various habituated and institutionalized experiences of groups within a dominant culture. It is, thus, in a way both beyond government and sustained by it in myriad ways that make a mockery of the ideological pretensions of liberal democracy.

Young lists, "among others, women, Blacks, Chicanos, Puerto Ricans and other Spanish-speaking Americans, American Indians, Jews, lesbians, gay men, Arabs, Asians, old people, working-class people, and the physically and mentally disabled" as "social groups" that experience one or more categories of oppression. Justice then means, first and foremost, the alleviation of the marginalization, or the powerlessness, or the cultural imperialism, and so on, afflicting these and other groups. Old people who are "laid off from their jobs and cannot find new work," young people, especially blacks or Latinos "who cannot find first or second jobs," single mothers "involuntarily employed," and American Indians on reservations, for example, are oppressed by "marginalization," being excluded from the means of livelihood and fulfillment in society. Working people lacking "professional" certification and, thus, denied status and respect, and women kept from promotion because of their gender, suffer from a "powerlessness" not experienced by professional white males. Perhaps most insidiously oppressive of all is "cultural imperialism," where the dominant group in a society (in the United States, white, professional, heterosexual males) imposes its norms on all others. Thus, differences such as those of "women from men, American Indians or Africans from Europeans, Jews from Christians, homosexuals from heterosexuals, workers from professionals, become reconstructed largely as deviance and inferiority." The various forms of oppression, moreover, not only separate the experience of these groups from that of the dominant culture, but also heighten "a sense of positive subjectivity" within the group that defines its own understanding of justice.[39] What W. E. B. Du Bois called a *double consciousness,* a "sense of always looking at one's self through the eyes of others, of measuring one's soul by the tape of a world that looks on in amused contempt and pity," "devalued, objectified, [and] stereotyped," brands the oppressed groups as "different, marked, or inferior."[40] This experience and double consciousness, however, create a sensibility and power within the group that both define its conception of justice and propel it against the norms of the dominant group. These groups must be understood, then, as the basic units in society and the foundation of the definition and quest for justice in any polity.

Though, like most postmodern thinkers, Young is deeply critical of liberal democracies as they exist in the United States and elsewhere, she sees some hope that, with major changes, a politics of difference might grow in them. Two particular revised directions are required. First, there must be "a positive sense of group difference, . . . which might be called democratic cultural pluralism, . . . [where] there is equality among socially and culturally differentiated groups, who mutually respect one another and affirm one another in their differences." In this understanding, at the core of one's sense of identity and fulfillment as a human being, one's "social existence," is "attachment to specific traditions, practices, language, and other culturally specific forms." The essence of oppression in human history, especially the implicit forms common in liberal democratic societies, is that, "in everyday interactions, images, and decisions, assumptions about women, Blacks, Hispanics, gay men and lesbians, old people, and other marked groups continue to justify exclusion, avoidance, paternalism, and authoritarian treatment." To correct this, not only must the oppressed groups ("often an 'affinity group' in a given situation with whom I feel most comfortable"), constructed in part by the very exclusions and denials that they have experienced, be acknowledged and accepted (Heidegger's otherness), but their self-identity, their social cohesion, their organization, and their "voice" in public affairs must be actively nourished and encouraged. Only then can any regime be meaningfully participatory and truly rest on the consent of the governed. Any political understanding that denies this and assumes, instead, that citizens are or should be rational, autonomous decisionmakers oriented toward universal ideals or the common good, or even assumes "rational choice" by individuals or special interests and then expects compromise among them, simply misunderstands and abuses the very nature of the political. Rather, given the realities of social existence in contemporary societies, group identities (especially of oppressed groups) must be heightened and foregrounded if there is to be justice.[41]

Second, as oppressed groups develop in their sense of identity, in their understanding of their just needs, in their social skills and organization, and in their orientation toward public affairs, they must also have a guaranteed voice in the public life of the polity. "In group-differentiated societies," Young observes, "conflict, factionalism, divisiveness, civil warfare, do often occur between groups." But, since these conflicts are caused mainly by "relations of domination and oppression . . . that produce resentment, hostility, and resistance" and that privilege those already skilled at manipulating and exercising power, the oppressed groups must have a special voice, perhaps even a veto, in matters of public policy that especially affect them. Thus, "a democratic public should provide mechanisms for the *effective* recognition and representation of the distinct voices and perspectives of those of its constituent groups that are oppressed or disadvantaged" (emphasis added). "Public resources" should support the "self-organization of group members . . . [to] achieve collective empowerment" and an understanding of where their experience and interests fit in society. Then, institutions are needed where group analysis, group perspectives, and group generation of policy are listened to, deliberated on, and taken into account when decisions are made. Finally, there must be "group veto power regarding specific policies that affect a group directly, such as reproductive rights policy for women, or land use policy for Indian reservations." Democracy thus means that otherness must be acknowledged and valued, that justice and equality are defined and understood as arising from the "narrative" and experience of oppressed groups, that these groups are made visible and given voice in ways suited to their cultural norms, though not necessarily in the privileged, articulated ways of the dominant group. Finally, groups must themselves have a decisive voice on policy questions affecting them most directly—even if that means something other than majority rule where that is merely the will of the dominant group.[42] (The idea is perhaps something like John C. Calhoun's notion of "concurrent majorities" where measures must gain not only the overall majority vote in a legislature but also the "concurring majority" of the representatives of the group most directly affected, as, e.g., representatives of fishermen, frontier farmers, or textile workers and cotton planters on, respectively, fishing rights treaties, land prices, and tariffs on imported cloth.)[43]

Young defends these procedures as different from and preferable to conventional "interest-group pluralism" (or conflict-of-interest politics) in that they require, not merely advocacy of self-interest and strategic compromise, but also deliberations that require explanations of the "social justice" grounds of the proposed perspectives and policies. She also insists that giving groups "veto power over policies that fundamentally and uniquely affect members of their group" will not necessarily simply stall decisionmaking but might facilitate and even "justify" it by altering "the structured relations of privilege and oppression." That is, people in oppressed groups, nourished, encouraged, and empowered to speak up and take part, by surfacing differences and conflicts, might enlarge overall understanding, identify points of convergence among previously oppressed and silent groups, and altogether level the playing field so that the engagement can proceed fairly. Even stalled decisionmaking might sometimes be "just" if it prevented the imposition of oppressive policies by the (previously) dominant group[44]—justice being understood as arising from the experience and felt needs of various oppressed groups, rather than as conformity to universal principles. John Dewey, of course, in another modernity, had made somewhat the same point in repudiating all conceptions of natural law.

In condemning universalism and upholding "democratic cosmopolitanism," Bonnie Honig raises the question of how much citizenship in a democratic nation might require allegiance to and even affection for the polity and for its allegedly universal principles—as, in the United States, "I pledge allegiance to the flag . . . and to the republic for which it stands" or in the pledges in naturalization rites and officeholding to honor and defend the Constitution. To Honig, this puts legal immigrants in the position of being valued "givers" of loyalty, energy, and productivity as they take up residence and become citizens. Illegal immigrants, including exploited migrant workers, are, on the other hand, seen as "takers," who, while contributing an "instrumental" productivity, take away from the affective loyalty that a committed citizenship embodies. Thus, what Honig calls "the myth of an immigrant America" sustains a view of the good or "model" immigrant who is welcome as over against the "bad" immigrant who needs to be deprivileged or sent away.

Honig wonders whether this myth might be "redeployed as part of a counter-politics of foreignness"—perhaps a version of Heidegger's presencing of otherness or of Young's politics of difference. Instead of supposing that the immigrant, legal or illegal, needs to be required to subscribe to the national myth by becoming a citizen of the democratic nation and taking part in its political practices (and sent away if he or she does not), Honig urges that democracy be understood as taking place prior to citizenship and in the act of being present in a place, even though outside national institutions. The ideas of membership in a polity and the assumption, thus, of political obligation, as in Lockean thinking, are absent. By his or her possession of a worthy cultural pluralism (prior to corruption by a greedy, self-centered, passive American consumer culture), the immigrant is positioned to act democratically (and patriotically) simply by being on the scene and able to act outside the flawed (non)democratic institutions set to coerce and require national membership. Thus, the "expansion of alien suffrage," for example, might encourage a "democratic cosmopolitanism" usefully corrective to the exclusion of diversity present in "Americanization" processes. "Promoting social and worker movements," Honig supposes further, "might help win for presently unrepresented populations a voice in institutional self-governance as well as greater autonomy in daily life." Finally, to further "denationalize democracy," Honig urges support for "transnational" groups such as Women Living under Islamic Law, Amnesty International, and Greenpeace that hold nations "accountable for their treatments of persons and public goods." The point of this "democratic cosmopolitanism," she concludes, "is not to replace the state with an international government," since the state was "an important potential and actual organizer of social welfare and justice as well as a potentially powerful ally to [struggling] citizens and groups." Rather, the need is for "social democrats to find ways to offset the still too singular power of the state." Instead, for example, of illegal immigrants being "criminalized and denationalized" by democratic nations (as often happens), their social and political energies should be mobilized into effective, probably transnational, action against the dominant not-really-democratic power—"workers [and migrants] of the world unite?"[45]

Honig's postmodern view of the state, especially the United States, then, is scorn for its past and present self-proclaimed but misnamed democratic liberalism and hope for ways to diminish the oppression and authoritarianism of its ideology and institutions—in the manner of Foucault. As with Lyotard, Young, and many other postmodern political theorists, the argument is not necessarily to abolish the state, or to turn away from the democratic form, but rather to seek ways to radically decentralize, populize, or even disempower it. These latter intentions are not completely foreign to second modernity democratic thinking, of course, but, because of assumptions of (according to Megill) "cultural crisis, a derelict present, [and] a nothing out of which everything must be created," the postmodern version of them focuses much more on criticism (deconstruction) than on reconstructive ideology or institution building.

Postmodern Democracy

Honig and Young seek to reconceive American democracy in what Young terms "a critique of the ideal of universal citizenship" and Honig calls the "too abstract universalism of America's democratic constitutionalism." "A general perspective does not exist," Young states, flatly denying Enlightenment universalism, "that all persons can adopt and from which all experiences and perspectives can be understood. . . . The existence of social groups implies different, though not necessarily exclusive, histories, experiences, and perspectives . . . and implies that they do not entirely understand the experience of other groups. No one can claim to speak in the general interest." The classical and Enlightenment models of rational citizens discerning the common good and applying universal principles of justice in their participation in public affairs (discussion, voting, officeholding, jury duty, community activism, etc.) are irrelevant in modern "group-differentiated societies," not only because many "citizens" are ignorant or biased, but also, and more basically, because there simply are no such principles. Any claims to them are only the "self-deceiving, self-interested" views of dominant groups, which always tend "to assert their own perspective as universal."[46] Young and Honig thus echo Nietzsche's assertions that "the will to a system is a lack of integrity" and that Kant's "categorical imperative smells of cruelty," Heidegger's insistence on "otherness" and "difference," Foucault's repudiation of "the inhibiting effect of global, *totalitarian theories,*" and Lyotard's "incredulity toward metanarratives." Postmodern conceptions of democracy, then, reject explicitly the Enlightenment ideals of natural (universal) law that undergirded first modernity democracy and the U.S. Constitution, the "scientific" reformulation of those principles in second modernity democracy, the universal-tending institutions and processes of the liberal corporate state of the twentieth century, and East Asian ideas of government resting on any modernized (including Communist) version of the mandate of heaven.

In fact, in a way harking back to the chasm between the Aristotelian and the Confucian understandings of government and modern, liberal, post-Hobbes-Locke ones, postmodernists simply approach the realm of the political and see the nature of the state differently—from both "ancients" and "moderns" (see chapters 2 and 4). "If by democracy one means," theorizes Honig, "a set of arrangements that perpetually generates popular (both local and global) political action as well as generating the practices that legitimate representative institutions," then the assumption by those whom she terms *virtue theorists* (Kant, John Rawls, and Michael Sandel, e.g.) "that it is possible and desirable to contain or expel the disruptions of [conflictual] politics has antidemocratic resonances." That is, when seekers after universal ideals of self-government, whether Enlightenment believers in natural law or modernist upholders of conflict-containing (and enfolding) democratic processes, have their way, the Other, which is always present in any configuration of public life, "is then dehumanized, criminalized, or ostracized" by an (otherwise inclusive) political community. The "outside others," the "remainders" of any and every real political process (always productive of argument and conflict), are "depoliticalized" by the "disavowing [of] their political genealogy [i.e., group identity, in Young's terms], function, or significance." Hence, the democratic rationales of the first and second modernities are, in their efforts to enshrine themselves in natural law or liberal metanarratives, in effect "antidemocratic." The understandings of government as embodied in the U.S. Constitution, the "refounding" of the American polity in the Progressive era, and the British social democracy of the twentieth century, for example (see chapters 5 and 6), by "displacing politics with bureaucratic administration, jurocratic rule, or communitarian consolidation," have simply betrayed politics by substituting the "cruelty" of hegemonic rules (government itself?) for the conflict and populist unfolding (not enfolding) of real politics. A postmodern "democratic politics of augmentation," on the other hand, must "seek out the [inevitable] rifts and fissures of foundational identities and constitutions, . . . not consolidate them; . . . calls up for contest [group] identities; . . . saves spaces of alternative perspectives and forms of life; . . . resists the states' organization of politics into approved spaces and formats; . . . [and] decenters the state as the owner and licensor of politics."[47] Altogether, then, postmodern rationales of democracy, rather than authorizing forms and processes of self-*government,* authorize attitudes and practices of populist democracy as much outside the state as the liberal corporate state makes necessary.

John Locke, Thomas Jefferson, and J. S. Mill are not so much repudiated as simply set aside. Liberal democracy is not assaulted and overturned in the manner of either Mussolini or Lenin, for example (though some of their critical analyses are accepted), but rather "deconstructed," its fundamental assumptions and processes challenged and invalidated. There is no quest for a "führer" or for a single, supreme party, conceptions abhorrent to postmodern tendencies toward otherness, differentiation, decentralization, and devolution of power. Instead, there is persistent effort to reaffirm the diversities and multiplicities of ordinary folk around the globe. In fact, though postmodern political thinking generally sets aside talk of "human nature," if that implies that there might be something common or universal about humankind, it nonetheless embodies a potent understanding of the human species. Somewhat in the fashion of Locke's insistence on the sense-impressions-created diversity of human beings, and of Mill's idea of "individuality," and of Dewey's of an infinitude of "felt needs," and of Laski's "inexpungable variety of human wills," postmodernism (like previous modernisms) rests on parts and eschews or condemns wholes. Indeed, the whole is often understood, not even as the sum of the parts, but often as rather less than the sum. Postmodernism adds, however, a vastly enlarged emphasis on the socialized and "genealogized" human being situated in social groups formed most fundamentally by the experience of marginalization and other oppressions by dominant forces (something like Marxist alienation of workers). Such groups, not the autonomous, rights-possessing individuals of liberal or rational choice theory, are the basic elements of any modern society. The study of humankind, then, must seek to understand the narratives and situations and identities of these groups and their problematic relation to metanarratives (philosophy, cosmology, ideology, scientific method, religion, historicism, etc.) and to "metainstitutions" (especially the modern state). Throughout, the emphasis is on openness, acceptance, awareness of the Other and of infinite, indelible, unpremeditated differentiation—a sort of uncompetitive Darwinism.

Thus, there is no center, no convergence of reason, no universal principle, no history, no scripture, no God, from which to derive an idea of a good or just society applicable anywhere anytime. Mosaic tablets, the New Testatment, the Qur'an, the Confucian mandate of heaven, the (secular) heavenly city of the eighteenth-century philosophers, the Declaration of Independence, and, of course, a Hegelian "state as God marching through history" or a Marxist dialectical materialism, all are deconstructed and set aside as dangerous delusions and impositions, varieties of "the will to a system," cultural imperialism, state hegemony, globalization, and so on. Rather, justice derives from the genealogy, situation, and experience of oppression of the many groups that make up any modern society. Only that narrative and experience, moreover, can define justice (as felt by any group). Though elements of need and intention may be overlapping among groups, the sense of justice remains specific to each group, is only incompletely communicable outside the group, and is resisted persistently by the dominant power because the group claim is always corrosive of its dominion. Hence, the "good society" is one where (oppressed) groups are enabled and encouraged to understand and sustain their particular identities and where the ethos is one of accepting otherness and differentiation—diverse and multicultural. Cross-cultural understanding, cross-group experience, cultural diversity, toleration, openness, and the presencing of otherness become the hallmarks of the good society and the essence of justice.

Within this sense of human nature and its implications for a good or just society, the nature and purpose of government becomes problematic. On the one hand, the exposure of the mechanisms of oppression imposed through the state by the dominant forces in society would seem to require radical change, perhaps total reconception of the role and purpose of a nonetheless active government. On the other, the very idea of government, especially any idea that implies universality of application—for example, Thomas Paine's claim in *Common Sense* (1776) that "the cause of America is in great measure the cause of all mankind" or the call of *The Communist Manifesto* (1848) that the "workers of the world unite"—is called into question. So notions of government vary from a near anarchism required for genuine openness to the Other and to difference (government is, thus, seen as necessarily an instrument of conformity and dominance) to a potential instrument for the liberation of "affinity groups" from the domination of even a liberal corporate state—though how the power of government might unbind or liberate or presence diversities and othernesses without becoming itself a means and force of oppression and domination remains uncertain. (The approach to the law itself by critical legal studies, e.g., repeatedly illustrates the tension.)

In general, however, postmodern thinking seeks to move democracy away from centralizations of power and toward various ways to foreground, enhance, and empower previously stigmatized or marginalized groups. Provoked and horrified by the hegemonic language and the global intentions and institutions of both sides in the hot and cold wars from 1914 to 1989–1991 (as well as the hegemony of "the end of history" proclaimed in 1989), some postmodern theorists (or antitheorists) have turned away resolutely from all the powers and forms of government. Corporatized democratic regimes and totalitarian and authoritarian ones are seen as similarly, perhaps even equally, flawed—Bush-Cheney-Rumsfeld and Blair-Straw as bad as Saddam and "socialism with Chinese characteristics"?

This turning away from theories and the efficacy of government leaves postmodernism in a curious place in the Third World. Half a century after the general demise of the formal colonial empires and the designation of the Third World as the less developed, the "outsider" in the cold war between the First (free) and the Second (Communist) Worlds, its experience of modernization (or Westernization or economic development) has been problematic at best. Failure, instability, poverty, the persistence of traditional ways, and the presence of various forms of neocolonialism have left many societies and nations exceedingly skeptical of, even deeply hostile to, many of the modernities of the liberal corporate state held up as models. Making effective use of such staples of democratic polities as open elections, competitive political parties, legislative give-and-take, and freedom of expression has been especially uneven, in a way even highlighting the limitations of those devices in the First World. Socialist liberation movements, modernist in ideology and style, have not generally been more successful. Benedict Anderson and other scholars have pointed out that, in Southeast Asia at least, the very idea of the nation-state, to say nothing of its democratic version, is a Western intrusion that seeks to impose those universalisms—another cultural imperialism. Hence, the postmodern critiques of technological growth, corporate power, commercial ethos, social science engineering, bureaucracy, nationhood, and even democratic processes —all forms of hegemony—often resonate powerfully in Caracas, Tehran, Cairo, Calcutta, Lagos, and other centers struggling with and nearly overwhelmed by the compulsions of second modernity development and progress. Thus, "postmodern themes," Pauline Rosenau notes, "including anti-Enlightenment views, anti-modern attitudes, a return to fundamentalist indigenous spirituality, anti-science sentiments, and opposition to modern technology," seem often to be appropriate responses.[48] Even though liberal, democratic, market economy ideas and institutions have by no means become pervasive in the Third World, their ambiguity or failure and their sponsorship and even imposition by dominant Western powers make postmodern analysis seem on target.

The Third World reaction, for example, often sees modernity as having a corrupting, oppressive effect on indigenous cultures and diversities. In Salman Rushdie's *The Satanic Verses* (1989), a fictional fundamentalist religious leader (modeled on Ayatollah Khomeini?) declares the Western (second modernity) understanding of history and development "the creation and possession of the Devil, of the great Shaitan, the greatest of lies—progress, science, rights."[49] An Indian postmodernist, upset at the cultural imperialism of British colonial rule in India, even questions British-imposed laws against suttee, the Hindu custom of widows ascending the funeral pyres of their late husbands. Such laws, Gayatri Spivak asserts, deny to women a voice of their own that might understand their immolation as a fulfillment of marital fidelity and moral excellence. Without approving it, Spivak calls for the state to be neutral vis-à-vis suttee. Governments must not impose, require, or prevent in ways that judge or condemn difference or otherness or impose universal guidelines from the "hegemonic metanarratives" of dominant powers. In any case, the resolution of the question of suttee must come from within the differentiated culture of the group, not from an outside power, which necessarily lacks authority.[50]

The postmodern impulse in the Third World thus has as its initial message the nourishment of traditional, local mores in a way evocative of Heidegger's preference for the "plural, unstable, motile, and unhierarchial" and his repudiation of second modernity's "teleocratic, technocratic disposition over words, deeds, and things." The practical effect is to seek banishment of as much of the colonizing influence as possible and to look toward preservation of long-standing local, decentralized customs, values, and modes of social organization, whatever those might be. The organizational, intellectual, and technological power of the second modernity (and its characteristic liberal corporate state), however, is often sufficiently embedded, and sufficiently attractive to indigenous people, to prevent its irradication and, thus, often sustains huge and problematic contradictions amid local othernesses. Furthermore, the indigenous cultures themselves often possess or generate potent hegemonic metanarratives of their own with at least as much tendency toward oppression, exclusion, and denial of difference as those of the colonizing powers. (One is somehow reminded of the Japanese reaction to Tagore's effort to uphold Asian spiritual values against Western technology and materialism: that would simply deny Japan the benefits of second modernity industry and power and hinder the development of a Japanese nationalistic metanarrative [*kokutai*] able to survive in the modern world [see chapter 9].) Thus, postmodernism in the Third World both highlights some of the weaknesses and dangers of the second modernity outlook and second modernity institutions, including its rationale for democracy, and the difficulties present when Third World societies must nevertheless, so it seems, face the question of organizing and rationalizing government in the twenty-first century (see chapters 8 and 9).

The effort to bring postmodern guidelines into an understanding of government is in a way reminiscent of Locke's projection of first modernity thinking to form ideas of self-government. In *An Essay concerning Human Understanding* (1690), Locke pointed out that the formation of individual identity by a multitude of sense impressions results in a "variety of pursuits . . . wherein it will be no wonder to find variety and difference. . . . Though all men's desires tend to happiness, yet they are not all moved by the same object. Men may choose different things, and yet all choose right."[51] The postmodern analogue is the emphasis on differentiation and nonjudgment, though the unit is often the group, not the individual. If government suppresses these differences and blocks the various paths that persons choose for their happiness (their freedom), that, according to Locke, is tyranny and justifies rebellion, organization, and action to overthrow the regime. The postmodern analogue is the urge and need for oppressed groups to crystallize their own identities and to resist the power of the dominant group. Then Locke posits a "contract" where the freed people form a government protective of their rights and suited to their convenience—"just government derived from the consent of the governed." The postmodern ana-

logue is the repudiation of all the structures and forces of bureaucratic government (Foucault's "society of normalization") and the need to reconstitute
somehow on new premises that accept the presence of all differentiations
(Honig's "democratic cosmopolitanism"). In the Jeffersonian corollary to
Locke, the variety of men's desires and intentions in the "pursuit of happiness,"
and the contrary tendency of powerful states to manage or homogenize them,
requires a strong bias toward decentralization and local control. The postmodern analogue is, following Lyotard (and others), a "decentralized plurality of
democratic, self-managing groups and institutions whose members problematize the norms of their practice and take responsibility for modifying them as situations require." Though how this might be worked out in an actual frame and
rationale of government may not be precise and comprehensive (suspect anyhow because of affinity for metanarrative), certain corrective directions for
modern government are at least pointed out.

There must be, as Young explains, a deliberate presencing of previously
oppressed groups, an encouragement and facilitation of their sense of identity, an
attention to their narrative and situation, and a privileging of their voice in public
affairs to "level their place on the playing field" with the already-entrenched
dominant groups. Pressures and movements toward centralization, homogeni-
zation, bureaucratization, certification, even any exaltation of the idea of national
sovereignty itself, all must be resisted because of their strong tendency to repress
the very qualities and circumstances essential for ensuring justice to groups. *The
politics of difference* and *the politics of identity* become the watchwords, rather than
a politics of universal principles, or of *conflict of interest,* or even of *individual
rights.*[52] To again cite Lyotard, "legitimate principles of knowledge . . . [and] disciplines disappear," and an "immanent, . . . 'flat'" approach to the political realm
emerges. Any idea of the purpose of government itself, when deconstructed, very
nearly loses intelligibility, leaving legitimate only such unpremeditated circumstances and procedures as emerge from the accepted presence and interaction of
the liberated groups.

The idea of democracy, then, has taken another step further along the path of
modernity laid out by Bacon and Locke in the seventeenth century, by Mill and
Dewey two centuries later, and then by Fukuzawa and Liang in East Asia. In this
fourth conception, the basic "parts" are understood, not as individuals, but as
affinity groups oppressed, not just, as traditionally, by tyrants, but also by the
very nature of contemporary society and liberal government. Thus, the just or
good society is one responsive to the needs and integrity of the oppressed groups
rather than to any allegedly universal values or institutions that define right and
justice from above or outside. Marxism, Islam, divine right monarchy, the Confucian mandate of heaven, Enlightenment natural law, the UN "Universal Dec-

laration of Human Rights," and even twentieth-century procedural democracy are all proscribed as being "foundational," "hegemonic," "closed." Thus barred from imposing any universal guidelines or even procedures, and confined to "situational" responses to the senses of justice of oppressed groups, the purpose of government is limited in a way analogous to the laissez-faire dimension of second modernity thinking: governments should do very little because almost anything that they might attempt will simply interfere with the (private, idiosyncratic) needs and fulfillments of the diverse parts of society. At most, governments might remove barriers, level inequities, open paths previously closed, and otherwise facilitate survival and justice as defined by the needs and aspirations of groups. On the other hand, this liberating function might, in the eyes of some groups, require large, enforced interventions in existing circumstances, which very quickly raises scepters of power and hegemony and authority and structure that have been identified in postmodern thinking as the very essence of oppression and tyranny. In any case, the understanding of, and rationale for, democracy achieved in the last third of the twentieth century is a further modernization that both extends and profoundly alters earlier modern-tending efforts to conceive self-government as good government.

11

Comparing Rationales for Democracy

"There was, in the beginning, *no word,* but only myriad voices that could have been interpreted in any number of ways," one scholar has written,[1] to encapsulate postmodern, deconstructionist thought. The very essence of classical, Middle Eastern, and any other "logocentric" universalism, "In the beginning was the Word" (John 1:1), is consciously struck down. The "Word," whether Platonic idealism, whether Mosaic commandments, whether "made flesh" in Christianity, whether the Four Books and Five Classics of the Confucian tradition, or whether recorded in the Qur'an by the Prophet, was from on high, expressed in timeless, honored language, and set forth as universal, the beginning, the source, the foundation, the truth. One way or another, from Bacon to Derrida, various modernities challenged these universalisms, including secularized versions such as natural law philosophies and liberal humanism. Roughly, the universalisms objected to were Comte's age of theology (pre-Bacon), age of philosophy (the Enlightenment), and age of science (liberal, post-Darwinian scholarship). Each age, or modernity, provoked in response traditionalist "cries of the heart," pleas for "souls on fire," efforts to reassert "the center," and so on. Always, however, the target was the fragmenting, empirical, specializing, reductionist, or at best "scientific" systemizing tendency of the various modernities.

Transcendental and Empirical Critiques of Baconian Modernity

To minds like Bacon and Descartes—"nimble and versatile enough to catch the resemblances of things . . . [and to] distinguish their subtler differences" and intent on "learning what is new"—"ancient," more traditional, thinkers had opposed "forms," "argumentation," and "invented systems of the universe" (see chapter 4). The emphasis is often to assert unapologetically the wisdom of the time tested and the traditional, to take seriously the transcendental and even the mystical, and to see the cosmologies, ethics, and political theories thus embodied as universal truths. When, in 1802, William Blake asked England

> To cast off Bacon, Locke, and Newton from Albion's covering,
> To take off his filthy garments and clothe him with Imagination,

and pled,

> May God us keep, from Single vision and Newton's sleep,[2]

his target was precisely the "Single vision" of the first modernity (Baconian induction and science). It had engendered, Blake thought, both English empirical philosophy and the attendant revolutions—technological, commercial, and industrial—that had made Britain the wealthiest, most powerful "modern" nation in the world. As Ernest Gellner has put it, the inductive, scientific, technological, modern world we live in had begun to be defined, "above all, by the existence of a unique, unstable and powerful system of knowledge of nature, and its corrosive, unharmonious relationship to the other clusters of ideas ('cultures') in terms of which men live. . . . One particular style of knowledge . . . proved so overwhelmingly powerful, economically, militarily, administratively, that all societies have to make their peace with it and adopt it."[3] To Blake, and to others, however, it was a world of "dark Satanic Mills" and the single (mundane, scientific) vision where the human spirit was reduced to dissecting and calculating and mastering—recall Thoreau's scorn for the railroad and the ice cutters disturbing the deep reveries of Walden Pond.

Both the transcendental (or romantic or spiritual) and the ancient repudiations of the first modernity, then, rested on a sense of its narrowness, its superficiality, its lack of profundity, its mundaneness, its materialism, and altogether its immense incompleteness in understanding human nature and the human condition. As Theodore Parker had put it, the "sensational system . . . [of] Locke . . . Hobbes . . . Hume" was "quite insufficient." Instead, Parker found wisdom in the works of Kant and others who explained "certain great primal intuitions, . . . facts of consciousness given by the instinctive action of human nature itself" that sustained a depth and completeness of understanding missing in first modernity thought.[4] This sensibility, added to the continuing critique in the tradition of the Augustan ancients (see chapter 4), also insisting on the insufficiency and transitoriness of the "sensational system," carried forth a counterpoint to modernity, coming "from the outside." That is, they repudiated its emphasis on the parts, its inductive methodology, its scientific materialism, and its preoccupation with new knowledge. Instead, they turned to traditional and transcendental principles and insights with, they insisted, timeless and universal implications. Sustaining the Apollonian-Dionysian, the Confucian-Taoist, the Hellenic-Hebraic, and other millennia-old tensions, these compellingly articulated universalisms were always present as criticism and alternative to all versions of modernity.

Also present was an "internal" critique of the first modernity that claimed simply that it had not followed through consistently on its own guidelines. By not being rigorously modern enough, it had, in fact, fallen into the supposedly repudiated universal-oriented thinking (*metanarratives* in postmodern terminology) of the ancients and the transcendentalists (often overlapping and closely allied). Instead of less Bacon, more was needed; instead of less science, less "sensational system," more was needed. The danger, to these critics, was not that modern thought would lose any sense of center or certitude. Indeed, Baconian induction seemed to require such a loss. Rather, the danger was the tendency for the very intensity of pursuit of parts and of new knowledge, and the application of the new methodology, to spawn universal systems ("centers") of their own—systems that were necessarily inconsistent and illegitimate in the modern world of parts, analysis, critique, and discovery. One of Newton's disciples, for example, wrote: "Natural science is subservient to purposes of a higher kind. . . . To study Nature is to study into His [God's] workmanship; every new discovery opens up to us a new part of His scheme. . . . The philosopher, while he contemplates and admires so excellent a system [as the Newtonian universe], cannot but be himself excited and animated to correspond with the general harmony of Nature."[5] This and other elaborate conceptions of natural law and natural rights, nourished by Locke and the foundation of the eighteenth-century rationalism and universalism of Jefferson and others, were, even in the early analysis of David Hume, simply unwarranted projections. That there were, or could be, causal connections among physical and social phenomena that revealed higher harmonies or natural laws could not be sustained by an empirical outlook that insisted on the validity of only sense impressions—observations, facts, evidence, objectivity. Enlightenment universalism, natural law, and "the heavenly city of the eighteenth-century philosopher" were as much inadmissible products of rationalist "will to a system" as the "metanarratives" of Augustine and Aquinas themselves.

The basic critique by Hume and his successors, then, was that the projection to system and universal laws, especially in the social sciences, by followers of Newton violated the very empiricism that they claimed to have learned from Bacon. Hume had noted that many writers (he mentioned Locke, Shaftesbury, and Mandeville, among others) "have begun to put the science of man on a new footing," and he even subtitled his early *Treatise of Human Nature* (1740) *Being an Attempt to Introduce the Experimental Method of Reasoning into Moral Subjects.*[6] This tendency to projection came, it seemed, from the inability to escape from the deep need for and commitment to something more than the parts or even simply the sum of the parts. Having shown that even "natural religion," the idea of a reasonable, "watchmaker" God (deism), was incompatible with a consistent empiricism, Hume posited a fragmented, mundane, incomplete (though perhaps prosperous and sophisticated) world as the true legacy of the first modernity. "'Tis impossible," he wrote, "*upon any system* to defend either our understanding or senses; and we but expose them farther when we attempt to justify them in that manner" (emphasis added). Yet, though Hume's immediate targets were the various religious and philosophical "dogmatists" of his day, he could not abandon his own attention to the big questions of causation and universal principles: "I cannot forbear having a curiosity to be acquainted with the principles of moral good and evil, the nature and foundation of government, and the cause of those several passions and inclinations which actuate and govern me. I am uneasy to think I approve of one object, and disapprove another; . . . decide concerning truth and falsehood, reason and folly, without knowing upon what principle I proceed."[7] Even in his own espousing of a "new science of man" it seems that Hume failed, from the standpoint of Lyotard and other postmoderns, to follow through with a necessary "incredulity toward metanarratives" (see chapter 10). Indeed, Bacon himself had written of a "New Atlantis," a utopia where the "connection or concatenation" of all things led to "perpetual and uniform laws . . . [that] did ascend to unity . . . [and] which appeareth to be Metaphysic."[8]

Second Modernity Political Evolution in the United States

The political dimension of Hume's critique of "any system" came into view only very slowly in the American polity, where first modernity thought had had its most significant political manifestation (see chapter 5). The new American polity was founded squarely on Lockean concepts of empiricism, of the rights and the convenience of individuals, and of the need for mechanisms of government responsive to the consent of the governed. To justify independence, the Declaration of Independence said simply: "Let Facts be submitted to a candid World." The Preamble to the Constitution (1787) declared further that it was the parts, "we the people," who were forming "a more perfect union," a framework, in order to gain for themselves the many blessings of good government. Good government would come, "Publius" noted, from "reflection and choice," not, as from time immemorial, from "accident and force." The framers of the Constitution were in general, and in the case of James Madison and some others quite specifically, attentive to the theme of Hume's influential essay "That Politics May Be Reduced to a Science" (1752). Gordon Wood picked up the same theme in calling his commentary on the Constitution "The American Science of Politics."[9] The checks and balances built into the Constitution itself and the dynamic for the benign interaction of "so many interests and parties" (factions) explained by Madison in *Federalist* no. 10 all presupposed the inauguration of what George Washington in 1788 termed a *political machine* that would manage and enhance the welfare of the people according to their needs. The government was to be based on facts and on attention to individual rights and to a variety of interests—a matter of "reflection and choice." It would operate as a machine, that is, be modern.

But it was also to be, in the famous phrase of James Russell Lowell, "a machine that would go of itself," in accord with laws of nature that were themselves timeless and universal.[10] The Constitution and its explanation in the *Federalist Papers*, Washington declared, "will merit the Notice of Posterity . . . [and] will be always interesting to mankind so long as they shall be connected in Civil Society . . . [because they] so ably discuss the principles of freedom and the topics of government."[11] The Constitution was understood as higher law, in accord with natural law principles. Madison had examined the performance of "Ancient and Modern Confederacies" to weigh the evidence, pro and con, about the effectiveness of various ways to define, divide, and exercise powers of government. "Experience," he asserted, "is the oracle of truth; and where its responses are unequivocal, they ought to be conclusive and sacred."[12] In typical post-Newtonian Enlightenment fashion, Madison moved easily, without any sense of inconsistency, from a survey of the "facts of history" to propositions that he regarded as true, unequivocal, conclusive, and sacred, that is, universal. And these propositions, paramount and fundamental, were understood as embodied in the Constitution (including the Bill of Rights) even as it was also understood as framing a process of government open to experience, discovery, and, as time went by, the changing needs of those consenting to be governed. Jefferson himself declared, in 1816, that he did not regard constitutions "with sanctimonious reverence, . . . like the ark of the covenant, too sacred to be touched." In Baconian fashion, he insisted: "Laws and institutions must go hand in hand with the progress of the human mind. As that becomes more developed, more enlightened, as new discoveries are made, new truths disclosed, and manners and opinions change with the change of circumstances, institutions must advance also, and keep pace with the times."[13] To his mind, this was not inconsistent with holding certain "Truths to be self-evident" and with finding "the Law of Nature and of Nature's God" entitled to the respect of humankind.

Thus, the rationale for self-government that derived from first modernity thinking, though startlingly different from customary, ancient concepts of government and faithful to ideas of attention to the parts (individuals), of discovery of new "truths," and of changing needs and intentions, was also still caught powerfully in a "will to a system." This is evident in almost every sentence of the political writing of the founding era, federal as well as antifederal, Hamiltonian as well as Jeffersonian. Just as this universalistic thinking (embodied in Chief Justice John Marshall's opinions and, thus, writ large in American constitutional law) was, as Jefferson saw in a way, a kind of betrayal of first modernity inductive thought, it was also itself subject, almost from the beginning of government under the Constitution, to challenge by ideas and forces intent on "more modernity."

Traditional notions of nonpartisan leadership in the public interest (adhered to by the first six presidents), attached to universalist propositions, were accused of being (as postmodern critics would also say) instruments of domination by elite groups. Martin Van Buren, advocating a more modern dynamic for American politics, declared in 1820 that factions and political partisanship "arouse the sluggish to exertion, give increased energy to the most active intellect, excite a salutary vigilance over our public functionaries, and prevent that apathy which has proved the ruin of Republics." "The very discord thus produced," he concluded, "may in a government like ours, be conducive to the public good."[14] To Van Buren and others who formed the second party system in the United States after 1820, arousing and organizing all the diverse interests of the polity, and then welcoming contention in the public arena, was a fuller manifestation of democracy than the elite-guided, nonpartisan ideal of the founding era. Though he claimed fidelity to the ideals of the founders of the American polity, Van Buren actually shifted the theory and practice of government away from their universalist assumptions and toward what he regarded as a more consistent dynamic of responsiveness to the pluralism of the parts (like Bentham) and of acceptance of the benignness of their interaction. He was on the road to understanding American politics in a way that profoundly undermined the universalizing aspects of its founding. At the same time, he set forth new guidelines that pointed toward a second modernity politics. The Lockean, first modernity guidelines, perhaps inconsistently, had combined with more traditional and universal understandings to become the foundation for a republic that then itself seemed not entirely faithful to the diverse energy and "discord" implicit in any modernity. Van Buren and his Jacksonian colleagues, in insisting on these dimensions, moved American politics on toward a more thorough modernity. We might say that, what Hume was to the heavenly city of the eighteenth-century philosophers, Martin Van Buren and other Jacksonian era politicians were to the republican vision of the American founding: they insisted on accepting the partisanship and discord of a free and diverse people, for whatever it was worth in public life. The same general shift occurred in Great Britain as the reality of the contentious, dynamic party politics of Robert Peel, Disraeli, and Gladstone overtook the ideal, at least, of a parliament of king, lords, and commons consulting and acting together for the good of the realm as a whole.

The Critique of Second Modernity Liberalism

A similar pattern was evident as new rationales for democracy continued to develop under the influence of insistently modern thinking. As Bentham had acknowledged in his own repudiation of natural law, if one was a consistent, modern empiricist, attending only to the wants and needs of the individuals composing society (the greatest happiness of the greatest number), then the social guidelines and the laws of a self-governing polity would have to rest on a responsiveness to some kind of aggregation of those wants and needs—nothing else, and nothing more. When J. S. Mill emphasized freedom of expression, individuality, the clash of ideas, and the faithful representation of interests in parliaments in order to achieve progress (imperial China, stagnant, custom bound, and autocratic, was for Mill the obvious antithesis), he further elaborated the new rationale for self-government. Herbert Spencer's understanding of "man versus the state," seeing the very idea of government (in its traditional forms) as a dangerous "will to a system" oppressive to individual energies, further demystified the political realm, leaving it only minimal functions of preserving law and order. Spencer insisted that a scientific understanding of how human society actually worked, acknowledging all its diverse and evolutionary energies, precluded any government-sponsored grand or cosmological directions (metanarratives). Then, when T. H. Green, John Dewey, and others reclaimed government from what they regarded as Spencer's dogmatic scorn for it (laissez-faire was *his* metanarrative), they in effect recast it in its proper scientific, pragmatic, modern form—what Dewey termed a *new liberalism* (see chapter 6). Veblen, Holmes, Laski, the Webbs, and other second modernity thinkers regarded this formulation of democratic, science-based government as fundamentally critical of, and finally free from, the natural law assumptions, with their inadmissible universalisms, of first modernity models of self-government.

In East Asia, as Confucian-trained scholars sought to understand second modernity thought and to apply its precepts to their own nations, they saw it initially as a potentially powerful tool for upsetting the ancient thinking and stultifying traditions that made China and Japan so "backward" in a competitive, aggressive, and technologically advanced world. Fukuzawa thought it necessary to "rid our country of the influences of the Chinese [Confucianism] altogether" by introducing the Western "spirit of personal independence" so that people could "start a new enterprise" and otherwise work efficiently "for the benefit of the nation" (see chapter 8). Yan Fu thought that Spencerian ideas of enhancing the skill, the education, the energy, and the dynamism of the people, by liberating them from oppressive, stagnating circumstances, would gradually bring to China the wealth and power required for survival and progress in the modern world (see chapter 8). Notions of "science and democracy" thus stimulated Japanese and Chinese intellectual life and helped set East Asian politics on the road to traumatic changes in the twentieth century. Somewhat in the manner of Western ancients, however (one thinks, e.g., of Swift and Carlyle), some East Asian scholars and political leaders drew back from the more fragmenting, conflicting, and antistatist ideas rife in second modernity thought. To them, the traditional ideas of a harmonious common good and of the paramountcy of the political were simply too deeply foundational for them to find attractive precepts of conflict-of-interest politics, of emphasis on individual rights against the government, and of the absence of higher law. Their effect in the long run, Liang Qichao declared, "can only be conflict and murder . . . [and] the collapse of civilization."[15] A rationale for democracy in East Asia, it seemed, would have to include in some fashion ideas and means that would assure guidance, probably through strong leader-intellectuals, according to higher principles—analogous to the mandate of heaven?

The new-liberal rationale of democratic government, however, more and more dominated mainstream political thinking, first in Anglo-America, then in modernizing societies around the world. It became the theoretical foundation for the twentieth-century liberal corporate state. This rationale, moreover, was elaborated and crystallized in its century-long contest, ideologically and geopolitically, with the candidly antidemocratic dogmas (metanarratives) of fascism and communism. As F. A. Hayek, Barbara Ward, Karl Popper, Eric Hoffer, John Rawls, and a host of other political thinkers faced off against the totalitarianisms and illiberalities of their day, they formulated as well theories of modern, liberal democracy that more and more achieved an orthodoxy, a claim to universal validity, a metanarrative, of their own. From Popper's upholding of capitalist and socialist "open societies" against Platonic, Hegelian, fascist, and Marxist "closed societies" in the mid-twentieth century, to Francis Fukuyama's declaration at the end of the cold war that the triumph of liberal democracy was so complete (especially at the level of ideology) as to have achieved "the end of history," a remarkable hegemony developed. There seemed to be no viable or even visible antithesis to it, as political thinkers and leaders worked to complete the rationale for the liberal corporate states that had won the cold war. Profound and searching arguments among academic political theorists, liberals and conservatives, communitarians and libertarians, including Jean Bethke Elshtain, Alasdair MacIntyre, Michael Walzer, Sheldon Wolin, Joshua Cohen, Donald Moon, Stephen Macedo, Amy Guttman, Will Kymlicka, and Cass Sunstein, refined and critiqued the liberal corporate identity but, on the whole, worked within its parameters.[16]

The broad liberal orthodoxy of the late twentieth century was also a key part of the developing rationale for nationhood—what Benedict Anderson has called *imagined communities*—that has been an important part of the spread of modernities around the world. With traditional ideas of political community (those based on universal, bonding empires or dynasties) under attack, and as Locke and others fashioned a rationale for democracy suited to modernity, the concept of modern nationhood, a community shaped around a sense of a people gathered as an imagined polity for defense and outreach, became a dominant motif, first in Western Europe, then elsewhere in the world. With the slow but steady growth of more liberal, representative government in Great Britain and, then, the energetic projection of the French Revolution, especially as a romantic, people-based nationalism, amalgams of government of and for the people (and even by the people), with imagined nationhood, became the aspired-to political ideologies and forms of modern people everywhere. Thus, the ideology and polity that took shape in the United States—in its founding first modernity form, then in its progressive, majoritarian "liberal orthodox" form a century or more later—were an example not so much of a harking back to or debating of classical republican ideals as of a polity seeking to suit its evolving nationhood (imagined community) to the modern imperative of self-determination—and even of achieving good government for all the people. The critiques of second modernity democracy raised grave doubts about such an achievement, of course.

Like the previous antimodern critiques of Pope and Swift early in the eighteenth century and of Carlyle, Emerson, and Arnold in the mid-nineteenth century, the maturing of second modernity ideology and democracy in the twentieth century and the basically liberal debate over it also produced ancient and transcendent critiques raising more fundamental questions. Coming along with the anti-Establishment ethos of the 1960s, a New Romanticism burgeoned around the world that challenged, not only the institutions of the liberal corporate state, but also its intellectual underpinnings fashioned in four centuries of Western thought. Charles Reich, for example, heralded in 1970 what he termed *the greening of America* as an antidote to the shortcomings of the liberal corporate state. Taking up the theme of the 1962 Port Huron Statement of the Students for a Democratic Society (see chapter 7), Reich called for a total "change of consciousness" that would set aside the institutions, ideology, economy, and politics of the outmoded liberal corporate state. Americans needed to get beyond both individualistic "Consciousness I" (roughly equivalent to first modernity thinking) and corporate "Consciousness II" (second modernity understandings and institutions) to achieve a "transcendence." The corporate state as it existed in the United States in 1970, Reich asserted, was characterized by

> 1. Disorder, corruption, hypocrisy, war; 2. Poverty, disordered priorities, and law-making by private power; 3. Uncontrolled technology and the destruction of the environment; 4. Decline of democracy and liberty; powerlessness; 5. The artificiality of work and culture; 6. Absence of community; and 7. Loss of "self." Needed was "a new way to live" where "science and technology work for, and not against the interests of man, . . . [where] work is nonalienating, is the free choice of each person, is integrated into a full and satisfying life, . . . [where] a community [exists] in which love, respect, and a mutual search for wisdom replace the competition and separation of the past, . . . and each individual is liberated and enabled to grow toward the highest possibilities of the human spirit.[17]

Though he concentrated his attack on the second modernity, to Reich all the modernities, from Bacon to Foucault, were "dread Empire[s]" of "CHAOS" (Pope), "dark" and "Satanic" (Blake), and places where "ignorant armies clash by night" (Arnold). Except to condemn utterly the processes and institutions of the state as he saw them in 1970, however, Reich had little to offer for the realm of politics. It needed, it seemed, simply to be transcended—flowers put in the muzzles of all the guns.

In a work concentrating especially on ideas and state of mind, Theodore Roszak in 1972 saw the "greening" of America as a place "where the wasteland ends" and a new "politics and transcendence in postindustrial society" might begin (as his title put it). He identified a "well-developed intellectual tradition . . . aspiring to a quantified, objectified politics" that ran from Bacon, Hobbes, and "the seventeenth century statistician William Petty," through Saint-Simon, Bentham, Comte, and Veblen, to "J. B. Watson's behaviorists (including B. F. Skinner) [and] the systems analysts of our own day."[18] He directed his broadside criticism, that is, against nearly four centuries of modern thought that had dominated Western intellectual life as it offered successive rationales of democratic government (hence the attacks on the "best" universities). In making his critique of politics from a "transcendent" perspective, Roszak was in one sense simply elaborating the assaults of William Blake, Thomas Carlyle, and a host of other "romantics" as he fashioned a new transcendentalism for a "postindustrial" society of the 1960s and beyond. In seeing the tradition of Baconian, science-based thinking joined with the omnipresent liberal corporate state of the mid-twentieth century as a huge, monolithic metanarrative and metainstitution, Roszak highlighted the target of postmodernity (though he attacked modernist paradigms from the outside, rather than from within).

As Foucault and others paid more and more attention to the total system of modern thought and its alleged connection to the structure of the liberal democratic state, they elaborated on the nature of what Roszak called, following Blake, *the single vision.* But postmodernists generally repudiated the need for a transcendent alternative to the single vision, which, in their view, would simply nourish more metanarratives that would one way or another oppress and marginalize all thinking that was different or "other." Instead, they insisted on sustaining an "incredulity toward [all] metanarratives," including the dominant liberal, social scientific one: the Establishment condemned by Roszak and the 1960s "movement" around the world. The postmoderns, then, agreed with the "new transcendentalists" about the oppressive orthodoxy that second modernity thinking had become, but they further insisted, in the manner of Bentham and Veblen (see chapter 6), that the need was to avoid entirely the "will to a system" that, in fact, betrayed the critical, inductive, tentative, scientific, mundane guidelines of any modernist thinking (as Hume and, later, John Dewey had explained). Their critique of the legions of post-Darwinian social scientists, policy experts, and politicians of the twentieth century was that they had so systematized and expertized evidence, inductions, and understandings that they had imposed new ideas of normalization on society. The tenor of this mode of thought (captured most vividly in the word *deconstruction*) is, however, not simply to contest the validity of the single vision that modernity had become (as a Blake or a Thoreau would do), but rather to protest the metamorphosizing of modernity into any vision at all.

The social science scholars of the twentieth century (following in the footsteps of Comte, Marx, Mill, Spencer, and Weber), postmodern critics charge, because they submitted their accumulations of evidence, projections of social theory, and policy proposals to the needs and interests of existing or soon-to-be-dominant forces, were the most complicit offenders. Neither democratic liberalism nor reformist nor scientific socialism, postmodernists claimed, escaped a compulsion toward normalizing and bureaucratizing in ways that marginalized and oppressed "deviant" diversities. Worst of all was the way in which the "disciplines" of the social science scholars, the very mode of "discourse" that they used (their scientific, inductive, "objective" methodology), fastened on the life of the mind a pervasive tendency toward something like the heavenly city of the eighteenth-century philosophers. They assumed a secularized, rational choice version of modernity that imposed its own orthodox metanarrative. This perhaps rested less candidly on an idea of universal natural law than did its eighteenth-century analogue, but it was just as "cruel" and imperialistic in its treatment of the Other, what Arnold Toynbee had called *internal* and *external* *proletariats*—those within and without who did not share the dominant ethos and advantages.

The postmoderns, that is, saw two pathological episodes in Western intellectual history when self-proclaimed empirical and critical thought had lapsed into metanarrative and "will to a system." The inclination of "first moderns" toward universal natural laws and that of "second moderns" toward a liberal orthodoxy were both driven by the need for rationales of their own dominance, by a failure to presence diversity, and by habits of thought that, as Hume had noted, sought inconsistently to know "upon what principle I proceed." The need, then, was for more of the critical mood of Bacon and Dewey, not less, a more consistent modernity that finally abandoned "the thread of causality"—a supermodernity. When Theodore Lowi and others advocated a democratic "juridical" state to replace the flawed, stagnant, conflict-of-interest model that signaled the (dead) "end of liberalism" and some like Robert Nozick offered a new, minimalist theory that prioritized the rights of individuals to choose and pursue their own values and ends over utilitarian or distributive acts of government,[19] postmodernists declared them all difference-suppressing metanarratives toward which one should be "incredulous."

Postmodern thinkers were equally scornful of the vigorous (largely academic) debate between self-styled liberals and so-called communitarians or civic republicans. The liberals sought to fashion the tolerances, the procedures, and the public spirit of democratic government into a political theory that, if not explicitly universal in language, championed (without being uncritical) a system that claimed general applicability in human affairs. John Rawls's ideas of an "original position" behind a hypothetical "veil of ignorance" screening out biases and status prejudices and of a "political conception of justice" resting on a "constitutional consensus" that gives priority to rights, requires processes of "public reason," and encourages members of a political community to meet each other "halfway" set forth a "theory of justice" for "political liberalism" that speaks in universal terms. How else can we understand his definition of *justice* as "the principles that free and rational persons concerned to further their own interests would accept in an initial position of equality" and an explanation that these principles include benefits for the least advantaged: tolerance, and majority forbearance?[20] To postmodernists, of course, these were metanarratives, throwbacks to eighteenth-century, Kantian universalism of the most homogenizing, domineering (*cruel* in Nietzsche's language) kind. Postmodernists also made use of Nietzsche to link their critique of Kantian universalism to East Asian devotion to concepts of higher law. In *The Antichrist,* following a fierce attack on what he called the *theological instinct* in both Christianity and Kant to be humble before God and fearful of creative human life, Nietzsche declared that they "express the decline and the final enervation of life, the Chinese religion of Konigsberg"; that is, the devotion to a higher law found in the Confucian mandate of heaven and in Kant's adherence to universal principle represented similar examples of oppressive, dogmatic ideologies.[21] Despite professions of inclusiveness and openness, Rawls and other liberals nevertheless tended, like the Kantians that they often claimed to be, to exclude and marginalize those who did not share their universal, though largely procedural, assumptions and guidelines.

The Critique of Postmodernism

In language that sometimes echoed candidly ancient universalisms, communitarians accepted postmodern critiques of the liberal efforts to fashion a "procedural republic" into a comprehensive system, not because of the intention itself (misguided to postmodernists), but rather because the result did not provide a rich understanding of polity capable of providing good government. Communitarians, that is, saw the liberals as offering a flawed or failed metanarrative that thus left them merely modern (procedural). They saw the postmoderns, however, because they repudiated universalisms and any "will to a system," as themselves more thoroughly modern than universalizing liberals in their attention to genealogies, differentness, groups, and parts. Postmodernists thus utterly neglected the shared moral and political principles essential to good government of any kind, including self-government. Communitarians often felt a certain satisfaction in the postmodern critique of both the actual operation of the liberal corporate state and the "theory of justice" and other principled liberal defenses, but they had only contempt for the postmodern repudiation of the theorizing, universal-seeking, foundational enterprise itself. That enterprise left postmodernism in the same (even more extreme) shallow, empirical, unprincipled position that various moderns had occupied since the time of Bacon's *Advancement of Learning* (1605).

At the same time, some communitarians, some New Age intellectuals (*prophets* in Roszak's usage), some poets and writers, some religious enthusiasts, and some traditionalists, often turning to classical, medieval, or non-Western philosophies and religions, have renewed the time-honored responses of ancients, romantics, and spiritualists. They expose the inadequacies of refashioned liberalism, of East Asian modernity, and of postmodernism, that is, of second, third, and fourth modernity thinking. (Tagore's espousal of pan-Asian spirituality catches some of the mood of this response [see chapter 9].) Though none of these responses has yet achieved the force or coherence of the voices of, say, Swift (chapter 4), Carlyle (chapter 6), or Niebuhr (chapter 6), it is clear that the fourth modernity, postmodernism, as a "systematic skepticism" and "furtherest . . . development . . . of the Cartesian critical intellect,"[22] would be found wanting. How was it, the latest generation of critics asks, in Carlyle's phrases, that, though everything "has been probed, dissected, distilled, desiccated, and scientifically decomposed" (i.e., deconstructed), "the grand Tissues, . . . Man's soul . . . wherein . . . his whole Faculties work, his whole Self lives, moves, and has its being," "should have been quite overlooked?" Postmodern criticism and deconstruction, to sustain Carlyle's images, though perhaps highly useful as "the epitome of all Laboratories and Observations," is actually "but a pair of Spectacles behind which there is no Eye."[23] In the twenty-first century, the "Eye" may be difficult to conceive, vivify, or perhaps even understand, but the sense remains strong that some real, integrating, more comprehending "Eye" exists ("Man's soul . . . his whole Self"; *foundations* in traditional discourse) and is necessary to a fully human life. One is reminded of Max Weber's famous observation at the end of his *Protestant Ethic and the Spirit of Capitalism* (1904). Following the culture (Weber called it a *cage*) thus brought into existence, he noted, "new prophets may arise" (transcendent or romantic visionaries), or there might be "a great rebirth of old ideas and ideals" (ancients), thus continuing immemorial cycles of human thought. "If neither," Weber speculated, there might persist a culture of "mechanized petrification, embellished with a sort of convulsive self-importance," where "specialists without spirit, sensualists without heart," exist in a "nullity" that "imagines . . . it has attained a level of civilization never before achieved."[24]

The versions of democratic government that have most prominently accompanied postmodernism, the politics of identity, or difference, and "democratic cosmopolitanism," fall under a holistic, foundational criticism similar to that experienced by earlier modern rationales. Even from thinkers who understand themselves as postmodern, the complaint arises that postmodern political thinking must go beyond its critical power and the presencing of otherness. Stephen White, for example, notes that postmodern thought (following Heidegger) seeks "to release [us] from the compulsive need for a public life securely grounded in first principles." But, if this requires a politics that "has as its guiding spirit action without *any* goal, without any 'why,'" then this "glosses over" a vital human need. It is necessary, White argues, after accepting postmodern presencing and even privileging of the Other, to "work back toward the other side," toward a "thoroughgoing realignment of modern consciousness." "Learning to be at home in homelessness, reorienting ourselves to our own finitude, and [understanding] the meaning of otherness" (postmodern perspectives), White argues, can become an "intensified commitment" to replace "the anchors of modern certainties [that] increasingly lose their hold." A "mood of delight . . . [and] a deepened concern for fostering difference . . . [and] an affirmation of our own finitude" can be the "goals" and "whys" in the postmodern era, fulfilling the human need for commitment and cosmologies of meaning.[25] (Whether this would satisfy what Santayana called the human need to "learn to love . . . only what is eternal" remains a question.)[26]

A more thoroughly antimodern critique of the politics of identity/difference, however, contests flatly the assertions of Iris Young, Bonnie Honig, and others that, since "a general perspective does not exist, . . . no one can claim to speak in the general interest" and that there is no such thing as an "ideal of universal citizenship."[27] Rather, Young asserts, citizenship exists only as a dimension of group identity (and, since a person can be a member of many groups, one might have many "citizenships"), where one strengthens one's sense of group identity, feels and understands its presence and needs, participates in internal strengthening (educating, organizing, etc.) of the group's public stance, and then takes part in the larger (national) political process as a defender of and advocate for the group's interest. Since there is no "general interest," no common understanding of justice, and no presumption that a process of deliberation might lead to insights and policies transcending particular perspectives, there is no core, no higher law, no universal principles toward which "citizens" (or leaders) might seek or tend to converge. Honig's proposals to "seek out the rifts and fissures of foundational identities and constitutions" and resist "the states' organization of politics into approved spaces and formats" have the same basis.[28] The only convergence possible or necessary is for those previously dominant to genuinely presence the "other" groups, accept their group-derived understandings of needs and justice, and adjust public policy accordingly. In a way, this view is the culmination of Locke's autonomous individualism wherein "all may choose different things, and yet all choose right" (see chapter 4), of Mill's positing of the "sovereignty" of an individual over his own person (see chapter 6), and of John Dewey's emphasis on the need for society (and hence government) to be responsive to the "felt needs" of groups and individuals (see chapter 6), a further stage of modernity. (From a postmodern standpoint, of course, the flaw in each of these earlier modernities was their fatal, inconsistent will and tendency to universalize.)

It is possible, then, to circle back and find, even among generally repudiated liberal theorists, some ideas that would substantiate postmodern political thinking. In a notable 1998 postmodern reference to modernist thinking, for example, Richard Rorty writes of "Dewey between Hegel and Darwin." Dewey rejected, Rorty explains, "everything nonhistoricist in Hegel, especially his idealism," as is common in postmodern discourse. Dewey understood Hegel (as Marx had) as in "the modern secular and positivistic spirit . . . [inviting] the human subject to mastery of what is already contained in the here and now of the world." With Darwin, Hegel rejected the "essence-accident distinction and blurred the line between spirit and matter, emphasizing continuity over disjunction, and production of the novel over contemplation of the eternal." Then, following Darwin (and Dewey [see chapter 6]) further, Rorty asserts: "Biological evolution produces ever new species, and cultural evolution produces ever new audiences, but there is no such thing as the species which evolution has in view, nor any such thing as the 'aim of inquiry.'" Rorty explains that he, Dewey, and other pragmatists all "think that there are a lot of detailed things to be said about justification [explanations, reasons, arguments] to any given audience, but nothing to be said about justification in general." He finds Dewey's "antifoundationalism," drawn from Hegel's "modern secular and positivistic spirit" and from Darwin's mundane, uncontemplative evolutionism, entirely congenial to the postmodern sense that "there was, in the beginning, *no Word.*" Rorty sees himself, William James, and Dewey as representing an Anglo-American outlook akin to that of the "Continental" philosophy of Nietzsche, Foucault, and Derrida in that all are "antidualists" hostile to the idealist tradition stretching from Plato to Kant. Rorty insists, however, contrary to "Continental postmodernism" (and its Anglo-American followers), that pragmatism is not complicit in the metanarrative of the liberal corporate state but rather is a genuinely postmodern perspective without "aim of inquiry" or end in view.[29]

In thus linking second and fourth modernity antiuniversalism, Rorty explains how Dewey's understanding of liberal reformism within a democratic process is good postmodernism. He sees Dewey's open-ended, step-by-step, pragmatic view of democratic government, not as part of a liberal metanarrative, as Lyotard or Iris Young might claim, but as an appropriate political expression suited to postmodern insistence on indeterminacy, contextualism, and the presencing of diversity. Once intellectuals concede that "the only plausible answer to the question 'What is intrinsically good?' is 'human happiness', and . . . admit that the answer provides no guidance for choices between alternative human lives," Rorty points out, one must "conclude that democratic citizenship does not require agreement on the relative value of these sorts of lives" (or, as Honig argued, on pledged allegiance to constitutions?). Thus, one needs to "disjoin from both religion and science" when attending to the "utilitarian and pragmatic . . . projects of social cooperation." Terming such gathered projects (somewhat teasingly) "a liberal democratic utopia . . . much more likely to produce greater human happiness" than, say, fascist tyranny, Rorty foresees (again teasingly) "a perfected society [that] will not live up to a pre-existent standard [any universalism], but will be an artistic achievement, produced by the same long and difficult process of trial and error as required by any other creative effort." Echoes of Honig and Mill and Dewey and even Bacon are obvious, marks of Rorty's intention to claim standing as a postmodern pragmatist or, as he often puts it, a philosophical pluralist.[30]

In another attempt to explain what postmodern pragmatism implies for the idea of democracy, Rorty refers simply to "generalized Darwinism which is democracy," which rests on "the Moral of Darwinian biology": "The only justification of a mutation, biological or cultural, is its contribution to the existence of a more complex and interesting species somewhere in the future." In more specifically political terms, laws, or policies, or "projects of social cooperation," manifestations of the democratic process, can be understood as cultural mutations, adaptations to the social environment with no more reference to aims, or ends, or universal principles than biological mutations. The "purpose," Rorty explains, is to distinguish "between descriptions of the world and of ourselves which are less useful and those which are more useful." Rorty then recites the pragmatic catechism: When asked, "Useful for what?" the answer is, "Useful to create a better future." When asked, "Better by what criterion?" there is no specific answer, "any more than the first mammals could specify in what respects they were better than the dying dinosaurs." When, after explaining that *better* meant "containing more good and less . . . bad," asked, "What exactly do you consider good?" the answer is, "Variety and freedom, or . . . growth," concluding with Dewey that "growth itself is the only moral end."[31]

Rorty thus approves, as Dewey did, a version of the liberal corporate state that is pragmatic about the uses of government, seeing a considerable potential for "good" from its democratically based actions—"projects of social cooperation" as people adapt to the physical, social, and human environments. Rorty asserts, for example, that "from the days of Franklin Roosevelt to those of Lyndon Johnson [the United States] made enormous progress" toward such traditional liberal goals as racial equality, economic justice, and educational opportunity for all, while, under the Reagan and the second Bush administrations, "happiness" receded as "the interest of the rich" came to dominate public life. Rorty sees "no reason for optimism about the progress of democracy" at the end of the cold war, however, because there is (and, here, he departs from the imbued progressivism of thinkers such as Mill and Dewey) no reason, in evolutionary terms and in the absence of any idea of purpose or goal in human history, to suppose either that democracy will remain the best way of furthering human happiness or even that it will survive the twenty-first century, any more than dinosaurs or mammoths survived their eras.[32]

In a way, then, Rorty overcomes the postmodern tendency to have little to say about the uses of government by explaining how a Deweyan kind of active new-liberal democracy (see chapter 6) is compatible with postmodern guidelines of antifoundationalism, indeterminacy, and pluralism. Indeed, for Rorty, a Deweyan pragmatic, means-over-ends democratic process is less an inadmissible metanarrative, as postmodernists generally claim, than is their logocentrism of presencing the Other through a politics of identity. Rorty thus avoids the recurring postmodern dilemma of what to do about government by assimilating it to a second modernity understanding of its function and uses. At the same time, however, he subjects himself to the critique of Carlyle, Mumford, and others that his "biologistic" view of human nature may lack depth and completeness. It simply begs the question of to what words like *useful, better,* and *good* have reference: useful, better, or good for what? As Jürgen Habermas asks: "What is to happen to the normative character of reason [universalisms], and how counter-intuitive is [Rorty's] proposed neo-Darwinist self-description of rational beings?" That is, is not Rorty's neo-Darwinist ("biologistic") understanding of human nature, and his denial of universalism of any kind, counter to "the great primal intuitions of human nature" and the pursuit of "ideal right" and cultivation of a human "moral sense" espoused by transcendentalists (chapter 6), Jefferson (chapter 5), and others? Could Rorty, as Hume could not, "forbear having a curiosity [about] . . . upon what principle I proceed?" Though Rorty backs off from some postmodern "antigovernmentalism" by endorsing a Deweyan form of the liberal corporate state, he shares the pervasive postmodern antiuniversalism and is, thus, vulnerable to the critiques of cycles of antimoderns.[33]

These antimodern critics generally simply affirm the capacity and obligation, if one deeply understands human life and society, to universalize. When George Kateb observed in 1987 that "the hidden source of modern democracy may always have been the death of God,"[34] he was simply remarking on the profound connection between the repudiations of the whole, the universal, and the eternal and various manifestations of modernity in the preceding half millennium. Bacon's pleas to have "patience to doubt . . . [and] dissect [nature] into parts" (see chapter 4), Bentham's blunt assertion that "*natural rights* is simply nonsense" (see chapter 6), Veblen's denial of any "elaborate discipline of faith and metaphysics, over-ruling Providence, order of nature, natural rights, natural law, underlying principles" (see chapter 6), Nishi Amane's contempt for deductive logic and insistence that "scholars by all means must rely on the inductive method" (see chapter 8), Justice Holmes's conviction that "philosophy is only cataloguing the universe and the universe is simply an arbitrary fact" (see chapter 6), Laski's remark that "the most distinguishing feature . . . of modern life . . . [was] a multiplicity of wills which have no common purposes" (see chapter 6), and Lyotard's definition of postmodernism as an "incredulity toward metanarratives" that sustains only "a justice of multiplicities" (see chapter 10) are all repudiations at the core of modernist thinking. Though modern thought had sometimes developed natural laws and metanarratives of its own, beyond them always stood the more avowedly universal, ancient, and transcendental insistences that humanity was simply bereft without such dimensions. To all the modernist arguments that "nature," human nature, had no use for "worship" or "guiding visions" or "the eternal," that in the beginning there was no word, transcendent perspectives argued for and sought to convey the reality and importance of aspirations and experiences that they regarded as essential to human nature (again, postmoderns and Rorty simply say "no such thing").

In contemporary politics, the antimodern critique condemns, not only postmodern identity politics, but also mainstream conflict-of-interest practice and even "libertarianism" in either its "old liberal" or "neoconservative" guises. The basic flaws are seen as the repudiation of higher or universal principles and the denigration of the place of government in human life and society. Both propositions, critics assert, tend toward a conditioned, manipulable understanding of human nature itself and, particularly, a minimal, narrow, even cynical concept of citizenship. The libertarian outlook, resting on laissez-faire arguments that prosperity and progress (and even justice and peace) depend on the release of private energies and the minimizing of government interference with natural forces—"government is the problem, not the solution"—leaves little for citizens as such to do and often, in fact, supposes that they have little capacity for any serious public responsibility.

Conflict-of-interest politics, not dogmatic about big government, readily countenances various government programs that seem suited to the needs and interests of various "actors" able to find support in the political arena. The assumption is that human beings, as "members" of a self-governing society, are able to make "rational choices" about their own needs and interests and that they will then be able to make more rational choices about how to further them in the political process, perhaps by voting, perhaps by lobbying or demonstrating, perhaps by joining a political party or a civic association. Or perhaps, if they calculate that any activity on their part would "not do any good" or "be more trouble than it's worth" (in terms of their own self-interest), they would do nothing at all. One rational choice theorist argued that it was "irrational," that is, a poor calculation of one's self-interest, "to be politically well-informed" because it was time-consuming and led only to "inconsequential voting." In no case is there any presumption either that universal precepts exist that might define justice or the public good or that citizens might have capacities to discern them, discuss them, or act in accord with them. Claims that there are universally applicable "liberal virtues" (mutual respect, tolerance, openness, fair procedures, e.g.) or that the decisionmaking process itself is a universal value providing all the foundation that a democratic polity requires are to antimoderns just that much more evidence that advocates of an "economic theory of democracy," or of a "procedural republic," simply don't get it. Michael Sandel, for example, argues: "A procedural republic cannot contain the moral energies of a vital democratic life. It creates a moral void that opens the way for narrow, intolerant moralisms. And it fails to cultivate the qualities of character that equip citizens to share in self-rule."[35] It embodies, to repeat again Carlyle's image, spectacles without eyes.

An antimodern perspective is even more antagonistic to fourth modernity political projections than it is to second modernity libertarian and liberal politics because postmodernism is more complete in its repudiation of any and all notions of universal morality or of any history, social science, criticism, claim, or language that presupposes or even countenances the existence of any such ideas. Such postmodern notions as the simple unprejudiced presencing of otherness, finding justice in the needs of particular groups, seeing the benefits of devolved, diminished government (whether democratic or not), and using exclusively the critical methods of "incredulity to metanarrative" and deconstruction all clash with antimodern tendencies to validate the wisdom of traditional and transcendental insights. Postmodern public philosophy, if that term can have any relevance or positive meaning, is, again, simply bereft, incomplete, and misdirected if it understands government in those terms. It is, in a long perspective, antimodernists assert, neglectful of both the Aristotelian tradition that "a state exists for the sake of a good life, and not for the sake of life only," and the Judeo-Christian-Islamic tradition that insists on a higher law that proclaims, in the words of Saint Augustine, that "an unjust law is no law at all."[36] Moses, Jesus, and the Prophet Muhammad would all agree—as would Thomas Jefferson and Martin Luther King (see chapters 2 and 3).

As cycles of modernity, through four centuries or more, have set forth rigorously inductive, scientific, and critical modes of thought, then, they have spawned various rationales for democratic government. One after another, ideas of what self-government and citizenship can, should, or might mean in human society have been proposed and criticized. Repeatedly, a modernist assertion of the primacy of the parts, of the scientific method, and of immediate human need has engendered a mode of democratic thought endorsing more effective participation of (at least some of) the people in their own affairs. These modernist thought patterns and their democratic corollaries have provoked first antimodernist (traditional and transcendental) protests of the shallow, narrow-visioned, chaotic, merely methodological nature of the modernities and of their democratic offshoots. They have also provoked internal criticism from self-proclaimed "true moderns" that the "original moderns" had (inconsistently) betrayed the need to "dissect [nature] into parts" by succumbing to the human inclination to abstraction and universalism. The internal critique then established itself as a further, heightened modernity that often had as its most direct target more the alleged abstracting apostasy of the previous modernity than the ongoing, perhaps predictable ancient or transcendental reservations about the whole enterprise of modernity. The political ideology dimension of each modernity, successive rationales of democracy (and, in some fashion, accompanying practices), though in a way understanding themselves as extensions, logical follow-ups, of previous democratic theory, actually produced new rationales as deeply different from earlier ones as the cycles of modernity were from each other. The result has been patterns and critiques of democratic thought that both illuminate the problems and opportunities of self-government and reveal some of the depth and richness of human reflection on the nature of government itself. Perhaps if one looks carefully at this flux of thought, more viable understandings of human nature and rationales for democracy can emerge as the third millennium begins.

12

The Idea of Democracy in the Third Millennium

Varieties of Contemporary Political Thinking

By the beginning of the twenty-first century, then, four major rationales for democratic government undergird contemporary political thinking in the United States and around the world. Perhaps most directly
reflecting the spirit of the first, post-Baconian modernity as expressed
especially by John Locke and Adam Smith, a pattern of thought often
characterized as libertarian emphasizes the rights and the benign, competitive interaction of parts (people) to sustain a theory of limited government and maximum freedom of choice and of opportunity for
individuals and their organizations. From F. A. Hayek's *Road to Serfdom* (1944), to Milton Friedman's *Capitalism and Freedom* (1962) and
Robert Nozick's *Anarchy, State, and Utopia* (1974), and even to Dick
Armey's *Freedom Revolution* (1995),[1] the argument insists that almost
any and all law and government regulation infringes on the vital freedom of the parts to achieve and to create and to produce. Though there
are "public good" aspects in the thought of both Locke and Smith and
generally Locke and Smith set forth an ideology of natural law that
highlights universals and metanarratives, nonetheless their assumptions about differentiated individuals and rational seekers of self-interest
are thoroughly modern. That is, they begin with assumptions of autonomous individuals needing maximum scope for fulfillment—and,
hence, maximum freedom from compulsion, harassment, regulation,
or even guidance from overarching ideologies or governments of any
kind. Democracy thus consists of limited, though representative, government, legally protected rights for individuals, and wide opportunity
for enterprise, private investments, deviations, and idiosyncratic

achievement. In the United States at least, this has been the favored understanding of self-proclaimed conservatives from William Graham Sumner and Herbert Hoover to Barry Goldwater and Tom DeLay—though, in fact, the outlook is deeply liberal in the classic nineteenth-century way, a mixture of J. S. Mill and Spencer and Sumner as well as Locke and Smith and Jefferson.

The second, post-Darwinian modernity gave rise to what John Dewey termed the *new liberalism,* which in turn furnished the rationale for the corporate democratic state of the twentieth century. This liberalism undergirded all the mainstream ideas and programs of thinkers and political leaders from Theodore and Franklin Roosevelt to Lyndon Johnson and Richard Nixon and from Harold Laski and Karl Popper to Al Gore and Robert Reich (the 2001 George W. Bush administration seems to rest uneasily across the two modernities). The emphasis is on inclusion of all groups and interests in the political system, equitable representation, full and open public discussion, court protection of individual rights, coalition building among groups, conflict-of-interest politics in legislative bodies, and pragmatic use of government power. The idea is to assure to all access to the political process, to provide for social science analysis and guidance on policy (as opposed to more overtly ideological programs, Communist, fascist, or ecclesiastical), and to make all agencies of government responsive to the concerns and needs of a variegated public, the liberal corporate state. Good government and democracy in this understanding consist of "whatever can be arrived at democratically and not another thing." Walter Lippmann had stated the essence of the outlook in 1914: democratic government must "come under the scientific discipline, where men use language accurately, know fact from fancy, search out their own prejudice, are willing to learn from failures, . . . do not shrink from the long process of observation, . . . live forward in the midst of complexity, and treat life not as something given but something to be shaped."[2] Though second modernity democracy shaded into dogmatic socialism on the left and into libertarianism on the right, it consistently managed to distinguish itself, a "vital center," by its open-endedness, its pragmatism, its tendency toward "bureaus" and "administrations," and its rhetoric of populism, ready to abide by the various wills of the people.

The third rationale for democracy, derived as it is from the impact of second modernity thought in East Asia, tends generally to endorse a similar corporatized version of democracy, though with less emphasis on *liberal* and more on *corporate* in its understanding of government. The result is a theory of the state that, in formal ways, is nearly indistinguishable from the second modernity liberal corporate state but that, in practice (and in the understanding of both leaders and people), continues to reflect the ancient Chinese/Confucian emphasis on the wide responsibility of the state for the moral, qualitative condition of society.

The idea of a simply "open society" has less resonance. In modern Taiwan, Singapore, Hong Kong, and South Korea, for example, representative assemblies, elections, freedom of expression, and protection of rights exist in some form, though often more limited than in North America and Western Europe. All these elements, however, are overshadowed and often overawed by forceful, paternalistic, "above-party" or single-party rulers claiming to speak for the nation as a whole. The implicit rationale for democracy is, thus, both remarkably like and remarkably unlike second modernity Western ones. Taken together, and despite differences among them, the writings and programs of Lee Kuan Yew (Singapore), Kim Dae Jung (South Korea), and Lee Teng Hui (Taiwan) articulate the different rationale, a rationale present in Western-oriented East Asian thought since the days of Fukuzawa Yukichi and Yan Fu. Though Japan has since 1948 had a more fully developed Western-style liberal corporate state (one side of the Trilateral Commission), its actual practices of and attitudes toward government are, in fact, often notably similar to those of its East Asian neighbors. In the People's Republic of China, where the lack of liberal and democratic values and practices is much more extreme, the talk of and even small moves toward them often display an East Asian preference for top-down, paternalistic rule "for the people." The thought of Malaysian prime minister Dr. Mahathir Mohamad, though grounded in Islam, also reflects what he sees as "Asian values" (25 percent of the people of Malaysia are of Chinese origin), and his rule in Malaysia bears many marks of third modernity democracy.[3]

Fourth, a post-Foucaultian variety of political thinking about democracy is perhaps best characterized as *the politics of difference* or *the politics of identity*. The beginning point is again the parts that are present, groups thought of not so much as parts of a body politic as freestanding, experience-molded, self-defining entities. They are not and should not be understood as constituents of a polity that is itself the highest embodiment of civilization (the East Asian model) or even a procedural republic committed to the obligatory democratic processes of the liberal corporate state. Least of all are the self-defined groups to be subsumed within natural laws that are presumed to be universal, as first modernity democratic thought and practice tended to suppose (inconsistently, its critics insisted). All these "wills to a system" and tendencies toward metanarrative, imperialisms of thought and practice, though clothed in the rhetoric of self-government, are, in fact, thought to be as oppressive in their impact on the parts and groups present as immemorial tyrannies.

Instead, a genuinely democratic society (one hesitates to use *government* or even *polity*) *begins* with the needs of the different, oppressed identity groups whose narrative and experience define justice for them. As this narrative and experience are recovered and vitalized within each group, a sense of identity and worth crystallizes in ways that can permit equitable participation in such public life as seems fair and useful. This requires first and foremost the dismantling and deconstruction of the oppressive institutions and modes of thought that sustained the dominant forces, including, especially, those of the liberal corporate states of the twentieth century. Then, perhaps using political forms decidedly decentralized, devolved, and defederated, the senses of justice and the senses of social need of the previously oppressed identity groups can become truly present and be the basis for any necessary social interaction. Continuing the movement away from the "forms," the "argumentation," and the "invented systems of the universe" that Bacon had scorned four centuries earlier, postmodern democracy even resists the idea that majority rule is somehow a universally valid mode of decisionmaking that must always prevail. There are times, that is, when the needs and sense of justice of groups must have special acknowledgment and weight beyond what formal majority-rule processes might dictate. Special care must be taken, too, not to exclude, but to welcome immigrants (even illegal ones) and others not fully, formally citizens, thus creating, perhaps partly outside the state, a more inclusively populist "democratic cosmopolitanism." Since the very notion of government itself might be proscribed as "argumentation" and "invented system," alien to ideas of difference and group identity, postmodernism often constitutes more a supercritique of previous and existing rationales of democracy than a reformulated rationale. In any event, the Baconian project of "patience to doubt . . . readiness to reconsider" and to "distinguish . . . subtler differences" had reached another fulfillment.[4]

The Idea of Human Nature Revisited

Most fundamental in the four hundred years of the Baconian project has been the steady reduction of the understanding of human nature from one of essences within systems to one of differences among autonomous parts. As the early stages of modern political thought, in Hobbes and Locke, revealed, the initial positing of diverse, self-willed individuals was able to go in both autocratic and democratic directions. The more powerful political direction, however, as modernity broadened in commercial, religious, and social ways, was the one pointed to by Locke and Jefferson of the autonomous individuals becoming, for their own survival, convenience, and happiness, parts of a self-governing polity —the rationale for first modernity democracy and the American Constitution. Locke and Jefferson argued that individuals, possessing freedom and natural rights, could and ought to form "a government truly republican" where they would "understand" and "maintain" their rights and "exercise with intelligence their parts in self-government."[5] Though this early-modern view saw humans as possessing rights as individuals and, thus, emphasized their autonomy and differentness, it also supposed capacity for and inclination toward participating in self-government with "intelligence," that is, with reason that would furnish access to higher law. The tension between the differentiating self-will of individual autonomy and converging universal reason was contained in the complex understanding of human nature itself. Humans possessed both "inalienable rights" and the capacity to reason that would allow "deriving . . . just powers from the consent of the governed." The "will to a system" was, thus, preserved within the inductive method; Locke and Newton join Bacon in Jefferson's "trinity of immortals."

When, as the twentieth century began, Justice Oliver Wendell Holmes declared that "life was an end in itself and that the only question of it being worth living was whether you had enough of it" and that "the best test of truth is the power of thought to get itself accepted in the competition of the market,"[6] the emphasis on individuality remained intense but had been shorn of notions of essence, cosmic purpose, and higher law—unless one called the ceaseless struggle for survival in an open-ended, unplanned multiverse the *law* of nature. The model of the struggling, striving individual (rather than the reasoning, rights-bearing one), needing to adapt in a complex, Darwinian world, undergirded both Spencerian struggle outside (even against) the state and Deweyan striving, perhaps through the state, for an existence more responsive to and fulfilling of individual and group "felt needs." In Laski's terms, human nature consisted basically of "a multiplicity of wills which have no common purposes." But, acknowledging that "the average man is, in fact, a political animal," humans might, in a democratic state, "encounter and relate to each other . . . [to achieve] an inductive realization . . . of the enrichment of common life."[7] Everything still flows from the parts, but there is no longer any notion that the encountering and relating of the "political animals" might achieve more than "inductive realizations" of an enriched "common life"—no natural rights (Holmes "sneered" at them), no universal laws, no design in human affairs. (The difference between what Aristotle and what Laski thought their "political animals" could and should do in public life was stark.) There remains only the powerful, encompassing metanarrative of the open, liberal, democratic process, where, in Holmes's words, "the proximate test of a good is that the dominant power has its way."[8]

Postmodern thinking accepts the uncosmological view of human nature as a "multiplicity of wills" but sees even their organization within the democratic idea of majority rule, where the dominant power has its way, as simply a face of tyranny and oppression seen in the liberal corporate state and its attendant, complicit, ideologies, especially social science. This understanding of human nature emphasizes diversity, the incessant, multicultural existence of "otherness," and the equally incessant will to power of dominant forces—kings, bishops, capitalists, police, incarcerating institutions, universities, various majorities, Communists, fascists, nationalists, bureaucrats, social science methodologies, etc. Since there are no such things as universal guidelines, objective studies, or "neutral" states presiding over open societies, the idea of benign, "just" government loses meaning. Humans simply need to be accepted and presenced in their own historically and experientially conditioned identities for their idiosyncratic fulfillment. There is in their nature no need or any constructive capacity to engage with (through reason or any political process) humankind in general, with any of its overarching ideologies, or with any prospect of discerning or achieving a general public good, except perhaps in ways that transcend nation-states. Implications for government are anarchic or minimal, which generally defines the "best" that can be done in sustaining democracy. Philosopher-kings or Confucian-trained administrators might not be in order, but people (facilitators? diversity trainers? human resource managers?) sensitive to and responsive to the differentness and needs of various groups in society might open the way. There would be, of course, as little categorizing, regulating, stereotyping, certifying, and institutionalizing as possible—to say nothing of the "tax, conscript, command, prohibit"[9] powers usually claimed by governments. The understanding of both human nature (the concept itself being profoundly antithetical to postmodern thinking) and the group identity basis of human society makes liberal democracy and even the very idea of government itself highly problematic.

Thinking beyond the forms and critiques of the rationales for democracy spawned by the four modernities, then, has generally begun with reconsideration of the attendant or implicit concepts of human nature. From Locke's view that "men may chuse different things, and yet all chuse right,"[10] through Mill's emphasis on "individuality" and John Dewey's on "felt needs," to postmodern attention to identity and groups, the focus has been on diversity, individuals and groups so different from each other that there are no generalizations possible and no essential or universal standards or qualities that could characterize a "human" nature—though only the postmodern version of this emphasis explicitly repudiates the very idea. Perhaps the most basic counterpoint to this tendency, rather than disputing whether human nature is good or bad, or spiritual or mundane, or rational or irrational (or whether it is a meaningful concept at all), as though relatively simple categorizations were possible, is to acknowledge and understand the complexity, actual and potential, in any human being and in human society. Thus, humans might be understood as possessing, in varying degrees, benign and malevolent qualities in their natures, spiritual capacity as well as concern for worldly affairs, an ability to reason as well as emotional and impulsive tendencies, competitive as well as cooperative inclinations, private and public interests, and so on. All humans might possess some of any of these qualities, and the very great differences in quantities and combinations of them in any one person yields enormous diversity and complexity in individual behavior and aspirations, in personal relationships, in group dynamics, in social arrangements, and in economic activity.

In an understanding especially evident in Confucian thought, this complexity and potential in human nature is to a considerable degree malleable, capable of change, repression, or nourishment, in response to a variety of historical, cultural, and social circumstances. Family upbringing, formal education, and the guidance, perhaps even manipulation, of political systems take on potentially key roles. This echoes the Aristotelian dictum: "A state exists for the sake of a good life, and not for the sake of life only."[11] "Man is a political animal" as part of his nature, but, given his varied and ambiguous qualities, the means and long-range effect of his political dimension are complicated—and also hugely interesting and important. Thus, it seems that the shape, intent, and impact of government are of deep significance in human life and need to be attended to seriously, faithfully, and skillfully—the precise opposite of Emerson's absurd observation that "the appearance of character makes the state unnecessary."[12] This same emphasis on the important, guiding role of government, and its obligation to sustain moral character, is prominent in theocratic regimes, for example, the Islamic Republic of Iran. The difference from Aristotelian and Jeffersonian ideas of government arises, however, from their supposition that the guiding principles can come in some fashion from the reason and conscience of the people (educated by teachers, sages, and others, of course), while, in the Islamic case, the principles, laws, and customs come directly from Allah through the Prophet to the Qur'an to the ayatollahs, who then, in effect, govern. The need for higher guidance and for the significance of government is in important ways similar; the difference is in where the people fit in and in the suppositions about their nature, capacities, and flaws. The understanding and practice of government, then, we might say, are vital to human life, both as a dimension of our nature and as essential to the survival and fulfillment of the "good life" that the complexities of human nature make possible. The complexities, on the other hand, might, under some circumstances, hinder or threaten such fulfillment.

Reinhold Niebuhr captured the particular implications of this complex, problematic, but potentially fulfilling view of human nature for democratic government with his aphorism: "Man's capacity for justice makes democracy possible, but man's inclination to injustice makes democracy necessary."[13] The tough-minded thrust turned somber views of human nature often used to justify authoritarian government (Thomas Hobbes or John Winthrop) into foundations for democracy: since rulers themselves (including clergy) were not immune to the corruptions and abuse of power, there was no likely haven for justice in governments that put all power in one place. As Locke said in critique of Hobbes, it made no sense "to avoid what mischiefs may be done by polecats or foxes, but . . . think it safety, to be devoured by lions."[14] The only effective check on the exercise of power (always with humans tending toward selfish abuse) was its dispersal into so many hands that no one depository had enough to tyrannize over all the rest—and the ultimate, most safe division of power was that of a democracy where, theoretically at least, each person had one vote, one quantum of power, among hundreds or thousands or millions. This idea was at the core of Madison's famous argument in *Federalist* no. 10 that the enlargement of a republic to include many counteracting factions was the only way to prevent the tyranny of one or a few likely in a small polity. (It is also a basis for the emphasis on access and inclusion in modern rational choice and conflict-of-interest politics.) Democracy, then, is necessary to create the dispersal of power needed to cope with the part of complex human nature that tends toward corruption, self-love, and aggrandizement; and absolute power corrupts absolutely.

To leave the rationale for government, even self-government, at this point, however, is to overlook other human capacities associated with the word *justice*. When Mencius began a commentary on government with the observation that "man's nature is endowed with feelings which impel it toward the good," he meant that there were inclinations and sensibilities among humans of goodwill, social responsibility, and harmony that made the "noble" life, in accord with the mandate of heaven, possible.[15] The same idea undergirded Aristotle's dictum that "man is a political animal," that is, possessed of the capabilities that both inclined humans toward life within a polity and made it possible for their public affairs to be conducted rationally and according to standards of justice, beauty, and prosperity—Periclean Athens the prototype. The point, even without particular democratic implications, was that human beings were suited to social life, were inclined at least potentially toward interest in and attention to public life (politics), and were endowed with capacities that would allow at least some of them some of the time to govern with wisdom, justice, and public spirit.

The more democratic implications of these capacities (largely unattended to in classical Greece and even less so in traditional China) found fullest voice, at least in North America, in the thought of Thomas Jefferson. Following Lockean implications that humans had the right of self-government and that government would be safe (nontyrannical) only in their hands, Jefferson worked out a theory that would include all (qualified [see below]) people in the practice of government yet would still assert the indispensable qualities of wisdom, justice, and public spirit. He was fully cognizant of the need for limitation on the powers of government both through checks and balances and through a bill of rights, which he declared "the people are entitled to against every government on earth . . . and which no just government should refuse." He feared especially, since "human nature is the same on every side of the Atlantic," that corruption would spread, not only among the leaders, but by them "through the body of the people." Even legislatures elected by the people, unless checked by other parts of the government, might be tyrannical. "One hundred and seventy-three despots," he said, referring to the all-powerful legislature of the state of Virginia, "would surely be as oppressive as one." Even before addressing the complicated question of how to organize the active side of self-government, usually termed *political freedom,* he insisted on bills of rights and separation of powers as barriers against human tendencies toward corruption, power lust, and faction. He believed that the *Federalist Papers,* resting its defense of the new U.S. Constitution on a sober, realistic understanding of human nature, to be "the best commentary on the principles of government, which ever was written."[16]

Just as important for the long run was paying attention to, and nourishing in the people, the sociability, the capacity for reason, the moral dimension, the political understanding, and the sense of justice that would make good democratic government possible. Agreeing with Mencius that there were "good materials" inherent in human nature, Jefferson also emphasized the need for the cultivating, the nourishing, the drawing forth of these capacities in sustained and deliberate ways. People must not only understand and defend their rights but also be able "to exercise with intelligence their parts in self-government." Since this "exercise" was multifaceted and the people to carry it out were diverse, complex, and malleable, the dimensions of making it effective in any polity would be many and varied. Attention would be necessary to the sort of jobs that people might have (since employment had an effect on character development), the distribution of land and wealth (to ensure genuine independence), the forms of local government (to provide meaningful participation), the freedom of religion (to emphasize choice and conviction rather than dogmatism and hypocrisy), and, perhaps most important of all, the provision of universal public education. Not all these matters were likely to be fully attended to, and circumstances at different times and places would require manifold forms and adjustments, but the latent capacities of the people for the reason, justice, goodwill, and public responsibility essential to good government could be made manifest only through such concern. This supposed, of course, not that all people would possess in full measure all the latent tendencies, or that they were immune to the selfish, evil tendencies that were also part of human nature, but that there was enough of the justice-enabling qualities, if properly nourished, to make democracy, even good self-government, in some measure possible.

This many-sided outlook of Jefferson's, wholly accepting, as he understood them, of Locke's modern assumptions about diverse human nature, about the mundane purposes of the state, and about the need for self-government, was not, however, looking back toward some benign and prehistoric state of nature. Nor, despite his acknowledged debts to Aristotle, Cicero, and other ancients, was he in any sense a revivalist seeking to establish in North America some sort of classical or neoclassical republicanism. Rather, along with his "Bacon-Newton-Locke" modernism, he had deep in his nature a classicism that he had no trouble also bringing to his task of nation conceiving and nation building. As Dumas Malone has observed, Jefferson "knew more about the past and thought more about the future" than most political leaders.[17] That is, though he possessed both ancient wisdom and modern learning, he believed that "laws and institutions must go hand in hand with the progress of the human mind . . . [and that,] as new discoveries are made, new truths disclosed, . . . manners . . . opinions . . . [and] institutions must advance also."[18] Jefferson's understanding of American nationhood, even empire, thus always had in view a polity (regime) geared toward the future and resting on what James Madison in *Federalist* no. 37 said under the U.S. Constitution was "the inviolable attention due to liberty and to the republican form."[19] In that way Jefferson played an important role in defining a form of civic nationalism that looked forward to the spread of republican ideals first within the American states and nation (an "Empire of Liberty"), then in other nations, and finally in a revolutionized world order. The trick was not to somehow turn the clock back but, rather, to set in motion a model for the future, sustaining valued, universal ideals, classical as well as enlightened. Jefferson's first inaugural address (see chapter 5) thus both stated a litany of liberal democratic values and embodied a deeply classical republican understanding of leadership and citizenship that he offered as a mode of nationalism for the United States and for others. Though modern political analysis might see this as hugely inconsistent or improbable, it was a civic national ideal that has never lost its appeal in the world—or failed to be a prod for improvement in the face of derelictions in Jefferson's own country.[20]

Note, however, that Jefferson (and Niebuhr too) was expressing a conditional argument: good democratic government was possible *if* the people were rendered up to the task. Conversely, without that, democracy would likely not be good government. Not only did democratic government require checks and balances and bills of rights that would restrain selfish, evil tendencies (like the positive ones, distributed unevenly among people), but it would also need to encourage carefully the justice-tending ones. The argument is, thus, a complex, conditional, even tentative one that seeks to avoid both naïveté and cynicism and rest on realistic grounds—in accord with human nature itself, as it might exist both in fact and as potentiality. (In both cases, variations in behavior and in potential were large and complex within any particular individual, between individuals, and among the various groups that compose any society; some were very good, some were very bad, but most were spread across many spectrums in between.) The basic wager was that there was enough of the positive qualities (Niebuhr's "capacity for justice") among enough of the people enough of the time for modestly good (at least "not bad") government to go ahead most of the time. At the same time, the negative qualities (Niebuhr's "inclination to injustice") would be largely held in check by the widespread dispersal of power.

As this sort of complex, conditional thinking about human nature and democratic government works out its logic, it more and more validates an inclusiveness that defeats arguments for exclusion of any group or category of humans. In Jefferson's day, and in his own thought, for example, there were formidable categories of exclusion from participation in government. Jefferson was convinced that democratic government could be good government only if the parts, the citizens, were in some measure reasonable, equal, responsible, and public-spirited. He thought, in accord with eighteenth-century republican theory, that voters and officeholders should have a "stake in the community" manifested by ownership of property (preferably land). He tried to reconcile this with the equal imperative that just government derived from the consent of the governed—*all* the governed. He proposed, in Virginia at a time when states set franchise rules, that all citizens lacking property be given fifty acres of land or a town building lot, thus assuring their "stake," independence, and sense of responsibility. When Jefferson later agreed with James Madison that, "as a man is said to have a right to his property, he may equally be said to have a property in his rights,"[21] he accepted the extension of stake-in-society arguments to include vocation, need for security, and provision for family in a person's property. Everyone, that is, might have such a stake, or built-in sense of responsibility. The gradual elimination of land or money property requirements for voting and for officeholding, first in the United States, then in other democratic polities, thus became part of the rationale for democracy. Notice, however, that the idea of qualification itself did not disappear—that, instead, the property grounds of qualification broadened to near total inclusiveness.

Disqualification on grounds of condition of servitude (especially slavery) or race, widespread at the time of the founding of the American polity, also required modification as anthropological understanding and economic imperatives shifted. To Jefferson, the oppressed, degraded condition imposed by slavery (and even some forms of indentured servitude) seemed obviously to disqualify persons in those conditions from well-informed and responsible exercise of citizenship, even though the condition of slavery was unjust and inadmissible in a republic. Furthermore, a never entirely abandoned conviction of the inherent inferiority of Africans prevented him from believing that they could ever be fully qualified and equal citizens of a self-governing polity, as would be required if the polity was to be just and wisely governed. Also, assuming fundamentally different capacities in public matters, it would always be problematic and unjust for Europeans and Africans to coexist in the same polity. One race would oppress and the other resent the other, thus preventing the harmonious, equitable attention to public affairs by all citizens that good government required. Jefferson proposed, though never practically or effectively, that the end of slavery required strenuous efforts at preparing the to-be-freed slaves for their new condition as citizens—but also, since those efforts would never entirely remove the inequalities and animosities between the races, separate existence and separate polities for Africans, either in the American West or returned to Africa. His point was always that, however much freedom, justice, and fulfillment was the birthright of all peoples (and he believed it was), the need for responsible and reasonable interchange among citizens of a self-governing polity required as well the mutually respectful, fully equitable standing of each and every citizen—something that would be impossible in a society of unequal races. If anthropological understanding and moral conviction came to see the two races as equal, then, of course, neither second-class citizenship nor separation would be either necessary or justifiable.

Jefferson's understanding of Native Americans, about whom he did not harbor convictions of inferiority, led him to quite different views of their inclusion in a republican polity. He believed Native Americans, at least those of near parts of North America with whom he was acquainted, to be physically, morally, and intellectually not inferior to Europeans. He even declared that Native American societies (all on a small scale) that depended on customs, manners, and the moral sense for "control" were happier and less exposed to evil (especially tyrannical government) than were "civilized" Europeans subjected to "too much law." He expected that, as Native Americans abandoned the predatory nature and "the precarious resources of hunting and fishing" and, instead, became "disposed to cultivate the earth, raise herds of the useful animals, and to spin and weave, for their food and clothing," they would form settled communities fully capable of becoming part of the American polity. He proposed, then, that American government and civil society "teach them agriculture and the domestic arts, encourage them . . . [in] industry, . . . and prepare them in time for that state of society, which to bodily comforts adds the improvement of the mind and morals." Jefferson hoped altogether "to induce [the Indians] to exercise their reason, follow its dictates, and change their pursuits with the change of circumstances."[22] Native Americans were as inherently qualified to be fully equal citizens of a republican polity as were white Europeans. To do this, however, they needed to abandon culture and mores that made life predatory, unhealthy (especially for women), and precarious and, instead, become industrious, orderly yeoman farmers in the same way that that style of life helped Europeans become good republican citizens. This was the difference between "savage" and "civilized" existence, and Jefferson thought such a transformation necessary for any (inherently qualified) peoples to establish and take part in good self-government. Not able to accept and value Native American culture in its own right, just as he argued that a feudal, peasant society or crowded commercial or industrial cities would not nourish habits of democratic citizenship, Jefferson insisted that Native Americans abandon their indigenous culture in order to become civilized yeoman farmers, thus qualified to be responsible, self-governing citizens. All who achieved such melioration, whatever their race or cultural background, were capable of inclusion in the polity and, indeed, had to be included, both in justice to themselves and because of the contribution that they could, thus, make to the well-being of society. The facts that U.S. "Indian policy," in Jefferson's day and later, never overcame the aggressive, violent conditions on the frontier that killed or drove Native Americans westward and never mustered the effective or culturally sensitive measures necessary to nourish settled farming communities meant that the republicanizing theories were never really tested.

The inclusive tendencies of civic republican theory are also evident in the gradual achievement of the full civil rights of women in the United States and other democratic nations. In the eighteenth century, for example, as the new American polity was being established, women were not regarded as "members" of the body politic. They were considered, both inherently and because of their "place" in society, to be mentally, temperamentally, or psychologically unsuited to a political role. They were not thought to possess, generally or in very high degree, the skill in public reason and the tough, confrontational realism required in politics. In Aristotelian terms, they were not regarded as "political animals," suited to and destined for public life. Rather, as wives, mothers, family laborers, and homemakers, often thought to have special responsibility for the spiritual and moral life of the family, and fully occupied and burdened in its nurture, women remained outside the sphere, and incapable, of politics. After the American Revolution, in part to make use for republican purposes of the increasing recognition of women's moral and intellectual qualities, women were often assigned the partly political role of "republican mothers." As such, they were given special responsibility for raising sons to be good republican citizens. This required that they be well educated themselves in republican ideology and even politics (Abigail Adams was a prototype) and, thus, capable of training their children (especially sons) for public life, especially in its moral dimension.

Acknowledgment of this capacity and this role rendered their exclusion from direct public life more and more an anomaly. If they were capable of training their sons for public life, why could they not take part themselves? Indeed, if women possessed that ability, republican theory would seem to require their inclusion so that they could enrich the polity with their portion of reason, goodwill, and public understanding. As long as the economics of family life, and the masculine character of life outside the home, was insisted on as necessary and sacrosanct, however, women's participation in public life could be resisted and denied. As their capacity for reason and public interest was asserted and acknowledged, however, as would also be the case for non–property owners, slaves, and Africans, their inclusion in a self-governing polity would be both just and required.

Complex Human Nature and Higher Law

At the beginning of the twenty-first century, then, a complex, conditionally positive understanding of human nature, inclusive of any and all categories and groups but aware of flaws and weaknesses scattered through them all, furnishes the foundation for a rich understanding of self-government. This understanding accepts, as Joseph Tussman has put it, that "self-interest and competitiveness are ancient facts of life and not the invention of political theorists," but it denies that they are all the facts of life or that they are sufficient and to be celebrated. "There is something novel and bold," Tussman observes, "in seeing them not as tendencies to be curbed but as powers to be encouraged and harnessed," allegedly for the public good.[23] These selfish, competitive, even quarrelsome and aggressive qualities, emphasizing the energy and contribution of the parts, and often accepted and praised by liberal and procedural ideas of democracy, are, in a complex, conditional understanding, "tendencies to be curbed" or controlled, most directly in self-government by checks and balances, limitations on government (bills of rights), and other separations and dispersals of power. The idea, however, is not that these problematic aspects of human nature can be eliminated or even very much diminished but, rather, that, especially in a democratic society, they can be checked, counterbalanced, and arranged so as to do as little harm (and maybe even some good) as possible—but not unconditionally celebrated. In Niebuhr's words, people "must know the power of self-interest in human society without giving it moral justification."[24] The intent is to be realistic, accepting human nature as it is, and as it is understood in a post-Freudian world, but to repudiate the

Mandevillian argument that "Desires," "Appetites," and "Vices" are valuable, constructive qualities in public life.[25]

On the other hand, the more positive qualities in human nature—"capacity for justice" (or moral sense), an interest in the public, and the ability to reason and deliberate—need to be encouraged and drawn forth. With disuse, abuse, or oppression, over long or short periods of time, they can atrophy seriously. In fact, this second part of human nature is also a "second nature" that, in practice, needs to be taught, educed, surfaced as over against "first" (self-oriented) nature. This second nature, however, does not come from outside or need to be imposed. Rather, it is "there," in human nature in varying degrees, needing only to be released, activated, trained, in order to play its part in human affairs—and is critical, of course, in democratic polities. This understanding does not include a rose-colored view of the simple goodness of basic or "original" human nature (as one can find in, e.g., Rousseau or Thoreau or even Marx in a way), nor does it contest the myriad situations past and present where humans in political societies are supposed to be or are observed to have been selfish, ignorant, greedy, alienated, apathetic, irrational, violent, and so on. The more complicated, interesting, and important point is that human nature is varied enough to make good government vital to its control and fulfillment, to furnish ingenuity to devise means of good government, and to allow people, all people, properly circumstanced, to take part, more or less, safely and constructively. But the variety (the central feature of humanity) is also such that things can go terribly wrong, not only under tyrannies, but in self-governing societies as well. The key is the nourishing, the educing, the drawing forth of the widely varying potential among people to understand their rights and to take part responsibly in self-government.

Such an idea of citizenship, however, carries with it implications of higher law or universal standards: What do reason and conscience reveal? The most immediate answer is the traditions of civility that, as Jefferson put it in 1801, bring to "social intercourse that harmony and affection without which liberty and even life itself are but dreary things."[26] But these concepts themselves require for intelligibility "foundations," "essences" that bind human conduct and human interchange to certain standards and guidelines, anywhere, anytime. Though the statement and practice of such foundations or universals is not entirely the same in societies over time and around the world, there is powerful convergence both on the need for something of the sort if a society is to be well governed and on many of the substantial principles in them. The formal statements of rights adopted by revolutionary polities at the time of the French and American Revolutions, which were asserted to be derived from and to conform to human reason, copied by countless nations ever since, and implicit in Great Britain's "unwritten" constitution, are widely accepted formulations of natural or higher law. Sir William Blackstone in 1765 had defined "the law of nature" as "coeval with mankind, and dictated by God himself, . . . superior in obligation to any other": "It is binding over the whole globe, in all countries, and at all times. No human laws are of any validity, if contrary to this."[27] In 1943, Justice Robert Jackson declared for the U.S. Supreme Court: "The very purpose of a Bill of Rights was to withdraw certain subjects from the vicissitudes of political controversy, to place them beyond the reach of majorities and officials and to establish them as legal principles to be applied by the courts. One's right to life, liberty, and property, to free speech, a free press, freedom of worship and assembly, and other fundamental rights may not be submitted to vote; they depend on the outcome of no elections."[28] Religious or cultural codes such as those in the Ten Commandments, the Qur'an, or the Chinese *Book of Mencius* and *Great Learning* also function implicitly (or sometimes explicitly) as higher law. In the late twentieth century, Nelson Mandela, Václav Havel, Aung San Suu Kyi, and many other voices proclaimed their resistance to tyranny and their claim for self-government and a civil society in language with worldwide appeal and acceptance. The UN "Universal Declaration of Human Rights" (1948) is perhaps the most widely acknowledged effort to articulate universal sentiments.

It is true, of course, that no one of these versions of higher law is actually accepted universally either in theory or in practice. Anthropologists can find societies and cultures where they are absent or not applicable or contradicted, and philosophers can, in the manner of a Hume, a Dewey, or a Lyotard, discredit them as not universal, not logically consistent, or simply nonexistent. There are, it seems, exceptions, inconsistencies, lapses, and contingencies that call into question any particular statement of them. In a way, then, they are neither foundational nor pervasive. These complaints and criticisms, however, often have the character of chipping away at the edges of the universal law (there are societies, e.g., that practice and validate human sacrifice or infanticide) without really undermining its general acceptance. Sometimes, too, the critiques are abstract or technical objections to a seemingly self-evident or universal observation or idea; for example, Hume's famous argument that, in the case of the movement when one billiard ball strikes another, one cannot prove causality or universality empirically. The effect is, for common understanding, to leave the principle or generalization substantially intact, acceptable and right for all practical purposes. The same sense of general validity obtains for the moral conviction present in such declarations as Martin Luther's "To go against conscience is neither right nor safe. God help me," Emerson's "I will not obey it, by God," response to the Fugitive Slave Law, and Martin Luther King's declaration from Birmingham jail that "an unjust law is no law at all."[29] They claim universality, anytime, anywhere, in spite of exceptions and even theoretically sound limitations that can be raised. The center holds even if the edges fray.

The arguments (reasons) on behalf of higher, universal, or natural law can also be sustained if one understands that any human, temporally contingent statement of them is bound to be flawed or incomplete simply because of those always present circumstances. As Reinhold Niebuhr has noted, even though "every society needs working principles of justice as criteria for its positive law and system of restraints, . . . every historical statement of them is subject to amendment. . . . Natural-law theories which derive absolutely valid principles of morals and politics from reason, invariably introduce contingent practical applications into the definition of the principle."[30] Thus, attempts by humans to articulate or codify higher or natural law at any given time or place will always bear the imprint of human fallibility and be subject to the biases and contingencies of time and place. The tendency for religious dogma, constitutional principles, moral codes, and other allegedly universal propositions to change and evolve through history or to be differently understood or interpreted by different people at a given time and place, then, may argue not so much for nonuniversality as for the recognition of (varying degrees of) human fallibility and of the always contingent nature of any ideal formulation—which reflects the complex, imperfect, but potentially improvable nature of humanity. Abortion, gay rights, and prayer in the schools are but a few of the issues that illustrate shifting ways of understanding and applying what those for and against claim as just.

It may be, however, as evidenced by countless individuals and movements through history and around the world, that human beings possess (in varying degrees) what Lord Kames, Jefferson, and others called a *moral sense,* the substance of which, "feelings of sympathy, justice, gratitude, benevolence, and friendship," is inherent and universal. In Lord Coke's striking metaphor, these sentiments are "written with the Finger of God in the Heart of Man." As Kames and Jefferson, as well as Confucius, Cicero, Charlotte Perkins Gilman, Martin Luther King, and numerous other moralists would insist, however, serious and thorough processes of nurture and education and upbringing are necessary to draw forth and vivify these sentiments, especially for their public usefulness. In the Greek understanding, a person controlled only by appetites and instinct, by the first nature of survival, self-aggrandizement, and greed, is a barbarian, while those nurtured to and possessed of a second and civilized nature, those with (some) educed sense of the moral law, are fit to be citizens, participants in self-government.[31]

We may understand, then, that part of human nature is to have a "capacity for justice," a "moral sense," that is distributed in varying individual degrees (some, like Socrates or Jesus or Confucius, with much, others with little or even none) among all races, genders, groups, and classes but that, in any case, needs to be drawn forth, nourished, and articulated. This cultivation, moreover, allows discernment, perhaps evolutionary, but always partial and incomplete, of higher laws, universal principles, that can serve as guides for private and public life. This capacity, or potential, in large or small measure present in individuals in all categories or groups of people, is, thus, part of human nature and gives access to converging sentiments ("moral sense," conscience) that, however imperfectly understood, satisfy the human longing (part of our nature) for universal standards for individual and shared life. Also present, of course, is the tendency toward injustice or evil (including selfishness, the capacity to rationalize, and inevitable partiality toward one's own interests), again distributed unevenly among individuals in all groups and categories, that makes government, especially self-government in which all participate, interesting, important, and complex, fraught with peril as well as opportunity, the reason why democracy is necessary as well as possible. This contests, of course, the contrary views of human nature that have undergirded other rationales for democracy: the perhaps too simple, Enlightenment view of some first modernity thinkers such as Thomas Paine and Rousseau; the self-interested, rational-choosing individuals of the second modernity; the more passive, in-need-of-guidance citizens of third modernity strong leader regimes; and the group-oriented, margin-tending, uncenterable individuals of postmodern understanding.

Democratic Decisionmaking, Leadership, and Citizenship

Modes of making decisions, the role of leadership, the responsibilities of citizens, and other aspects of democratic government can be attuned to this complex understanding of human nature. Liberal, individualistic, conflict-of-interest versions of democracy, for example, suppose that self- or group advocacy, negotiation, compromise, horse-trading, voting, majority rule, and ongoing opposition seeking 50 percent plus 1 in the next vote are the best, perhaps the only way to make decisions in a free, democratic, pluralistic society. This accords with the self-interested, autonomous, rational choice understanding of human nature, more attuned to private than to public affairs, of second modernity thinking. Such persons would be well suited to a decisionmaking process based on majority rule in a legislative assembly, ready to take part effectively, likely to accept the pragmatic, for-the-time-being, partial results, and willing to go forward with public life on that basis.

The results, however, become problematic, especially in the long run. There is a slow but steady movement of public life away from large aspirations, wise conceptions, "vision," and thoughtful concern for the general welfare and toward stridency, power brokering, and a demeaned, fragmented idea of the nation's common life. As Jane Mansbridge has put it, the model of "adversarial democracy," the notion of "mechanical aggregation of conflicting desires," "verges on moral bankruptcy": "It accepts and makes no attempt to change the foundations of selfish desire."[32] In fact, the adversarial, brokering, special- and group-interest-responding model and rationale further call forth and sustain the very qualities of autonomous self-interest that have been assumed in the first place. As John Taylor of Caroline noted two centuries ago, "a bad form of government," that is, one depending largely on factional struggle within a system of checks and balances, "will often succeed in making good men bad" by requiring them to act partially and selfishly in order to succeed within the process.[33] The self-fulfilling circle is, thus, complete: as the system assumes and requires only the self-interested striving of its members to make it work, it nourishes the very factions and self-orientation that it assumes, and the attitudes and practices of the citizens, as well as the processes of government, are on a downward, reinforcing cycle of self-interest, partiality, conflict, and neglect of the public good.

A more complex understanding of human nature, however, makes available, and calls for, broader possibilities in making political decisions. The part of the nature of human beings that seeks self- or group interests responds to and behaves on political matters much as is the case for the conflict model and calls for some of the same political dynamic and processes. Democracy is, thus, necessary. But other dimensions of human nature, possessing a capacity for discerning and seeking justice, and aspiring to what Jefferson termed *ideal right* in public life (again in widely varying degrees among humans), suggest other possible modes of making decisions in a democratic society. Note, for example, James Madison's idealistic understanding, in *Federalist* no. 63, of how the Senate under the new constitution might work. He was pleased that it was a relatively small body (twenty-six at first) in office for long terms and elected by supposedly well-informed, public-spirited legislators in the various states. This carefully chosen body, then, would gather and look beyond the "blindness of prejudice" and the "corruption of flattery" often characteristic of large, frequently chosen, and directly elected assemblies to seek "the cool and deliberate sense of the community." The Senate might, thus, be able to "suspend the blow . . . against the people" that might arise in hasty, passion-driven assemblies until, through senatorial deliberation, "reason, justice, and truth can regain their authority over the public mind."[34] The essential part of their decisionmaking would take place within their deliberations, as the senators, from their enlarged perspective, discussed various public matters—legislation, appointments, and treaties. They would provide in the last case "advice and consent," words laden with implications of the potential good effects of public-spirited talk. Factionalism, horse-trading, small-mindedness, and partisan voting were probably inevitable in a free society, and could not be banished, and would prove to be often characteristic of the Senate's actual performance. Madison hoped, however, that the wisdom, sense of justice, and concern for the public good that were also in varying degrees part of human nature would also prove important.

The same point was made by Edmund Burke in the famous 1774 address to the Bristol constituents who had elected him to Parliament. He would not go to Westminster, he told them, as an advocate of their special interests, nor did he pledge himself in advance to back any particular measures. Parliament, he said, "is a *deliberative* assembly of *one* nation, with *one* interest, that of the whole—where not local purposes, not local prejudices, ought to guide, but the general good, resulting from the general reason of the whole." He intended to go there as a representative of "the commons" of all of Great Britain, to deliberate with other members on the affairs of the nation at large. He would, he said, be mindful of local interests, not to advocate them, but rather to offer them for consideration in the broader discussion. Then, with all interests and purposes before the House, he and the other members would talk them over, not each to gain as much as possible for the constituents, but to understand what was best for the country.[35] Indeed, before the Long Parliament (1640–1660), the members of the House of Commons were instructed to speak "their consciences in matters proposed in the House but with all due respect for your majesty." They seldom voted (or after long committee discussions often decided unanimously) and were regarded as an advisory body to the king, who was understood to speak for the nation as a whole. The point was not to "divide," as the House would often do in coming partisan days, but rather, through discussion, to reach agreement on the business of the realm. Though by Burke's day, and even under Charles I, the House of Commons had become an often bitterly partisan, contentious, and divided body that decided by majority vote (and elections were fought increasingly on local constituency issues), this was at the expense of a dynamic that sought agreement rather than division and that valued deliberation over debate.[36]

Modern democracies, of course, have long largely submitted to the partisan, majority-vote model as the politics of the parts has pushed aside the politics of the whole. From the practices of Athens and the writings of Aristotle and the speeches of Cicero, however, the idea that reason, deliberation, and the search for agreement on the public good could be a vital part of self-government has persisted. Some more recent philosophers and practitioners of democracy from Jefferson onward have sought both to retain the deliberative dynamic in the councils of government and to spread its constructive use among citizens by seeking to enlarge the pool of qualified, public-spirited participants, including those not usually or already heard in the public councils. It might still be possible, even in the twenty-first century, to invigorate this dynamic in some measure or some fashion, perhaps beginning by "deschooling" ourselves (and our children) of the idea that the partisan-conflict, majority-rule model is inevitable, benign, and sufficient. This, in any case, is a plausible possibility within a rationale for democracy that rests on a more complex, partly just and partly selfish conception of human nature. Moreover, it does not require an immediate, total, or unrealistic change in attitude or procedures. Rather, as sentiments expressed in public bodies, even by a few individuals, become more deliberative and less adversarial, or as groups from committees to legislatures practice seeking a "sense of meeting" instead of a majority-vote division, small bits of "the general reason of the whole" might come into play and, in some degree, move the proceedings toward the public good. The process might even produce immediate, small steps forward. In the Aristotelian formulation, "the many, of whom each individual may not be of a good quality, ... when they meet together may surpass ... the quality of the few best, if regarded not individually but collectively. . . . Each individual can bring his share of goodness and moral prudence; ... and when all meet together, they become something in the nature of a single person ... with many qualities of character and intelligence."[37]

Such decisionmaking possibilities also suggest altered purposes and styles of leadership. The leader-as-broker model generally assumes, explicitly or implicitly, a human nature that is self-oriented and manipulable. Individuals and groups in the polity have their own interests and agendas and are participants in the political process in order to get as much of what they want, or what they consider is just for themselves, as possible. While it is assumed that individuals and groups will try to gain influence and power for themselves, there is also general acknowledgment that the process works best when all have access to it and when advocacies and interactions are open and effective, "on an even playing field." Clear and potent concepts of equality and freedom are, thus, embodied: equal access of all to political processes and freedom for all to seek as best they can their own interests and concerns; this is what democracy means and is intended to be in the liberal corporate state.

Within this context, the goal and task of the political leader is to somehow arrange that all interests and concerns are attended to as much as possible and that his or her own standing and power (his or her self-interest) are made as secure as possible. Leaders cannot claim legitimately to be seeking an objective justice because no such conception exists, and, if it is claimed, it is always a rationalization of the claimer's own power and position of dominance. Since it is, thus, assumed that there is no such thing as an overarching public good, the leader's role is not to offer some grand scheme of things to which others might be attracted and by which they might be persuaded but, rather, to accommodate and compromise among the various interests in a way that provides enough satisfaction and gains enough backing for the brokering leader to achieve and retain political power. In the realities of politics in a free society, this can be a necessary and useful role, but it is not enough if rule in a self-governing society is to achieve its potential. For that, the leader must also provide *leadership*, offer goals and plans and aspirations, even "the vision thing" (George H. W. Bush, scornfully, in 1992), that can articulate for the people what Aristotle had in mind in noting that "a state exists for the sake of a good life, and not for the sake of life only." It is what Jefferson had in mind in 1801 when he noted that, though it was "impossible to advance the notions of a whole people suddenly to ideal right," it was still the duty of the president (which office he had recently entered) to lead toward as much "good . . . [as] the nation could bear." Theodore Roosevelt's statement of the same idea was: "I simply made up my mind what the people ought to think, and then did my best to get them to think it."[38]

The president—the leader, that is—if democracy is to rise above lowest common denominators and above being a mere arena for the interaction of interests and groups, must articulate noble, inspiring ideas that call forth the higher and better and more just potentialities in human nature and open up prospects that would, in the words of the ancient oath of the Athenian citizen, "quicken the sense of public duty . . . [and] transmit this city not less but greater, better and more beautiful than it was transmitted to us."[39] Such an understanding of the U.S. presidency, for example, would suggest a less partisan, more public-spirited idea of the office. Though campaigning with party support and with an eye to the needs and interests of various groups throughout the country is probably both practically necessary and a useful way to gather and organize support, campaign energy should focus political parties, interest groups, and the public at large on programs responsive to the question, What is in the public interest of the nation as a whole? The campaigns of Theodore Roosevelt and Woodrow Wilson in 1912 urging a "New Nationalism" and a "New Freedom," for example, were largely of that kind. They understood and spoke to each other, and the public understood that each was responding to the question, What is good for the nation as a whole? while the widely perceived candidate of special interests, President William Howard Taft, was thought irrelevant and shunted to the sidelines.

Once in office, the president should as much as possible leave partisanship and catering to special interests at the White House door. Though those of the president's party, and perhaps even some special-interest advocates, would probably be prominent among cabinet and other officers because of like-mindedness, those of other parties and groups, not necessarily allies during the campaign, would also be invited to the councils insofar as they could serve the public good. Relations with Congress would follow the same pattern: using fellow party members as much (probably substantially) as policy agreement made effective, but also appealing across party and interest group lines for support for a program of "as much good as the country could bear." This might have the effect of helping gather and even mobilize popular support for the "good" programs and aspirations that the president might lay before the nation. This would not, in a free society, create unanimous agreement or end partisan and special-interest disagreement and competition, but it would encourage and help foreground the notion of public-spiritedness in the nation's public life. At the same time, of course, the president would cease fund-raising and other explicitly party-building enterprises that compromise his standing as the leader of the country as a whole. The effect again might be to enhance the president's power and authority, rather than diminish it as party conflict theory generally supposes, by heightening his standing among a people responding positively to a manifestly above-party perspective and intention. In any case, such an understanding and style of leadership are attuned to a complex idea of human nature possessing in some degree a "capacity for justice" as well as an inevitable tendency toward self-interestedness. It can also be part of a rationale for democracy that might counteract millennia-old critiques insisting on its tendencies toward mindless mob rule and toward endless bickering and special-interest pandering.

The most fundamental reorientation required by a rationale for democracy resting on human complexity, however, is that of the citizens themselves. The connection between the part of human nature, the capacity for justice, that makes democracy possible and the implications and possibilities that this opens up for the nature and practice of citizenship is crucial. Just as an emphasis on the self-seeking and self-aggrandizing part of human nature, brought into the public sphere, validates a democratic participation oriented toward maintenance of individual rights and achieving special interests, the justice-tending part looks toward a citizenship focused on the public good. This is not to say, of course, that private seeking can or needs to be abandoned. It needs simply to be modulated in ways that prevent the obscuring of the public dimension. One might think of the individual rights-seeking, self-oriented part of our nature as that which finds legitimate fulfillment living in a free, liberal society—nothing wrong with that.

A capacity for justice and for attention to the public good, however, suggests that, as a member of a self-governing society, one must fulfill "the office of the citizen," that is, be part of the "ruling class" responsible for the good of the whole. Only by understanding and, in some measure, fulfilling this role can one really enjoy political freedom and be the "political animal" that Aristotle insisted was an essential part of human nature. This does not require, however, that the United States, for example, become a nation of 300 million Aristotles. Rather, it supposes that some attention to the "office of the citizen," whether many hours, a few hours, or even a few minutes a week, when one thinks and perhaps acts as publicly and as disinterestedly as possible, is what is meant by exercising *political* freedom—a different enterprise from the also valued idea of *personal* liberty. As Thomas Pownall explained in the years following the American Revolution, the "ancient Legislators and Institutors of Republics" in Greece and Rome had restricted "personal liberty, the inalienable rights of the individual," in order to "force nature" (one thinks of Platonic "gentle persuasion") toward the cultivation of good rulers (citizens) practicing political freedom. In the United States, however, personal liberty was to be protected and valued even as political freedom was exercised in a public-spirited way by every citizen taking part in the affairs and decisions of the polity. "As members of the constitutional community," Michael Perry writes, "we participate in a form of life that is both a personal and a collective good . . . a form of life that enables us . . . to make progress . . . in realizing our true selves and in achieving well being. Were we deprived of or cut off—alienated—from the constitutional community [as in totalitarian societies] we would . . . be seriously diminished."[40]

The ideal is something like the combining of private and public qualities in the Confucian model of the noble or exemplary person, *chüntzu (junzi)* (see chapter 2). For the *chüntzu,* as David L. Hall and Roger T. Ames explain, "self-cultivation necessarily entails active participation in the family and the extended order of the community [public life] as a means of evoking the compassion and concern that leads to one's own personal growth." Though the ideal is for the exceptionally noble person and, thus, not thought of as embodying qualities that might characterize masses of ordinary people (citizens), it was a model that could be achieved by one of any race, class, or category and that emphasized the indispensable public part of one's being. "The Confucian model of personal realization," Hall and Ames point out, "does not permit severe distinctions between ethics and politics, between the personal and social, between the private and public. . . . The private/public distinction that has been so basic to Western political theories is largely absent."[41] Within this understanding, the citizen is not a basically private entity, perhaps occasionally entering the public arena for self-oriented reasons, but rather one whose personal fulfillment is found at least in part in concern for and improvement of circles of relationship extending out from family to community and nation and the world.

When Benjamin Franklin noted at the Constitutional Convention of 1787 that "the virtue and public spirit of our common people" would be the key to the good operation of the new constitution, he identified the essence of its undergirding concept of citizenship. He was urging that the franchise be broad so that as many people as possible would gain the sense of participation and public competence that might be nurtured by the experience of voting. He hoped for a beneficent circle that depended on some capacity for justice: if the people were accorded the trust and responsibility implied in the grant of the franchise, this might help educe the "virtue and public spirit" that would in turn make their participation constructive and useful to the common good. Without this, Franklin implied, the United States would be in the same position as Great Britain and other undemocratic governments where the people had no part to play and, thus, were not drawn forth in a public-spirited way.[42] Government in the public interest, Franklin was saying, began with an interest in the public by citizens, which could be heightened by the experience of participating in self-government.

Attention to the powerful impact of occupations and social life on the habits and attitudes of the people is also crucial to a stronger, deeper idea of citizenship. A preponderance of occupations that nourish inherently (or at least do not stifle or cause to atrophy) the sense of responsibility, diligence, purposeful effort, independence, self-reliance, honesty, and social cooperativeness vital to good citizenship is essential in any self-governing polity. Jefferson's extolling of the lifestyle of the yeoman farmer rested on this proposition, as did Franklin's encouragement of the thrifty, honest habits of "Poor Richard" among urban artisans. Oppositely, Jefferson declared, an occupation of dependence or stultification "begets subservience and venality, suffocates the germ of virtue, and prepares fit tools for the designs of ambition." For similar reasons, Jefferson was uneasy about lawyers trained to advocate what they did not believe and merchants tempted to cheat as they bought cheap and sold dear.[43] In a later age, factory workers schooled in "participatory" democracy through autonomous unions, women practiced in family management, and myriad operatives, tradespeople, and technicians trained to be "professional," that is, to be competent, responsible, honest, and efficient, would also have essential fostering and practice in the arts of citizenship. The movement for an eight-hour day had as one of its objectives "relief from Hours of Labor, which use up in the service of others, the whole day, leaving us no time to comply with the public duties" of citizenship. "The charm of the eight hour system," one advocate argued, was that it would give ignorant, downtrodden, exhausted workers leisure to become "wiser fellows" by studying political and social science and, thus, to learn, as citizens, about "the prevention of crime, women's wages, war, and the ten thousand schemes with which our age [1902] teems for the amelioration of the condition of man."[44] Furthermore, part of the training for any job or profession, in order to meet public as well as private need, would have to include, in Puritan terms, attention not only to the "particular calling," the skills of a specific vocation, but also to the "general calling," or its place in a larger, moral scheme of things of which responsible citizenship would be a crucial part.[45] In any case, a political economy inured in occupations not congenial to the traits of a rich and strong citizenship would be unlikely to sustain good democratic government. The direction of the American labor movement away from arguments on behalf of improved citizenship and toward trade union emphasis on shorter hours, better working conditions, and higher wages in order to give workers more time, energy, and resources to improve their individual lives, strengthen their bargaining power, and increase demand in the national economy, of course, accorded with the second modernity ethos of the liberal corporate state.

Even if many occupations in a society had few rhythms conducive to the needs of citizenship or of a "general calling," some of the disadvantages could be counteracted if there was easy and effective participation in a wide variety of associations. "Americans make associations," Tocqueville observed, "to give entertainments, to found seminaries, to build inns, to construct churches, to diffuse books, to send missionaries to the antipodes; they found in this manner hospitals, prisons, and schools." (Exactly the trouble, Michel Foucault would point out.) As those who "happen to have a common interest . . . meet, they combine, and thus by degrees, they become familiar with the principle of association. . . . Political life [then] makes the love and practice of association more general." Such associations "may therefore be considered as large free schools where all members of the community go to learn the general theory of association," that is, the practice of a rich and public-spirited citizenship.[46] Contemporary social scientists make the same point. Robert Putnam, for example, notes that the existence of large amounts of "social capital," that is, "features of social organization such as networks, norms, and social trust that facilitate coordination and cooperation for mutual benefit," are important for effective democratic government. Churches, labor union halls, fraternal organizations, school associations, Scouts and the Red Cross, neighborhood groups, volunteer efforts, sports clubs, and even bowling leagues, Putnam argues, have formed a vital part of the "citizenship training" of Americans ever since Tocqueville noticed them nearly two centuries ago.[47] Equitable deliberation, social cooperation, and the opportunity to consider matters of public concern, the very essence of a rich understanding of citizenship, are, thus, nourished in habits of association, perhaps overtly political or perhaps not, that seem vital to good democratic government. The general absence of such associations, as the totalitarian state and its omnipresent party monopolized all activity, of course, is often thought to be the greatest obstacle to the achievement of genuine democracy in the post–Soviet Empire states.

This important capacity for civic association of all kinds, atrophied in societies supposed to rest on simple economic determinism (whether capitalist or Marxist), depends itself on a more complex understanding of human nature that makes room for a capacity for justice suited to the formation of organizations that nourish "social trust" and "mutual benefit." Like the civically useful occupations, civic associations provide critical opportunities for evoking the attributes of a rich and strong citizenship. These mobilized capacities, moreover, undergird a citizenship that is not minimal or advocacy oriented but, rather, deliberative, participatory, and public-spirited, likely as important in the twenty-first century as it was when Franklin, Jefferson, and others explained its vital connection to good democratic government two hundred years ago. The perhaps countereffect of so-called bad associations neither cancels the good effects explained by Tocqueville, Putnam, and others nor challenges an understanding of human nature that acknowledges as well the huge capacity of organizing for evil purposes likely present in a free society.

Perhaps most central of all to the nurturing of the human capacity for justice into a strong citizenship is public education, that is, tutelage to meet the *public* need for qualified citizens. Jefferson's explanation merits repetition: "I know of no safe depository of the ultimate power of society but the people themselves, and if we think them not enlightened enough to exercise their control with a wholesome discretion, the remedy is not to take it from them, but to inform their discretion through education."[48] A carefully designed, formally required, and publicly supported system of schools, perhaps supplemented with private schools held to the same public purposes, is the critical capstone to the proper occupations, responsibility for localities, associational maturity, sense of "general calling," and moral training also important in a self-governing community. This requires, once again, citizens-to-be "qualified to understand their rights, to maintain them, and to exercise with intelligence their parts in self-government." The idea is to draw forth the latent capacity for justice, for social cooperation, and for public understanding, perhaps understood as a human second nature, that can then modulate or harness the first nature of self-preservation and self-interest and take part constructively in democratic government (Aristotelian and Confucian echoes abound). Not to do this, as Horace Mann noted in 1848, would be as disastrous as foreign invasion "because the general prevalence of ignorance, superstition, and vice, will breed Goth and Vandal at home, more fatal to the public well-being, than any Goth or Vandal from abroad."[49]

Mann proposed both compulsory education (in public, private, or parochial schools) and the inclusion in that education of explicit attention to training in responsible citizenship. As time passed, this came to require either the implanting of the idea of education for public purposes throughout the curriculum or the creation of specific courses for "responsible citizenship" and "participation in government," or perhaps both. John Dewey's combining of democracy and education (in his 1916 *Democracy and Education*) led to emphasis on using classroom procedures themselves as "learning by doing" for constructive socialization. One of Dewey's disciples, W. H. Kilpatrick, explained in 1926 that school courses should teach "knowledge, insight, sensitivity, ideals, attitudes, and habits" essential to democratic citizenship.[50] A mid-twentieth-century emphasis on civics courses in high school and a responsible-citizenship requirement in college, however, largely fell victim to emphasis on specialization and vocational training later in the century (a kind of second modernity thinking). As a new century begins, however, there is a revived understanding of the need for civic or character education for American young people if they are to fill properly the "office of citizen" in a democratic society. One report, worried that, "as a nation, we are becoming civically illiterate, . . . drifting unwittingly into a new kind of Dark Age, . . . [when] democratic government [is] . . . replaced by a technocracy or the control of policy by special interest groups," calls for colleges to institute "a carefully crafted general education program for all students that focuses on those experiences that integrate individuals into a community."[51]

Education for participation in government, that is, requires more than learning the formal structure and processes of government (federal, state, and local), knowing how to research, draft, and implement public policy, and understanding and practicing the techniques of advocacy for special or group interests. These may be, to yet again evoke Carlyle's image, the "Spectacles" of the good citizen, but they cannot be the "Eye" that sees purposes and aspirations pointed toward the common good. To understand and maintain rights means more than seeing how rights can be sustained and used for personal fulfillment. It means as well understanding how a sense and practice of human rights can improve, even ennoble the character of an individual and, even more basic, undergird principled participation in public life. Freedom of religion and expression and the rights to due process of law and trial by jury are, of course, vital personal liberties, but understanding and possessing them are also essential to conscientious citizenship. Then the culmination of civic education comes with young people learning to "exercise with intelligence their parts in self-government." What does that mean and require? It means knowledgeable, wise, thoughtful, moral, public-spirited exercise of all the public offices of administration, deliberation, the franchise, and civic association. At the college level, this requires both a broad liberal arts education (to understand human nature and the world we live in) and thoughtful concern for public affairs and, at lower levels, constant attention to the civic dimensions of all branches of study. Only then will citizens have the "intelligence," the thoughtful, well-informed concern for public affairs, that is essential to all aspects of citizenship. Some such enriched citizenship is what Joseph Tussman in *Obligation and the Body Politic* (1960), Benjamin Barber in *Strong Democracy* (1984), Michael Sandel in *Democracy's Discontent* (1996), Peter Levine in *The New Progressive Era* (2000), and others in the last half century have had in mind as the sense of the flaws of various "minimal," "rational choice," and "procedural" citizenships has become more apparent.[52]

A concept of citizenship suited to a rationale for democracy that rests on a complex idea of human nature having some "capacity for justice" as well as for "injustice," then, is one that needs careful social nourishment. It depends on the prevalence of occupations and professions conducive to the habits of good citizenship, on the existence of associations of all kinds that afford practice in deliberative interaction, and on effective education in the virtues, values, and means of participation in self-government. It does not suppose, of course, that members are able completely to set aside their private and selfish interests. In fact, it assumes in a free and open society an incessant presentation and advocacy that bring to public discussion the varied concerns of all elements of a diverse society. It merely supposes that, with the aid of constructive vocations, civic associations, and public education, citizens will, some of the time, in some ways, also be able to take some interest in the public and attend to its affairs and advocacies with an eye to the common good. This public-spiritedness exists in the midst of a welter of vigorous special-interest and group concerns and demands affecting in some way every member of society. No citizens are perfectly public-spirited, nor are many totally bereft, at least potentially. There is, however, enough inherent capacity and potential social nourishment to allow enough fulfillment of the office of citizen to make self-government work deliberatively in some measure for the good of the whole—at least so theorists and practitioners of democracy from Thomas Jefferson to Nelson Mandela and Aung San Suu Kyi have argued.

A Post-Postmodern Rationale for Democracy

Where, then, does this leave rationales for democracy? After the contributions of four cycles of modernity and the critical responses to them, is there available for the twenty-first century a viable understanding of democratic government that can help make it good government? From the first modernity associated with Francis Bacon, emphasizing the need to begin with and somehow understand and agglomerate the facts or the parts, notions of *self*-government, also beginning with the parts, the people, have come persistently to the fore. Thus, the first rationale for democracy (though not so-called, positively, in the seventeenth and eighteenth centuries) took into account the varied needs and concerns of the people and, in some degree and fashion, accepted their participation. In the manner of Locke and Jefferson, however, the parts, the interests and convenience of the people, were still argued to be, using human reason, subsumed within patterns of natural, universal law. As an early New England Lockean put it: "Reason is congenate with [man's] nature, . . . by a law immutable instampt upon his frame. . . . We acknowledge the law of nature to be the dictate of right reason. . . . The way to discover the Law of Nature . . . is by a narrow watch and accurate contemplation of our natural condition, and propensions."[53] Though this version of democracy led to notable trials of self-government, especially that inaugurated under the U.S. Constitution of 1787–1791, it also spawned critiques from within and outside first modernity thought. From within came the argument that the natural law framework of the Constitution and the Bill of Rights was inconsistent with the strict, inductive guidelines of Baconian thought; one could not derive natural law, or any cause-and-effect certainty, from mere observation of facts and collection of data. From outside came the claim that, even with the Lockean natural law projection of first modernity thought, it was too mundane, too mechanical, too empirical (cf. Emerson's "our science is sensual, and therefore superficial"),[54] to do anything like draw forth and fulfill the moral, aesthetic, and spiritual dimensions of human nature. The rationale and practice of democracy had achieved remarkable liberations from immemorial tyrannies and oppressions (*metanarratives* in postmodern terms), but there was uneasiness about both democracy's consistency and ultimate implications in its own terms and its capacity to take into account and nurture the full range of human moral and spiritual potential.

These powerfully expressed critiques propelled both another, second modernity rationale for democracy and further reservations. This second rationale, responding to the internal critique, explicitly abandoned the natural, higher law aspects of democratic thought and focused instead on an allegedly more consistent attention to the calculus of the parts ("greatest happiness of the greatest number"), emphasis on the "individuality" of each person, and response to the felt needs of individuals and groups in any given polity. This had the useful effect of turning attention directly and mundanely to the more immediate needs of the people (all the people) in a society, but it also heightened the sense that neglecting the higher capacities and guidelines in affairs of government was deeply problematic and bypassed hugely important human potential (Carlyle called economics *the dismal science*). Indeed, it raised the question of whether second modernity thought was really suited to the varied dimensions of human nature.

The shortcomings of the second modernity rationale for democracy were highlighted when Confucian-trained scholars and statesmen in East Asia absorbed and made use of second modernity thought. Though such thought seemed highly useful in resisting ancient tyrannies and hierarchies and likely to help in achieving the wealth and power needed for survival and progress in the modern world, it also upset profound moralities and cosmologies that had for centuries guided life in East Asia. Hence came the Japanese slogan "Eastern morals and Western science." The problem seemed to be, as scholars understood and pursued the implications of Western thought, that it supposed a correlation between the mundane knowledge and understandings of "the people" in a society (collected democratically) and the higher laws (the Chinese mandate of heaven) of social existence that simply did not exist. Confucian precepts of the moral responsibilities of the state and of the need for learning and wisdom to guide the councils of statecraft seemed incompatible with the idea of government by the people in a participatory democracy, especially taking into account what the scholars saw as the ignorant, passive, utterly unpracticed circumstances of the common people of China and Japan as the twentieth century dawned. There developed in East Asia, then, an idea that wise, public-spirited, authoritarian leadership was necessary until the education and activeness of the people reached levels likely to make democratic government good government. Thus, the course of democratic government in East Asia, from the earliest partial trials in Meiji Japan in the 1870s to the continued movement toward meaningful democracy in South Korea, Taiwan, and even a little in the People's Republic of China 130 years later, has set forth a more leader-oriented, less participatory rationale for democracy. It has also offered an often-telling critique of the more unguided, quarrelsome, special-interest-pandering procedures of the liberal corporate state of the West.

Another critique of second modernity democracy, however, came from postmodernity, which, in the manner of Jeremy Bentham and Thorstein Veblen, insisted that the previous modernity had been too unrigorous, not sufficiently "incredulous to metanarrative." Instead of being thoroughly critical and unfoundational, as any modernity seemed to require, second modernity rationales for democracy in the hands of John Dewey, Harold Laski, and others had fashioned a "will to a system," a metanarrative that undergirded, not an open society, but a liberal corporate state as foundational, oppressive, and hostile to difference and otherness as any of the more obvious but less insidious tyrannies of history. The need, in government, was to dismantle the enormous bureaucracies, enforcement agencies, international corporations, certifying systems, and even nongovernment organizations that controlled and dominated so much of the lives of ordinary people and over which they had almost no control—self-government, that is, was a fraud and a farce. Though postmodernism does not incline toward any systematic new rationale of democracy (indeed, it cannot do so in faithfulness to its own denial of metanarrative), it does offer trenchant arguments on behalf of decentralization, lifting of regulations and certifications, acknowledging and presenting of excluded or marginalized "others," and the opening and even privileging of such groups in whatever political system, perhaps a more participatory, locally grounded self-government, might replace the oppressive liberal corporate state. Though some postmodern thought in seeking to "wither away" the state is, thus, properly understood as neo-Marxist, there is only scorn for Leninist or statist versions of Marxism. In any event, the focus is more on criticism and deconstruction than on a new rationale, another further development of "the Cartesian critical intellect [at] its furtherest point of development, . . . applying a systematic skepticism to every possible meaning."[55]

Critics of postmodernism from the outside see much the same sort of flaws that Swift saw in the empirical worldview of Bacon and Locke, that Carlyle and Niebuhr saw in the mundane reasonings of Bentham and Dewey, and that Liang Qichao came eventually to see in the logic and social science of J. S. Mill and Herbert Spencer. The various moderns simply did not comprehend the moral or spiritual dimensions of human nature or the normative prospects for government that a full understanding of the human condition makes possible. Even worse, all versions of modernity seemed to suffer from a sort of presumptuousness in the projection and extrapolation of their own thought. Baconian induction and scientific understanding of nature, that is, seemed to require and herald the complete dissection and then dominion of the physical world, even to the point of ignoring or overriding all other dimensions of life. Similarly, Comtian social science and Dewey's exalting of means over ends seemed to leave no room for the divine, the transcendent, the purposeful, the all-encompassing, the eternal, or the universal inclinations of human nature. Advocates of "science and democracy" in China in the twentieth century, whether fascist, Communist, or democratic, simply rushed on toward systems of "wealth and power" without much sense either of possible restraints imposed by ancient "mandates" or of possible disadvantage or disaster in the determined effort to seek a Baconian (or Spencerian) domination of nature. Finally, the critical studies of postmodernism, thoroughly reductionist and deconstructive, accept no restraints or evaluations deriving from traditional patterns of thought (inadmissible "logocentrisms" [see chapter 10]) but, instead, push ahead in "supermodern" fashion to declare all "texts" words without meaning beyond what can be understood subjectively from the critical theories themselves. The critical, unfoundational, postmodern world itself, that is, where there is, "in the beginning, *no word,* but only myriad voices that could have been interpreted in any number of ways,"[56] finds in its own methods no grounds for not going ahead on its path that leads to subjectivity, reductionism, mere acceptance, meaninglessness, and cynicism—literally nihilism.

Successive modernities, it seems, have left their rationales for democracy with very little place to stand except for an increasingly procedural, nonjudgmental, open, and differentiated circumstance. This has led to progress toward inclusion of all peoples and groups in the political process, the reduction of built-in and traditional privileges and inequalities, and a heightened emphasis on the rights, procedural and substantive, of all individuals. It has not, however, notably advanced the theory or practice of good government. These inclusions, reductions, and emphases, valid enough in their own right, have often proved to be "neutral," sometimes useful and sometimes not, in their impact on the "good life" and on effective government in any particular polity. This may be because the modern rationales themselves, over four centuries or more, have increasingly tended to bracket, to set aside, notions of higher law, of moral purpose, of capacities for justice, of spiritual quest—metanarratives of any kind. The bracketing of these matters, moreover, arises and grows most fundamentally because the successive rationales, faithful to reigning modernities, have insisted on their nonexistence in fact and on their pathological effect when societies have taken them seriously. The result has been a steady advance in one kind of thinking about democracy (inclusive, equitable, rights protecting) but the increasing neglect of, even scorn for, the active, qualitative life of the self-governing community.

Good democratic government in the twenty-first century, then, may depend on the development of a rationale that accepts the valid aspects of the various modern rationales but as well takes into account a more complex understanding of human nature that makes room for purpose, justice, and higher law. Democracy may limp along as the "least bad" of governments, but it is not likely to achieve good government if it is understood merely as a process for exercising majority rule and a means for protecting personal rights while celebrating the unique identity, the self-interestedness, and the ability to make rational choices of individuals and groups. Social and political arrangements, furthermore, that aspire to the demise of most institutions and structures of control, especially centralized ones, and that emphasize simply the presencing, the acceptance, and perhaps the privileging of previously oppressed groups, thus enlarging conceptions of tolerance and anti-imperialism, also seem unlikely to provide anything like good *government* in the contemporary world. Time-immemorial understandings of the importance of the political, and of the capacities of human beings to be "political animals" and, thus, to nourish a shared "good life," loom too largely and too profoundly to make either a procedural republic or a politics of identity and difference seem anything like a fulfillment of the potential for self-government.

Rather, democracy needs to nourish and make use of the human capacity for justice, understood as the reasoned and conscientious insight that makes good government possible. This reason and conscience, what Jefferson termed *the moral sense*, is present in some degree in all persons, though, in some—indeed, perhaps, most—societies, past and present, circumstances may have severely restrained, deadened, or atrophied it, among all or part of the people. Though there is, thus, wide variation in the effective presence of reason and conscience among individual human beings, there is no abundance or denial of it to groups defined by race, class, gender, ethnicity, culture, or creed. In that sense, all humans are equal and provisionally qualified for participation in self-government. At the same time, of course, greed, inattention, irrationality, and lust for power loom very large in human affairs and form part of the "pretension of pride," the "corruption of inordinate self-love," and the tendency to rationalize that are also indelible, though variable, parts of complex human nature. The harmless egotism of Adam Smith, the rational egotism of the utilitarians, and even the non-egotism of Marx's classless society all underestimate the power of self-interest in human society that makes democracy necessary as well as possible.[57] All power in human hands needs, in government, the "auxiliary precautions" of democratically arranged checks and balances to prevent abuse.

The point, however, is not to simply let democratic government rest on the outcome of the checks and balances among self- and group interests as liberal conflict-of-interest politics and, in a way, identity politics suppose is sufficient. Rather, a system of government must "neutralize" self-interests enough to make room for the expression and pursuit of the reasoned and conscientious capacities also present in human nature—or at least potentially present in sufficient degree among enough people to allow self-government to be good government. This supposes, of course, that the exercise of human reason and conscience leads in some general way toward widely understood and accepted guidelines for public life, universals that exist within the metanarratives of customs, cultures, religions, "mandates of heaven," and laws of right reason around the world. There is no complete agreement among these varied metanarratives, but humans have often discerned a core of convergence, at many levels, that sets forth concepts of the common good, applicable in some fashion for all humankind. The inclusion of some sort of this sensibility, embedded in a complex understanding of human nature, may be the best foundation for a rationale for democracy that can help make self-government good government in the twenty-first century.

INTRODUCTION

1. Alfred North Whitehead, *Science in the Modern World* (1925; New York: Mentor, 1948), 2.

1. PROSPECTS FOR GOVERNMENT IN 1989

1. Paul Kennedy, *Preparing for the Twenty-first Century* (New York: Random House, 1993); Immanuel Wallerstein, "The Three Instances of Hegemony in the History of the Capitalist World-Economy," *International Journal of Comparative Sociology* 24 (1983): 1–2; Thomas L. Friedman, *The Lexus and the Olive Tree: Understanding Globalization* (New York: Anchor, 2000), esp. 437–75.
2. Francis Fukuyama, "The End of History?" *The National Interest,* summer 1989, 3–18.
3. Samuel P. Huntington, "The Clash of Civilizations," *Foreign Affairs,* summer 1993, 22–49.
4. Robert L. Heilbroner, *An Inquiry into the Human Prospect* (New York: Norton, 1980), 13 and, generally, 166–78.
5. Samuel P. Huntington, *The Third Wave: Democratization in the Late Twentieth Century* (Norman: University of Oklahoma Press, 1991), 18–26.

2. ARISTOTELIAN AND CONFUCIAN INSIGHTS

1. Aristotle, *Politics,* trans. Benjamin Jowett (New York: Modern Library, 1943), bk. 3, chap. 9, p. 142.
2. David L. Hall and Roger T. Ames, *The Democracy of the Dead: Dewey, Confucius, and the Hope for Democracy in China* (Chicago: Open Court, 1999), 209.
3. Excerpts from the Four Books—the *Analects* of Confucius, the *Great Learning,* the *Doctrine of the Mean,* and the *Book of Mencius*—can be found in Wing-tsit Chan's *A Source Book in Chinese Philosophy* (Princeton, N.J.: Princeton University Press, 1963) and are summarized in Herrlee G. Creel's *Chinese Thought from Confucius to Mao Tse-tung* (Chicago: University of Chicago Press, 1953), David M. Earl's *Emperor and Nation in Japan: Political Thinkers of the Tokugawa Period* (Seattle: University of Washington Press, 1964), and many other excellent works.
4. The *Great Learning* quoted in Huston Smith, *The World's Religions* (San Francisco: Harper, 1991), 174.
5. The *Great Learning* quoted in Hall and Ames, *Democracy of the Dead,* 174.
6. Edwin O. Reischauer, *The Japanese* (Tokyo: Charles Tuttle, 1978), 44–45.
7. Benjamin Schwartz, *The World of Thought in Ancient China* (Cambridge, Mass.: Harvard University Press, 1985), 96.
8. Aristotle, *Politics,* bk. 1, chap. 2, p. 54.
9. Ibid., bk. 4, chaps. 1–5.

10. Benjamin Franklin, speech of August 7, 1787, before the Federal Convention, in Ralph Ketcham, ed., *The Political Thought of Benjamin Franklin* (Indianapolis: Bobbs-Merrill, 1965), 398.

11. Thucydides, *The Peloponnesian War*, trans. Crawley (New York: Modern Library, 1934), bk. 2, chap. 6, p. 105.

3. TENSIONS OF CITIZENSHIP

1. H. Mark Roelofs, *The Tension of Citizenship: Private Man and Public Duty* (New York: Rinehart, 1957).

2. I am referring here to Aquinas's *On the Training of Princes* (1266) and Erasmus's *The Education of a Christian Prince* (1516).

3. Roger Williams, "The Bloody Tenent yet More Bloody" (1652), in E. S. Morgan, ed., *Puritan Political Ideas* (Indianapolis: Bobbs-Merrill, 1965), 217.

4. Martin Luther King, "Letter from Birmingham Jail" (1963), in Henry J. Silverman, ed., *American Radical Thought* (Lexington, Mass.: D. C. Heath, 1970), 398; Henry David Thoreau, "Civil Disobedience" (1849), in ibid., 64.

5. Thoreau, "Civil Disobedience," 64.

4. THE FIRST ERA OF MODERN THOUGHT

1. Pico della Mirandola, *Oration on the Dignity of Man* (1486), in J. B. Ross and M. McLaughlin, eds., *The Portable Renaissance Reader* (New York: Penguin, 1968), 476.

2. Reinhold Niebuhr, *The Nature and Destiny of Man*, 2 vols. (New York: Scribner's, 1964), 1:61.

3. Alfred North Whitehead, *Science in the Modern World* (1925; New York: Mentor, 1948), 2.

4. Francis Bacon, *Advancement of Learning* (1605) and "The Four Idols" and "The New Method of Induction" from *Novum Organum* (1620), in Daniel S. Robinson, ed., *An Anthology of Modern Philosophy* (New York: Thomas Y. Crowell, 1931), 99–107, "Natural and Experimental History for the Foundation of Philosophy" (1622), in Fulton Anderson, ed., *Francis Bacon: The New Organon and Related Writings* (Indianapolis: Bobbs-Merrill, 1960), xiv–xv, and "Proem" (1605), quoted in Catherine D. Bowen, *Francis Bacon: The Temper of a Man* (Boston: Atlantic Monthly Press, 1963), 105.

5. Descartes, *Discourse on Method* (1637), pts. 1, 2, and 6, and *Rules for the Direction of the Mind* (ca. 1637), rule 4, quoted in John H. Randall, *The Making of the Modern Mind* (Boston: Houghton Mifflin, 1926), 215, 222–24; and Daniel Boorstin, *The Seekers* (New York: Vintage, 1999), 168.

6. Thomas Hobbes, *The Leviathan* (1650), quoted in Sheldon Wolin, *Politics and Vision* (Boston: Little, Brown, 1960), 247; and William Lucy, "Observations . . . of Notorious Errours in Mr. Hobbes' His Leviathan" (London, 1663), quoted in Joyce Appleby, *Capitalism and a New Social Order* (New York: New York University Press, 1984), 20.

7. C. B. Macpherson, *The Political Theory of Possessive Individualism* (Oxford: Oxford University Press, 1962). Also H. Mark Roelofs, *Ideology and Myth in American Politics* (Boston: Little, Brown, 1976).

8. Joseph Levine, *The Battle of the Books: History and Literature in the Augustan Age*

(Ithaca, N.Y.: Cornell University Press, 1991); and Paul Rahe, *Republics Ancient and Modern: Classical Republicanism and the American Revolution* (Chapel Hill: University of North Carolina Press, 1992).

9. Alexander Pope, "Epilogue to the Satires" (1738), lines 161–62, in W. K. Wimsatt, ed., *Alexander Pope: Selected Poetry and Prose* (New York: Holt, Rinehart, & Winston, 1962), 296; and Jonathan Swift, writing in *The Examiner* (London), December 28, 1710, quoted in J. R. Moore, *Daniel Defoe: Citizen of the Modern World* (Chicago: University of Chicago Press, 1958), 307.

10. Bernard Mandeville, *The Fable of the Bees; or, Private Vices, Publick Benefits* (1714; 6th ed., 1732), ed. F. B. Kaye, 2 vols. (Oxford: Oxford Univesity Press, 1924), 1:24, 36; Pierre Bayle quoted in Thomas A. Horne, *The Social Thought of Bernard Mandeville: Virtue and Commerce in Early Eighteenth-Century England* (New York: Columbia University Press, 1978), 30–31; and Daniel Defoe, *A Plan for English Commerce* (London, 1728), 68.

11. Henry St. John, First Viscount (Lord) Bolingbroke, "Reflections on the State of the Nation" (1749), in *The Works of Lord Bolingbroke*, 4 vols. (Philadelphia: Carey & Hart, 1841), 2:458–59.

12. Alexander Pope, "The Dunciad" (1743), bk. 4, lines 653–56, in Wimsatt, ed., *Pope: Poetry and Prose*, 449; Pope on Bacon quoted in Bowen, *Bacon*, 5.

13. Benjamin Constant, "The Liberty of the Ancients Compared with That of the Moderns" (1819), in *Benjamin Constant: Political Writings*, trans. and ed. Biancamaria Fontana (Cambridge: Cambridge University Press, 1988), 326–28.

5. THE UNITED STATES AND FIRST MODERNITY DEMOCRACY

1. Carl Becker, *The Heavenly City of the Eighteenth-Century Philosophers* (New Haven, Conn.: Yale University Press, 1932). For the "rethinking of the American Revolution," see "Forum," *William and Mary Quarterly* 52 (April 1996): 341–86.

2. John Adams to Timothy Pickering, 1823, quoted in Carl Becker, *The Declaration of Independence* (1922; New York: Vintage, 1942), 24; Thomas Jefferson to Henry Lee, May 8, 1825, in Adrienne Koch and William Peden, eds., *The Life and Selected Writings of Thomas Jefferson* (New York: Modern Library, 1993), 656.

3. James Otis, "The Rights of the British Colonies Asserted and Approved" (1764), and Thomas Jefferson, "A Summary View of the Rights of British America" (1774), in Merrill Jensen, ed., *Tracts of the American Revolution, 1763–1776* (Indianapolis: Bobbs-Merrill, 1967), 32–33, 258, 275–76.

4. Thomas Paine, *Common Sense* (1776), in ibid., 434.

5. *Journals of the Continental Congress, 1774–1789*, ed. Worthington C. Ford et al., 34 vols. (Washington, D.C., 1904–1937), 4:342 (May 15, 1776); John Adams to Abigail Adams, July 3, 1776, in L. H. Butterfield et al., eds., *Adams Family Correspondence*, 6 vols. (Cambridge, Mass.: Harvard University Press, 1963–1973), 2:28; broadside (Evans no. 15115), July 26, 1776, quoted in Merrill Jensen, "The American People and the American Revolution," *American Historical Review* 57 (June 1970): 29; Pennsylvania Constitution of 1776, in F. N. Thorpe, ed., *The State and Federal Constitutions*, 9 vols. (Washington, D.C., 1909), 5:3084–92.

6. Massachusetts Constitution of 1780, in Thorpe, ed., *State Constitutions*, 3:1888–

1911; Samuel Adams quoted in W. W. Wells, *The Life and Public Services of Samuel Adams,* 3 vols. (Boston: Little, Brown, 1865), 3:90–96.

7. When I discuss eighteenth-century political thought, I put *liberal* in quotation marks because it was not then a term in use with connotations that it came to have in the nineteenth and twentieth centuries. It was not, e.g., in Jefferson's political vocabulary.

8. *Federalist* no. 78, in Clinton Rossiter, ed., *The Federalist Papers* (New York: Mentor, 1961), 469.

9. *Federalist* no. 1, in ibid., 33.

10. *Federalist* nos. 62 and 63, in ibid., 381, 379, 390.

11. Aristotle, *Politics,* trans. Benjamin Jowett (New York: Modern Library, 1943), bk. 3, chap. 9, p. 142.

12. *Federalist* no. 10, in Rossiter, ed., *The Federalist Papers,* 77–84.

13. Thomas Paine, *Common Sense* (1776), in Jensen, ed., *Tracts,* 404.

14. Melancton Smith, speech at New York Convention, June 21, 1788, in Ralph Ketcham, ed., *The Antifederalist Papers* (New York: Mentor, 1986), 344.

15. James Madison to Thomas Jefferson, October 17, 1788, in Robert A. Rutland et al., eds., *The Papers of James Madison,* 17 vols. (Charlottesville: University Press of Virginia, 1962–1991), 11:299; Madison Resolution, House of Representatives, June 8, 1789, in Helen Veit et al., eds., *Creating the Bill of Rights* (Baltimore: Johns Hopkins University Press, 1991), 12.

16. Thomas Jefferson to Walter Jones, March 3, 1801, in H. A. Washington, ed., *The Works of Thomas Jefferson,* 9 vols. (Washington, D.C., 1853–1854), 4:392–93.

17. Arthur O. Lovejoy, "The Chinese Origins of Romanticism," in *Essays in the History of Ideas* (1948; New York: Capricorn, 1960), 105–10 (quoting Leibniz).

18. Thomas Jefferson to Henry Lee, May 8, 1825, in Koch and Peden, eds., *Writings of Jefferson,* 657.

19. Thomas Jefferson, "Autobiography" (dated January 6, 1821), in ibid., 52.

20. See Voltaire, *Philosophical Letters* (1732), trans. Ernest Dilworth (Indianapolis: Bobbs-Merrill, 1961), 46–65.

21. Thomas Jefferson, "First Inaugural Address" (March 4, 1801), in Koch and Peden, eds., *Writings of Jefferson,* 322.

22. Ibid., 322–23. See also Noble E. Cunningham, *The Inaugural Addresses of President Thomas Jefferson, 1801 and 1805* (Columbia: University of Missouri Press, 2001).

23. Jefferson, "First Inaugural Address," 324.

24. Ibid., 324–25.

6. THE SECOND MODERNITY

1. Woodrow Wilson, *Constitutional Government in the United States* (New York: Columbia University Press, 1908), 56–57.

2. Theodore Parker, "Theodore Parker's Experience as a Minister" (1859), in Perry Miller, ed., *The Transcendentalists* (Cambridge, Mass.: Harvard University Press, 1950), 485.

3. Keats, "Lamia" (1819), pt. 2, lines 229–37, in James Stephens et al., eds., *English Romantic Poets* (New York: American Book Co., 1952), 605.

4. Carl Becker, *The Heavenly City of the Eighteenth-Century Philosophers* (New Haven, Conn.: Yale University Press, 1932), 40.

5. Jeremy Bentham, *Anarchical Fallacies* (1824), art. 2, and *Principles of Morals and Legislation* (1822), quoted in John H. Randall, *The Making of the Modern Mind* (Boston: Houghton Mifflin, 1926), 360–62.

6. J. S. Mill, *On Liberty* (1859), ed. C. V. Shields (Indianapolis: Bobbs-Merrill, 1956).

7. J. S. Mill, *Representative Government* (1861), in *Utilitarianism, Liberty, and Representative Government* (London: Everyman, 1948), 207–18.

8. J. S. Mill, *Principles of Political Economy* (London: J. W. Parker, 1848), bk. 2, chap. 1, and *Autobiography* (New York: Oxford University Press, 1924), 133.

9. Auguste Comte, *The Positive Philosophy* (1853), trans. Harriet Martineau (1853; London: Kegan Paul, 1893), in Daniel S. Robinson, ed., *An Anthology of Modern Philosophy* (New York: Thomas Y. Crowell, 1931), 98, 702, 711.

10. Ibid., 713–16, 719, 721, 717.

11. Ibid., 701.

12. Stephen Jay Gould, *Triumph and Tragedy in Mudville* (New York: Norton, 2003), 203.

13. Thorstein Veblen, "Why Is Economics Not an Evolutionary Science?" *Quarterly Journal of Economics,* vol. 12 (July 1898), in Max Lerner, ed., *The Portable Veblen* (New York: Viking, 1950), 215–40, 216, 220–26.

14. Ibid., 235–40.

15. Perry Miller, introduction to Perry Miller, ed., *American Thought: Civil War to World War I* (New York: Holt Rinehart, 1954), xv.

16. William Graham Sumner, "The Scientific Attitude of Mind" (1905), in Robert C. Bannister, ed., *On Liberty, Society, and Politics: The Essential Essays of William Graham Sumner* (Indianapolis: Liberty Fund, 1992), 336.

17. Lester F. Ward, *Dynamic Sociology,* 2 vols. (New York: D. Appleton, 1883), 1:8, 12, 103.

18. Sidney Webb and Beatrice Webb, *Industrial Democracy* (London, 1913), 592, quoted in Shirley Robyn Letwin, *The Pursuit of Certainty: David Hume, Jeremy Bentham, John Stuart Mill, Beatrice Webb* (Indianapolis: Liberty Fund, 1998), 405–6.

19. Beatrice Webb, diary entry, June 11, 1898, quoted in ibid., 409.

20. John Dewey, *The Influence of Darwin on Philosophy* (New York: Henry Holt, 1910), 1.

21. Ibid., 3–4.

22. Ibid., 5, 7–9.

23. Thomas Carlyle, "Preliminary," bk. 1, chap. 1, and "Pure Reason," bk. 1, chap. 10, of *Sartor Resartus* (1834; New York: Greystone, n.d.), 3, 36–37.

24. Thomas Carlyle, "Aristocracies," bk. 4, chap. 1, and "The English," bk. 3, chap. 5, of *Past and Present* (1843), in George Woods et al., eds., *The Literature of England,* 2 vols. (Chicago: Scott, Foresman, 1947–1948), 2:489, 493.

25. John Grote, *An Examination of the Utilitarian Philosophy* (Cambridge: Deighton Bell, 1870), 1–2, 350.

26. Ibid., 110, 352.

27. Matthew Arnold, "Sweetness and Light," chap. 1 of *Culture and Anarchy* (1869),

in G. Anderson and R. Warnock, eds., *The World in Literature* (Chicago: Scott, Foresman, 1951), 238–44.

28. Ibid., 245–48.

29. Alexander Pope, "The Dunciad" (1743), in W. K. Wimsatt, ed., *Alexander Pope: Selected Poetry and Prose* (New York: Holt, Rinehart, & Winston, 1962), 449; Matthew Arnold, "Dover Beach" (1867), in Woods et al., eds., *The Literature of England,* 2:744.

30. Lewis Mumford, *The Golden Day* (New York: Boni & Liveright, 1926), in Gail Kennedy, ed., *Pragmatism in American Culture* (Boston: D. C. Heath, 1950), 36–49, 54–57.

31. Reinhold Niebuhr, *The Nature and Destiny of Man,* 2 vols. (New York: Scribner's, 1964), 1:70–72.

32. Ibid., 1:72–74.

33. Ibid., 1:94, 110–11.

34. Reinhold Niebuhr, "Intellectual Autobiography" (1955), in Charles Kegley and Robert Bretall, eds., *Reinhold Niebuhr: His Religious, Social, and Political Thought* (New York: Macmillan, 1961), 13.

35. Reinhold Niebuhr, *The Children of Light and the Children of Darkness* (New York: Scribner's, 1944), 70–71.

36. George Santayana, "Odes" and "The Genteel Tradition in American Philosophy" (1913), in *Complete Poems,* ed. William Holzberger (Lewisburg, Pa.: Bucknell University Press, 1979), 140–41, 158.

37. Harold Laski to O. W. Holmes, September 9, 1916, Holmes to Laski, September 15, 1916, July 30, 1917, January 18, 1918, Laski to Holmes, February 22, 1918, Holmes to Laski, April 12, 1917, January 11, 1924, in Mark DeWolfe Howe, ed., *Holmes-Laski Letters,* 2 vols. (New York: Atheneum, 1963), 15, 19, 71, 95, 100, 57–58, 406.

38. *Lochner v. New York* (1905), *Schenck v. United States* (1919), and *Abrams v. United States* (1919), in Max Lerner, ed., *The Mind and Faith of Justice Holmes* (Boston: Little, Brown, 1951), 149, 296–97, 312.

39. O. W. Holmes, "Montesquieu" (1900) and "John Marshall" (1901), in ibid., 378–83; and Robert Faulkner, *The Jurisprudence of John Marshall* (Princeton, N.J.: Princeton University Press, 1968), 256.

40. Harold Laski to O. W. Holmes, January 2, 1917, January 15, 1917, April 18, 1917, December 8, 1917, in Howe, ed., *Holmes-Laski Letters,* 35, 41, 59, 86.

41. Harold Laski, *A Grammar of Politics* (London: George Allen, 1925), 31–34.

42. Ibid., 10, 34–43.

43. John Dewey, *Individualism Old and New* (1930; New York: Capricorn, 1962), 9, 36, 76, 81, 83, 97, 99.

44. John Dewey, *Liberalism and Social Action* (1935; New York: Capricorn, 1963), 4, 6, 8, 13, 40 (quoting J. S. Mill, *Logic* [1843], bk. 4, chap. 9).

45. Ibid., 44, 43, 55, 92.

46. Ibid., 61, 71.

47. Lester Frank Ward, *Psychic Factors of Civilization* (Boston: Ginn, 1893), 278–79, 319–27.

48. Sidney Webb and Beatrice Webb, *Socialist Commonwealth* (1920), *Our Partner-*

ship (1948), and *Soviet Communism* (1947), quoted in Letwin, *Pursuit of Certainty,*
408–9.

49. Arthur F. Bentley, *The Process of Government* (1908; Cambridge, Mass.: Harvard University Press, 1967), 208–9, 258–59.

50. Ibid., 370–94.

51. Harold Lasswell, *Politics: Who Gets What, When, How* (New York: McGraw-Hill, 1936); Paul Appleby, *Big Democracy* (New York: Knopf, 1945).

52. Karl Pearson, *The Grammar of Science* (1892; London: Everyman, 1937), 11, 13.

53. John Dewey, *The Public and Its Problems* (1927; Denver: Alan Swallow, 1954).

54. Charles Beard, *An Economic Interpretation of the Constitution of the United States* (New York: Macmillan, 1913).

7. LIBERAL DEMOCRACY IN THE TWENTIETH CENTURY

1. Herbert Croly, *The Promise of American Life* (1909; New York: Macmillan, 1919), 43–45.

2. Croly, *Promise of American Life,* 51.

3. Peter J. Coleman, *Progressivism and the World of Reform: New Zealand and the Origins of the American Welfare State* (Lawrence: University Press of Kansas, 1987), esp. 76–97.

4. Karl Popper, *The Open Society and Its Enemies* (Princeton, N.J.: Princeton University Press, 1950).

5. Arthur H. Schlesinger Jr., *The Vital Center* (Boston: Houghton Mifflin, 1949).

6. Arthur F. Bentley, *The Process of Government* (1908; Cambridge, Mass.: Harvard University Press, 1967), 380.

7. Theodore Lowi, *The End of Liberalism: The Second Republic of the United States* (New York: Norton, 1969), esp. 50–60, 295–98.

8. "The Port Huron Statement" (1962), in Henry J. Silverman, ed., *American Radical Thought* (Lexington, Mass.: D. C. Heath, 1970), 358–62.

9. Ibid., 362–66.

10. Herbert Marcuse, *One Dimensional Man* (Boston: Beacon, 1964), 107.

11. Robert P. Wolff, "Beyond Tolerance," in *A Critique of Pure Tolerance* (Boston: Beacon, 1965), 52.

12. Anthony Sampson, *The New Anatomy of Britain* (London: Hodder & Stoughton, 1971), 14.

13. Milton Friedman, *Capitalism and Freedom* (Chicago: University of Chicago Press, 1962); and Milton Friedman and Rose Friedman, *Freedom to Choose* (New York: Harcourt Brace Jovanovich, 1980).

14. William Brennan, *The Constitution of the United States: Contemporary Ratification* (Washington, D.C.: Georgetown University Press, 1985), 5, 6, 10, 15.

15. Francis Fukuyama, "The End of History?" *The National Interest,* summer 1989, 18.

16. Aristotle, *Politics,* trans. Benjamin Jowett (New York: Modern Library, 1943), bk. 3, chap. 9, p. 142; Thomas Carlyle, "Aristocracies," bk. 4, chap. 1, and "The English," bk. 3, chap. 5, of *Past and Present* (1843), in George Woods et al., eds., *The Literature of England,* 2 vols. (Chicago: Scott, Foresman, 1948), 2:489, 493.

17. The literature is vast, but see, e.g., Brennan, *Constitution of the United States;* and Robert Bork, *The Tempting of America* (New York: Simon & Schuster, 1990).

18. Liang Ch'i-ch'ao, *History of Chinese Political Thought* (1922), trans. L. T. Chen (1930; New York: AMS, 1969), 7, 43–44, 56–57.

19. Instead of, as in previous chapters, letting political theorists and other intellectuals carry most of the rationale and critique of democracy in the last half of the twentieth century, I have left that to the performance and assessment of democracy in major "First World" countries where it received searching attention. The victory of 1945, outside the Soviet sphere, in the "West" and in most of the former colonial world, was seen as one for democracy, which left its sustenance and support largely in the hands of Western theorists and practitioners operating in the mainstream, the vital center, of world politics. The idea of democracy, then, has had its most significant and even profound development in the realm of public rather than academic discussion. Thus, this chapter has dealt largely with public affairs (in deed and word). The more strictly academic debate has been left largely for the comparisons of chapter 11.

8. SECOND MODERNITY THOUGHT IN JAPAN AND CHINA

1. Louise Lavathes, *When China Ruled the Seas: The Treasure Fleet of the Dragon Throne, 1405–1433* (New York: Oxford University Press, 1994), 173.

2. This paragraph and the following are based largely on Arnold H. Rowbotham, *Missionary and Mandarin: The Jesuits at the Court of China* (Berkeley: University of California Press, 1942), 37–167. See also Jonathan Spence, *The Memory Palace of Matteo Ricci* (New York: Penguin, 1984).

3. Rowbotham, *Missionary and Mandarin,* 157.

4. Leibniz, Voltaire, and Temple quoted in Arthur O. Lovejoy, "The Chinese Origins of Romanticism," in *Essays in the History of Ideas* (1948; New York: Capricorn, 1960), 105–10. See also Alfred Owen Aldridge, *The Dragon and the Eagle: The Presence of China in the American Enlightenment* (Detroit: Wayne State University Press, 1993); Jonathan Spence, *The Chan's Great Continent: China in Western Minds* (New York: Norton, 1998), esp. 19–100.

5. Jonathan Spence, *The Search for Modern China* (New York: Norton, 1990), 121–23, quoting J. L. Cranmer-Byrg, ed., *An Embassy to China: Lord Macartney's Journal, 1793–1794* (London, 1962), 340, 191, 212–13.

6. Masao Maruyama, *Studies in the Intellectual History of Tokugawa Japan* (Princeton, N.J.: Princeton University Press/Tokyo University Press, 1974), esp. 135–85.

7. Fukuzawa Yukichi, *The Autobiography of Fukuzawa Yukichi,* trans. Eiichi Kiyooka (Tokyo: Hokuseido, 1960), 215; Chuhei Sugiyama and Hiroshi Mizuta, eds., *Enlightenment and Beyond: Political Economy Comes to Japan* (Tokyo: University of Tokyo Press, 1988), 75–76.

8. Fukuzawa Yukichi, *An Encouragement of Learning,* trans. David Dilworth and Umeyo Hirano (Tokyo: Sophia University, 1969), 1, 3, 35.

9. Sugiyama and Mizuta, eds., *Enlightenment and Beyond,* 48, 77–78.

10. Liang Ch'i-ch'ao (Liang Qichao), *History of Chinese Political Thought* (1922), trans. J. T. Chen (1930; New York: AMS, 1969), 10; Fukuzawa, *Encouragement of Learning,* 17–20, 30.

11. Fukuzawa, *Encouragement of Learning,* 40, 43.

12. *Fukuzawa Yukichi on Education,* trans. and ed. Eiichi Kiyooka (Tokyo: University of Tokyo Press, 1985), 132.

13. Ibid., 237–38, 231.

14. Carmen Blacker, *The Japanese Enlightenment: A Study of the Writings of Fuku-zawa Yukichi* (Cambridge: Cambridge University Press, 1964).

15. Fukuzawa, *Autobiography,* 91.

16. Thomas R. H. Havens, *Nishi Amane and Modern Japanese Thought* (Princeton, N.J.: Princeton University Press, 1970), 7, 43–44 (quoting a letter, Nishi Amane to Matsuoka Rinjiro, June 12, 1862).

17. Ibid., 42–56 (quotation on 48).

18. Nishi Amane, *Hyakugaku renkan* (Links of all sciences encyclopedia) (ca. 1870–1873), quoted in Havens, *Nishi,* 108.

19. Nishi Amane, *Jinsei sanpōsetsu* (Theory of the three human treasures) (1875–1880), quoted in ibid., 144–47.

20. Nishi, *Tōei Mondo* (Dialogue of enlightenment) (1870–1873), quoted in ibid., 87–90.

21. Nishi, *Kyomonron* (On religion) (1874), quoted in ibid., 180.

22. Nishi, *Hokkyu sōkagi ichidoi* (One topic in the refutation of the general public opinion) (1874) and *Mōra giin no setsu* (Discussion of a collective assembly) (1875), quoted in ibid., 187–89.

23. Imperial proclamation quoted in Robert Scalapino, *Democracy and the Party Movement in Pre-War Japan: The Failure of the First Attempt* (Berkeley: University of California Press, 1953), 59–60. See also *Meiroku Zasshi Journal of the Japanese Enlightenment,* trans. W. R. Braisted (Cambridge, Mass.: Harvard University Press, 1976).

24. Kato Hiroyuki's response to the 1874 petition is quoted in E. H. Norman, *Origins of the Modern Japanese State* (New York: Random House, 1975), 456.

25. Imperial Constitution of 1889, chap. 2, arts. 28 and 29, and "Count Ito on the Constitution" (1889), quoted in Scalapino, *Democracy in Pre-War Japan,* 83–86.

26. Joseph Pittou, *Political Thought in Early Meiji Japan, 1868–1889* (Cambridge, Mass.: Harvard University Press, 1967), 90.

27. Ito Hirobumi, speech of February 15, 1889, quoted in Scalapino, *Democracy in Pre-War Japan,* 88.

28. Fukuzawa, *Autobiography,* 190–91.

29. Tadashi Aruga, "The Declaration of Independence in Japan: Translation and Trans-plantation, 1854–1997," *Journal of American History* 85, no. 4 (March 1999): 1411–12.

30. Motoda Eifu's memorandum is quoted in Donald Shively, "Motoda Eifu: Confu-cian Lecturer to the Meiji Emperor," in D. S. Nivison and A. P. Wright, eds., *Confucianism in Action* (Palo Alto, Calif.: Stanford University Press, 1959), 303–33.

31. The first of the Five Articles is quoted in Watanabe Hiroshi, ". . . the West as Seen through Confucian Eyes in Nineteenth-Century Japan," in Tu Wei-ming, ed., *Confucian Traditions in East Asian Modernity* (Cambridge, Mass.: Harvard University Press, 1996), 128; Motoda Eifu, "Kokken taiko" (General principles of the constitution) (1880), quoted in Pittou, *Meiji Japan,* 94.

32. Spence, *Search for Modern China*, 216–22.

33. Benjamin Schwartz, *In Search of Wealth and Power: Yen Fu and the West* (Cambridge, Mass.: Harvard University Press, 1964), 22–41.

34. Ibid., 42–43.

35. Yan Fu, "Yüan-ch'iang" (On strength) (1895), quoted in ibid., 45, 36.

36. Schwartz, *Yen Fu*, 70–75.

37. Yan Fu's commentary is quoted in ibid., 114–19.

38. J. S. Mill, *On Liberty* (1859), ed. C. V. Shields (Indianapolis: Bobbs-Merrill, 1956), 87.

39. Yan Fu, "I-shih li-yen," introduction to vol. 2 of his 1900 Japanese translation of Adam Smith's *Wealth of Nations,* quoted in Schwartz, *Yen Fu*, 124.

40. Yan Fu, "Translator's Directions to the Reader," in his 1903 translation of Mill's *On Liberty,* quoted in ibid., 131–34.

41. Noted in Jerome B. Greider, *Intellectuals and the State in Modern China* (New York: Free Press, 1981), 241.

42. Yan Fu quoted in Schwartz, *Yen Fu*, 140.

43. From the "Principles of Compilation" of the elementary school ethics texts issued in April 1904 by the Japanese Ministry of Education, in Kaigo Tokiomi, ed., *Collection of Japanese Textbooks* (Tokyo: Kodansha, 1962), 3:355–56, quoted in Samuel Hideo Yamashita, "Confucianism and the Japanese State, 1904–1945," in Tu, ed., *Confucian Traditions,* 143.

44. Yan Fu quoted in Schwartz, *Yen Fu*, 141.

45. Mill, *On Liberty*, 140–41.

46. Douglas F. Challenger, *Durkheim through the Lens of Aristotle* (Lanham, Md.: Rowman & Littlefield, 1994), 85–104.

47. Thorstein Veblen, "Why Is Economics Not an Evolutionary Science?" *Quarterly Journal of Economics,* vol. 12 (July 1898), in Max Lerner, ed., *The Portable Veblen* (New York: Viking, 1950), 235.

48. Yan Fu's commentary on bk. 8 of *Spirit of the Laws* quoted in Schwartz, *Yen Fu*, 158.

49. Commentary on bk. 17, quoted in ibid., 171–72.

50. See ibid., 158, 172–73.

51. Yan Fu's translation of Edward Jenks's *History of Politics* (London, 1900) quoted in ibid., 185.

52. Yan Fu's *Ming-hsüch* (1905), his translation of J. S. Mill's *Logic,* pt. 1, bks. 1 and 2, quoted in ibid., 187, 191–92, 195.

53. Yan Fu, *Hou-kuan yen-shih'ping-tien Lao-tsu* (Commentaries on Lao-tsu) (1903), quoted in ibid., 199, 209.

54. Yan Fu, "A Critique of the *Social Contract,*" in *Justice* (1914), letters to Hsiung Chún-ju published in *Hsüch Heng* (1922–1923), and "An Introduction to *Ito's Commentaries on the Japanese Constitution,*" quoted in ibid., 222, 224, 230, 232, 235.

55. Jiang Zemin, policy address to Chinese leaders, August 13, 1999, quoted in *New York Times,* August 14, 1999, A7.

56. Yan Fu in *Hsüch Heng* (Shanghai), no. 18 (1923), quoted in Herrlee G. Creel, *Chinese Thought from Confucius to Mao Tse-tung* (Chicago: University of Chicago Press, 1953), 237.

57. Philip C. Huang, *Liang Ch'i-ch'ao and Modern Chinese Liberalism* (Seattle: University of Washington Press, 1972), 11–35.

58. Zhang Zhidong, "Exhortation to Learn" (1898), quoted in ibid., 42.

59. Y. C. Wang, *Chinese Intellectuals and the West* (Chapel Hill, N.C.: University of North Carolina Press, 1966), 510.

60. Liang Qichao quoted in Huang, *Liang Ch'i-ch'ao,* 50.

61. Liang Qichao, *Hsin-min shu* (The new citizen) (1902), quoted in ibid., 58. Stephen N. Hay, *Asian Ideas of East and West: Tagore and His Critics in Japan, China, and India* (Cambridge, Mass.: Harvard University Press, 1970), describes the outlook of Inoue Tetsujiro, Kato Hiroyuki, and other Germanized Japanese intellectuals.

62. Liang Qichao, *Tzu-yu shu* (Notes on freedom) (1899), quoted in Huang, *Liang Ch'i-ch'ao,* 63.

63. Liang's citations of the *Great Learning (Ta hsüeh)* and the *Book of Mencius (Meng-tsu)* in his *Hsin-min shu* are quoted in ibid., 65–66.

64. Liang, *Tzu-yu-shu,* quoted in ibid., 72–74.

65. Liang Qichao, *Hsin-min shu* and *Enlightened Despotism,* quoted in ibid., 79–82.

66. Liang Qichao quoted in Chou Tse-tsung, *The May Fourth Movement: Intellectual Revolution in Modern China* (Cambridge, Mass.: Harvard University Press, 1960), 328.

67. Liang, *History of Chinese Political Thought,* 7, 43–44, 56–57.

68. Ibid., 10.

69. Edwin O. Reischauer, *The Japanese* (Tokyo: Charles Tuttle, 1978), 44–45.

70. *Analects* 13.23, 15.22, 4.16, quoted in David L. Hall and Roger T. Ames, *The Democracy of the Dead: Dewey, Confucius, and the Hope for Democracy in China* (Chicago: Open Court, 1999), 193, 196.

9. AN ASIAN THIRD MODERNITY

1. Sun Yatsen, *San Min Chu I: The Three Principles of the People,* trans. Frank W. Price, ed. L. T. Chen (Shanghai, 1927), 348–50.

2. Ibid., 351–55.

3. Ibid., 359–60, 357–58.

4. Jonathan Spence, *The Gate of Heavenly Peace: The Chinese and Their Revolution, 1895–1980* (New York: Penguin, 1982), 206.

5. Chou Tse-tsung, *The May Fourth Movement: Intellectual Revolution in Modern China* (Cambridge, Mass.: Harvard University Press, 1960). *John Dewey: Lectures in China, 1919–1920,* ed. and trans Robert Clopton and Tsuin-Chen Ou (Honolulu: University of Hawaii Press, 1973), prints many of Dewey's lectures (all delivered in English) by retranslating into English the notes taken in Chinese at the time by Dewey's listeners and translators, often including Hu Shi himself. Philip Short, *Mao: A Life* (New York: Henry Holt, 1999), 107–13.

6. Clopton and Ou, eds., *John Dewey,* 166.

7. Hu Shi's introduction to his *Science and Philosophy of Life* (1923), quoted in Sung-Peng Hsu, "Hu Shih," in Donald H. Bishop, ed., *Chinese Thought* (Delhi: Motilal Banarsidass, 1985), 375–76.

8. Hu Shi's "Study More Problems, and Talk Less about Theories" (1919) quoted in

Jerome B. Greider, *Intellectuals and the State in Modern China* (New York: Free Press, 1981), 328.

9. Hu Shi quoted in Bishop, ed., *Chinese Thought*, 389.

10. Hu Shih [Hu Shi], "Confucianism" (1937), quoted in Herrlee G. Creel, *Chinese Thought from Confucius to Mao Tse-tung* (Chicago: University of Chicago Press, 1953), 241; John Dewey, "Transforming the Mind of China" (1919), in J. A. Boydston, ed., *John Dewey: The Middle Works, 1899–1924*, 15 vols. (Carbondale: University of Southern Illinois Press, 1976–83), 11:213.

11. Jerome B. Greider, *Hu Shih and the Chinese Renaissance: Liberalism in the Chinese Revolution, 1917–1937* (Cambridge, Mass.: Harvard University Press, 1970), describes Hu Shi's career and thought. David L. Hall and Roger T. Ames, *The Democracy of the Dead: Dewey, Confucius, and the Hope for Democracy in China* (Chicago: Open Court, 1999), discuss Dewey's thought in a Chinese context.

12. Minutes of the People's Congress, Central Committee of the Guomindang, Beijing (May 1930), and Chiang Kaishek, "Why Do We Join the Party and Propose to Rule the Country by the People's Party?" (1930), quoted in Chuxuan Zheng, *A Comparison between Western and Chinese Political Ideas* (Lewiston, Maine: Mellen University Press, 1995), 235–37.

13. Liu Shaoqi, "On the Cultivation of a Communist Party Member" (1939), quoted in Graham Young, "Liu Shaoqi and the Sinification of Leninism," in Soren Clausen et al., eds., *Cultural Encounters: China, Japan, and the West* (Aarhus: Aarhus University Press, 1995), 394. (Readers should note that Liu's title is usually translated as "How to Be a Good Communist.")

14. Liu Shaoqi, tracts, 1937–1944, quoted in ibid., 396–402.

15. Liu Shaoqi, "Democratic Spirit and Bureaucratism," quoted in ibid., 408 n. 6.

16. Mao Zedong's "On the Correct Handling of Contradictions among the People," from which these quotations are taken, was first published on February 27, 1957. It is cited here from John Wilson Lewis, ed., *Major Doctrines of Communist China* (New York: Norton, 1964), 98–105.

17. Ibid., 86–88.

18. This paragraph and the next are taken largely from Jonathan Spence, *The Search for Modern China* (New York: Norton, 1990), 653–711.

19. Editorials, *People's Daily*, March 15, 1977, and January 3, 1979, and *Zhexue Yanjui* (Philosophical research), January 31, 1979, quoted in Merle Goldman, *Sowing the Seeds of Democracy in China: Political Reform in the Deng Xiaoping Era* (Cambridge, Mass.: Harvard University Press, 1994), 29–35.

20. "Political Questions Can Be Discussed," *People's Daily*, November 19, 1979, and editorial, *People's Daily*, July 5, 1979, quoted in ibid., 52–53, 60–61.

21. See ibid., 49.

22. Zhao quoted in Andrew Nathan, "The Tiananmen Papers," *Foreign Affairs*, January/February 2001, 13. See also Spence, *Search for Modern China*, 738–47.

23. Motoda Eifu is quoted in Donald Shively, "Motoda Eifu: Confucian Lecturer to the Meiji Emperor," in D. S. Nivison and A. P. Wright, eds., *Confucianism in Action* (Palo Alto, Calif.: Stanford University Press, 1959), 301.

24. Li Peng, statement of May 18, 1989, quoted in Michael Oksenberg et al., *Beijing*

Spring, 1989 (Armonk, N.Y.: M. E. Sharpe, 1990), 311; banner cited in Minzhu Han, ed., *Cries for Democracy: Writings and Speeches from the 1989 Chinese Democracy Movement* (Princeton, N.J.: Princeton University Press, 1990), 68; Deng's remarks quoted in Nathan, "Tiananmen Papers," 20.

25. L. H. M. Ling, "Rationalization for State Violence in Chinese Politics: The Hegemony of Parental Governance," *Journal of Peace Research* 31 (1994): 393–405; Nathan, "Tiananmen Papers," 13, 19.

26. Robert Scalapino, *Democracy and the Party Movement in Pre-War Japan: The Failure of the First Attempt* (Berkeley: University of California Press, 1953), 353.

27. Yoshida Shigeru, "Chichi to haha . . ." (Father and mother: Matters of my youth), *Kaizo*, January 1950, 108, quoted in John W. Dower, *Empire and Aftermath: Yoshida Shigeru and the Japanese Experience, 1878–1954* (Cambridge, Mass.: Harvard University Press, 1979), 23.

28. Edwin O. Reischauer, *The Japanese* (Tokyo: Charles Tuttle, 1978), 44–45.

29. Edwin O. Reischauer, *The Japanese Today* (Cambridge, Mass.: Harvard University Press, 1988), 234.

30. Yukio Mishima, *After the Banquet*, trans. Donald Keene (New York: Perigree, 1963), 185.

31. Nakane Chie, *Japanese Society* (1970; London: Penguin, 1973), 149–54.

32. Mao quoted in Orville Schell, *Mandate of Heaven* (New York: Simon & Schuster, 1994), 179.

33. Deng quoted in Mark Borthwick, ed., *Pacific Century* (Boulder, Colo.: Westview, 1992), 324.

34. Okakura Kakuzo, *The Ideals of the East, with Special Reference to the Art of Japan* (London, 1903), quoted in Stephen N. Hay, *Asian Ideas of East and West: Tagore and His Critics in Japan, China, and India* (Cambridge, Mass.: Harvard University Press, 1970), 39–40.

35. Bertrand Russell, *The Problem of China* (New York: Century, 1922), 14.

36. Rabindranath Tagore, "India's Message to Japan" (June 1916) and "Visva-Bharati" (1922), quoted in Hay, *Asian Ideas*, 63–66, 133.

37. Rabindranath Tagore to William Rothenstein, August 2, 1916, quoted in ibid., 75.

38. Mitsui Koshi quoted in Kiyozawa Iwao, "How Famous Men Regard Tagore" (1916), quoted in ibid., 87.

39. Inoue Tetsujiro, "Concerning Tagore's Lecture" (July 1916), quoted in ibid., 107.

40. Tanaka Oda, "I Discuss Mr. Tagore's Views of Japan" (September 1916) and "Tagore Came and Then Left" (October 1916), and *Yorozu chōhō* (Universal news), August 1916, quoted in ibid., 109–10, 121.

41. Spence, *Gate of Heavenly Peace*, 172–74; and Greider, *Intellectuals and the State*, 203–79 and passim.

42. Xu Zhimo quoted in Hay, *Asian Ideas*, 145, 148.

43. Liang Qichao, "China's Debt to India," trans. Xu Zhimo, *Visva Bharati Quarterly* (October 1924), and Rabindranath Tagore, "The Rule of the Giant" (May 9, 1924), quoted in ibid., 157, 169.

44. Leaflet entitled "Farewell Tagore" and distributed in Beijing on May 10, 1924, quoted in ibid., 171. See also Spence, *Gate of Heavenly Peace*, 213.

45. Mao Dun and Guo Moruo quoted in Spence, *Gate of Heavenly Peace,* 214–15.

46. Hu Shi's "Our Attitude toward Modern Western Civilization," a compilation of conversations and lectures conducted in China in 1925 and 1926, quoted in Hay, *Asian Ideas,* 217; Hu Shih [Hu Shi], *The Chinese Renaissance* (Chicago: University of Chicago Press, 1933), x.

47. Gu Hongming in the *Shanghai Mercury,* May 30, 1924, quoted in Hay, *Asian Ideas,* 206–7, 383n. See also Greider, *Intellectuals and the State,* 220–21.

48. Russell, *Problem of China,* 205; Lin Yutang, *The Wisdom of India and China* (New York: Random House, 1942), 377; and Liang Shuming, *The Cultures of East and West,* 7th ed. (1926), quoted in Hay, *Asian Ideas,* 208.

49. Russell, *Problem of China,* 205; Liang, *Cultures of East and West,* quoted in Greider, *Intellectuals and the State,* 264–65.

50. Liang, *Cultures of East and West,* quoted in Greider, *Intellectuals and the State,* 264–65. See generally Guy Alitto, *The Last Confucian: Liang Shu-ming and the Chinese Dilemma of Modernity* (Berkeley and Los Angeles: University of California Press, 1979); and Shiping Hua, *Scientism and Humanism: Two Cultures in Post-Mao China, 1978–1989* (Albany: State University of New York Press, 1995), 109–11.

51. Benjamin Schwartz, *China and Other Matters* (Cambridge, Mass.: Harvard University Press, 1996), 114.

52. *Book of Mencius,* bk. 6, pt. 1, quoted in Lin, *Wisdom of India and China,* 774–75.

53. Michael Davis, "The Case for Chinese Federalism," *Journal of Democracy* 10, no. 4 (April 1999): 124–37 (see esp. n. 2); Fareed Zakaria, "Culture Is Destiny: A Conversation with Lee Kuan Yew," *Foreign Affairs,* March/April 1994, 109–26 (quote on 119).

54. *Asahi shimbun* (Tokyo), March 24, 2002, English ed.; Arthur Balfour, introduction to Walter Bagehot, *The English Constitution* (1928; Oxford: Oxford University Press, 1982), xxiv.

55. Yonung Kwŏn, "The Royal Lecture and Confucian Politics in Early Yi Korea," *Korean Studies* (East-West Center, Honolulu) 6 (1982): 41–62.

56. Jongwoo Han, "Origins of the Developmental State in Korea" (Ph.D. diss., Syracuse University, 1997).

57. Tokugawa Ieyasu and the "Code of Keicho" (1615) quoted in A. L. Sadler, *The Maker of Modern Japan: The Life of Tokugawa Ieyasu* (Tokyo: Tuttle, 1978), 311, 375.

58. Scalapino, *Democracy in Pre-War Japan,* 54–55, 150–51, 380–81; Dower, *Yoshida Shigeru,* 274, 490; Kenneth Pyle, *The Making of Modern Japan,* 2d ed. (New York: D. C. Heath, 1996), 229–30.

59. Leibniz and Voltaire quoted in Arthur O. Lovejoy, "The Chinese Origins of Romanticism," in *Essays in the History of Ideas* (1948; New York: Capricorn, 1960), 105–10.

10. POSTMODERNISM AND A FOURTH MODERNITY DEMOCRACY

1. Allan Megill, *Prophets of Extremity: Nietzsche, Heidegger, Foucault, Derrida* (Berkeley and Los Angeles: University of California Press, 1985), 18, 183.

2. William Butler Yeats, "The Second Coming" (1920), in M. L. Rosenthal, ed.,

Selected Poems and Two Plays of William Butler Yeats (1962; New York: Collier, 1966), 91.

3. Richard Tarnas, *The Passion of the Western Mind* (New York: Ballantine, 1991), 399.

4. Friedrich Nietzsche, *The Birth of Tragedy* (1872/1886), in Walter Kaufmann, ed., *Basic Writings of Nietzsche* (New York: Modern Library, 1968), 34. See also Megill, *Prophets of Extremity,* 55–57, 95–109.

5. Megill, *Prophets of Extremity,* 20, following J. Hillis Miller, "Tradition and Difference," *Diacritics* 2 (winter 1972): 11.

6. Friedrich Nietzsche, *On the Genealogy of Morals* (1887), essay 2, pt. 6, in Mitchell Cohen and Nicole Fermon, eds., *Princeton Readings in Political Thought* (Princeton, N.J.: Princeton University Press, 1996), 472, and *The Antichrist* (1930; New York: Arno, 1972), par. 11, p. 13.

7. Immanuel Kant, *Critique of Practical Reason* (1788), bk. 1, chap. 6, in T. M. Greene, ed., *Kant Selections* (New York: Scribner's, 1929), 302.

8. Dennis Schmidt, *The Ubiquity of the Finite: Hegel, Heidegger, and the Entitlements of Philosophy* (Cambridge, Mass.: MIT Press, 1988), xiii; and Stephen K. White, *Political Theory and Postmodernism* (Cambridge: Cambridge University Press, 1991), 59.

9. White, *Political Theory and Postmodernism,* 46, 59.

10. Manfred Stanley, *The Technological Conscience* (Chicago: University of Chicago Press, 1978), 137; White, *Political Theory and Postmodernism,* 47.

11. White, *Political Theory and Postmodernism,* 47.

12. Martin Heidegger, *An Introduction to Metaphysics* (1953), trans. Ralph Manheim (New Haven, Conn.: Yale University Press, 1959), 37–38; Heidegger on "global technology" quoted in Megill, *Prophets of Extremity,* 140.

13. Martin Heidegger quoted in Reiner Schürmann, *Heidegger on Being and Acting: From Principles to Anarchy,* trans. Christine-Marie Gros (Bloomington: Indiana University Press, 1987), 38.

14. White, *Political Theory and Postmodernism,* 49–51.

15. Michel Foucault, "Two Lectures" (January 1976) and "The Art of Telling" (ca. 1980–1984), in Michael Kelly, ed., *Critique and Power: Recasting the Foucault/ Habermas Debate* (Cambridge, Mass.: MIT Press, 1994), 19–21, 147; and "Interview with Michel Foucault" (1980), quoted in Edward Said, review of Michel Foucault, *Power* (2000), *New York Times Book Review,* December 17, 2000, 17.

16. Foucault, "Two Lectures," 21–25.

17. Ibid., 25.

18. Ibid., 39.

19. Ibid., 40–45.

20. Hubert L. Dreyfus and Paul Rabinow, *Michel Foucault: Beyond Structuralism and Hermeneutics,* with an afterword by Michel Foucault (Chicago: University of Chicago Press, 1982), viii, use this phrase to characterize Foucault's critiques in *The Order of Things* (1966) and *The Archaeology of Knowledge* (1969) (see *The Order of Things and The Archaeology of Knowledge,* trans. A. M. Sheridan Smith [London: Tavistock, 1972]).

21. Michel Foucault, *Discipline and Punish: The Birth of the Prison* (1975), trans. Alan Sheridan (New York: Pantheon, 1977), 205.

22. Megill, *Prophets of Extremity,* 192–93.

23. Ibid., 199 (quoting Michel Foucault, *Madness and Civilization: A History of Insanity in the Age of Reason* [1961], trans. Richard Howard [New York: Pantheon, 1965]), 200.

24. Foucault, "The Art of Telling," 43–45.

25. Foucault, *Discipline and Punish,* 210; Bonnie Honig, *Political Theory and the Displacement of Politics* (Ithaca, N.Y.: Cornell University Press, 1993), 73.

26. Jean-François Lyotard, *The Postmodern Condition: A Report on Knowledge* (1979), trans. Geoff Bennington and Brian Massumi (Minneapolis: University of Minnesota Press, 1984), xxiv–xxv.

27. Jean-François Lyotard, "The Differend, the Referent, and the Proper Name," *Diacritics* 13 (fall 1984): 4–14, and *The Postmodern Condition,* 35, 39.

28. Honig, *The Displacement of Politics,* 9; Linda Nicholson, *The Play of Reason: From the Modern to the Postmodern* (Ithaca, N.Y.: Cornell University Press, 1999), 103.

29. Jean-François Lyotard, "Adamo as the Devil," *Telos,* no. 19 (1974): 136, quoted in Calvin O. Schrag, "Rationality between Modernity and Postmodernity," in Stephen K. White, ed., *Life-World and Politics* (South Bend, Ind.: University of Notre Dame Press, 1989), 103.

30. Jacques Derrida, *Writing and Difference,* trans. Alan Bass (Chicago: University of Chicago Press, 1978), 279, 35, quoted in Megill, *Prophets of Extremity,* 216, 218.

31. Megill, *Prophets of Extremity,* 316, 320.

32. Jacques Derrida, "Declaration of Independence," *New Political Science* 15 (1987): 9–12.

33. A. Heller and F. Feher, *The Postmodern Political Tradition* (Cambridge, England: Polity, 1988), 17, 5, quoted in Simon Thompson, "Postmodernism," in Adam Lent, ed., *New Political Thought* (London: Lawrence & Wishart, 1998), 149–51.

34. Gianni Vattimo, "Bottle, Net, Truth, Revolution, Terrorism, Philosophy," *Denver Quarterly* 16, no. 4 (1982): 25, quoted in Pauline M. Rosenau, *Post-Modernism and the Social Sciences* (Princeton, N.J.: Princeton University Press, 1992), 143.

35. Thompson, "Postmodernism," 148.

36. Iris M. Young, *Justice and the Politics of Difference* (Princeton, N.J.: Princeton University Press, 1990), 7–8, 3.

37. Ibid., 88–92.

38. Ibid., 91, 40–41.

39. Ibid., 53–60.

40. W. E. B. Du Bois, *The Souls of Black Folk* (1903; New York: New American Library, 1969), 45.

41. Young, *Politics of Difference,* 163–64, 172.

42. Ibid., 184.

43. John C. Calhoun, *A Disquisition on Government* (1850), in Ross M. Lence, ed., *Union and Liberty: The Political Philosophy of John C. Calhoun* (Indianapolis: Liberty Fund, 1992), 23–43.

44. Young, *Politics of Difference,* 188–91.

45. Bonnie Honig, *Democracy and the Foreigner* (Princeton, N.J.: Princeton University Press, 2001), 98–106.

46. Iris M. Young, *Throwing like a Girl and Other Essays* (Bloomington: Indiana University Press, 1990), 121, 135.

47. Honig, *The Displacement of Politics*, 4, 12–13.

48. Benedict Anderson, *The Spectre of Comparisons: Nationalism, Southeast Asia, and the World* (London: Verso, 1998), 29–74, 318–30; Rosenau, *Post-Modernism and the Social Sciences*, 152–55.

49. Salmon Rushdie, *The Satanic Verses* (New York: Viking, 1989), 210–11.

50. Gayatri Spivak, "Can the Subaltern Speak," in C. Nelson and L. Grossberg, eds., *Marxism and the Interpretation of Culture* (Chicago: University of Chicago Press, 1988), 271–313, quoted in Rosenau, *Post-Modernism and the Social Sciences*, 154.

51. John Locke, "On Power," bk. 2, chap. 21, par. 55 of *An Essay concerning Human Understanding* (1690), ed. Peter H. Nidditch (London: Oxford University Press, 1975), 269–70.

52. Bonnie Honig (*The Displacement of Politics*, 14, 214 n. 5), e.g., notes that her arguments "converge at crucial points" with those of other mostly postmodern scholars, suggesting important linkages among thinkers: Stuart Hampshire (via Machiavelli) in *Innocence and Experience* (Cambridge, Mass.: Harvard University Press, 1989); Sheldon Wolin (via Tocqueville and Hannah Arendt) in *The Presence of the Past: Essays on the State and the Constitution* (Baltimore: Johns Hopkins University Press, 1989); Nancy Fraser (via Jürgen Habermas) in "Rethinking the Public Sphere: A Contribution to the Critique of Actually Existing Democracy," *Social Text* 25/26 (1991): 56–80; William Connolly (via Nietzsche and Foucault) in *Identity/Difference: Democratic Negotiations of Political Paradox* (Ithaca, N.Y.: Cornell University Press, 1991); Stanley Cavell (via Emerson) in *Conditions Handsome and Unhandsome: The Constitution of Emersonian Perfectionism* (Chicago: University of Chicago Press, 1990); Michael Walzer (via Rousseau) in *Spheres of Justice* (New York: Basic, 1983); Judith Butler (via Foucault and Derrida) in *Gender Trouble* (London: Routledge, 1990); Isaiah Berlin (via J. S. Mill) in *Four Essays on Liberty* (Oxford: Oxford University Press, 1969) and *The Crooked Timber of Humanity* (New York: Knopf, 1991); Bernard Williams (via Berlin) in *Problems of the Self and Moral Luck* (Cambridge: Cambridge University Press, 1983); and Richard Flathman (via Michael Oakeshott, Ludwig Wittgenstein, and Nietzsche) in *Willful Liberalism: Voluntarism and Individuality in Political Theory and Practice* (Ithaca, N.Y.: Cornell University Press, 1992).

11. COMPARING RATIONALES FOR DEMOCRACY

1. Rosemarie Tong, *Feminist Thought* (Boulder, Colo.: Westview, 1989), 233.

2. William Blake, "When Happiness Stretched across the Hills" (1802), and "To Thomas Butts, 22 November 1802," in David V. Erdman, ed., *The Complete Poetry and Prose of William Blake* (Berkeley and Los Angeles: University of California Press, 1982), 722.

3. Ernest Gellner, *Postmodernism, Reason, and Religion* (London: Routledge, 1992), 60–61.

4. Theodore Parker, "Theodore Parker's Experience as a Minister" (1859), in Perry Miller, ed., *The Transcendentalists* (Cambridge, Mass.: Harvard University Press, 1950), 485.

5. Colin Maclaurin, *An Account of Sir Isaac Newton's Philosophical Discoveries* (1742?), quoted in John H. Randall, *The Making of the Modern Mind* (Boston: Houghton Mifflin, 1926), 275.

6. See Charles W. Hendel, ed., *David Hume's Political Essays* (Indianapolis: Bobbs-Merrill, 1953), xi.

7. David Hume, *A Treatise of Human Nature* (1740), quoted in Shirley Letwin, *The Pursuit of Certainty: David Hume, Jeremy Bentham, John Stuart Mill, Beatrice Webb* (Indianapolis: Liberty Fund, 1998), 68–69.

8. Francis Bacon, *Advancement of Learning* (1605), quoted in Fulton Anderson, ed., *Francis Bacon: The New Organon and Related Writings* (Indianapolis: Bobbs-Merrill, 1960), xxvi.

9. *Federalist* no. 1, in Clinton Rossiter, ed., *The Federalist Papers* (New York: Mentor, 1961), 33; Douglass Adair, "'That Politics May Be Reduced to a Science': David Hume, James Madison, and the Tenth *Federalist*," *Huntington Library Quarterly* 20 (1956–1957): 343–60; Gordon Wood, *The Creation of the American Republic, 1776–1787* (1969; Chapel Hill: University of North Carolina Press, 1998), 593–615.

10. Michael Kammen, *A Machine That Would Go of Itself* (New York: Knopf, 1986), 18.

11. George Washington to Alexander Hamilton, August 28, 1788, in W. B. Allen, ed., *George Washington: A Collection* (Indianapolis: Liberty Fund, 1988), 416–17.

12. *Federalist* no. 20, in Rossiter, ed., *The Federalist Papers*, 138.

13. Thomas Jefferson to Samuel Kercheval, July 12, 1816, in Adrienne Koch and William Peden, eds., *The Life and Selected Writings of Thomas Jefferson* (New York: Modern Library, 1993), 615–16.

14. Van Buren quoted in Michael Wallace, "Changing Conceptions of Party in the United States: New York, 1815–1828," *American Historical Review* 74 (1968): 487–89. See also Ralph Ketcham, *Presidents above Party: The First American Presidency, 1789–1829* (Chapel Hill: University of North Carolina Press, 1984), 141–54.

15. Liang Ch'i-ch'ao (Liang Qichao), *History of Chinese Political Thought* (1922), trans. J. T. Chen (1930; New York: AMS, 1969), 43–44, 56–57.

16. See n. 20 below.

17. Charles Reich, *The Greening of America* (New York: Bantam, 1970), 4–19.

18. Theodore Roszak, *Where the Wasteland Ends: Politics and Transcendence in Postindustrial Society* (1972; Garden City, N.Y.: Anchor, 1973), 226.

19. Theodore Lowi, *The End of Liberalism: The Second Republic of the United States* (New York: Norton, 1969); and Robert Nozick, *Anarchy, the State, and Utopia* (New York: Basic, 1974).

20. John Rawls, *A Theory of Justice* (Cambridge, Mass.: Harvard University Press, 1971), 11, 136–37, and *Political Liberalism* (New York: Columbia University Press, 1993), 13, 161–63. The still generally second modernity debate among liberals, communitarians, civic republicans, and libertarians (which sometimes shades into postmodernism) has produced a huge and impressive bibliography. In addition to works otherwise cited, some highlights are Bruce Ackerman, *Social Justice in the Liberal State* (1980); Benjamin Barber, *Strong Democracy* (1984); Brian Barry, *Theories of Justice* (1989); Seyla Benhabib, *Critique, Norm, and Utopia* (1986); Joshua Cohen, ed., *For Love of Country* (1996); Robert Dahl, *Democracy and Its Critics* (1989);

Ronald Dworkin, *A Matter of Principle* (1985); Jean Bethke Elshtain, *Democracy on Trial* (1995); Amitai Etzioni, ed., *Rights and the Common Good: The Communitarian Perspective* (1995); William Galston, *Liberal Purposes* (1991); Carol Gilligan, *In a Different Voice* (1991); Amy Gutmann, *Democratic Education* (1987), and *Identity in Democracy* (2003); Will Kymlika, *Liberalism, Community, and Culture* (1989); Alasdair MacIntyre, *Whose Justice? Which Rationality?* (1989); Stephen Macedo, *Liberal Virtue* (1997); J. Donald Moon, *Constructing Community* (1993); Martha Nussbaum, *The Fragility of Goodness* (1986); Susan M. Okin, *Justice, Gender, and the Family* (1989); Carol Pateman, *The Problem of Political Obligation: A Critique of Liberal Theory* (1979); Nancy Rosenblum, ed., *Liberalism and the Moral Life* (1989); Amartya Sen and Bernard Williams, eds., *Utilitarianism and Beyond* (1982); Cass Sunstein, *After the Rights Revolution* (1990); Charles Taylor, *Sources of the Self: The Making of the Modern Identity* (1989); Michael Walzer, *Spheres of Justice* (1983); Cornel West, *American Erosion of Philosophy: A Genealogy of Pragmatism* (1989); and Sheldon Wolin, *Politics and Vision* (1960).

21. Friedrich Nietzsche, *The Antichrist* (1930; New York: Arno, 1972), par. 11, p. 13.

22. Richard Tarnas, *The Passion of the Western Mind* (New York: Ballantine, 1991), 399.

23. Thomas Carlyle, "Preliminary," bk. 1, chap. 1, and "Pure Reason," bk. 1, chap. 10, of *Sartor Resartus* (1834; New York: Greystone, n.d.), 3, 36–37.

24. Max Weber, *The Protestant Ethic and the Spirit of Capitalism* (1904), trans. Talcott Parsons, with a foreword by R. H. Tawney (New York: Scribner's, 1958), 182, quoted, e.g., in Allan Megill, *Prophets of Extremity: Nietzsche, Heidegger, Foucault, Derrida* (Berkeley and Los Angeles: University of California Press, 1985), vi; and in Christopher Lasch, *Revolt of the Elites and the Betrayal of Democracy* (New York: Norton, 1995), 235.

25. Stephen K. White, *Political Theory and Postmodernism* (Cambridge: Cambridge University Press, 1991), 52–53, 129, 146–47.

26. George Santayana, "Odes," in *Complete Poems,* ed. William Holzberger (Lewisburg, Pa.: Bucknell University Press, 1979), 140–41.

27. Iris M. Young, *Throwing like a Girl and Other Essays* (Bloomington: Indiana University Press, 1990), 121, 135.

28. Bonnie Honig, *Political Theory and the Displacement of Politics* (Ithaca, N.Y.: Cornell University Press, 1993), 4, 12–13.

29. Richard Rorty, *Philosophy and Hope* (London: Penguin, 1999), xxxii, 14, 38.

30. Ibid., 267, 270.

31. Ibid., 275, 27–28.

32. Ibid., 259, 274.

33. Jürgen Habermas, "Richard Rorty's Pragmatic Turn," in Robert B. Brandom, ed., *Rorty and His Critics* (Oxford: Blackwell, 2000), 50.

34. A comment made by George Kateb in 1987.

35. Anthony Downs, *An Economic Theory of Democracy* (New York: Harper Bros., 1957), 259; Michael Sandel, *Democracy's Discontent: America in Search of a Public Philosophy* (Cambridge, Mass.: Harvard University Press, 1996), 24.

36. Aristotle, *Politics,* trans. Benjamin Jowett (New York: Modern Library, 1943), bk. 3, chap. 9, p. 142; Saint Augustine quoted in Martin Luther King, "Letter from

Birmingham Jail" (1963), in Henry J. Silverman, ed., *American Radical Thought* (Lexington, Mass.: D. C. Heath, 1970), 398.

12. THE IDEA OF DEMOCRACY IN THE THIRD MILLENNIUM

1. F. A. Hayek, *The Road to Serfdom* (Chicago: University of Chicago Press, 1944); Milton Friedman, *Capitalism and Freedom* (Chicago: University of Chicago Press, 1962); Robert Nozick, *Anarchy, the State, and Utopia* (New York: Basic, 1974); Dick Armey, *Freedom Revolution* (Washington, D.C.: Regnery, 1995).

2. Walter Lippmann, *Drift and Mastery* (1914; Englewood Cliffs, N.J.: Prentice-Hall, 1961), 150–51.

3. Mahathir Mohamad, *Politics, Democracy, and the New Asia* (Subang Jaya: Pelanduk, 2000), esp. 139–46.

4. Francis Bacon, *Advancement of Learning* (1605) and "The Four Idols" and "The New Method of Induction" from *Novum Organum* (1620), in Daniel S. Robinson, ed., *An Anthology of Modern Philosophy* (New York: Thomas Y. Crowell, 1931), 99–107.

5. Thomas Jefferson, "Autobiography" (dated January 6, 1821), in Adrienne Koch and William Peden, eds., *The Life and Selected Writings of Thomas Jefferson* (New York: Modern Library, 1993), 52.

6. O. W. Holmes Jr., "Life as Joy, Duty, End" (1900) and *Abrams v. United States* (1919) (Holmes dissenting), in Max Lerner, ed., *The Mind and Faith of Justice Holmes* (Boston: Little, Brown, 1951), 43, 312.

7. Harold Laski, *A Grammar of Politics* (London: George Allen, 1925), 42–43.

8. O. W. Holmes, "Montesquieu" (1900), in Max Lerner, ed., *The Mind and Faith of Justice Holmes* (Boston: Little, Brown, 1951), 378.

9. Walter Lippmann, *The Public Philosophy* (New York: Mentor, 1955), 15.

10. John Locke, "On Power," bk. 2, chap. 21, par. 55 of *An Essay concerning Human Understanding* (1690), ed. Peter H. Nidditch (London: Oxford University Press, 1975), 270.

11. Aristotle, *Politics*, trans. Benjamin Jowett (New York: Modern Library, 1943), bk. 3, chap. 9, p. 142.

12. Ralph Waldo Emerson, "Politics" (1844), in William H. Gilman, ed., *Selected Writings of Ralph Waldo Emerson* (New York: New American Library, 1965), 357.

13. Reinhold Niebuhr, *The Children of Light and the Children of Darkness* (New York: Scribner's, 1944), xiii.

14. John Locke, *Second Treatise on Civil Government* (1690), sec. 93, in Ernest Barker, ed., *Social Contract: Locke, Hume, Rousseau* (New York: Oxford University Press, 1960), 55.

15. *Book of Mencius* (ca. 300 B.C.E.), 6.1.6, quoted in Herrlee G. Creel, *Chinese Thought from Confucius to Mao Tse-tung* (Chicago: University of Chicago Press, 1953), 88.

16. Thomas Jefferson to James Madison, December 20, 1787, November 18, 1788, and Thomas Jefferson, "Notes on Virginia" (1782), in Koch and Peden, eds., *Writings of Jefferson*, 405, 418, 222–23.

17. Dumas Malone, speech; Rotunda, University of Virginia, March 16, 1981.

18. Thomas Jefferson to Samuel Kercheval, July 12, 1816, in Koch and Peden, eds., *Writings of Jefferson*, 615–16.

19. *Federalist* no. 37, in Clinton Rossiter, ed., *The Federalist Papers* (New York: Mentor, 1961), 226.

20. See generally Peter S. Onuf, *Jefferson's Empire: The Language of American Nationhood* (Charlottesville: University Press of Virginia, 2000), 1–17.

21. James Madison, "Property" (1792), in Robert Rutland et al., eds., *The Papers of James Madison*, 17 vols. (Charlottesville: University Press of Virginia, 1962–1991), 14:266.

22. Thomas Jefferson, First Annual Message, December 8, 1801, Jefferson to Powtewatamies and Weeauks, January 7, 1802, and Jefferson, Second Inaugural Address, March 4, 1805, in Koch and Peden, eds., *Writings of Jefferson*, 302, 308, 315.

23. Joseph Tussman, *Obligation and the Body Politic* (New York: Oxford University Press, 1960), 112.

24. Niebuhr, *Children of Light*, 40–41.

25. Bernard Mandeville, *The Fable of the Bees; or, Private Vices, Publick Benefits* (1714; 6th ed., 1732), ed. F. B. Kaye, 2 vols. (Oxford: Oxford University Press, 1924), 136.

26. Jefferson, First Inaugural Address, March 4, 1801, in Koch and Peden, eds., *Writings of Jefferson*, 298.

27. Sir William Blackstone, *Commentaries on the Laws of England* (Oxford, 1765), introduction, sec. 1, "Of the Nature of Laws in General."

28. *West Virginia Board of Education v. Barnette*, 591 U.S. 638 (1943).

29. Martin Luther's statement in defense of his teachings was made before the Imperial Diet of Worms in 1521; Ralph Waldo Emerson, journal entry, [spring(?) 1851], in Stephen E. Whicher, ed., *Selections from Ralph Waldo Emerson* (1957; Boston: Houghton Mifflin, 1960), 355; Martin Luther King, "Letter from Birmingham Jail" (1963), in Henry J. Silverman, ed., *American Radical Thought* (Lexington, Mass.: D. C. Heath, 1970), 398.

30. Niebuhr, *Children of Light*, 74.

31. Jean M. Yarborough, *American Virtues: Thomas Jefferson and the Character of a Free People* (Lawrence: University Press of Kansas, 1998), 193; Sir Edward Coke, Calvin's Case, *Coke Reports*, vol. 7, pt. 12 (1606), quoted in Gordon Schochet, *Patriarchalism in Political Thought* (New York: Basic, 1975), 91; Lippmann, *Public Philosophy*, 106–8.

32. Jane Mansbridge, *Beyond Adversary Democracy* (1980; Chicago: University of Chicago Press, 1983), 18.

33. John Taylor of Caroline to Thomas Jefferson, June 25, 1798, in *John P. Branch Historical Papers* (Lynchburg, Va.: Randolph-Macon College, 1908), 271–72.

34. *Federalist* no. 63, in Rossiter, ed., *The Federalist Papers*, 384.

35. Edmund Burke, "Speech to the Electors of Bristol" (November 3, 1774), in *The Writings and Speeches of Edmund Burke*, 12 vols. (Boston: Little, Brown, 1901), 2:96.

36. Mark Kishlansky, "The Emergence of Adversarial Politics in the Long Parliament," *Journal of Modern History* 49 (1977): 17–40.

37. Aristotle, *Politics*, bk. 3, chap. 11, quoted in Douglas F. Challenger, "A More Per-

fect Union: Aristotle on Deliberation, Diversity, and Citizenship," in Oto Luthar et al., eds., *Liberal Democracy, Citizenship, and Education* (Oakville, Ont.: Mosaic, 2001), 176–202.

38. Aristotle, *Politics* (Jowett), bk. 3, chap. 9, p. 142; Thomas Jefferson to Walter Jones, March 3, 1801, in H. A. Washington, ed., *The Works of Thomas Jefferson*, 9 vols. (Washington, D.C., 1853–1854), 4:392–93; Theodore Roosevelt, ca. 1910, quoted in E. J. Hughes, *The Living Presidency* (New York: Coward, McCann & Geohegan, 1972), 166.

39. I take the text of the oath from a tablet in the Maxwell School of Citizenship and Public Affairs, Syracuse University. The oath appears in public buildings throughout the United States.

40. Thomas Pownall (1784) quoted in Paul Rahe, *Republics Ancient and Modern: Classical Republicanism and the American Revolution* (Chapel Hill: University of North Carolina Press, 1992), 49; Michael Perry, *Morality, Politics, and Law* (New York: Oxford University Press, 1998), 158–59.

41. David L. Hall and Roger T. Ames, *Thinking from the Han: Self, Truth, and Transcendence in Chinese and Western Culture* (Albany: State University of New York Press, 1998), 155–61.

42. Benjamin Franklin, speech of August 7, 1787, in Ralph Ketcham, ed., *The Political Thought of Benjamin Franklin* (Indianapolis: Bobbs-Merrill, 1965), 398–99.

43. Jefferson, "Notes on Virginia," 259.

44. Ira Steward, "Poverty," *American Federalist* 9 (1902): 159–60, quoted in Michael Sandel, *Democracy's Discontent: America in Search of a Public Philosophy* (Cambridge, Mass.: Harvard University Press, 1996), 191.

45. William Perkins, "On Calling" (1603), in E. S. Morgan, ed., *Puritan Political Ideas* (Indianapolis: Bobbs-Merrill, 1965), 36–50.

46. Alexis de Tocqueville, *Democracy in America* (1835), pt. 2, bk. 2, chap. 5, in Richard Heffner, ed., *A Documentary History of the United States* (New York: New American Library, 1956), 198–206.

47. Robert Putnam, *Bowling Alone: The Collapse and Revival of American Community* (New York: Simon & Schuster, 2000), 18–23.

48. Thomas Jefferson to W. C. Jarvis, September 28, 1820, in Edward Dumbauld, ed., *The Political Writings of Thomas Jefferson* (Indianapolis: Bobbs-Merrill, 1955), 93.

49. Horace Mann, "Twelfth Annual Report" (1848), in S. A. Rippa, ed., *Educational Ideas in America* (New York: David McKay, 1969), 202.

50. John Dewey, *Democracy and Education* (New York: Macmillan, 1916); W. H. Kilpatrick, *Education for a Changing Civilization* (New York: Macmillan, 1926), iv.

51. Ernest L. Boyer and Fred M. Hechinger, *Higher Learning in the Nation's Service* (Washington, D.C.: Carnegie Foundation, 1981), 47, 60–61.

52. Tussman, *Obligation and the Body Politic*; Benjamin Barber, *Strong Democracy* (Berkeley and Los Angeles: University of California Press, 1984); Sandel, *Democracy's Discontent*; Peter Levine, *The New Progressive Era: Toward a Fair and Deliberative Democracy* (Lanham, N.H.: Rowman & Littlefield, 2000).

53. John Wise, "A Vindication of the Government of New England Churches" (1717), in Morgan, ed., *Puritan Political Ideas*, 254.

54. Ralph Waldo Emerson, "The Poet," in Brooks Atkinson, ed., *The Selected Writings of Ralph Waldo Emerson* (New York: Modern Library, 1968), 325.

55. Richard Tarnas, *The Passion of the Western Mind* (New York: Ballantine, 1991), 399.

56. Rosemarie Tong, *Feminist Thought* (Boulder, Colo.: Westview, 1989), 233.

57. Niebuhr, *Children of Light*, 17–30.

small, 104, 105–106
strong, 11
traditional, 35–37, 38, 39
weak, 11
See also Modernity; Self-government
Grammar of Politics, A (Laski), 79, 99
Grant, Ulysses, 67, 79
Great Britain, 34, 35, 37, 94–95, 96, 100, 127, 130, 218, 250
constitution, 245
and old liberalism, 103
party politics, 94, 95, 216
Great Cultural Revolution (China), 157
Greatest good of the greatest number, 2, 81–82
Great Learning (Confucius), 12, 14, 15, 129, 140
Great Society, 96
Greece (ancient), 4, 17, 18, 19, 24, 27, 238, 252
Green, T. H., 216
Greening of America, The (Reich), 218–219
Greenpeace, 201
Gregory VII (pope), 26
Grote, John, 71–72
Gu Hongming, 172
Gulliver's Travels (Swift), 36, 37, 56, 74
Guomindang (Nationalist Party, China), 142, 149, 154
Guttman, Amy, 218

Habermas, Jürgen, 4, 192, 227
Haiti, 9
Hall, David, 13, 254
Hamilton, Alexander, 79, 93, 94
Handicapped Americans Act, 97
Happiness, 58, 60, 208
Harmony, 14
Hartsfield, William, 97
Hastert, Dennis, 107
Havel, Václav, 9, 246
Hayek, F. A., 217, 231
Heath, Edward, 95, 102
Hegel, Georg W.F., 15, 68, 69, 119, 153, 224–225
Hegemony, 203, 209. *See also* Liberal corporate state
Heidegger, Martin, 182, 184–186, 187, 206–207
Henry IV (Holy Roman emperor), 25–26
Hesse, Herman, 185
High Noon (film), 24
Hinduism, 5, 8–9, 25, 168
History of Politics (Jenks), 134

Hitlerism, 185
Hobbes, Thomas, 9, 15, 17, 33, 34, 37
Niebuhr on, 74
Ho Chi Minh, 98
Hoffer, Eric, 217
Holmes, Oliver Wendell, 75, 77–79, 80, 86, 90, 92, 107, 227, 235
on Arnold, 78
Holy men, 18
Holy Roman Emperor, 25–26, 141
Hong Kong, 166, 176, 233
Honig, Bonnie, 191, 192, 196, 200–203, 208, 224, 225
Hoover, Herbert, 96, 232
House of Commons, 250
House of Representatives, 45
Hsu Kuang-ch'i (Paul), 113
Humanism, 30, 34, 60
Human nature, 16, 17, 72, 76, 204, 211, 227, 230, 235–238, 240–241, 244–248, 249, 262, 264
Human rights, 50, 245
Hume, David, 36, 44, 50, 56, 65, 212–213, 214
Niebuhr on, 74
Hungary, 99
Husband-wife relationship, 13, 14
Hu Shi, 125, 151–154, 158, 170, 172
Hu Shi's New Decalogue, 152–153
Hussein, Saddam, 205
Hutu, 9
Huxley, Thomas H., 64, 70, 72
impact on Asian thought, 111, 127
translation into Chinese, 127
Hu Yaobang, 158, 159, 160

Idealism, 57, 249–250
Ideal right, 249, 252
Ideals of the East, The (Okakura), 168
Idea of a Patriot King (Bolingbroke), 36
Imagined communities, 218
Iman, 18
Immigration, 200–201
India, 9, 170, 206
Individual conscience, 28, 30
Individuality/individualism, 30–31, 33, 34, 35, 38, 39, 41, 51, 57, 60, 76, 82, 91, 104, 224, 231
"new," 81
Individual rights, 41, 44, 52, 105, 213, 214, 234–235, 254
Indonesia, 10
Inductive method, 31, 33, 34, 50, 60, 62, 70, 76, 79, 82, 120, 134, 211–212

Malaysia, 233
Malgovernment, 9, 10
Malone, Dumas, 240
Malthus, Thomas, 66
Mandate of heaven. *See under* China
Mandela, Nelson, 246, 259
Mandeville, Bernard, 36, 37, 245
Mann, Horace, 257
Mansbridge, Jane, 249
Man vs. the State (Spencer), 104
Mao Zedong, 16, 99, 125, 145, 152, 156–157, 158, 167
Marcuse, Herbert, 102
Marginalized and excluded, 3, 197–200, 204, 221, 222
Marshall, Alfred, 64
Marshall, John, 79, 92, 215
Marshall, Thurgood, 92
Marx, Karl, 4, 19, 51, 60, 62, 68, 75, 115, 183, 184, 245, 264
Marxism, 4, 156, 171, 185, 186, 187, 208
Marxism-Leninism, 15, 153, 155, 156, 192
  -Mao Zedong thought, 157, 158
Massachusetts Constitution, 43
Materialism, 57, 211–212
Material well-being, 104
May 4 movement. *See under* China
McKinley, William, 91, 123
Medieval spirituality, 30
Megill, Allan, 182, 193, 202
Meiji Six Society, 121
Mencius, 130, 136, 138, 140, 153, 156
Menzies, Robert, 99
Mercantilism, 34
Metanarratives, 183, 192, 196, 204, 207, 212, 216, 217, 220, 263, 264
Metaphysics, 184. *See also* Philosophy
Mexico, 10
Middle class, 91
Militaristic authoritarian regimes, 9, 10
Military-industrial complex, 100
Mill, John Stuart, 2, 17, 55, 58–60, 64, 71, 79, 81, 134–135, 166, 183, 204, 216, 224
  impact on Asian thought, 111, 115, 116, 120, 127, 152–154
  translated into Chinese, 127, 130–131, 134
  translated into Japanese, 141
Miller, Perry, 66
Mills, C. Wright, 100
Minorities, 100, 102, 105. *See also* Marginalized and exluded
Minority, 52
Mishima, Yukio, 164

Modernity, 4, 21, 30, 33, 38, 39, 40, 229–230, 263
  factors, 38
  first, 1, 30–39, 51, 55, 99, 118, 211–213, 215, 259–260
  first, critics of, 56–57, 211–212, 216
  politics as casualty of, 191
  second, 2, 55, 74, 80–81, 83–84, 89, 90, 93, 97, 101, 106, 107, 122, 180, 181, 183, 188, 206, 216, 232, 248, 260–261 (*see also under* China; Japan; Korea)
  second, critics of, 72–77, 101, 183, 190, 219, 260–261
  third, 2, 89, 110, 133, 166, 174–181, 182, 248
  third, hybrid, 111
  fourth, 2–3, 89, 110, 182–191, 225, 248 (*see also* Antifoundationalism; Deconstruction; Postmodernism)
Monarchies, 34
Moon, Donald, 218
Montesquieu, Charles, 4, 44, 133
  translated into Chinese, 127, 132–133, 163
Moral order, 16, 17
Moral sense, 247
Morgan, J. P., 67
Motoda Eifu, 125–126, 161
Muhammad (prophet), 24, 33
Mulroney, Brian, 104
Multiculturalism, 196
Multinational corporations, 105
Mumford, Lewis, 73–74
Mundaneness, 30, 31, 211, 240
Municipal research institutes, 93
Muslims, 8, 9, 10

Nähe, 184
Nakane Chie, 165, 166
Nakasone Yasuhiro, 104
Napoléon I (emperor of the French), 141
Nation building, 42
Nationhood, 218
Nationalism, 3
  New, 91, 252
Nationalizations, 95
National Labor Relations Board, 92
Native Americans, 242–243
Natural law, 2, 36, 40, 54, 62, 63, 64, 68, 69, 75, 77, 78, 84, 88, 90, 92, 133, 183, 190, 208, 212, 214, 216, 246–247, 260
  Laski on, 79
  as old liberalism, 99, 104
Natural rights, 50, 98, 109, 212
  Bentham on, 58, 227

Natural selection, 63, 65
"Nearness," 184
Nehru, Jawharlal, 98
"New Age," 101, 122
New citizen, 140–141, 145, 146–147
New Deal, 34, 91, 92, 94, 96
    critics, 94
New Freedom program, 91, 252
New orthodoxy, 104
New Progressive Era, The: Toward a Fair and Deliberative Democracy (Levine), 259
Newton, Isaac, 36, 40, 50, 55, 212
Newtonian anthropology, 192
New Zealand, 94, 104
Niebuhr, Reinhold, 31, 74–76, 82, 237, 241, 244
Nietzsche, Friedrich, 32, 60, 182, 183, 191, 193, 221, 222
Nishi Amane, 4, 119–122, 126, 141–142, 145, 164, 227
Nixon, Richard M., 19–20, 96–97, 100, 102, 232
Non-English language use, 102
Normalization, 188, 190, 191
Novissima Sinica (Leibniz), 113
Nozick, Robert, 221, 231
Nuclear arms race, 100

Objectivity, 189
Obligation and the Body Politic (Tussman), 259
Occupational Safety and Health Administration, 97
Occupations, 19, 53, 255–256
"Of Individuality, as One of the Elements of Well-Being" (Mill), 131
Okakura Kakuzo, 167
Okuma Shigenobu, 123, 162
Older sibling-yonger sibling relationship, 13
On Liberty (Mill), 58, 130, 131, 132, 141
On the Boundaries of the Rights of Society and the Individual (Yan translation of *On Liberty*), 131–132
On the Genealogy of Morals (Nietzsche), 183
"Open societies." *See* "Closed and open societies"
Open Society and Its Enemies, The (Popper), 95
Opium Wars (1840–1842), 114, 127
Oppression, 197–198, 205, 208. *See also* Marginalized and excluded

Opzoomer, C. W., 120
Oration on the Dignity of Man (Pico), 30–31
Order, 14
Origin of Species (Darwin), 63, 68
Organization for Economic Cooperation and Development, 97
Otherness/difference, 182, 184, 186, 189, 196, 199, 204, 208, 223
Otis, James, 42

Paine, Thomas, 40, 42, 44, 46, 50, 205, 248
Pan-Asianism, 139, 168, 170, 172, 222
Park Chung Hee, 166
Parker, Theodore, 56, 211
"Patriot king," 181
Paul, Saint, 17
Peace, 14
Pearson, Karl, 87–88
Peel, Robert, 95, 216
Pennsylvania Constitution, 43
People of color, 9
People's Daily (CCP), 158
Pericles, 21, 51, 238
Perot, Ross, 107
Perry, Michael, 254
Peru, 10
Philosophical Letters (Voltaire), 50
Philosophy, 60, 61, 73, 78
Pico della Mirandola, 30, 31
Pinyin romanization (China), 125
Plato, 17, 32, 33, 42, 68, 96, 102, 108, 184
Pleasure, 58
Pluralism, 215, 227. *See also* Cultural pluralism
Plutarch, 72
Plutocracy, 84
Poland, 99
Political economy, 116–117
Political Economy (Mill), 64
Political freedom, 239
Political participation, 20, 43, 53, 90, 91, 103, 251
    exclusions, 53
Political parties, 86–87, 102, 156, 163
Political science, 69, 84
Politics (Aristotle), 12, 17, 51, 96
Politics: Who Gets What, When, How (Lasswell), 87
Politics of difference, 195, 198, 233–234
Politics of identity, 195, 208, 233–234
Polity, 16, 17, 21, 49, 144
Poll taxes, 92
Polo, Marco, 112

Roszak, Theodore, 219–220, 222
Rousseau, Jean Jacques, 4, 62, 135, 176, 245, 248
Rulers, 21, 141, 175, 238
    bad, 17
    and education, 17–18, 19, 25
Rushdie, Salman, 206
Russell, Bertrand
    in China, 152
    influence on Asian thought, 111, 152, 168, 173, 180
Russia, 10, 257
    czarist, 67, 138
    See also Soviet Union
Russo-Japanese War (1905), 67
Rwanda, 9

Saint-Simon, Claude, 62
Saionji Kinmochi (Japanese prince), 179
Sameness, 189
Sandel, Michael, 203, 259
Santayana, George, 69, 75, 76–77, 84, 184
Satanic Verses, The (Rushdie), 206
Sato Eisaku, 100
Scalia, Antonin, 107
Schlesinger, Arthur, Jr., 95, 96
School and Society, The (Dewey), 82
Schröder, Gerhard, 106
Schwartz, Benjamin, 16, 174
Science, 60, 61, 62–63, 66, 68–69, 74, 76, 85–86, 90, 91, 130, 169, 171, 180, 183, 210, 212
    and catastrophe, 142
    as totalitarian ideology, 190
Science in the Modern World (Whitehead), 31
"Science of Society," 67
Scientific method, 31, 35–36, 63, 72, 107
Scotus, Johannes, 113
SDS. See Students for a Democratic Society
Secondariness, 193
Second Treatise on Civil Government (Locke), 36
Second World, 8, 98, 99, 106, 205
Secular individualism, 30
Secularism, 30, 33
Securities and Exchange Commission, 92–93
Self-consciousness, 74
Self-determination, 98, 104, 218
Self-expression, 80
Self-government, 1–2, 10, 30, 35, 42, 46, 50, 53–54, 82, 83, 89, 90, 94, 97, 99, 107,

116, 117, 133, 147, 209, 215, 216, 230, 239, 245, 248, 255, 259, 262
    and China, 150
    defects of, 196–197
    in First World, 10–11
Self-Help (Smiles) translated into Japanese, 140
Self-interest, 38, 41, 46, 75, 129, 130–131, 244, 264
Self-rule, 41
Senate, 45–46, 47
    direct elections for, 91
Sensational system, 211–212
Separation of powers, 44
Shaw, George Bernard, 95
Shotoku (Japanese prince), 124
Sidney, Algernon, 49, 50
Silk road, 112
Singapore, 166, 233
Sinophiles, 49, 114
Skinner, B. F., 219
Slavery, 241–242
Slavs, 8
Smiles, Samuel, 140
Smith, Adam, 34, 40, 41, 44, 49, 64, 92, 104, 115, 118, 131, 133, 183, 190, 264
    translation into Chinese, 127, 130–131
Smith, Huston, 4
Social Contract (Rousseau), critique of, 135–136
Social Darwinism, 49, 81, 127, 128–129, 133, 134, 135, 136, 139
Social democracy, 90, 94, 159, 160
Social evolution, 66–67, 78, 134
Socialism, 97, 171, 206
    and China, 151, 205
    Fabian, 89, 95, 96
Socialness of human nature, 16, 17
Social physics. See Sociology
Social progress, 82, 88
Social sciences, 62–63, 64, 65, 66, 67, 76, 77, 84, 85, 93, 98, 102, 120, 212, 220–221, 256
Social Security Administration, 92
Social utility, 58
Social welfare, 85
Society for Lectures on the New Learning, 170
Sociocracy, 67, 84, 85
Sociocrats, 85
Sociology, 60, 84
Socrates, 27–28
    Nietzsche on, 183
Somalia, 9

assault on the "Establishment," 100
challenged (*see* Postmodernism)
conservatives, 232
and good government, 11, 42, 218
and modern democracy, 40–54, 90–94,
102, 213–216, 226
presidency, 252–253
See also under Japan
U.S. Steel (company), 92
Universal Declaration of Human Rights
(UN), 208–209, 246
Universalism, 56, 57, 58, 132, 215, 227
Universal manhood suffrage, 163
Universal rights, 50, 246
Universities, 101, 115, 119, 152, 258
Utilitarianism (Mill), 71, 120
Utilitarians/utilitarianism, 17, 57–58, 71,
72, 121, 264

Van Buren, Martin, 215
Veblen, Thorstein, 2, 56, 60, 64–65, 68,
132–133, 183, 190
Versailles Treaty (1919), 135
Vietnam War, 100, 101
Virginia, 48, 49, 50, 241
Vissering, Simon, 120
Virtue, 72, 183–184, 255
theorists, 293
Vital Center, The (Schlesinger), 96
Voltaire, François, 5, 49, 50
on China, 113, 181
Voting age, 92, 101
Voting rights, 91, 93, 101, 163, 241, 255

Walpole, Robert, 37
Walzer, Michael, 218
War, 7, 136
Ward, Barbara, 217
Ward, Lester Frank, 60, 66–67, 82, 84–85,
93, 103
War on poverty, 101
Warren, Earl, 105
Washington, George, 214
Watson, J. B., 219
Way, The (Lao-tsu), 135
Wealth of Nations (Smith), 64
translated as *Book of Smith* by Yan, 130
Webb, Beatrice, 60, 67, 82, 85, 95
Webb, Sidney, 60, 67, 78, 82, 85
Weber, Max, 4, 185, 223
Webster, Daniel, 79

Welfare corporate state, 196
Welfare state, 3, 90, 95, 97
"What Social Classes Owe to Each Other"
(Sumner), 66
Whigs, 40
White, Morton, 69
White, Stephen, 223
White, Walter, 92
Whitehead, Alfred North, 1, 31
Whites, 9
"Why Economics Is Not an Evolutionary
Science" (Veblen), 56, 64
Wilberforce (bishop), 64, 70
"Will to a system," 182–183, 190, 220, 221,
222, 235, 261
Williams, Roger, 26
Wilson, Harold, 95, 99, 100
Wilson, Woodrow, 55, 79, 91, 92, 252
Winthrop, John, 26
Wolff, Robert, 102–103
Wolfius, 49
Wolin, Sheldon, 218
Women
enfranchisement of, 91, 93
and rights, 102, 206, 243–244
See also Marginalized and excluded
Women Living under Islamic Law, 201
Wood, Gordon, 214
Wordsworth, William, 70
World War I, 135, 136, 142
Wright, Chauncey, 77

Xavier, Francis, 112, 113
Xu Zhimo, 170–171

Yamagata Aritomo, 162
Yan Fu, 4, 111, 127–137, 145, 176, 180–181, 217
Yeats, W. B., 182
Yin and Yang, 171
Yoshida Shigeru, 164, 165, 179
Young, Iris M., 196–200, 202, 208, 224
Youth, 100–101
Yuan Shikai, 135, 142
Yugoslavia, 99

Zaire, 9
Zhang Junmai, 170
Zhang Zhidong, 138
Zhao Ziyang, 159, 162
Zheng He, 112
Zhu Xi, 115, 152, 153

JC423 .K4128 2004
The idea of democracy in
modern era